ACCA
STUDY TEXT

Certificate Paper 5

Information Analysis

New in this June 1998 edition

- Recent developments in hardware and software, and issues such as Windows 98, Windows NT v Unix, legacy systems and Year 2000

- The forthcoming Data Protection Act 1998 and the new data protection principles

- New material on developments in programming

- Revised and updated material on the Internet, outsourcing, audit trails, database design and administration, passwords, viruses, the project manager and his team, and systems performance

- Many new illustrations and case examples

FOR DECEMBER 1998 AND JUNE 1999 EXAMS

BPP Publishing
June 1998

First edition 1993
Sixth edition June 1998

ISBN 0 7517 0129 7 (Previous edition 0 7517 0069 X)

British Library Cataloguing-in-Publication Data
A catalogue record for this book is available from the British Library

Published by

BPP Publishing Limited
Aldine House, Aldine Place
London W12 8AW

http://www.bpp.co.uk

Printed and bound by Progressive Printing (U.K.) Limited, Leigh-on-Sea, Essex.

We are grateful to the Association of Chartered Certified Accountants for permission to reproduce in this text the syllabus and teaching guide of which the Association holds the copyright.

We are also grateful to the Association of Chartered Certified Accountants, the Institute of Chartered Accountants in England and Wales and the Chartered Institute of Management Accountants for permission to reproduce past examination questions in our Exam Question Bank. The Exam Answer Bank has been prepared by BPP Publishing Limited.

HOW TO USE THIS STUDY TEXT

Aims of this Study Text

To provide you with the knowledge and understanding, skills and applied techniques required for passing the exam

The Study Text has been written around the ACCA's Official Syllabus and the ACCA's Official 1998-9 Teaching Guide (reproduced below, and cross-referenced to where in the text each topic is covered).

- It is **comprehensive**. We do not omit sections of the syllabus as the examiner is liable to examine any angle of any part of the syllabus - and you do not want to be left high and dry.

- It is **up-to-date as at 1 June 1998**, which means that it more than fulfils the requirement for the December 1998 exams that students should be up-to-date as at 1 June 1998.

- And it is **on-target** - we do not include any material which is not examinable. You can therefore rely on the BPP Study Text as the stand-alone source of all your information for the exam, without worrying that any of the material is irrelevant.

To allow you to study in the way that best suits your learning style and the time you have available, by following your personal Study Plan (see below)

You may be studying at home on your own until the date of the exam, or you may be attending a full-time course. You may like to (and have time to) read every word, or you may prefer to (or only have time to) skim-read and devote the remainder of your time to question practice. Wherever you fall in the spectrum, you will find the BPP Study Text meets your needs in designing and following your personal Study Plan.

To tie in with the other components of the BPP Effective Study Package to ensure you have the best possible chance of passing the exam

Recommended period of use	Elements of BPP Effective Study Package
3-12 months before exam	**Study Text** Acquisition of knowledge, understanding, skills and applied techniques
1-6 months before exam	**Practice and Revision Kit** Tutorial questions and helpful checklists of the key points lead you into each area. There are then numerous Examination questions to try, graded by topic area, along with realistic suggested solutions prepared by BPP's own authors in the light of the Examiner's Reports. June 1999 examinees will find the 1999 edition of the Kit invaluable for bringing them up-to-date as at 1 December 1998, the cut-off date for the June 1999 examinable material
last minute - 3 months before exam	**Passcards** Short, memorable notes focused on what is most likely to come up in the exam you will be sitting

Settling down to study

By this stage in your career you are probably a very experienced learner and taker of exams. But have you ever thought about *how* you learn? Let's have a quick look at the key elements required for effective learning. You can then identify your learning style and go on to design your own approach to how you are going to study this text - your personal Study Plan.

Key element of learning	Using the BPP Study Text
Motivation	You can rely on the comprehensiveness and technical quality of BPP. You've chosen the right Study Text - so you're in pole position to pass your exam!
Clear objectives and standards	Do you want to be a prizewinner or simply achieve a moderate pass? Decide.
Feedback	Follow through the examples in this text and do the Questions and the Quick quizzes. Evaluate your efforts critically - how are you doing?
Study Plan	You need to be honest about your progress to yourself - don't be over-confident, but don't be negative either. Make your Study Plan (see below) and try to stick to it. Focus on the short-term objectives - completing two chapters a night, say - but beware of losing sight of your study objectives
Practice	Use the Quick quizzes and Chapter roundups to refresh your memory regularly after you have completed your initial study of each chapter

These introductory pages let you see exactly what you are up against. However you study, you should:

- **read through the syllabus and teaching guide** - this will help you to identify areas you have already covered, perhaps at a lower level of detail, and areas that are totally new to you

- **study the examination paper section**, where we show you the format of the exam (how many and what kind of questions etc) and analyse all the papers set so far under the syllabus.

Key study steps

The following steps are, in our experience, the ideal way to study for professional exams. You can of course adapt it for your particular learning style (see below).

Tackle the chapters in the order you find them in the Study Text. Taking into account your individual learning style, follow these key study steps for each chapter.

Key study steps	Activity
Step 1 *Chapter topic list*	Study the list. Each numbered topic denotes a numbered section in the chapter
Step 2 *Introduction*	Read it through. It is designed to show you *why* the topics in the chapter need to be studied - how they lead on from previous topics, and how they lead into subsequent ones
Step 3 *Knowledge brought forward boxes*	In these we highlight information and techniques that it is assumed you have 'brought forward' with you from your earlier studies. If there are matters which have changed recently due to legislation etc then these topics are explained in full. Do not panic if you do not feel instantly comfortable with the content - it should come back to you as we develop the subject for this paper. If you are really unsure, we advise you to go back to your previous notes
Step 4 *Explanations*	Proceed methodically through the chapter, reading each section thoroughly and making sure you understand. Where a topic has been examined, we state the month and year of examination against the appropriate heading. You should pay particular attention to these topics.
Step 5 *Key terms* and *Exam focus points*	• **Key terms** can often earn you *easy marks* if you state them clearly and correctly in an appropriate exam answer (and they are indexed at the back of the text so you can check easily that you are on top of all of them when you come to revise) • **Exam focus points** give you a good idea of how the examiner tends to examine certain topics - and also pinpoint *easy marks*
Step 6 *Note taking*	Take brief notes if you wish, avoiding the temptation to copy out too much
Step 7 *Examples*	Follow each through to its solution very carefully
Step 8 *Case examples*	Study each one, and try if you can to add flesh to them from your own experience - they are designed to show how the topics you are studying come alive (and often come unstuck) in the real world
Step 9 *Questions*	Make a very good attempt at each one
Step 10 *Answers*	Check yours against ours, and make sure you understand any discrepancies
Step 11 *Chapter roundup*	Check through it very carefully, to make sure you have grasped the major points it is highlighting

 BPP Publishing

Key study steps	Activity
Step 12 *Quick quiz*	When you are happy that you have covered the chapter, use the **Quick quiz** to check your recall of the topics covered. The answers are in the paragraphs in the chapter that we refer you to
Step 13 *Examination question(s)*	Either at this point, or later when you are thinking about revising, make a full attempt at the **Examination question(s)** suggested at the very end of the chapter. You can find these at the end of the Study Text, along with the **Answers** so you can see how you did. We highlight for you which ones are introductory, and which are of the full standard you would expect to find in an exam

Developing your personal Study Plan

Preparing a Study Plan (and sticking closely to it) is one of the key elements in learning success.

First you need to be aware of your style of learning. There are four typical learning styles. Consider yourself in the light of the following descriptions. and work out which you fit most closely. You can then plan to follow the key study steps in the sequence suggested.

Learning styles	Characteristics	Sequence of key study steps in the BPP Study Text
Theorist	Seeks to understand principles before applying them in practice	1, 2, 3, 4, 7, 8, 5, 9/10, 11, 12, 13 (6 continuous)
Reflector	Seeks to observe phenomena, thinks about them and then chooses to act	
Activist	Prefers to deal with practical, active problems; does not have much patience with theory	1, 2, 9/10 (read through), 7, 8, 5, 11, 3, 4, 9/10 (full attempt), 12, 13 (6 continuous)
Pragmatist	Prefers to study only if a direct link to practical problems can be seen; not interested in theory for its own sake	9/10 (read through), 2, 5, 7, 8, 11, 1, 3, 4, 9/10 (full attempt), 12, 13 (6 continuous)

Next you should complete the following checklist.

Am I motivated? (a) [ ]

Do I have an objective and a standard that I want to achieve? (b) [ ]

Am I a theorist, a reflector, an activist or a pragmatist? (c) [ ]

How much time do I have available per week, given: (d) [ ]

- the standard I have set myself
- the time I need to set aside later for work on the Practice and Revision Kit and Passcards
- the other exam(s) I am sitting, and (of course)
- practical matters such as work, travel, exercise, sleep and social life?

Now

- take the time you have available per week for this Study Text (d), and multiply it by the number of weeks available to give (e)

  (e) [   ]

- divide (e) by the number of chapters to give (f)

  (f) [   ]

- set about studying each chapter in the time represented by (f), following the key study steps in the order suggested by your particular learning style.

This is your personal **Study Plan**.

Short of time?

Whatever your objectives, standards or style, you may find you simply do not have the time available to follow all the key study steps for each chapter, however you adapt them for your particular learning style. If this is the case, follow the Skim Study technique below (the icons in the Study Text will help you to do this).

Skim Study technique

Study the chapters in the order you find them in the Study Text. For each chapter, follow the key study steps 1-3, and then skim-read through step 4. Jump to step 11, and then go back to step 5. Follow through steps 7 and 8, and prepare outline Answers to Questions (steps 9/10). Try the Quick quiz (step 12), following up any items you can't answer, then do a plan for the Examination question (step 13), comparing it against our answers. You should probably still follow step 6 (note-taking), although you may decide simply to rely on the BPP Passcards for this.

Moving on...

However you study, when you are ready to embark on the practice and revision phase of the BPP Effective Study Package, you should still refer back to this Study Text:

- as a source of **reference** (you should find the list of key terms and the index particularly helpful for this)

- as a **refresher** (the Chapter roundups and Quick quizzes help you here)

And remember to keep careful hold of this Study Text when you move on to the next level of your exams - you will find it invaluable.

ACCA OFFICIAL SYLLABUS

Introduction

This paper introduces the different types of information systems and how they can contribute to the management =decision making processes. It includes coverage of the development, introduction and use of computer-based information systems and the advice that might be given regarding control, privacy and security procedures. Students' appreciation of the role of IT in the organisation will be reinforced in Paper 12, where the strategic implications of IT are examined. Students are assumed to be familiar with the basic components of computer systems – hardware and software – and have the ability to relate to business the basic structure of a computer, computer peripherals and communication devices.

Covered in chapter

1   Systems to handle and process information

(a)   Systems theory, classification of systems and the nature of feedback and control. The emphasis here will be on the use of these concepts in a business context and in relation to financial information systems.   3
   (i)   an outline of general systems theory
   (ii)   definition of a system
   (iii)   types of system
   (iv)   basic elements of systems control
   (v)   positive and negative feedback
   (vi)   delays in systems.

(b)   The nature of systems needed for transaction processing   4, 5, 14
   (i)   data capture
   (ii)   batch systems
   (iii)   on line systems
   (iv)   data storage.

2   Forms of financial and related information systems

This section covers the different types of organisational structures and the different types of information systems.

(a)   Organisational structures.   1

(b)   Structures of information systems and their appropriateness to different organisational structures.   1, 2, 6

   (i)   development of different types of system
   (ii)   independence of data structures from the organisational structure
   (iii)   formal and informal information systems.

**Covered in
chapter**

(c) Types and nature of information systems for operational, tactical and strategic planning and control.   1, 2

(i) management information systems
(ii) internal reporting systems
(iii) decision support systems
(iv) executive information systems
(v) strategic information systems
(vi) expert systems

3   Systems analysis and design

This section covers the design and use of human computer interfaces and the legal requirements of data protection legislation.

(a) Basics of human computer interface design   9, 14

(i) means of interacting with a computer
(ii) prototyping
(iii) implications of poor design
(iv) preferences of type of interface from novice and experienced users
(v) validation and verification of data
(vi) security measures depending on the type of system.

(b) The requirements of data protection legislation   9

(i) principles of the Data Protection Act 1984
(ii) privacy of information
(iii) accuracy of information
(iv) accessibility of information
(v) purpose for which the data is to be used
(vi) ability of individuals to correct data held about them
(vii) organisations distributing information should ensure the reliability of the information
(viii) effect of EC legislation

(c) Use of feasibility studies   7, 11, 12, 16

(i) assessment of the feasibility/desirability of potential computer projects from the viewpoints of technical, social, operational and economic feasibility including the use of cost benefit analysis.
(ii) the production of a feasibility report and project plan.

Use of appropriate fact-finding techniques in order to establish client's system requirements in terms of:

- processes to be carried out
- outputs to be produced
- functional areas to be covered

To consider aspects such as:
- client requirements
- need for internal controls
- client competence
- cost, budget and timescale constraints
- compatibility

Identification and application of appropriate systems analysis and design tools and techniques such as:
- data analysis
- database management systems
- structured methodology
- prototyping
- CASE tools
to enable production of programme specifications, database structures, network specifications, document/screen layouts, dialogue design etc.

4   Systems evaluation

This section provides the criteria for evaluating potential and actual systems against performance criteria.

(i)   systems proposals
(ii) software design and documentation tools
(iii) bench marking
(iv) conversion plans.

                                                                                Covered in
                                                                                chapter

(b)   Evaluating potential suitable systems and packages against agreed   8, 18
criteria.

        (i)   needs analysis
        (ii)   systems development life cycle
        (iii) upgrade paths for hardware and software
        (iv) switching costs and costs of locking into manufacturers.

(c)   Designing and implementing procedures for systems operation and   6, 9, 10, 15
control

        (i)   the application of administrative controls to the acquisition,
              development, use and maintenance of data processing resources
        (ii)   the application of operational controls built into individual
              computer applications
        (iii) the issues raised by the concepts of privacy, data protection and
              computer misuse
        (vi) the use by internal or external auditors of computer-based audit
              techniques.

(d)   Drawing conclusions from the evaluation and proposing an optimal   6, 8, 18
system

        (i)   the possibility of creating an optimum system
        (ii)   judging whether an optimum system has been achieved
        (iii) costing of different systems options
        (iv) prioritising needs
        (v)   political considerations
        (vi) trade-off between strategic needs and impact on IT strategy
        (vii) cost of information and cost of lack of information.

(e)   Explaining, negotiating, agreeing and documenting systems   18
modifications.

5   Implementation of systems

This section covers the life cycle of a system and the backup systems
needed for a system and also considers the role of the system developer in
giving and seeking advice.

(a)   Negotiating and agreeing procedures and plans for the implementation,   16, 17
monitoring and maintenance of a new system

        (i)   need for project management
        (ii)   the tools of project management
        (iii) project team concepts
        (iv) monitoring criteria
        (v)   organisation control
        (vi) systems changeover

Covered in chapter

(b)   Informing and advising on relevant aspects of the nature, purpose, functions and operation of the system to appropriate personnel **16, 17**

    (i)   software upgrades
    (ii)   role of database administrator
    (iii)   system/network manager
    (iv)   external impacts on IT system
    (v)   advise on the appropriateness and completeness of user, administrator, software and hardware documentation

(c)   Minimising the possibility of system failures **15**

    (i)   backup systems
    (ii)   log file systems

(d)   Obtaining and analysing information on the operation of the system **10, 18**

    (i)   the need for measures of performance
    (ii)   error detection and correction
    (iii)   meeting new user requirements

    (iv)   flexibility and adaptability
    (v)   integrity
    (vi)   effect of increasing volumes of transactions and users

(e)   Systems modifications **17, 18**

    (i)   create criteria for the changing and upgrading of systems
    (ii)   effort expended in relation to the upgrading and improvement of systems
    (iii)   fault rectification
    (vi)   systems records
    (v)   alignment with manufacturers' upgrades
    (vi)   training and retraining
    (vii)   help lines
    (viii)   user groups
    (ix)   advantages and disadvantages of experts/contractors

ACCA OFFICIAL 1998-1999 TEACHING GUIDE

This is the official 1998-1999 Teaching Guide, for the December 1998 and June 1999 exam.

SECTION ONE: THE NATURE AND ROLE OF INFORMATION SYSTEMS

Syllabus reference

Sessions 1/2   Organisational systems

2a, b

- information flow in an organisation
- modelling information flow
- non-financial systems: order processing, inventory control and personnel and recruitment records
- financial systems: accounts and payroll
- the links and integration between the systems described above

Sessions 3/4   Information and decision making

2b, c

- discuss the nature of the decision-making process and the role of information in this process
- differentiate between informal and formal information systems
- distinguish between data and information and define the 'qualities' of good information
- distinguish between structured and unstructured decisions
- explain how the type and quality of information varies according to the level of decision making
- explain the principles of Executive Information Systems, Management Information Systems, Decision Support Systems and Expert Systems
- describe the components of Office Automation and explain how these components have changed the structure and operation of office work

Session 5   Systems theory and its application

1a

- explain the philosophy of the systems approach
- describe the systems view of an organisation
- differentiate between open, closed, deterministic and probabilistic systems
- explain the concept of positive and negative feedback, filtering, coupling and decoupling, requisite variety and entropy in the context of organisational and financial systems

Session 6   The characteristics of information technology

1b

- describe the basic components of a computer system
- describe typical input, output and secondary storage devices
- appreciate the role and functions of the Operating System
- describe typical communication devices
- distinguish between batch, on-line and real-time systems
- appreciate current trends in Information Technology

SECTION THREE: SYSTEMS DEVELOPMENT

Sessions 14/15/16   Systems analysis   3c, d, f

- describe the evolution of the development lifecycle with particular reference to structured analysis and design methodologies
- explain the various phases normally present in the structured lifecycle
- explain the relevance and importance of a standard approach to systems development
- describe the various fact finding techniques that can be employed to determine information system requirements
- construct and interpret levelled dataflow diagrams
- construct and interpret entity relationship models (Logical Data Structures)
- construct and interpret entity life histories
- understand the principles and application of normalisation
- use Structured English, decision trees and decision tables to define the logic of a process

Sessions 17/18/19   Systems design   1b, 3a, e, f, 4b

- describe input and output technologies and the principles of effective input and output design
- discuss the principles of file and database design
- explain the advantages of the database approach over conventional file organisation
- describe the three major database structures - hierarchical, network and relational
- describe the content and role of the data dictionary
- describe different ways of structuring a dialogue between the system and its users
- explain what factors contribute to a 'user-friendly' system
- contrast the advantages and disadvantages of bespoke development against a software package solution
- select an appropriate software package solution
- explain the use, significance and major features of CASE tools
- explain the principles of prototyping and the potential role of Fourth Generation Languages in this approach

Session 21   Security design and operation   1e, 4c, 5c

- explain the need and principles of backup and recovery procedures
- explain the importance of controls
- identify the basic types of clerical and software controls
- describe the main methods of fraud and how to discover the nature of a fraud
- describe the operation of a password system
- explain the role and operation of a logical access system
- explain the dangers stemming from hackers, viruses and electronic eavesdropping
- understand the role of encryption techniques

    BPP Publishing

SECTION FOUR: SYSTEMS IMPLEMENTATION, MANAGEMENT AND EVALUATION

Sessions 22/23/24   Project management

3c, 5a, b

- describe the major problems likely to arise in the management of computer-based projects
- describe the likely contents of a Terms of Reference for the project
- explain the phases outlined in a project management plan
- discuss the need for accurate estimating for costing and resource allocation
- construct and interpret a Network Chart
- construct and interpret a Gantt Chart
- understand the significance of the Critical Path
- define the features of commonly used project management tools
- discuss the advantages which may accrue from the use of project management software tools
- explain the possible structure of a project team
- discuss the human resource management issues concerned with project teams
- explain the nature of a risk management exercise
- identify the threats to the successful implementation of an information system
- discuss measures to reduce such threats

Sessions 25/26   Systems management

4a, 5a

- select the implementation strategy appropriate to a given situation
- ensure the adequacy of testing, training, documentation and support services for the new system
- discuss the need for training
- identify the types and levels of training required
- devise a plan for the complete training requirement
- define the documentation required to support the delivered system
- recognise the need and problems of file conversion and creation

Sessions 27/28   Systems maintenance and evaluation

4b, e, 5d, e

- distinguish between systems maintenance and system redevelopment
- describe the concepts of corrective, perfective and adaptive maintenance
- identify the causes of systems maintenance
- construct a system maintenance lifecycle
- outline the need for user groups and help lines
- explain the structure and function of user groups
- evaluate the benefits stemming from user groups
- suggest methods of providing adequate help and advice facilities
- describe how the evaluation of an information system is performed
- explain the role of computer-based monitoring
- describe ways and means of measuring and improving information systems performance
- explain the need and structure of post-implementation reviews

THE EXAMINATION PAPER

Assessment methods and format of the paper

		Number of marks
Section A	Compulsory questions based on a case study	55
Section B	3 (out of 5) questions of 15 marks each	45
		100

Time allowed: 3 hours

Analysis of past papers

The following topics have been examined in papers set under the syllabus for Paper 5 *Information Analysis*. You should note that the new examiner set the December 1995 and subsequent papers.

December 1997

Section A (Compulsory)

Case study - electrical product supplier
1   Post - implementation review
2   Software acquisition
3   Systems performance
4   Project management

Section B (3 questions to be answered)
5   Decision tables and structured English
6   Outsourcing and organisation structure
7   Information and decision making
8   Data dictionary and database administration
9   Passwords and audit trails

June 1997

Section A (Compulsory)

Case study - Payroll system
1   Compare parallel running and direct changeover
2   Options for training
3   Maintenance contracts and user groups
4   Information for, and explanation of, network diagrams

Section B (3 questions to be answered)
5   Feedback, coupling and decoupling, and entropy
6   Validation checks and input design principles
7   Relational databases, SQL and normalisation
8   Feasibility studies
9   Maintenance and user-friendliness

December 1996

Section A (Compulsory)

Case study - hospital recruitment

1 Interpret Data Flow Diagram
2 Development standards and structured walkthroughs
3 Data protection principles
4 Risk analysis

Section B (3 questions to be answered)

5 Office automation
6 Investigation techniques
7 Prototyping and 4GLs
8 Qualities of information and decisions
9 Evaluating software acquisition proposals

June 1996

Section A (Compulsory)

Case study - administration of examinations

1 Benefits and costs of integrating systems
2 Advantages and disadvantages of methods of assessing the economic feasibility of an IS project
3 Data collection methods
4 Determining the operational feasibility of a project

Section B (3 questions to be attempted)

5 Entity relationship model
6 Project management
7 CASE tools and systems development
8 Mini-case: off the shelf packages v tailored packages
9 Data validation and data verification

December 1995

Section A (Compulsory)

Case study - large public authority

1 Decentralisation and its advantages
2 Centralisation and its advantages
3 Funding options for IS: cost centre or separate company
4 Structured methods

Section B (3 questions to be attempted)

5 Features of user-friendly software
6 Functions and advantages of a DBMS; explanation of aspects of a relational DBMS
7 Negative feedback; spreadsheets and decision making; end-user computing
8 Testing and file conversion
9 Preparation of a decision table; decision trees

An official pilot case study, devised by the new examiner for this paper, was published in the March 1995 Students' Newsletter *and covered the following topics. It is included as the final question in the exam question bank at the end of this Study Text.*

Pilot case study: Accounting Academy
1   Areas of the business to be included in a feasibility study
2   Business benefits of computerisation of areas identified
3   Off-the-shelf package or bespoke solution
4   Security and audit issues raised by implementation of network
5   Preparation of a dataflow diagram December 1994

June 1995

Section A - Case study: Mediserve Health Centre
1   Problems of reliance on manually based systems
2   Processes and functions suitable for IT investment
3   Suitability of networked PCs or minicomputer and terminals
4   'Responsibilities of ownership': data integrity, security and risk management
5   Preparation of a dataflow diagram

Section B
6   Planned approach to identification and selection of computer projects
7   Process specification tools: structured English; decision tables; decision trees
8   Types of decision and decision making; use of a decision support system
9   Project management: network charts and Gantt charts; activities in systems implementation
10 Acquisition of hardware and software: contents of an invitation to tender; evaluation of tenders received; financing methods

Prior to June 1995 the exam did not feature a case study.

December 1994

1   Expert systems; prototyping
2   Decisions, decision making and decision support systems
3   Systems theory and feedback
4   Devolved authority for acquisition of PCs
5   Implementation and post-implementation review
6   Analysis and design tools; CASE techniques
7   Acquisition of hardware and software: cost-benefit analysis and sources of finance

June 1994

1   Systems replacement: speed of development; use of computers to control projects; user participation
2   Categories of system; their use in sales and marketing and in finance
3   System characteristics against which a system can be evaluated
4   Preparation of a dataflow diagram; process specification tools
5   Types of maintenance; system documentation
6   Feasibility study; fact-finding techniques
7   The effects of computerisation

Further guidance from the ACCA

The ACCA provides the following further guidance on the examination paper for Paper 5 *Information Analysis*.

The objective of the Certificate Stage

This stage continues the introduction of the new subject areas, develops students' analytical skills and introduces students to the problems and situations that they will meet at work.

The Certificate Stage tests the application of the theory in the context of recognisable problems and conceptual understanding. It will consolidate knowledge of current principles, practices and techniques and begin to develop students' ability to criticise current practices. Questions will present practical scenarios requiring students to select the best answer from a range of available solutions in order to achieve the specified objective.

This stage will establish links between subjects, for example coverage of mathematical topics will be wholly in the context of their use in management accounting or financial management.

Skills to be tested in the Certificate Stage

Students should be able to demonstrate the ability to:

- analyse and evaluate information;
- apply concepts and principles flexibly in a variety of circumstances;
- identify, define and rank problems;
- interpret results;
- criticise proposed solutions or practices.

Aim of paper 5

To ensure students appreciate the contribution of information systems to meeting the goals and needs of the business and understand procedures for the development, introduction and use of computer-based systems.

On completion of this paper students should be able to:

- describe different types of information systems, with particular reference to financial systems, and understand their role in the decision-making process and their relationship to the organisation

- describe and apply the main tools and techniques of systems analysis and design

- evaluate the performance of information systems

- describe systems for the security of data and applications

- describe the tools available to assist in efficient project management

- discuss the procedures to enable systems maintenance to be carried out in an accurate and timely manner

- demonstrate the skills expected at the Certificate Stage.

Prerequisite knowledge

Students are assumed to be familiar with the basic components of computer systems (hardware and software) and the basic structure of a computer, computer peripherals and communication devices from their study of paper 3 *Management Information* and from their practical work experience. If students are exempt from paper 3 and do not have this background knowledge of information technology, they are recommended to read the relevant chapter in a suitable text.

Development of paper 5 topics in subsequent papers

The table below shows the papers in which the support topic, information technology (IT), is developed and integrated with its application in core topics.

	SUPPORT SUBJECT
CORE SUBJECT	Information Technology
Financial Accounting	Paper 1
Management Accounting	Papers 3 and 9
Auditing	Papers 6 and 10
Management	Paper 12

Students will apply their knowledge of IT in an auditing context in paper 6 *Audit Framework* and paper 10 *Accounting and Audit Practice* where more advanced study of computer-assisted audit techniques will be tested.

Students' appreciation of the role of IT in the organisation will be reinforced in paper 12 *Management and Strategy* where the importance of linking information systems development and management to improve business performance will be emphasised.

Extent of integration

Paper 5 will incorporate the provisions of legislation relevant to privacy and computer misuse. Questions will be set on principles and good practice and will not make specific reference to the UK legislation to ensure non UK students are not disadvantaged.

General note

Students are advised to read the 'Exam Notes', published in the *Students' Newsletter* as these contain details of examinable legislation, changes in the syllabuses and other useful information for each examination session.

Part A

The nature and role of information systems

Chapter 1

ORGANISATIONAL INFORMATION SYSTEMS

Chapter topic list	Syllabus reference
1 Information flow in an organisation	2(a), 2(b)
2 Transactions processing and management information	2(a), 2(b), 2(c)
3 Order processing and inventory control	2(b)
4 Financial systems	2(b)
5 Personnel and payroll	2(b)
6 Integrated systems	2(b)

Introduction

This chapter provides an introduction to the topic of **information** as it is used in **organisations**. Many of the organisational systems that we describe will be familiar from your earlier studies of accounting, but here we are particularly interested in how the different systems link up.

1   INFORMATION FLOW IN AN ORGANISATION

1.1   The aim of this book, and of paper 5 as a whole, is to ensure that you appreciate the contribution of **information systems** to meeting the goals and needs of **businesses**.

Businesses and communication

1.2   Any business has three major components. In simple terms these are:

(a)   **people** (who have skills and knowledge);
(b)   **things** (such as buildings, equipment, materials);
(c)   **goals** (such as making a profit or helping the public).

To achieve the business's goals, the people, with the help of the things that the business provides, use their skills and knowledge to carry out activities.

Step 1.   A salesperson might persuade a customer to order an item that her organisation produces.

Step 2.   The order details will be sent to another person in the organisation who acts as a sales administrator.

Step 3.   That person will notify somebody who can make this item to the customer's requirements.

Step 4.   The maker will follow the customer's instructions and use the things provided by the organisation to make the item.

Step 5. He will tell the sales administrator when the item has been made and sent.

Step 6. The sales administrator will then ask the customer to pay for the item.

1.3 This is a very simple description of the typical activities of a commercial organisation, but look at the activities that are described: persuade, send an order, notify, follow instruction, tell, ask. These are all aspects of **communication**. Communication is central to anything that happens in an organisation. Without communication it would be impossible for an organisation to achieve its goals.

> **KEY TERM**
>
> **Communication** means transmitting or exchanging **information**. An information **system** is something that manages the task of transmitting and exchanging information.

Resources

1.4 What we have described as people and things may be more formally referred to as **resources**. An organisation takes inputs of resources and converts them into outputs. In a manufacturing organisation the following resources might be encountered.

(a) Metal, plastic, and other raw materials
(b) Machinery and equipment to mould and assemble the raw materials
(c) The skills of people (for example, designers, managers and machine operators)
(d) Money to pay for the materials, machinery and people

> **KEY TERM**
>
> **Resources** are conventionally referred to as the four Ms: materials, machinery, men (ie people) and money. But we also need to add time (perhaps the scarcest resource of all), and space (land and buildings), and, above all, **information**.

1.5 Information is a resource in every sense, because you might have to **pay for it** (buying a mailing list, say), you have to **process it** (analyse the mailing list to find all customers in Barnsley, say), and because it **can be sold** as an output (a newspaper, this book, or a set of accounts produced by an accountant are all examples).

1.6 Information is also used to **manage** the other resources (stock records, personnel records, accounting records).

Question 1

What does an organisation do with its resources of time and space? What information is needed to manage these resources?

Information flows

1.7 There are lots of different and separate activities within an organisation, which is why organisations have a structure of departments or functions. For example, a manufacturing organisation will have amongst other things, a **production** department and a **sales** department. The sales department liaises with customers. The production department makes the goods. These activities appear completely distinct. Many of the personnel working for the sales department will have little or no contact with the production workforce.

1.8 However, these two functions are vitally linked, and, to different degrees in different organisations, each activity depends on information **exchanges** with other activities to function effectively.

(a) There is no use promising customers goods which cannot be supplied, so the selling activity depends on the production activity to come up with the goods. Likewise, it is thoroughly wasteful to produce goods which no one wants to buy. So, for the **production activity** to function effectively, it **must be linked** in some way to the **selling activity**.

(b) The organisation might be able to sell a large number of goods at a low price; or a small number of goods at a high price. This sort of information will be **collected from the environment** by the selling staff. However, it is the production staff who know the cost of the goods to be purchased. A selling price has to be determined, but this must be one which ensures that the costs of production are met.

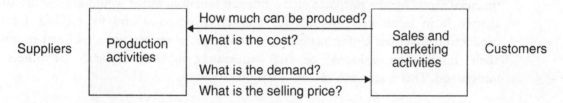

1.9 We can draw out a few conclusions from this simple example.

(a) The sales and production departments need to exchange information about their requirements and capacities. Put another way, there needs to be a **flow of information** between these different activities.

(b) The sales and production departments are, as it were, mini-organisations in their own right within the organisation as a whole, yet inevitably, they must be linked in some way. All organisations therefore display some sort of **structure**, with varying degrees of formality, linking the various forms of activity within the organisation.

Modelling information flow

1.10 The diagram above is a very simple example of how information flows can be modelled. Later in this book we shall be looking at more formal procedures, notably data flow diagrams (DFDs).

Organisation structures and information flows

1.11 Organisations will adopt different structures depending on their size, on what their task is, and on how managers like to manage things. There is no ideal structure for a given set of circumstances, although we can make some generalisations.

Geographically based structures

1.12 A **geographically based structure** might be adopted by an organisation whose task could be done better by people with **local** knowledge, for example a French division and a German division. It is also the most common structure within a national **salesforce**, to cut down on travelling, and is obviously the best option when there is a need to use local resources (Scottish springwater, say).

1.13   In the past a geographical structure may have given rise to **communication problems** due to the time it would take information to flow around the organisation and the lack of personal contact between people in different parts of the business. Advances in telecommunications and faster transport have lessened these difficulties. Information may have to be gathered on a regional basis and then consolidated to gain an overall view of what is happening in the organisation. This could cause **delays** and make it **difficult to see patterns** such as sales trends emerging. Systems would need to be designed to overcome these difficulties.

Functionally based structures

1.14   **Functionally based structure** is very commonly adopted to take advantage of people's different specialisms and skills.

1.15   **Information problems** would centre on the **sharing** of information collected for different purposes. For example sales invoice information would need to be analysed in financial terms for the purposes of the **finance** function, but it would also be useful to analyse it in terms of customers for **marketing** purposes and by product for the **production** function. Unfortunately, functional specialists are often inclined to guard 'their' information jealously, or else deliberately make it difficult for others to understand. This is seen as a means of self-preservation.

Other structures

1.16   Other possibilities are a **product or brand-based structure**, which makes sense for organisations that produce a relatively small number of high volume products, and a **customer or market segment-based structure**, where the organisation can identify significant groups that it wants to target.

1.17   In both cases, once again, the main danger is that information **collection** will be **fragmented** and it will be difficult to get a picture of what is happening in the organisation **as a whole**. There may well be some **duplication** of information collection and processing, which is inefficient.

1.18   We can conclude that an information system may be, or become, ineffective if it is too closely modelled on the prevailing structure of the organisation. It needs to **cut across the organisation structure** wherever possible and be capable of changing to respond to the changing needs of the business.

Exam focus point

The material in Section 1 of this chapter is unlikely to be at the centre of an exam question, but it is relevant background information for almost **all** questions, since all are set in the context of an organisation.

2   TRANSACTIONS PROCESSING AND MANAGEMENT INFORMATION

2.1   An organisation's information systems might be used to perform a number of tasks simultaneously.

(a) **Initiating transactions** (for example automatically making a purchase order if stock levels are below a specified amount)

(b) **Recording transactions** as they occur (for example a sale is input to the sales ledger system)

(c) **Processing** data

(d) Producing **reports**

(e) Responding to **enquiries**

Transactions processing

2.2 Transactions processing systems, or data processing systems, are the lowest level in an organisation's use of information systems. They are used for **routine tasks** in which data items or transactions must be processed so that operations can continue. Handling sales orders, purchase orders, payroll items and stock records are typical examples.

2.3 Transactions processing systems provide the raw material which is often used more extensively by management information systems, databases or decision support systems. In other words, transactions processing systems might be used to produce **management information**, such as reports on cumulative sales figures to date, total amounts owed to suppliers or owed by debtors, total stock turnover to date, value·of current stock-in-hand, and so on, but the main purpose of transaction processing systems is as an integral part of day-to-day operations.

Management information

KEY TERM

A **management information system (MIS)** is a system to **convert data** from internal and external sources into **information** and to communicate that information, in an appropriate form, to **managers** at all levels in all functions to enable them to make timely and effective decisions for planning, directing and controlling the activities for which they are responsible.

2.4 An MIS is good at providing **regular formal information** gleaned from normal commercial data. For example, an MIS relating to sales could provide managers with information on the following.

(a) Gross profit margins of particular products
(b) Success in particular markets
(c) Credit control information (aged debtors and payments against old balances)

2.5 It may be less efficient at presenting information which is relatively **unpredictable**, or **informal**, or unstructured. So, for example, an MIS could not provide information relating to the sudden emergence of a new competitor into the market.

2.6 As we shall see in the next chapter, while an MIS may not be able to provide all the information used by management, it should be sufficiently flexible to enable management to incorporate unpredictable, informal or unstructured information into **decision-making** processes. For example, many decisions are made with the help of financial models (such as spreadsheets) so that the effect of new situations can be estimated easily.

Exam focus point

The meaning and nature of a MIS featured in several questions set by the old examiner (prior to December 1995). There is more on this, and on other categories of system, such as decision support systems, in the next chapter.

3 ORDER PROCESSING AND INVENTORY CONTROL

3.1 There are two types of **order processing** system, one for items to be **bought**, the other for items to be **sold**.

3.2 In terms of the **information** needed they are fairly similar. They are frequently **linked** together by **inventory control** systems.

Exam focus point

In the exam you are unlikely to be asked 'What is an order processing system', but you may well be given a scenario that describes a **faulty** order processing system and asked to identify what is missing. Moreover, most exam questions have in their background a typical business system such as an order processing or inventory control system.

This section and the ones that follow in this chapter give **practical** illustrations of the key elements of organisational systems in any business, so this is a point to return to and think about if ever you are feeling bogged down by details and cannot see how the information we are providing fits into the overall scheme of things.

Purchase order systems

3.3 If you want to buy something personally you need to know what **specification** of thing you want (size 9 shoes in black, for instance), what it will be **used for** (for work or for casual wear, say), **where or from whom** to buy it from (Dolcis locally, perhaps, or through a mail order catalogue) and **how much** money you are going to need (you might want particularly good quality shoes and be prepared to pay extra).

3.4 In a **business,** a purchase order system is similar to this.

3.5 See how many of the purchase criteria noted in paragraph 3.3 you can spot in the illustration below, from a computerised Purchase Order Processing (POP) system. This is a purchase order that might have arisen because the company concerned is low on stocks of WIDGET2000, which may be a **component** that they use to make another product (if they are a **manufacturing** business), or something that they **stock for resale** to customers (if they are a **retailer**).

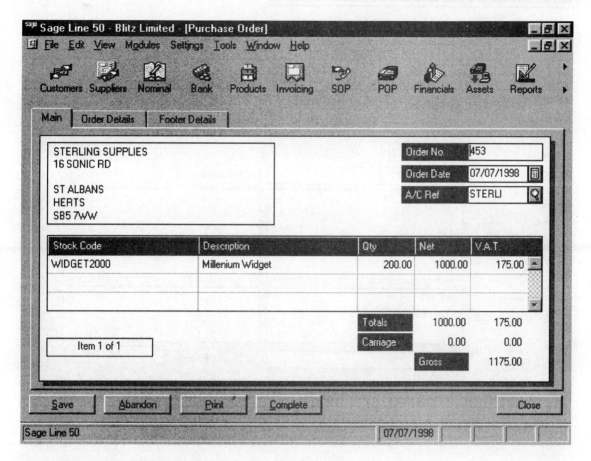

3.6   There are several important points to note initially.

    (a)   In a business all orders are **numbered and dated**. This is to help identify them at a later date in case of any query about what was ordered.

    (b)   The supplier has a **code** –the A/C Ref, STERLI –and so does the product – the Stock Code, WIDGET 2000.

    (c)   This is only an **order**. The records will be updated to show that 200 items are **On order** but have not yet been received, and so are not available for immediate use or resale.

3.7   The **codes** are used because this is an **integrated** system which links up with other systems. The information shown here, for instance, derives partly from a separate but linked system of supplier details.

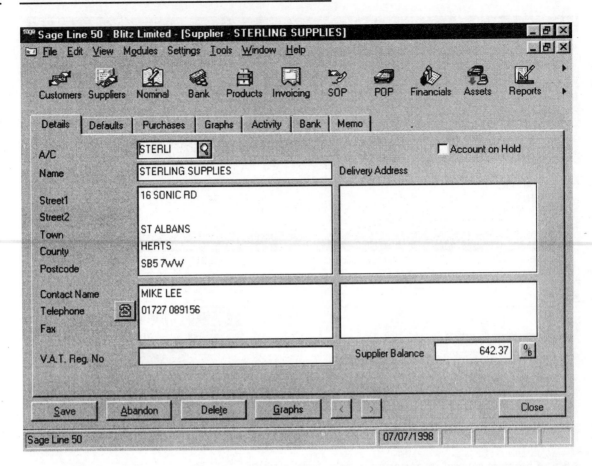

3.8   The user of this system simply needs to enter the code STERLI into the A/C Ref box to bring up in the box on the left hand side the full name and address details for that supplier.

Integrated systems

3.9   Purchase order systems do not necessarily *need* to be linked up (**integrated**) with other systems. In a very **small business**, for instance, Employee A, who makes the final product, may mention (at tea-break) to Employee B, who is in charge of buying materials, that she is about to run out of Widgets and could Employee B please buy the best Widgets available. Employee B would happen to know that Sterling Supplies was currently offering the best deal on Widgets and place the order accordingly.

3.10 In a very **large business**, using millions of different parts and making many different products, this is impractical. For one thing Employee A would not even meet Employee B at tea-break: they may be on different sites. For another, Employee B could not possibly remember off the top of his or her head who the best supplier for a particular component might be, and certainly would not remember their name and address details.

3.11 An integrated computerised purchase order system, however, could:

(a)   automatically notify the purchase order department that stocks of Widgets were low and fresh supplies were needed;

(b)   automatically be updated with and provide the details of suppliers offering the best deal on Widgets.

3.12 The stock level details would be drawn from an **inventory system**, as we shall see in a moment, and the best supplier details would be drawn from the inventory system via the **accounting system**, again as we shall see.

Sales order systems

3.13   A sales order is processed when a customer rings up, or sends an order by post, or comes in personally and asks for a specific item. For instance, if we assume that our business buys WIDGET2000s from a wholesaler and then **resells** them, here is how a sales order might look.

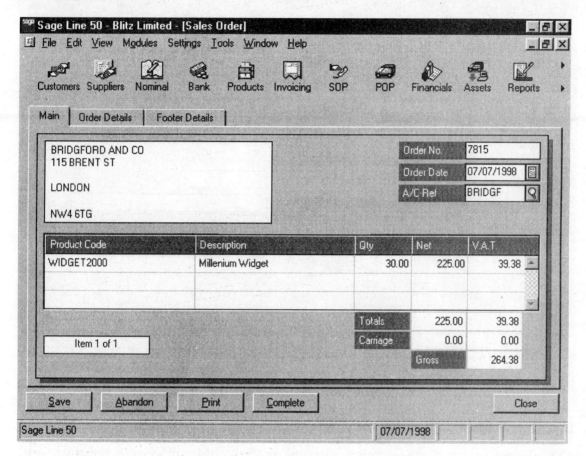

3.14   Note again that details are recorded that enable the transaction to be **traced** easily if necessary. Note also that the customer details are taken, if possible, because the business then has the necessary **marketing** information to inform relevant customers of new products that they might be interested in buying, such as WIDGET 2001s.

(This is why supermarkets want you to sign up for their 'loyalty' cards, such as Tesco **Clubcard or** Safeway **ABC** cards).

Integrated systems

3.15   Again sales order systems do not *necessarily* need to be integrated with other systems. Some customers like dealing with very **small** businesses, such as the corner shop, because the owner **remembers** their name or what they look like, and takes the trouble to get in things for them or keep them aside specially, knowing that the customer is bound to come in again.

3.16   **Larger** businesses may not have this luxury, and may not find it economic to deal with very small orders for unusual items. They need records of all their **customer details** (identical to the supplier details illustrated for Sterling Supplies above) and they need to develop systems that force them to **Allocate** stock that has been ordered by particular customers. (This too will become clearer when we look at inventory control, below.)

3.17   A particularly important issue for sales order systems is that orders are not accepted from customers who might not pay for them, and therefore a system that recognises **credit limits** is required.

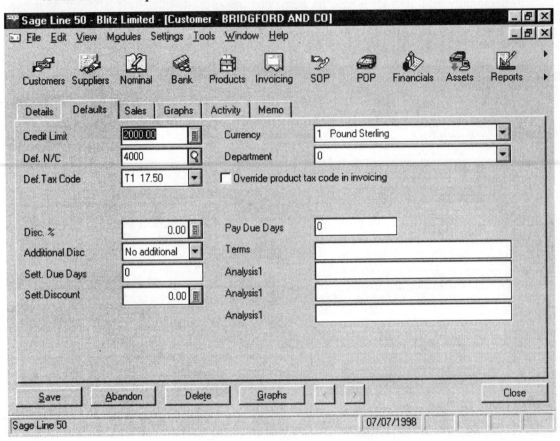

Inventory control

3.18   Central to both purchase order processing and sales order processing, therefore, is a system of controlling what **stock** is held.

> **KEY TERM**
>
> **Inventory** is just another name for stock.
>
> Stocks might be **raw materials** for incorporation into other products, work that is partially completed (**work-in-progress**), products that are finished (**finished goods**) or things bought solely to sell on to others, like baked beans in a supermarket (**goods for resale**).

3.19   Here is the stock record for the WIDGET2000, reflecting the sales order and purchase order that we have looked at already. Make sure you do the Question that follows to ensure that you understand the value of **integrated** records.

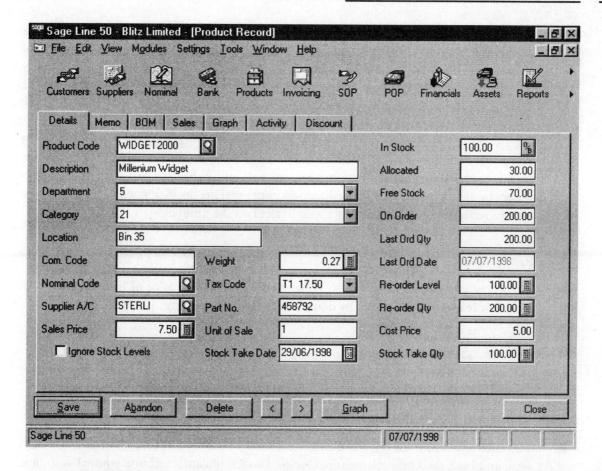

Question 2

In a number of ways this stock record reflects the purchase order and the sales order that we have looked at already.

In what ways does it do this? What else does it show?

Answer

These are the most important points, though there are others.

(a) It shows the best **supplier** for this product. When a purchase order for WIDGET2000s is initiated the system will automatically use this supplier unless the user specifies otherwise.

(b) It has details of the **purchase cost** of individual items (£5). This means that when a purchase order is entered the user does not need to go looking through catalogues and price lists for the relevant information. Also, the quantity ordered can be multiplied by the price **automatically**, so there is not even any calculation to do. (**Audit the figures, to check**.)

(c) It has details of the normal **reorder quantity** (calculated using, say, the EOQ model, that you have learned about in your studies for Paper 3 or Paper 8), so that when a purchase order is entered this figure (200 units) is suggested automatically.

(d) It has a **re-order level,** which could generate a computer message telling the purchase order assistant when stocks fell down to the re-order level.

(e) It shows stock **on order** from Sterling Supplies (200 units).

(f) It shows stock **allocated** to Bridgford, though not yet despatched.

(g) It shows the **selling price** of a unit of stock, so again once quantities are entered the total figure does not need to be calculated by hand (**audit the figures**).

(h) It shows the amount of **free stock.** This will mean that if someone orders more than 70 units before the next delivery is received the system will generate a message alerting the sales order processing assistant that the customer will not be able to have their full order immediately.

(i) It shows where the stock is **physically located** (Bin 35) in the warehouse.

3.20 In a manufacturing company inventory control may be reliant upon a highly complex **production system.** For example BOM in the illustration above stands for **Bill of Materials.** This would be used by a company that makes a product using a wide variety of raw materials and components, so that the cost of that product is the sum of all the material inputs, and there would be a separate record linked to the main WIDGET2000 record, for each item used to make a WIDGET2000.

3.21 The **production system** may have its own records for individual **machines** (time in use, energy inputs, maintenance required and so on), and either as part of the production system or as a separate **time-recording/personnel** system finished goods cost would also need to reflect the cost of the people who worked on the product.

4 FINANCIAL SYSTEMS

4.1 You know what a financial system is, so we will not spend a lot of time on it. It is a system of **ledgers** co-ordinated by **double-entry** and comprising:

- sales ledger
- purchase ledger
- nominal ledger

Sales ledger and purchase ledger

4.2 The sales ledger and the purchase ledger are **fed by** order processing systems, as we have seen, and both **feed into** the nominal ledger via debtors and creditors **control** accounts. Both will include details of individual customers or suppliers, as we have seen, and store up cumulative data about transactions, partly to fulfil legal obligations and partly for **management reporting** purposes. The commonest report is an **aged analysis.**

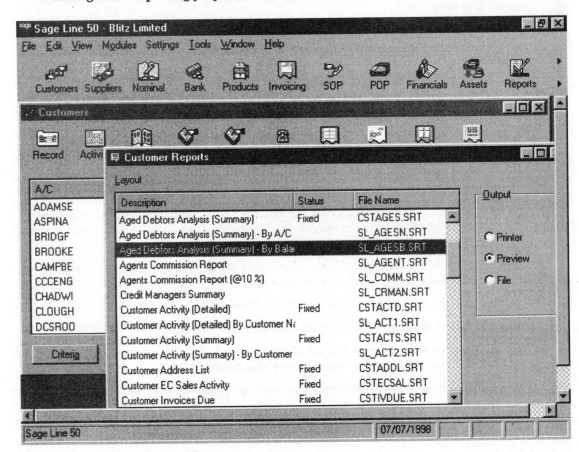

Nominal ledger

4.3   The nominal ledger contains records of **sales and expenses** by type. In an integrated system an invoice posted to a Purchase Ledger account for, say, *The Battersea Guardian*, would also update the **advertising expense** account in the nominal ledger.

4.4   Also subsidiary to the **nominal ledger** are the **cash book,** the **fixed asset** system and the **inventory control** system. See how many of these elements you can spot in the illustration below.

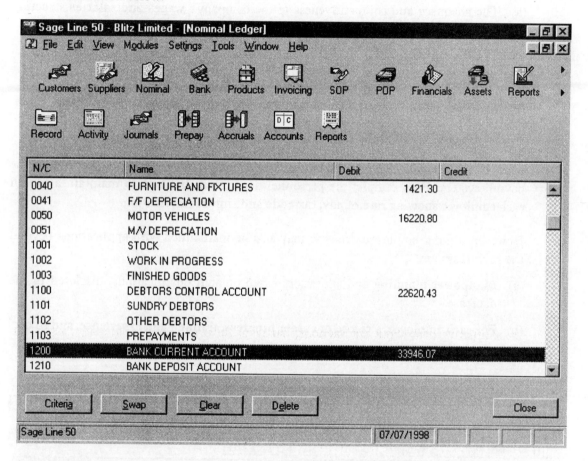

Other financial systems

4.5   The finance function is also responsible for controlling and co-ordinating a number of areas besides accounting, which affect most or all other functions. These include the following.

- Budgeting and standard costing
- Forecasting
- Producing management accounts
- Reporting financial results

5   PERSONNEL AND PAYROLL

5.1   The principal assets of some organisations (such accountants and solicitors) are the **people** who work for them, and there clearly need to be systems to support the management of people and their **time**.

5.2 The personnel system will be concerned with issues such as the following.

 (a) The adequacy and competitiveness of the company's **wages and salaries** structure (and therefore also for staff grading)

 (b) **Training** of staff

 (c) Pension plans, and other **employment benefits**

 (d) Maintenance of personnel **statistics** such as labour turnover

 (e) Attendance and **time** records

5.3 Some of the data kept by a personnel department will overlap with the data used in the payroll system. For example, the personnel department is likely to maintain a file on each employee showing **rate of pay, tax code** and similar information.

5.4 However, a fuller employee database may also be maintained with applications beyond the payroll system.

 (a) **Manpower planning** and allocation, based on staff qualifications, disclosed in the database.

 (b) For each employee, a record of **career progress**, training and experience, and so on.

 (c) Selection of appropriate staff for further **training** and/or promotion.

 (d) Preparation of statistics on sickness, injuries and absenteeism.

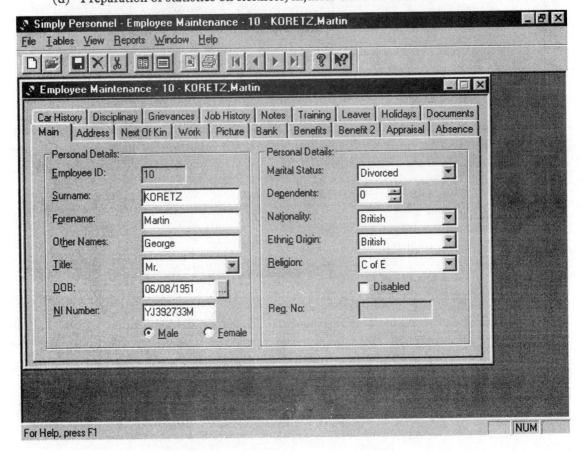

Question 3

Look at the illustration above and see how many of the features we have mentioned you can spot.

Payroll

5.5 A payroll system would be **linked** to whatever time-recording and personnel systems are in operation and also perhaps to production and stock or work-in-progress control systems.

5.6 **Unique records** in a payroll system would be things like tax code, and bank details. The system would also need to hold details of current legislation and tax and NI rates.

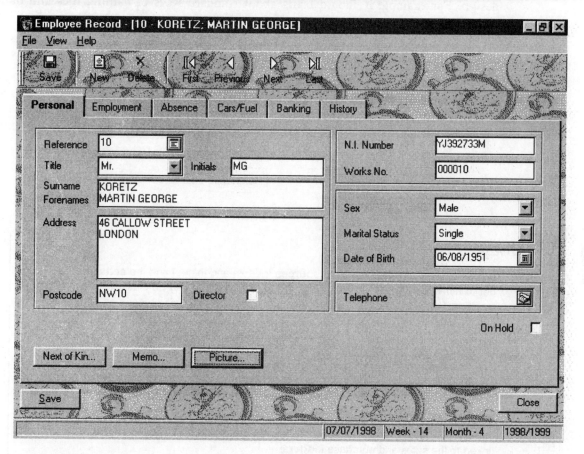

6 INTEGRATED SYSTEMS

> ### KEY TERM
>
> **Integrated systems** can be defined as a number of systems which, although capable of autonomous operation, may be linked closely to form a comprehensive and single view to the user. The use of common files or records by the individual systems is a feature of integration.

6.1 The advantages of integrated processing are as follows.

  (a) Each part of the system can be used **separately**, or in a **combination** of the parts, or as a **total** system.

(b) A transaction item only has to be **entered once** to update all parts of the system. **Duplication of effort** is avoided, and so is the need to store the same data in several different places (**data redundancy**).

(c) Integration of data means that all departments in a company are using the same information and inter-departmental disagreements based on differences about 'facts' can be avoided.

(d) **Managers** throughout the organisation should have access to fully **up-to-date information** drawn from sources right across the organisation, not just from one source. This ought to improve the breadth of vision and quality of management decisions.

(e) Integration will require **standardisation** and better defined and documented system design. For example it should bring about standard ways of naming files and of constructing spreadsheets.

6.2 The diagram below might make all this more clear. It deals with stock control, sales order and purchases applications.

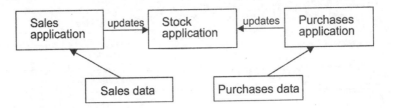

Chapter roundup

- An organisation is composed of **resources** (people and things) and the **activities** it carries out to achieve its goals. The resources of an organisation can be classified as materials, machines, men and money. Time, space and information are also resources.

- **Information** is necessary to convert these resources for use in the organisation's activities.

- The **structure** of an organisation is usually based on tasks or functions, but whatever the basis there are implications for **information systems**, which need to be **flexible** enough to serve the **entire** organisation and respond to **changes**.

- **Order processing systems** (purchase orders and sales orders) contain and use information about customers, suppliers and products. In an integrated system they will be linked to the sales and purchase **ledgers**.

- **Inventory control systems** record details about raw materials, work-in-progress and goods for resale such as supplier name, amount in stock and on order, cost and selling price. They may be linked to a **production** system and a **time**-recording system.

- **Financial systems** comprise the standard financial accounting ledgers and possibly also budgeting systems and other management accounting systems. There may be links to **asset management** systems and **personnel** and **payroll** systems as well as to order processing and inventory control.

- **Integrated systems** have many advantages over separate systems, in particular because they avoid duplication of effort and data.

Quick quiz

1   Why is information a resource? (see paras 1.5 – 1.6)

2   How should an information system reflect organisation structure? (1.18)

3   What are information systems used for? (2.1)

4   What is the link between transaction processing and management information? (2.3)

5   Describe what features you might find in a purchase order system. (3.5)

6   Why do systems use codes? (3.7)

7   What is meant by 'allocated' stock? (3.17)

8   Describe what features you might find in an inventory control system. (3.19)

9   What are the principal elements of a financial system? (4.1)

10   What type of information might be recorded in a personnel system? (5.2 - 5.4)

11   What records might be unique to a payroll system? (5.6)

12   What are the advantages of integrated processing? (6.1)

Question to try	Level	Marks	Time
1	Introductory	n/a	30 mins

Chapter 2

INFORMATION AND DECISION MAKING

Chapter topic list	Syllabus reference
1 The nature of decision making	2(b)
2 Formal and informal information systems	2(b)
3 Data and information	2(b)
4 Types of decision	2(b), 2(c)
5 How information systems support decision making	2(b), 2(c)
6 Types of management information system	2(c)

Introduction

Everything we do involves decisions, and decisions require information. For instance, if you are about to go out you need to decide what coat to wear, if any, and to make that decision you need information about what the weather is like.

This chapter considers what is involved in decision making, what different types of decision there are, and how information varies depending on how it is used for decision making. Particularly important are the **qualities of good information**. This is likely to be useful background knowledge for practically every Paper 5 question you encounter.

1   THE NATURE OF DECISION MAKING

The decision making process

1.1   The stages in making a decision are as follows.

Step 1.   Problem recognition.

Step 2.   Problem definition and structuring.

Step 3.   Identifying alternative courses of action.

Step 4.   Making and communicating the decision.

Step 5.   Implementation of the decision.

Step 6.   Monitoring the effects of the decision.

Problem recognition

1.2   Decisions are not made without **information**. The decision maker needs to be informed of a problem in the first place. This is sometimes referred to as the **decision trigger**.

Problem definition and structuring

1.3   Normally **further information** is then required. This further information is **analysed** so that the problem can be **defined** precisely.

1.4 Consider, for example, a company with falling sales. The fall in sales would be the **trigger**. **Further information** would be needed to identify where the deficiencies were occurring. The company might discover that sales of product X in area Y are falling, and the problem can be **defined** as:

> 'Decline of sales of product X in area Y due to new competitor: how can the decline be reversed?'

1.5 One of the purposes of **defining** the problem is to identify the **relationships** between the **various factors** in it, especially if the problem is complex.

Identifying alternative courses of action

1.6 Where alternative courses of action are identified, **information** is needed about the likely effect of each, so they can be assessed.

1.7 As a simple example, if our company wishes to review the price of product X in area Y, information will be needed as to the effect of particular price levels on demand for the product. Such information can include external information such as market research (demand at a particular price) and the cost of the product, which can be provided internally.

Making and communicating the decision

1.8 The decision is **made** after review of the information relating to alternatives. However, the decision is useless if it is not **communicated**. So, in our example, if the **marketing director** decides to lower the price of product X and institute an intensive **advertising** campaign, nothing will happen unless the advertising department is informed, and also the **manufacturing** department, who will have to prepare new packaging showing the lower price.

Implementation of the decision

1.9 The decision is then **implemented**. For large-scale decisions (for example to relocate a factory 100 miles away from its current site), implementation may need substantial **planning**, detailed information and very clear communication.

Monitoring the effects of the decision

1.10 Once a decision has been implemented, information is needed so that its effects can be **reviewed**. For example, if a manufacturing organisation has installed new equipment in anticipation of savings in costs, then information will need to be obtained as to whether these are going to be achieved in practice.

Exam focus point
There was a question in **December 1994** about the phases of decision making. This was set by the previous examiner (pre December 1995).

Information and decision-making

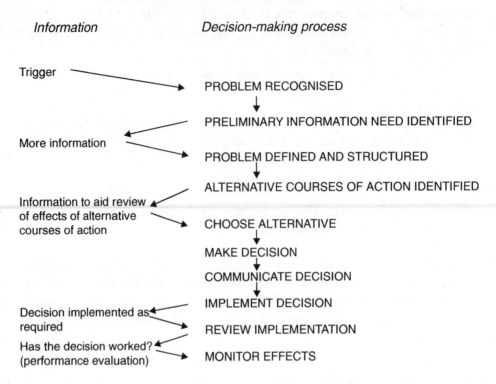

2   **FORMAL AND INFORMAL INFORMATION SYSTEMS**

2.1   Most information systems in organisations grow up **informally**, with each user making sure that he gets all the information he thinks he needs to make decisions. It is virtually taken for granted that the necessary information flows to the job, and to a certain extent this is so.

2.2   Much accounting information, for example, is easily obtained, and users can often get along with frequent **face-to-face contact** and **co-operation** with each other. Such an informal system works best in **small companies**, but is inadequate in a large company, especially one which spreads over several industries, areas or countries.

2.3   However, management should try to design the information system for their organisation with care. If they allow the information system to develop without any formal planning, it will almost certainly be **inefficient** because data will be obtained and processed in a random and disorganised way and the communication of information will also be random and hit-and-miss.

2.4   For example, without formal planning and design of the information system, the following situations are likely.

(a)   Some managers will prefer to **keep data in their heads** and will not commit information to paper. When the manager is absent from work, or is moved to another job, his stand-in or successor will not know as much as he could and should about the work because there would be no information to help him.

(b)   **Not all data is collected** and processed that ought to be, and so valuable information that ought to be available to management would be missing from neglect.

(c)   Information is available but **not communicated** to the managers who are in a position of authority and so ought to be given it. The information would go to waste because it would not be used. In other words, the wrong people would have the information.

(d) Information is **communicated late** because the need to communicate it earlier is not understood and appreciated by the data processors.

The value of informal systems

2.5 The **formal** system of communication in an organisation is **always** supplemented by an **informal** one: talks in the canteen, at the pub, on the way home, on the telephone etc. This is unavoidable and not necessarily undesirable.

2.6 The **danger** with informal communication is that it might be malicious, full of inaccurate rumours or wild speculation. This type of gossip in the organisation can be unsettling, and make colleagues mistrust one another.

2.7 Formal systems do, nevertheless, **need** the support of a good - accurate - informal system, which might be encouraged by:

(a) setting up 'official' communications to **feed information** into the informal system, eg house journals or briefings, (though these will have to earn the attention and trust of employees); and

(b) encouraging and offering opportunities for **'networking'**. A network is a collection of people, usually with a shared interest, who tend to keep in touch to exchange informal information. Ordinary social exchanges should not be stifled at work (unless they start interfering with performance, eg by distracting or delaying an employee in the middle of seeing a customer.)

2.8 Since the grapevine exists, and cannot be got rid of, management should learn both to **accept it** and to **use it**: to harness it towards achieving the objectives of the organisation. It is important for managers themselves to 'hook into' the grapevine, to be aware of what is going on - and what their subordinates think is going on.

3   DATA AND INFORMATION

Distinction between data and information

3.1 First, some definitions: in normal everyday speech the terms **data** and **information** are used interchangeably. However, in the context of data processing and information systems the terms have distinct meanings.

> **KEY TERMS**
>
> **Data** is the raw material for data processing. Data relates to facts, events, and transactions and so forth.
>
> **Information** is data that has been processed in such a way as to be meaningful to the person who receives it.

3.2   EXAMPLE, DATA AND INFORMATION

A typical market research survey employs a number of researchers who request a sample of the public to answer a number of questions about a new product, say. Several hundred questionnaires may be completed. The questionnaires are input to a system. Once every questionnaire has been input, a number of processing operations are performed on the data.

- Classifying
- Sorting
- Calculating
- Summarising

3.3 Individually, a completed questionnaire would not tell the company very much, only the views of one consumer. In this case, the individual questionnaires are **data**.

3.4 Once they have been processed, and analysed, however, the resulting report is **information**: the company will use it to inform its decisions regarding the new product. If the report revealed that consumers disliked the product, the company would scrap or alter it.

Good information

3.5 The **quality of source data** affects the **value of information**. Information is worthless if the source data is flawed. If the researchers filled in questionnaires themselves, inventing the answers, then the conclusions drawn from the processed data would be wrong, and **poor decisions** would be made.

3.6 Different levels of management take different types of decision and often require different **types** of information. However, the information provided to them can be good or bad, and in fact information which is **good** information at one level can be **bad** information at another. We shall now go on to describe the factors which are important for the successful conversion of data to information.

The qualities of good information

3.7 The qualities of good information are as follows.

(a) It should be **relevant** for its purpose.

(b) It should be **complete** for its purpose.

(c) It should be sufficiently **accurate** for its purpose.

(d) It should be **clear** to the user.

(e) The user should have **confidence** in it.

(f) It should be **communicated** to the right person.

(g) It should not be excessive - its **volume** should be manageable.

(h) It should be **timely** - in other words communicated at the most appropriate time.

(i) It should be communicated by an appropriate **channel** of communication.

(j) It should be provided at a **cost** which is less than the value of the benefits it provides.

Exam focus point

A question in the **December 1996** exam asked how you would **apply** the qualities of good information to a particular type of decision. Think through some typical decisions that may be made in an accounts department and try to work out what good information would be for the decision. This will help you to develop application skills.

A question in **December 1997** could have been answered by picking out qualities of good information and **applying** them to information needed for operational decisions (see below).

Relevance

3.8   Information must be relevant to the purpose for which a manager wants to use it. The consequences of irrelevant data are that managers might be confused by the data and might waste time.

Completeness

3.9   An information user should have all the information he needs to do his job properly. If he does not have a **complete picture** of the situation, he might well make bad decisions.

3.10   Suppose that the debt collection section of a company is informed that a customer owes £10,000 and the debt is now 4 months old and overdue. The debt collection section therefore decides to write a strongly-worded letter to the customer asking for immediate payment. Now suppose that an important piece of information had been kept from the debt collection section, for example that the debt had already been paid or that the customer had negotiated special credit terms of 6 months. In these circumstances, sending a strongly-worded demand for payment would be a mistake and likely to create badwill that might harm the prospects of future sales to the customer.

Accuracy

3.11   Information should obviously be accurate because using incorrect information could have serious and damaging consequences. However, information should only be **accurate enough for its purpose** and there is no need to go into unnecessary detail for pointless accuracy.

   (a)   **Supervisors and office workers** might need information that is accurate **to the nearest penny**, second or kilogram. For example, a cashier will do a bank reconciliation to the exact penny and purchase ledger staff will pay creditors exactly what they are owed. Much financial accounting information for day-to-day transactions must indicate amounts to the exact penny.

   (b)   **Middle managers** might be satisfied with revenues and costs **rounded to the nearest £100 or £1,000**, since greater detail would serve no purpose. For example, in budgeting, revenue and cost figures are often rounded to the nearest £1,000 because trying to be more exact would usually only give a **spurious accuracy**.

   (c)   **Senior managers** in a medium-sized to large organisation might be satisfied with figures to the **nearest ten thousand pounds**, or even hundred thousand or million pounds. Estimates to the nearest pound at this level of decision-making would be so inappropriate that they would seem ridiculous and so, oddly enough, perhaps undermine the user's confidence in the accuracy of estimates.

Clarity

3.12 Information must be clear to the user. If the user **does not understand** it properly he **cannot use** it properly. Lack of clarity is one of the causes of a breakdown in communication, which is referred to in information system theory as 'noise'.

Confidence

3.13 Information must be **trusted** by the managers who are expected to use it.

    (a) Information **sources** will not be used if they have proved **unreliable** in the past.

    (b) Even if it has a good source, not all information is **certain**. Information relating to the **future** or to the **external environment** is uncertain. However, if the assumptions underlying it are clearly stated, this might enhance the confidence with which the information is perceived.

Communication

3.14 Information that is needed might be **communicated to the wrong person**. In other words, it might be communicated to a person who does not have the authority to act on it, or who is not responsible for the matter and so does not see any need to act on it.

Volume

3.15 There are physical and mental limitations to what a person can read, absorb and understand properly before taking action. An enormous mountain of information, even if it is all relevant, cannot be handled: it leads to **information overload**. Reports to management must therefore be clear and concise and in many systems action is taken on the 'exception' principle.

KEY TERM

Exception reporting can be defined as a system of reporting based on the exception principle which focuses attention on those items where performance differs significantly from standard or budget.

Timing

3.16 Information which is not available until **after a decision** is made will be useful only for comparisons and longer-term control, and may serve no purpose even then.

3.17 Information prepared **too frequently** can be a serious disadvantage. If, for example, a decision is taken at a monthly meeting about a certain aspect of a company's operations, information to make the decision is only required once a month, and weekly reports would be a time-consuming waste of effort.

3.18 In a well designed management information system, the frequency with which information is provided will depend on the needs of:

    (a) the differing levels or status of persons to whom it is provided;

    (b) the differing functional groups.

Channel of communication

3.19   There are occasions when using one particular method of communication will be better than others. For example, job vacancies should be announced in a **medium** where they will be brought to the attention of the people most likely to be interested. The channel of communication might be the company's in-house journal, a national or local newspaper, a professional magazine, a job centre or school careers office.

3.20   Some information is best communicated informally by telephone or word-of-mouth, whereas other information ought to be formally communicated in writing or figures.

Cost

3.21   The **benefits** obtainable from the information must exceed the **costs** of acquiring it, and whenever management is trying to decide whether or not to produce information for a particular purpose (for example whether to computerise an operation or to build a financial planning model) a **cost/benefit study** ought to be made.

3.22   For information to have **value**, it must lead to a decision to take action which results in reducing costs, eliminating losses, increasing sales, better utilisation of resources, prevention of fraud (audit requirements) or providing management with information about the consequences of alternative courses of action.

3.23   The cost of **collecting** information does not give it value. An item of information which leads to an actual increase in profit of £90 is not worth having at all if it costs £100 to collect. The value of information lies in the **action taken** as a result of receiving it.

Question 1

What questions might you ask in order to make an assessment of the value of information?

Answer

(a)   What information is provided?

(b)   What is it used for?

(c)   Who uses it?

(d)   How often is it used?

(e)   Does the frequency with which it is used coincide with the frequency with which it is provided?

(f)   What is achieved by using it?

(g)   What other relevant information is available which could be used instead?

An assessment of the value of information can be derived in this way, and the cost of obtaining it should then be compared against this value. On the basis of this comparison, it can be decided whether certain items of information are worth having.

ACCURATE

3.24   You might like to try a mnemonic to remember the points above. This does not fit the list in paragraph 3.7 exactly, but should certainly enable you to recall the key issues.

Information should be:

A ccurate

C omplete

C ost-beneficial

U ser-targeted

R elevant

A daptable (in terms of communication)

T imely

E asy to use

4   TYPES OF DECISION

Structured and unstructured decisions

4.1   A distinction can be drawn between structured, semi-structured and unstructured problems and decisions.

> **KEY TERMS**
>
> A **structured problem** is one in which there is a defined number of elements, and it is possible to go about solving the problem in a systematic way.
>
> An **unstructured problem**, on the other hand, is less easy to analyse as it appears to lack any obvious logic, underlying procedures or rules for solving it.

4.2   A **structured** decision can also be described as a **programmable** decision, in that unambiguous decision rules can be specified in advance. Structured decisions can often be characterised as **routine** and **frequently repeated**.

4.3   Little or **no human judgement** is required. An organisation can prepare a **decision procedure** for a structured decision. This consists of a series of steps to be followed, and may be expressed in the form of, for example, a flowchart or a decision table.

4.4   An **unstructured** decision is said to be **non-programmable**. It cannot be pre-planned in the same way that a structured decision can be. It will usually occur less frequently and will be non-routine. There is **no** pre-prepared decision **procedure** for an unstructured decision, either because it does not occur frequently enough to warrant one or because it is too complex. Data requirements cannot be fully known in advance. Unstructured decisions usually involve a high degree of **human judgement**.

4.5   A **semi-structured** decision falls somewhere between the two categories described. It is likely to involve an element of **human judgement** and to have characteristics of **standard procedures** with some programmed elements.

4.6   Also relevant in this context are two types of decision making. These depend largely on the characteristics of the decision maker, rather than the nature of the decision itself.

KEY TERMS

An **analytic** decision maker relies on information that is systematically acquired and evaluated and make a choice that is **information based**. Such a decision maker learns by analysing a particular situation, is methodical, and values quantitative information.

An **heuristic** decision maker may make use of guidelines, but decisions will generally be **experience-based** (for example 'milk in first' when making a cup of tea). Such a decision maker relies on common sense or uses trial and error to find a solution.

Exam focus point

Structured, semi-structured and unstructured decisions featured in the **December 1994, June 1995** and **December 1996** exams, so it is a popular topic with both old and new examiners.

Levels of decision making

4.7 Writers commonly identify three **areas of decision making**.

(a) Strategic planning
(b) Tactical control
(c) Operational control

(This is sometimes referred to as the **Anthony hierarchy**, after the writer Robert Anthony. Note that these terms used to be used to refer to top, middle and junior **management** levels. This is no longer a valid distinction in many modern businesses.)

KEY TERM

Strategic planning is a process of deciding on objectives of the organisation, on changes in these objectives, on the resources used to attain these objectives and on the policies that are to govern the acquisition, use and disposition of these resources.

4.8 Strategic decision making:

- is medium to **long-term**
- involves high levels of **uncertainty** and risk (the future is unpredictable)
- involves situations that **may not recur**
- deals with **complex** issues

KEY TERMS

Tactical planning/control (also called **management control**) means ensuring that resources are obtained and used effectively and efficiently in the accomplishment of the organisation's objectives.

- **Efficiency** means that resources input to a process produce the optimum (maximum) amount of outputs;

- **Effectiveness** means that the resources are used to achieve the desired ends.

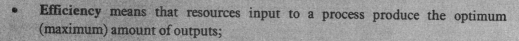

4.9 Tactical control decisions are taken within the framework of strategic plans and objectives which have previously been made, or set.

> **KEY TERM**
>
> Operational control ensures that specific tasks are carried out effectively and efficiently. It focuses on individual tasks, and is carried out within the strictly defined guidelines issued by strategic planning and tactical control decisions.

4.10 Many operational control decisions can be **automated** or programmed. 'Programmed control' exists where the relationship between inputs and outputs is clearly defined, so that an optimal relationship can be specified for every activity. **Mathematical models** can be designed to provide optimal solutions to problems, and many physical procedures can be controlled by automatic devices. Programmed control will always be a form of operational control.

Decision level	Structured	Semi-structured	Unstructured
Operational	Stock control procedures	Selection of new supplier	Hiring supervisor
Tactical	Selection of products to discount	Allocation of budget	Expanding into a new design
Strategic	Major investment decisions	Entry to new market; new product line	Reorganisation of whole company

Question 2

Consider management decisions as they affect work in a purchase ledger department. Classify each of the following three decisions according to the three types of decision identified by Anthony.

(a) The payment cycle will be extended by five days to improve cash flow.

(b) On receipt of an invoice, the purchase order form and goods received note relating to the order must be checked to the invoice. Specified details must be checked, and the invoice stamped to show that the checks have been carried out fully and satisfactorily.

(c) Suppliers who supply over £50,000 worth of goods per annum will be asked to join the company's EDI network.

Answer

The first is a tactical control decision, the second is an operational control decision and the third is a strategic planning decision.

> **Exam focus point**
>
> Operational and tactical decisions were most recently examined in **December 1997** in conjunction with a question about the qualities of information. Note that decision types is an area of the syllabus that comes up very regularly.

5 HOW INFORMATION SYSTEMS SUPPORT DECISION MAKING

Operational information

5.1 Operational information is used to ensure that specific tasks are planned and carried out properly within a factory or office.

5.2 In the payroll office, for example, operational information might include the hours worked **each week** by each employee, his rate of pay per hour, details of his deductions, and for the purpose of wages analysis, details of the time each person spent on individual jobs during the week.

5.3 More urgent operational information, such as the amount of raw materials being input to a production process, may be required **daily, hourly**, or in the case of automated production, **second by second**.

5.4 Operational information:

- is derived almost **entirely** from **internal** sources;
- is highly **detailed**, being the processing of raw data;
- relates to the **immediate** term;
- is **task-specific**;
- is prepared constantly, or very **frequently**;
- is largely **quantitative**.

Tactical information

5.5 Tactical information is used to decide how the resources of the business should be employed, and to monitor how they are being, and have been, employed.

5.6 Such information includes **productivity measurements** (output per man hour or per machine hour) **budgetary control** or variance analysis reports, and **cashflow forecasts, manning levels** and **profit** results within a particular department of the organisation, **labour turnover** statistics within a department and short-term **purchasing** requirements.

5.7 Tactical information therefore:

- is primarily generated from **internal** sources;
- is **summarised** although a report might include raw data as backup;
- is relevant to the **short and medium term**;
- describes or analyses **activities** or **departments**;
- is prepared **routinely** and **regularly**;
- is based on **quantitative** measures.

5.8 A variety of systems can be used at this level, and there may be a greater reliance than at operational level on **exception** reporting, **informal** systems and some **external** sources.

5.9 Tactical information may be generated in the same processing operation as operational level information. For example, tactical level information **comparing** actual costs incurred to budget can be produced by a system in which those costs are **recorded**.

Strategic information

5.10 Strategic information is used to plan the **objectives** of their organisation, and to assess whether the objectives are **being met** in practice.

5.11 Such information includes **overall profitability**, the profitability of different segments of the business, future **market prospects**, the availability and cost of raising **new funds**, total cash needs, total manning levels and **capital equipment needs**.

5.12 Strategic information is therefore:

- derived from both **internal and external** sources;
- **summarised** at a high level;
- relevant to the **long term**;
- deals with the **whole organisation** (although it might go into some detail);
- often prepared on an 'ad hoc' basis;
- both **quantitative and qualitative**;
- **uncertain**, given that the future cannot be predicted.

5.13 At strategic level the information system is likely to be **informal**, in the sense that it is not possible always to quantify or program strategic information, and much of the information might come from environmental sources. The MIS will provide summary high level data from transactions processing. **Human judgement** is used more often at this level, as many strategic decisions cannot be programmed

5.14 Section summary

A table showing typical inputs, processes and outputs at each level of a management information system is provided below.

	Inputs	*Processes*	*Outputs*
Strategic	Plans Competitor information Market information	Summarise Investigate Compare Forecast	Key ratios Ad hoc market analysis Strategic plans
Tactical	Historical data Budget data	Compare Classify Summarise	Variance analyses Exception reports
Operational	Customer orders Programmed stock control levels	Update files Output reports	Updated files Listings Invoices

Exam focus point

The 'operational, tactical, strategic' hierarchy was a favourite topic of the previous examiner (pre December 1995), but will probably appear less frequently under the new examiner.

6   TYPES OF MANAGEMENT INFORMATION SYSTEM

Decision support systems

6.1 Decision support systems are used by management to assist in making decisions on issues which are **unstructured**, with high levels of uncertainty about the true **nature** of the problem, the various **responses** which management could undertake or the likely **impact** of those actions.

6.2 Decision support systems are intended to provide a wide range of alternative **information gathering** and **analytical tools** with a major emphasis upon **flexibility** and **user-friendliness**.

6.3 The term decision support system is usually taken to mean computer systems which are designed to produce information in such a way as to help managers to make better decisions. They are now often associated with information 'at the touch of a button' at a manager's personal computer or workstation. DSS can describe a **range of systems**, from fairly simple information models based on **spreadsheets** to **expert systems**.

6.4 Decision support systems **do not make decisions**. The objective is to allow the manager to consider a number of **alternatives** and evaluate them under a variety of potential conditions. A key element in the usefulness of these systems is their ability to function **interactively**. This is a feature, for example, of spreadsheets, which were described in an earlier chapter. Managers using these systems often develop scenarios using earlier results to refine their understanding of the problem and their actions.

6.5 Some decision support computer systems are composed of three elements. These subsystems then combine to provide the capabilities required for an effective decision support system.

(a) A **language subsystem** used by the manager to communicate interactively with the decision support system.

(b) A **problem processing** subsystem which provides analytical techniques and presentation capabilities.

(c) A **knowledge subsystem** which holds internal data and can access any needed external data.

Executive information systems

6.6 An executive information system (EIS) is a type of DSS which gives the senior executive easy access to key internal and external data'. An EIS is likely to have the following features.

(a) Provision of **summary-level** data, captured from the organisation's main systems.

(b) A facility which allows the executive to **drill down** from higher levels of information to lower).

(c) **Data manipulation** facilities (for example comparison with budget or prior year data, trend analysis).

(d) **Graphics**, for user-friendly presentation of data.

(e) A **template** system. This will mean that the same type of data (eg sales figures) is presented in the same format, irrespective of changes in the volume of information required.

Exam focus point
The previous examiner was fond of questions asking students to distinguish between, say, a transactions processing system, a management information system, an executive information system and a decision support system.

6.7 At the heart of an executive information system is a **corporate model**, which holds key information about the organisation. This model provides the interface between the database and the executive, who as a result does not have to define how information should be displayed. The corporate model contains **rules** as to how the information should be **presented** and **aggregated**. The model can be amended if required.

6.8   EXAMPLE: DRILLING DOWN

Many **accounting packages** still mirror manual reporting systems in that they provide **details first and totals last**. The format of a report from a package, whether displayed on screen or printed out, is usually a list of transactions with totals at the end of the list.

6.9   This does not fit well with the principle of **management reporting by exception**. For example, a sales manager monitoring sales in six different regions would first of all wish to view the sales totals for each region with a comparison of budget against actual. If totals for five regions are in line with budget, he will not immediately wish to review the underlying detail; he will be more concerned with the performance of the sixth region.

6.10   On selecting the relevant region for further investigation, he will still not wish to see an individual sales transactions listing, but will prefer to look at, for example, a report of budget against actual **by product group**, or perhaps **by customer type**. Only when he has identified the individual product group, or customer type, which is **responsible for the difference** between actual and budget, will he wish to look at individual products, or customers, to see where the difference lies.

6.11   An EIS will reflect the manager's real information needs. This approach has several advantages.

(a) It incorporates the principle of **exception reporting**.

(b) It reduces the amount of data to be reviewed (**no information overload**).

(c) It is **screen-based**, with print-outs only being required for specific matters.

Artificial intelligence and expert systems

6.12   **Artificial intelligence** has been called the study of how to make computers do things at which, at the moment, **people are better**. For example, people are much better than computers at:

(a) **learning** from experience;

(b) **making sense** out of information that seems to be ambiguous or contradictory;

(c) responding in an appropriate way to a completely **new situation**;

(d) recognising the **relative importance** of different aspects of a situation;

(e) understanding **other people's behaviour**, which may not always be rational or which may be motivated by things that are not part of the problem as defined.

6.13   Artificial intelligence software works by creating a **knowledge base** that consists of facts, concepts and the relationships between them and then **searches** it using pattern-matching techniques to 'solve' problems.

(a) **Rules of thumb** or ('heuristics') are important. A simple example might be 'milk in first' when making a cup of tea: this is a rule of thumb for tea making that saves people having to rethink how to make a cup of tea every time they do so. A simple business example programmed into many accounting packages might be: 'Don't allow credit to a customer who has exceeded their credit limit'.

(b) **Pattern-matching** finds similarities between objects, events or processes that may not be clear if items are only understood in terms of their differences. Tea and coffee are different things but they both serve the same purpose if the problem is that you want a refreshing hot drink. Conventional computer systems are not programmed to make this sort of logical leap.

6.14 Artificial intelligence is still in its infancy but some applications have been developed in a variety of fields, such as linguistics, psychology, and optics. The main commercial applications however, are known as **expert systems**.

Expert systems

6.15 Expert systems are a form of DSS that allow users to benefit from expert knowledge and information. The system will consist of a **database** holding specialised data and **rules** about what to do in, or how to interpret, a given set of circumstances.

6.16 For example, many financial institutions now use expert systems to process straightforward **loan applications**. The user enters certain key facts into the system such as the loan applicant's name and most recent addresses, their income and monthly outgoings, and details of other loans. The system will then:

(a) **check the facts** given against its database to see whether the applicant has a good previous credit record;

(b) **perform calculations** to see whether the applicant can afford to repay the loan;

(c) **match up other criteria**, such as whether the security offered for the loan or the purpose for which the loan is wanted is acceptable, and to what extent the loan applicant fits the lender's profile of a good risk (based on the lender's previous experience).

6.17 A decision is then suggested, based on the results of this processing. This is why it is now often possible to get a loan or arrange insurance **over the telephone**, whereas in the past it would have been necessary to go and speak to a bank manager or send details to an actuary and then wait for him or her to come to a decision.

6.18 There are many other **business applications** of expert systems.

(a) **Legal** advice

(b) **Tax** advice

(c) **Forecasting** of economic or financial developments, or of market and customer behaviour

(d) **Surveillance**, for example of the number of customers entering a supermarket, to decide what shelves need restocking and when more checkouts need to be opened, or of machines in a factory, to determine when they need maintenance

(e) **Diagnostic systems**, to identify causes of problems, for example in production control in a factory, or in healthcare

(f) **Project management**

(g) **Education and training** (diagnosing a student's or worker's weaknesses and providing or recommending extra instruction as appropriate).

Question 3

If you are studying at a college you might like to annoy your tutor by having a class discussion about whether he or she could be replaced by an expert system!

Question 4

An exam question could ask you to explain how an expert system could help with the activities of a company described in a scenario.

Give some thought to this for different sorts of organisation, for example a local authority, a transport company, a manufacturer of fast-moving consumer goods, a firm of accountants and so on.

6.19 An organisation can use an expert system when a number of conditions are met.

   (a)   The problem is **reasonably well defined**.

   (b)   The expert can define some **rules** by which the problem can be solved.

   (c)   The problem cannot be solved by **conventional** transaction processing or data handling.

   (d)   The **expert could be released** to more difficult problems, in the case of certain types of work. (An actuary in an insurance company is an example. Actuaries are very highly paid.)

   (e)   The **investment** in an expert system is cost **justified**.

6.20 This is a diagram of an expert system.

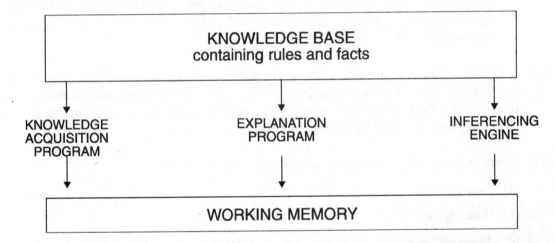

   (a)   The **knowledge base** contains facts (assertions like 'a rottweiler is a dog') and rules ('if you see a rottweiler, then run away'). Some facts contradict rules, of course, or even each other ('all birds can fly' is contradicted by the existence of ostriches and kiwis).

   (b)   The **knowledge acquisition program** is a program which enables the expert system to acquire new knowledge and rules.

   (c)   The **working memory** is where the expert system stores the various facts and rules used during the current enquiry, and the current information given to it by the user.

(d) The **inferencing engine** is the software that executes the reasoning. It needs to discern which rules apply, and allocate priorities.

> **Exam focus point**
>
> A question in the **December 1994** exam included a brief scenario about a company that serviced marine engines and asked how an expert system used in conjunction with portable PCs could help its on-the-road engineers.

Advantages and limitations of expert systems

6.21 Advantages include the following.

(a) Artificial intelligence and expertise is **permanent**, whereas human experts may leave the business.

(b) It is **easily copied,** so that one bank branch say, can have access to the same expertise as any other branch.

(c) It is **consistent,** whereas human experts and decision makers may not be.

(d) It can be **documented**. The reasoning behind an expert recommendation produced by a computer will all be recorded. Experts may have what seem to them to be inspired ideas out of the blue, not fully realising the thought processes that they have been going through while they have been mulling the problem over.

(e) Depending on the task the computer may be much **faster** than the human being.

6.22 There are severe limitations, however.

(a) Systems are **expensive**, especially if they have to be designed from scratch, as they often would be.

(b) The technology is still **in its infancy** in many areas. Understanding of how the human mind works is also still fairly limited.

(c) It is very **difficult to develop** a system in the first place, and the system will need extensive testing and debugging before it can be trusted.

(d) **People are naturally more creative.** If a computer system can be creative at all, it can only be so to the extent that creativity has been programmed into it: arguably this is not creativity at all.

(e) Systems have a very **narrow focus**, whereas human experts can bring the whole of their experience to bear on a problem.

(f) **Managers will resist** being replaced by computers, or at least will sometimes be **reluctant to believe** the advice of an expert system.

Chapter roundup

- One of the key uses of information is in decision making. The making of a decision has a number of **identifiable stages**.

- Most information systems grow up **informally**. Informal communication cannot be avoided, and is often to be **encouraged**, but it can lead to **inefficient** systems and misunderstandings. A formal system should be designed to support the informal one.

- An important distinction can be made between data and information.

    o **Data** is the complete range of raw facts and measurements which exist within and outside an organisation.

    o **Information** is data which has been processed in some way so as to make it meaningful to the person who receives it.

    o **Good information** has a number of specific qualities, for which **ACCURATE** is a useful mnemonic.

- Types of decision include **structured, unstructured** and **semi-structured** decisions.

- There is a hierarchy of decision making, which comprises the three areas of **strategic planning**, **management (or tactical) control** and **operational control**.

- In general, **strategic** information is used to plan objectives and assess whether they are being met, **tactical** information is used to decide how to employ the resources of the business and monitor their use, and **operational** information is used to ensure that specific tasks are planned and carried out properly.

- There are a number of different types of information system to **support decisions,** including **executive information** systems and **expert systems**.

Quick quiz

1   What are the six stages in making a decision? (see para 1.1)

2   What might happen if an information system has no formal planning and design? (2.4)

3   What are the qualities of good information? (3.7, 3.24)

4   How accurate should information be? Give examples. (3.11)

5   How much should information cost? (3.21 – 3.23)

6   What are the characteristics of a structured decision? (4.2 – 4.3)

7   What is tactical planning? (4.9)

8   What are the characteristics of operational information? (5.4)

9   What are the characteristics of strategic information? (5.12)

10   What are the features of an EIS? (6.6)

11   Give some examples of expert systems (6.18)

12   What are the advantages and disadvantages of expert systems? (6.21 – 6.22)

Question to try	Level	Marks	Time
2	Introductory	n/a	20 mins
3	Exam standard	15	27 mins

Chapter 3

SYSTEMS THEORY

Chapter topic list	Syllabus reference
1 Systems theory	1(a)
2 The systems view of organisations	1(a)
3 Types of system	1(a)
4 Systems concepts	1(a)

Introduction

In this chapter we provide an introduction to **systems theory** and, in the last section of the chapter, to **control theory**. You may find it a bit dry in parts, but you will encounter these ideas frequently in your present and later studies so it is worth mastering them now.

There are lots of new **terms** and **concepts** to learn, but remember that in the exam you are likely to be asked to give practical business **examples** or apply the theory to a practical scenario, so it is important to take note of the numerous examples that we give too.

1   SYSTEMS THEORY

1.1   The term **system** is very hard to define because it is so widely used - the 'respiratory system', the 'political system', the 'long ball system', and so on.

1.2   Possibly the most useful and illuminating definition says simply that 'system' means **connections**.

Question 1

Apply the idea of connections to any 'systems' you can think of - the London Underground system, a computer system, the idea of working 'systematically', or anything else that comes to mind.

KEY TERMS

More formally, a **system** is set of interacting components that operate together to accomplish a purpose.

A **business system** is a collection of people, machines and methods organised to accomplish a set of specific functions.

Why study systems theory?

1.3   An understanding of the concepts of systems theory is relevant to the design of **financial and management accounting systems** and it presents a particularly useful way of describing and analysing **computer systems**. The application of systems theory may achieve the following.

(a)   Create an awareness of **subsystems** (the different parts of an organisation), each with potentially conflicting goals which must be brought into line with each other.

(b)   Help in the design and development of **information systems** to help **decision makers** ensure that decisions are made for the benefit of the organisation as a whole.

(c)   Help identify the effect of the **environment** on systems. The external factors that affect an organisation may be wide ranging. For example, the government (in all its forms), competitors, trade unions, creditors and shareholders all have an interactive link with an organisation.

(d)   Highlight the **dynamic aspects** of the business organisation, and the factors which influence the growth and development of all its subsystems.

Exam focus point

The recently appointed examiner is more likely to test your understanding of systems theory as it can be **applied** to businesses than to ask for straightforward regurgitation of the theory. So take careful note of all the practical examples we give in this chapter.

The component parts of a system

1.4   A system has three component parts: inputs, processes and outputs.

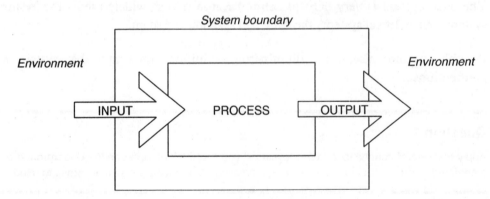

Inputs

1.5   Inputs **provide the system with what it needs** to be able to operate. Input may vary from matter, energy or human actions, to information.

- Matter might include, in a manufacturing operation, adhesives or rivets

- Human input might consist of typing an instruction booklet or starting up a piece of machinery.

1.6   Inputs may be **outputs from other systems**. As we have seen, the output from a transactions processing system is part of the input for a management information system.

Processes

1.7   A process **transforms an input into an output**. Processes may involve tasks performed by humans, plant, computers, chemicals and a wide range of other actions.

1.8   Processes may consist of **assembly**, for example where electronic consumer goods are being manufactured, or **disassembly**, for example where oil is refined.

1.9   There is **not necessarily a clear relationship** between the number of inputs to a process and the number of outputs.

Outputs

1.10   Outputs are the **results of the processing**. They could be said to represent the **purpose** for which the system exists.

1.11   Many outputs are used as **inputs to other systems**.

1.12   Alternatively outputs may be discarded as **waste** (an input to the ecological system) or **re-input** to the system which has produced them, for example, in certain circumstances, defective products.

The system boundary

1.13   Every system has a boundary that **separates it from its environment**. For example, a cost accounting department's boundary can be expressed in terms of who works in it and what work it does. This boundary will separate it from other departments, such as the financial accounts department.

1.14   System boundaries may be natural or artificially created (an organisation's departmental structures are artificially created).

1.15   There may be **interfaces** between various systems, both internal and external to an organisation, to allow the exchange of resources. In a commercial context, this is most likely to be a reciprocal exchange, for example money for raw materials.

The environment

1.16   Anything which is outside the system boundary belongs to the system's environment and not to the system itself. A system **accepts inputs** from the environment and **provides outputs** into the environment. The parts of the environment from which the system receives inputs may not be the same as those to which it delivers outputs.

1.17   The environment exerts a considerable influence on the behaviour of a system; at the same time the system can do little to **control** the behaviour of the environment.

Question 2

The environment affects the performance of a system. Using a business organisation as an example of a system, give examples of environmental factors which might affect it.

Answer

(a)   Policies adopted by the government or ruling political body.
(b)   The strength of the domestic currency of the organisation's country of operation.
(c)   Social attitudes: concern for the natural environment.
(d)   The regulatory and legislative framework within which the company operates.

(e)   The number of competitors in the marketplace and the strategies they adopt.

(f)   The products of competitors; their price and quality.

Subsystems

1.18   Every system can be broken down into **subsystems** In turn, each subsystem can be broken down into **sub-subsystems**. Separate subsystems **interact** with each other, and **respond** to each other by means of **communication** or observation.

1.19   Subsystems may be **differentiated** from each other by, for example:

(a)   function;

(b)   space;

(c)   time;

(d)   people;

(e)   formality; or

(f)   automation.

Question 3

Using each of the above six factors by which subsystems may be differentiated, give examples of how an organisation may be structured. (For example, an organisation structured by function might have a production department, a sales department, an accounts department and a personnel department.)

Answer

(a)   Functional departments might include production, sales, accounts and personnel.

(b)   Differentiation by space might include the geographical division of a sales function (subsystem) into sales regions (sub-subsystems).

(c)   A production system might be subdivided into three eight-hour shifts.

(d)   The hierarchy may consist of senior management, middle management, junior (operational) management and the workforce.

(e)   There may be a formal management information system and a 'grapevine'.

(f)   Some systems might be automated (sales order processing, production planning), while others may be 'manual' (public relations, staff appraisal).

1.20   Often, whether something is a system or a subsystem is a matter of definition, and depends on the context of the **observer**. For example, an organisation is a social system, and its 'environment' may be seen as society as a whole. Another way of looking at an organisation would be to regard it as a *subsystem* of the entire social system.

1.21   As we have hinted at several points, what links up the different subsystems in an organisation is **information**.

2   THE SYSTEMS VIEW OF ORGANISATIONS

2.1   A typical manufacturing company or service organisation can be viewed as a system. **Inputs** are received and **processed** by people and machines to produce **outputs** of goods and services. The **objectives** of the organisation are thereby fulfilled.

The systems approach

2.2   The systems approach uses three steps.

(a)   It starts by identifying what the **whole system** is.
(b)   It identifies the overall **objectives** of the system as a whole.
(c)   It makes **plans** with these objectives in mind.

2.3   For example, in a business, the total system is the **business as a whole**. Its objective might be to **maximise profits**. The plans for the business should then be made with this objective in view.

2.4   To achieve systems objectives, it is usually necessary to set objectives and targets for **individual parts** of the system. The systems approach involves development of plans and controls for subsystems within the framework of the overall objectives of the total system.

2.5   However, the organisation must also remain sensitive to its **external environment**, with which it is in constant interaction: it must respond to threats and opportunities, restrictions and challenges posed by markets, consumer trends, competitors, the government and so on. Changes in input will influence output.

Hierarchy of systems

2.6   The organisation as system can be viewed as being composed of subsystems arranged in a **system hierarchy**.

Corporate level

2.7   Corporate systems support the organisation as a whole. They are concerned with its **strategic** outlook and its relationship with the external elements and systems in the environment. Systems at this level might include business and economic **forecasting** systems and corporate **financial planning** systems.

Divisional level

2.8   Many organisations are divided into a number of distinct units which may operate in different industrial sectors, provide different services or sell different products. Legally, these units may be divisions of a single company or separate subsidiary companies or a combination of the two. Systems at this level might include **market analysis** systems and **industry performance** forecasting systems.

Departmental level

2.9   At departmental level, the emphasis is on the implementation of the organisation's strategy. This involves managing available resources within the constraints imposed. Systems at this **tactical** level include **credit control** and **quality control** systems.

Operational level

2.10   At **operational** level, the emphasis is on the control of day-to-day operations. The systems usually found at this level are **transaction processing systems**, such as sales order processing or production control systems.

Socio-technical systems

2.11 Another point of view suggests that an organisation is a 'structured **sociotechnical** system', that is, it consists of at least three sub- systems.

   (a) A **structure**

   (b) A **technological system** (concerning the work to be done, and the machines, tools and other facilities available to do it)

   (c) A **social system** (concerning the people within the organisation, the ways they think and the ways they interact with each other)

3   TYPES OF SYSTEM

Open systems and closed systems

3.1 In systems theory a distinction is made between open systems and closed systems.

> **KEY TERM**
>
> A **closed system** is a system which is isolated from its environment and independent of it, so that no environmental influences affect the behaviour of the system, nor does the system exert any influence on its environment.
>
> Some scientific systems might be described as closed systems. An example of a closed system is a chemical reaction in a sealed, insulated container. Another is the operation of a thermostat.

3.2 However, all **social** systems, including business organisations, have some interaction with their environment, and so cannot be closed systems.

> **KEY TERM**
>
> An **open system** is a system connected to and interacting with its environment.
>
> It takes in influences (or 'energy') from its environment and also influences this environment by its behaviour (it exports energy).

3.3 Open and closed systems can be described by diagram as follows.

Closed system

Open system

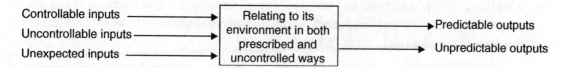

3.4   For example, a **business** is an open system where management decisions are influenced by or have an influence on suppliers, customers, competitors, society as a whole and the government.

3.5   Employees are obviously influenced by what they do in their job, but as members of society at large, they are also a part of the **environment**, just as their views and opinions expressed within the business are often a reflection of their opinions as members of society at large.

3.6   As noted earlier, every system has a boundary. An open system will have considerable cross-influences with its environment **across its boundary**, whereas a closed system's boundary would shut it off from its environment.

Deterministic systems

3.7   A deterministic system is one in which various states or activities follow on from each other in a completely **predictable** way, ie A will happen, then B, then C. A fully-automated production process is a typical example. A computer program is another.

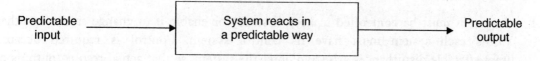

Probabilistic systems

3.8   A probabilistic system is one in which, although some states or activities can be predicted with certainty, others will occur with **varying degrees of probability**. In business, many systems can be regarded as probabilistic systems.

    (a)   A company's **credit control department** can analyse customers' payment schedules as 10% cash with order, 50% within 1 month of invoice and 40% within 2 months of invoice.

    (b)   A **purchasing department** might assess a supplier's delivery times as 0.75 on schedule, 0.20 one week late and 0.05 two weeks late.

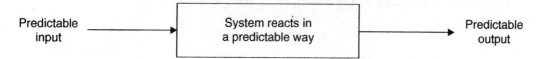

Exam focus point

Open and closed systems and deterministic and probabilistic systems featured in a question set by the old examiner in **December 1994**, together with positive and negative feedback, which we shall discuss in a moment.

Self-organising systems

3.9 A self-organising system is one which **adapts and reacts** to a stimulus. The way in which it adapts is uncertain and the same input (stimulus) to the system will not always produce the same output (response). Social and psychological systems come within this category. Examples might be as follows.

(a) A bank which pays a rate of interest to depositors depending on the amount of money in the deposit account. Interest calculations (the output of the system is the calculated interest) will **vary** as the money in each depositor's account goes up or down.

(b) A stock re-ordering system where the quantity of a stock item that is ordered from a supplier **varies** according to changes in the usage of the item. For example, if consumption of stock item 12345 goes up by 20% per week, the reorder quantity of the item will be increased.

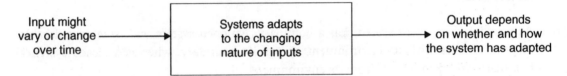

3.10 The three classifications are **not mutually exclusive**, and a system may contain elements of all three types.

4   SYSTEMS CONCEPTS

Control systems

4.1 A system must be **controlled** to keep it steady or enable it to change safely, in other words each system must have its control system. Control is required because unpredictable disturbances arise and enter the system, so that actual results (outputs of the system) deviate from the expected results or goals.

4.2 Examples of **disturbances** in a business system would be the entry of a powerful new competitor into the market, an unexpected rise in labour costs, the failure of a supplier to deliver promised raw materials, or the tendency of employees to stop working in order to chatter or gossip.

4.3 A control system must ensure that the business is **capable of surviving** these disturbances by dealing with them in an appropriate manner.

4.4 To have a control system, there has to be a plan, **standard** - budget, rule book or some other sort of target or guideline towards which the system as a whole should be aiming. The standard is defined by the **objectives** of the system.

4.5   A control system can be represented in a model, as shown below.

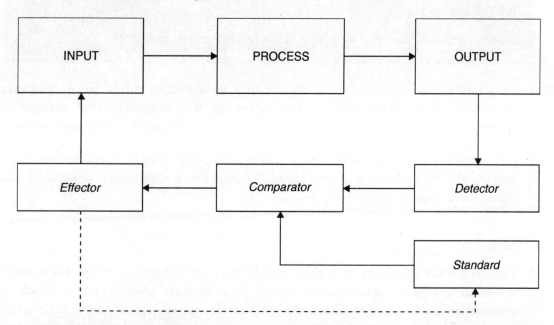

4.6   The terms here need explanation.

> **KEY TERM**
>
> A **sensor** is the device by which information (or data) is collected and measured.

4.7   Although an automatic meter is commonly cited as an example of a sensor, it is more appropriate for managers to think of a sensor as the **means by which information is recorded** on paper or computer file, or transmitted by telephone or computer screen.

4.8   A sensor may be **inefficient** because it does not record information as completely or accurately as required, or because it is too complete or unnecessarily accurate. It may not record information at the most appropriate time, or it may break down and fail to record anything (for example, a night-watchman might fall asleep, or a TV camera or computer might break down).

4.9   Some sensors are more efficient than others. A document that can be read by a scanner, for example, is better than a manually prepared computer input document because it **saves data collection time**, and **reduces errors**.

> **KEY TERM**
>
> A **comparator** is the means by which the actual results of the system are measured against the pre-determined plans or system objectives.

4.10   In a business organisation, the arithmetic of comparison (for example the calculation of variances, or productivity ratios) might be done by computer. **Managers**, however, will be the comparators who are expected to make some judgement on the results of the comparison, to decide whether investigation of the variances is advisable, and then (after investigation) whether control action is required.

4.11 In a production department, an effector may be a component in some automatic equipment which **regulates** the functioning of the equipment (for example a **thermostat**). An effector may also be a manager's instruction and a subordinate's action.

4.12 Just as any sensor may be **inefficient,** so too might a comparator or an effector do its job imperfectly. In designing a control system, it should be a requirement to optimise the efficiency of these control items.

Feedback

4.13 Feedback is the return of part of the output of a system to the input as a means towards improved quality or correction of errors. In a business organisation, feedback is information produced from **within** the organisation (for example management control reports) with the purpose of helping management and other employees and triggering control decisions.

4.14 In the control model described above part of the output is **fed back,** so that the output can initiate **control** action to change either the activities of the system or the system's input. A feedback system or a **feedback loop** carries output back to be compared with the input. This is also called a **closed loop system.**

4.15 You might like to think of a **budgetary control** system in a company, by which results are monitored, deviations from plan are identified and control (corrective) action taken as appropriate.

Negative feedback

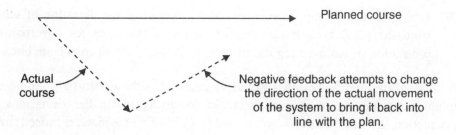

4.16 Thus, if the budgeted sales for a department for June and July were £100,000 in each month, whereas the report of actual sales in June showed that only £90,000 had been reached, this negative feedback would indicate that **control action** was necessary to raise sales in July to £110,000 in order to get back on to the planned course. Negative feedback in this case would necessitate July sales exceeding the budget by £10,000 because June sales fell short of budget.

Positive feedback

> **KEY TERM**
>
> **Positive feedback** results in control action which causes actual results to maintain (or increase) their path of deviation from planned results.

4.17 Much positive feedback would be considered **harmful**, because deviations from the plan are usually adverse and undesirable.

4.18 Positive feedback occurs when there is some kind of **problem in the feedback loop**.

- The **sensor** may measure the **total volume** of units produced instead of the number of **good** units (as opposed to faulty ones). Positive feedback that indicated that total volume had fallen might result in control action to stretch resources and make the system produce more units, but in reality this might mean an increase in the number of **faulty** units and a fall in the overall number of good units.

- The **standard** may be set at the wrong level. For example a sales person might be set a sales target of £20,000 per **month**. If sales people find they can achieve £20,000 of sales in **three weeks** they may decide to reduce their inputs (the number of hours they work).

Question 4

See if you can think of examples of similar problems with the comparator and the effector.

4.19 There are occasions however when positive feedback is **beneficial**. Suppose, for example, that a company budgets to produce and sell 100 units of product each month, maintaining an average stock level of 40 units. Now if actual sales exceed the budget, and show signs of sustained growth, it will obviously be in the company's interests to produce and sell as much as possible (provided additional output earns extra contribution to profit).

(a) Positive feedback in the first month might show that sales are above budget, selling costs are a little higher than budget and that stocks have been run down to meet demand.

(b) Action should attempt to increase sales (ie promote the deviation of actual results from the plan) even if this requires extra selling costs for advertising or sales promotion (ie maintaining the adverse deviation of actual costs from budget).

4.20 Additional production volumes would be required, although initially, some extra sales might be made out of remaining stocks (resulting in further deviations from the production and finished goods stocks budgets.) Positive feedback is indeed fundamental to the growth of any system.

Exam focus point

Feedback has featured in questions set in **December 1995** and **June 1997**.

Filtering

KEY TERM

Filtering means removing 'impurities' such as excessive detail from data as it is passed up the organisation hierarchy.

4.21 We met this concept in the context of good information. Operational staff may need all the detail to do their jobs, but when they report to higher and higher subsystems the data can be progressively **summarised**. Extraneous detail is filtered out leaving only the important points.

4.22 The **problem** with this is that sometimes the 'filter' may let through unimportant information and/or remove important information, with the result that the message is **distorted** at the next level.

Coupling and decoupling

4.23 If systems or subsystems are very closely connected or **coupled** this may cause difficulties.

4.24 For example, in order to sell goods, a manufacturing company must first of all make them. If the sales and production subsystems are closely coupled the company will produce in any week exactly the amounts required for sales. However the system would be prone to inefficiency through 'mishap', such as a late delivery of raw materials, a machine breakdown, or a strike, so that goods would not be available to meet sales demand.

4.25 From a traditional point of view greater efficiency is achieved between the production and sales systems by **decoupling** them. This means reducing the immediacy of the interaction between them by creating a finished goods stock for meeting sales orders.

4.26 From a modern point of view holding finished goods stock is expensive, and greater efficiency is achieved by adopting **quality management** philosophies to try to ensure that mishaps do not occur. If this is successful this means that a **just-in-time (JIT)** approach to production and purchasing can be adopted. JIT closely couples the sales and production subsystems and closely couples one organisation's purchasing function with another's supplying function.

Requisite variety

4.27 The so-called 'law' of requisite variety is a principle of general system theory, developed by Ross Ashby.

> **KEY TERM**
>
> The **law of requisite variety** states that the variety *within a system* must be at least as great as the *environmental variety* against which it is attempting to regulate itself.

4.28 In other words, if there is **variety** in the environmental influences in the system, then the system itself must be suitably varied and variable to adapt itself successfully to its environment.

4.29 If a system does not have the requisite amount of variety, it will be **unable to adapt to change** and will eventually die or be replaced. History is full of examples of political systems that could not adapt to social, economic or political changes, and so were overthrown.

4.30 The law of requisite variety applies to self-regulating systems in general, but one application of the law relates to control systems. A control system (which is a sub-system of a larger system) must be sufficiently flexible to be able to deal with the variety that occurs naturally in the system that it is attempting to control.

Case example

A company making heavy equipment suddenly found its raw materials and in-process inventory climbing, but, at the same time, it was experiencing reduced sales and reduced production. The system was out of control.

The cause was traced to the materials analysts who made the detailed inventory decisions. They had been furnished with decision rules for ordering, cancelling, etc, under normal conditions, but they had no rules governing how to handle the inventory when production was decreasing and production lots were being cancelled.

In other words, the system did not provide the requisite variety of control responses. In this case, the urgency of remedy did not allow new rules to be formulated and validated. Instead, each materials analyst was treated as a self-organising system, given a target inventory, and told to achieve it. With the analysts given the freedom to generate control responses, the inventory was reduced in a few months.'

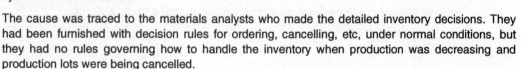

4.31 Way of introducing the requisite variety into a control system include the following.

(a) **Allowing a controller some discretion,** to judge what control action is needed

In a business system, managers should not be instructed that a problem must be handled in a particular way, especially when the problem involves labour relations, disciplinary procedures, motivating the workforce or any other such 'behavioural' matters. The response of individuals to control action by managers will be variable because people are different, and even one person's moods change from day to day. The control system must be flexible enough to use different methods to achieve the same ends.

(b)   **Introducing tolerance limits**

When actual results differ from planned results, control action should not be instigated automatically in every instance. Control action should only be applied when the variance becomes excessive and exceeds allowable tolerance limits. Tolerance limits recognise that plans are based on an 'average' or 'norm' of what is expected to happen, and some variation around this average will be due to 'natural' causes which there should be no reason to get alarmed about.

Entropy

4.32   A final important term in information and systems theory is entropy.

> **KEY TERM**
>
> **Entropy** is the amount of disorder or randomness present in any system.

4.33   Entropy arises because of the natural tendency of objects, and systems, to fall into a state of disorder. All inanimate systems display this tendency to move towards a state of disorder. If they remain unattended they will gradually lose all motion and degenerate into an inert state. When this state is reached and no observable systems activity can be discerned, the system has reached maximum entropy.

4.34   The term entropy is therefore used as a measure of *disorganisation*. A system will increase its entropy unless it receives **negative entropy** in the form of information or inputs from the environment.

4.35   For instance if a business does not listen to its customers' complaints about its products it will eventually fail because it will not be able to sell what it produces. The system will fall into a state of disorder, in the sense that it is ignoring its purpose, which is to sell things not just to produce them. Negative entropy is needed in the form of new or improved products or perhaps new, more open-minded management.

Chapter roundup

- **Systems theory** is relevant to the study of information analysis because general system principles apply to any type of system, including an information system such as a computer system and a sound system such as a business organisation.

- A system receives **inputs** which it **processes** and generates into **outputs**. Any system can be thought of in terms of inputs, processing and outputs.

- A system exists in an environment. An environment surrounds the system but is not part of it, and a **systems boundary** separates the system from its environment. Systems are affected to different degrees and in various ways by their environments, and systems can therefore be classified according to how they are influenced by or respond to (communicate with) their environments.

- An **open** system has a relationship with its environment which has both prescribed and uncontrolled elements. A **closed** system is shut off from its environment and has no relationship with it.

- In a **deterministic** system, the value of certain variables and/or the relationship between them is known. **Probabilistic** systems use probability distribution to predict an expected outcome, or a range of possible outcomes. **Self-organising** systems adapt in an uncertain way to a stimulus.

- **Control** in a system is needed to ensure that the system's operations go according to plan. Control cannot be applied unless there is information about the operations of the system.

- In a control system **sensors** collect data, **comparators** measure data against system objectives or plans, and **effectors** implement any control action that needs to be taken.

- **Feedback** is control information generated by the system itself, and involves a comparison of actual results against the target or plan. Feedback may be **negative** or **positive** depending upon what control action it initiates.

- The terms **coupling** and **decoupling** relate to how closely one system depends on another.

- The law of **requisite variety** states that the variety within a system must be at least as great as the environmental variety against which it is attempting to regulate itself.

- **Entropy** is the amount of disorder or randomness there is in a system. Systems tend to fall into disorder unless they receive negative entropy in the form of information or inputs from the environment.

Quick quiz

1   Why study systems theory? (see para 1.3)

2   What are the component parts of a system? (1.4 – 1.12)

3   What is a sub-system? (1.18)

4   Explain the systems approach to organisations. (2.2)

5   What is a socio-technical system? (2.11)

6   Define the terms open system and closed system. (3.1, 3.2)

7   What is a deterministic system? (3.7)

8   What is a probabilistic system? (3.8)

9   Draw a diagram of a control system. (4.5)

10   What is an effector? (4.11)

11   What is negative feedback? (4.16)

12   Give an example of coupling. (4.23 – 4.26)

13   How can requisite variety be introduced into a control system? (4.31)

14   Give an example of entropy. (4.35)

Question to try	Level	Marks	Time
4	Exam standard	15	27 mins

Chapter 4

THE BASICS OF COMPUTING IN THE LATE 1990s

Chapter topic list	Syllabus reference
1 Computers	(1b), Prerequisite knowledge
2 The processor	(1b), Prerequisite knowledge
3 Input devices	(1b), Prerequisite knowledge
4 Output devices	(1b), Prerequisite knowledge
5 Storage devices	(1b), Prerequisite knowledge
6 The operating system	(1b), Prerequisite knowledge
7 Data processing with a computer	(1b), Prerequisite knowledge

Introduction

This is a lengthy chapter but you may have covered many aspects of it in your earlier studies, for instance in **Paper 3**. If it is some time since you did this we recommend that you at least glance through this chapter, because the world of computers is a **fast-changing** one. This is one reason why we have covered the topics in full. The other is because many lecturers like to be assured that their students have the required basic computer knowledge.

Much of the chapter is **background** knowledge, which will not be examined directly, but will make it easier for you to understand more complex matters that are dealt with in subsequent chapters. At the very least, read the **exam focus points** so that you understand how this brought forward knowledge – such as document reading methods – is cropping up in exam questions.

1   COMPUTERS

1.1   To many people in the late 1990s a computer is probably something with a **screen** like a TV, a **box** for the screen to sit on (with some slots to put disks in), a **keyboard,** and a **mouse**. It may have a pair of **speakers,** too, if it has been bought in the last year or two.

1.2   What we describe is actually a PC, which is certainly a **type** of computer—it is the type that now most regularly sits on desks in the average office or home. However, larger computers are still common, and these days there are also 'computers' in cars and planes and even in some domestic appliances.

KEY TERM

A **computer** is a device which will accept input data, process it according to programmed logical and arithmetic rules, store and output data and/or calculate results. The ability to store programmed instructions and to take decisions which vary the way in which a program executes (although within the defined logic of the program) are the principal distinguishing features of a computer.

(CIMA, *Computing Terminology*)

1.3   Let's look more closely at this definition.

(a)   The **device** is actually a group of electronic and electromechanical devices working together to accept or retrieve **inputs** (some figures, say), **process** them and give you the **output**.

In terms of a PC, the computing device is a collection of electronic circuits, with electrons rushing to and fro along cables: perhaps **from** things like impact-sensitive keyboards **to** things like 'cathode ray tubes' (the screen) and/or **to** the magnetic surface of floppy discs (or **vice versa**, rushing from disk, via the circuits, to the screen).

(b)   A computer **accepts** and then **processes** input data according to the instructions it is given.

(c)   A computer's operations are performed 'according to **programmed** logical and arithmetic rules.' The **arithmetic** element might be as simple as x + y = z. The **logic** will be something along the lines of 'if x + y **does not** = z, **then** add 3 to x and try again'.

KEY TERM

A **program** is a set of coded instructions which tells the computer what to do.

1.4   A **computer** is therefore a mixture of physical, **tangible** things like keyboards, mice, screens, circuits and cables (**hardware**) and **intangible** arithmetic and logic (**software**). Using electrical impulses, the two are connected and communicate with each other.

1.5   The main types of **software** will be covered later in this Chapter and in subsequent chapters.

Hardware

KEY TERM

Hardware means the various physical components which comprise a computer system, as opposed to the non-tangible software elements.

CIMA, *Computing Terminology*

1.6   Most of these physical components are physically separate from, or **peripheral** to, the main circuitry that does the arithmetical and logical processing, but they are the most familiar bits of a computer: keyboards, screens, disks and so on. These are described at greater length later in this Chapter. Developments in **communications** devices and terminology are covered in Chapter 5.

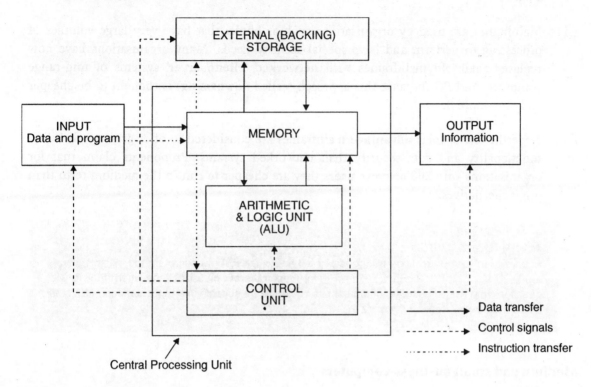

Central Processing Unit

Types of computer

1.7 Computers can be **classified** as follows, although the differences between these categories are becoming increasingly **vague**.

(a) Supercomputers
(b) Mainframe computers, now sometimes called 'enterprise servers'.
(c) Minicomputers, now often called 'mid-range' computers
(d) Microcomputers, now commonly called PCs

We shall group (c) and (d) together as 'small business computers'.

Supercomputers

1.8 A supercomputer is used to process **very large amounts of data** very quickly. They are particularly useful for occasions where high volumes of calculations need to be performed, for example in meteorological or astronomical applications. Manufacturers of supercomputers include Cray and Fujitsu. They are **not used commercially**.

Mainframes

1.9 A mainframe computer system is one that has at its heart a **very powerful central computer,** linked by cable or telecommunications to hundreds or thousands of **terminals,** and capable of accepting simultaneous input from all of them. A mainframe has many times more processing power than a PC and offers very **extensive data storage facilities.**

1.10 **Older** systems are typically very large in terms of size and very sensitive to fluctuations in temperature and air quality, requiring them to be housed in a **controlled environment**. However, the main **modern example** (the **IBM S/390**) uses the same kind of components that are used in PCs, may not be much larger than a fridge-freezer, and has far less need for a specialised environment. The basic IBM S/390 costs around **£50,000**.

1.11 Mainframes are used by organisations such as **banks** that have very large volumes of processing to perform and have special security needs. Many organisations have now replaced their old mainframes with **networked 'client/server'** systems of mid-range computers and PCs because this approach (called **downsizing**) is thought to be cheaper and offer more flexibility.

1.12 Nevertheless, to their **advantage** mainframes are considered to offer greater reliability, functionality and data security than networked systems. Proponents claim that for organisations with **200 or more users** they are cheaper to run in the medium term than other alternatives.

Exam focus point

Scenarios in exam questions will generally tell you what sort of computers the organisation is presently using. It is important to know about these different classifications when dealing with questions that ask what sort of computer system would be suitable in a particular case. We shall come back to this issue in **Chapter 6**.

Medium and small business computers

Minicomputers

1.13 A minicomputer is a computer whose size, speed and capabilities lie somewhere between those of a mainframe and a PC. The term was originally used before PCs were developed, to describe computers which were cheaper but less well-equipped than mainframe computers (which had until then been the only type of computer available). The advent of more powerful chips now means that some 'superminis', and even PCs linked in a network, can run more powerfully than some older mainframes.

1.14 With the advent of PCs, and with mainframes now being physically smaller than in the past, the definition of a minicomputer has become rather vague. There is really **no definition** which distinguishes adequately between a PC and a minicomputer. Price, power and number of users supported have been used to identify distinguishing features, but these differences have tended to erode as microchip technology has progressed. Manufacturers of minicomputers include IBM with its **AS400**, ICL and DEC.

PCs

1.15 The **'personal' computer** (or **'microcomputer'**) market was first developed by companies like **Apple** Computers, but a key event was the launch of the **IBM PC** in August 1981. In the early years of the development of the PC, the Apple Macintosh (technically not a PC) became the standard for graphics-based applications and the IBM PC and a host of IBM-compatibles, or clones, were chosen for text-based (business) applications. However, as chips have become more powerful, the difference in emphasis has become less important. Apple have recently introduced the PowerPC, which **is** IBM-compatible.

1.16 PCs are now the **norm** for small to medium-sized business computing and for home computing. Often they are linked together in a **network** to enable sharing of information between users.

File servers

1.17 A file server is more powerful than the average desktop PC and it is dedicated to providing **additional services** for users of networked PCs. We shall discuss these in more detail in Chapter 6.

1.18 A very large network is likely to use a 'mainframe' computer as its server, and indeed mainframes are beginning to be referred to as '**enterprise servers**'.

Portables

1.19 The original portable computers were heavy, weighing around five kilograms, and could only be run from the mains electricity supply. Subsequent developments allow true portability.

  (a) The **laptop** is powered either from the electricity supply or using a rechargeable battery. It uses 3½" disks and CD-ROMs, a liquid crystal or gas plasma screen and is fully compatible with desktop PCs.

  (b) The **notebook** is about the size of an A4 pad of paper. Some portables are now marketed as 'sub-notebooks'.

  (c) The **pocket computer** or handheld, may or may not be compatible with true PCs. They range from machines which are little more than electronic organisers to relatively powerful processors with DOS compatibility and communications features.

1.20 While portable PCs are becoming more popular (even in the office, as they save precious space on crowded desks), they have some **disadvantages**, in particular the following.

  (a) Keyboard **ergonomics** (ie keys which are too small, or too close together, for easy, quick typing).

  (b) **Battery power** (although manufacturers are trying to reduce power consumption).

Workstations

1.21 Originally, a workstation was a computer used by one person, particularly for graphics and design applications (like Computer Aided Design) and was used primarily in **engineering**. It had a fast and powerful central processor, a high resolution monitor, and a large memory. This enabled complex designs to be easily manipulated.

1.22 These characteristics, however, are no longer unique to workstations. High performance personal computers can offer very similar services; so the distinction is a historical one. Personal computers are generally fitted with some kind of **graphics expansion card** — a circuit board containing the necessary electronics.

A typical PC specification

1.23 Here is the specification for a **fairly powerful PC**, extracted from an advertisement that appeared in the *Times* in Spring 1998. This PC cost **around £1,200** (including VAT) at this time.

Exam focus point

In the exam you will **not** be expected to know about terms like IDE or UART shown below, so don't let it scare you. We include this information because you might well want to have such things demystified if you are buying a PC for work or personal use.

```
┌─────────────────────────────────────────────────────────────────┐
│                        PC SPECIFICATION                           │
│                                                                   │
│   Intel 233 MHz Pentium Processor      4MB 3D 64-bit SUPER Graphics│
│   55.6 kbps internal fax modem         Accelerator Card including  │
│                                        MPEG software               │
│                                                                   │
│   High performance 82440FX chipset     3.5" (1.44MB) Floppy Disk   │
│   motherboard (4 PCI, 4 ISA slots,     Drive                       │
│   1 shared)                                                        │
│                                                                   │
│   High speed 64-bit data path to memory PCI Enhanced IDE Controller│
│                                                                   │
│   512K CPU Cache                       105 Key UK Windows 95       │
│                                        Keyboard                    │
│   64MB Fast EDO RAM (expandable to                                 │
│   512MB)                               Logitech 2 button mouse     │
│                                                                   │
│   6.4GB hard disk drive                Midi Tower Case 3 × 5.25"&  │
│   15" SVGA Colour Monitor LR, NI up to 3 × 3.5" drive bays, 2      │
│   1024 × 768 & Energy Star compliant   serial ports (16550 UART),  │
│                                        1 parallel port             │
│   32 Speed IDE CD ROM                  Windows 95                  │
└─────────────────────────────────────────────────────────────────┘
```

1.24   By the end of this Chapter you should understand most of the terms used here.

2   THE PROCESSOR

2.1   The processor is the 'brain' of the computer.

KEY TERM

The **processor** is the collection of circuitry and registers that performs the processing in a particular computer and provides that computer with its specific characteristics. In modern computers the CPU comprises a single (albeit increasingly sophisticated) chip device but this is supported by other chips performing specialist functions.'

(CIMA, *Computing Terminology*)

2.2   The processor (sometimes referred to as the **central processing unit** (or **CPU**)) is divided into three areas:

(a)   the **arithmetic and logic unit**;
(b)   the **control unit**;
(c)   the main store, or **memory**.

The set of operations that the processor performs is known as the **instruction set**, or repertoire, and this determines in part the speed at which processing can be performed.

Chips with everything

2.3   In modern computer systems the processing unit may have all its elements - arithmetic and logic unit, control unit, and the input/output interface-on a single '**chip**'. A chip is a small piece of silicon upon which is etched an integrated circuit, which consists of transistors and their interconnecting patterns on an extremely small scale.

2.4   The chip is mounted on a carrier unit which in turn is 'plugged' on to a circuit board - called the **motherboard** - with other chips, each with their own functions.

Arithmetic and logic unit

2.5 The ALU is the part of the central processor where the arithmetic and logic operations are carried out. These include **arithmetic** (for example adding and multiplying) and **logical** functions such as comparison, branch operations (a branch instruction changes the order of program instructions) and movement of data. The operations are all simple but, as we shall see in a moment, the significant feature of computer operations is the very rapid speed with which computers can perform vast numbers of simple-step instructions, which combine to represent quite complex processing.

Control unit

2.6 The control unit receives program instructions, one at a time, from the main store and decodes them. It then sends out **control signals** to the peripheral devices.

MHz and clock speed

2.7 The signals are co-ordinated by a **clock** which sends out a 'pulse' - a sort of tick-tock sequence called a 'cycle' - at regular intervals. A clock pulse indicates to some circuits that they should **start** sending data on their wires and at the same time indicates to others, when the data from the previous pulse should have **arrived**. This ensures that devices do not start the next stage of processing until all the data that is needed has arrived in the right place.

2.8 This sounds rather laborious until you realise the phenomenal speed at which computers work. The number of cycles produced per second is usually measured in **MegaHertz** (MHz).

1 MHz = one **million** cycles per **second**.

A typical modern business PC might have a specification of 166 MHz, but models with higher clock speeds (eg 200, 233, and 266MHz) are now common. To show you the speed of development, note that a 300 MHz model was released at the end of 1997 and a 400 MHz model was released in Spring 1998.

> **Exam focus point**
> Just to reassure you again, we are providing this information about Mhz and clock speeds because it is useful to know about these things in practice. You will **not be asked** to explain them in the exam.

Getting the bus

2.9 A signal travels along a path that is called a **bus** in computer jargon. A 'local bus' is a particularly fast route. The terms PCI and ISA in the PC advertisement refer to different industry standards for buses.

Intel inside

2.10 If you have been working for some time you have probably noticed the shift from '386' processors to the **'Pentium'** processors common today. This refers to the chips made by the Intel company. Each generation of Intel CPU chip has been able to perform operations in **fewer clock cycles** than the previous generation, and therefore works more quickly.

2.11   For example, suppose an accounting program were trying to add up a column of numbers.

> A **386** CPU requires a minimum of 6 clock ticks to add two numbers.
>
> A **486** CPU can generally add two numbers in 2 clock ticks.
>
> A **Pentium** CPU can add two numbers in 1 clock tick.
>
> A **Pentium Pro** can add **three** numbers in 1 clock tick, **and** if it discovers that one of the numbers will take longer than others to retrieve from memory, it will request that number and then skip ahead to add later numbers further down the column, coming back to include the missing number when it arrives.

2.12   **You need not remember the precise details** here: just be aware that a Pentium of any kind is much faster than a 486 or a 386.

The widely advertised Pentium **MMX** technology offers enhanced sound and graphics capabilities. This technology is incorporated into the latest Intel processor (at the time of publication) the **Pentium II**.

2.13   Other manufacturers of processors include IBM, with their **6×86 chip** (similar to a Pentium) and Digital with their **Alpha** chip (perhaps twice as powerful as a Pentium).

Memory

2.14   Just as humans can work more quickly if they can **remember** the rules for doing something rather than having to look them up, a computer's processing is much faster if it has the information it needs readily to hand. The computer's **memory** is also known as main store, internal store or immediate access storage. This is circuitry which is used to store data within the processing unit whilst the computer is operating.

2.15   The memory will hold the following.

(a)   **Programs**. The control unit acts on program instructions that are held in the store; these program instructions include the operating system.

(b)   Some **input data**. A small area of internal store is needed to take in temporarily the data that will be processed next.

(c)   A **working area**. The computer will need an area of store to hold data that is currently being processed or is used for processing other data.

(d)   Some **output data**. A small area of store is needed to hold temporarily the data or information that is ready for output to an output device.

Bits and bytes

2.16   Each individual storage element in the computer's memory consists of a simple circuit which can be switched **on** or **off**. These two states can be conveniently expressed by the numbers **1** and **0** respectively. Any piece of data or instruction must be coded in these symbols before processing can commence.

> **KEY TERMS**
>
> Each 1 or 0 is a **bit**.
>
> Bits are grouped together in groups of eight to form **bytes**.
>
> A byte may be used to represent a **character**, for example a letter, a number or another symbol.
>
> The characters formed can be grouped together to form **words**. A word may be a number (in binary form), a computer instruction, or a group of characters.
>
> A byte coding system that is commonly used in microcomputers is **ASCII**.

2.17 Since a byte has 8 bits, there are 2^8, or 256, different combinations of 1s and 0s, which is sufficient to cover numeric digits, upper and lower case alphabets, punctuation marks and other symbols. Business PCs now make use of **16 or 32 bit** processors. This means that data travels around in groups of 16 or 32 bits, and so modern PCs operate considerably faster than the original 8 bit models introduced in the early 1980s.

2.18 The processing capacity of a computer is in part dictated by the capacity of its memory. Capacity is calculated in **kilobytes** (1 kilobyte = 2^{10} (1,024) bytes) and **megabytes** (1 megabyte = 2^{20} bytes) and **gigabytes** (2^{30}). These are abbreviated to Kb, Mb and Gb.

2.19 The reason for holding programs in the memory is to **speed up processing**. The transfer of data, such as program instructions, within memory is faster than the transfer of data between the processor and peripheral devices. However, a computer's memory is limited in its size, and can only hold a certain volume of data at any time. A program can be too big for some computers, because the computer's memory is not large enough to hold it.

2.20 A distinction can be made between two main types of memory, **RAM** and **ROM**. The term **cache** is also important.

RAM

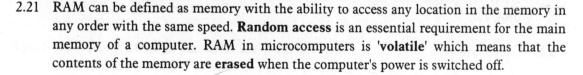

> **KEY TERM**
>
> **RAM (random access memory)** is memory that is directly available to the processing unit. It holds the data and programs in current use. Data can be written on to or read from random access memory.

2.21 RAM can be defined as memory with the ability to access any location in the memory in any order with the same speed. **Random access** is an essential requirement for the main memory of a computer. RAM in microcomputers is '**volatile**' which means that the contents of the memory are **erased** when the computer's power is switched off.

2.22 The reference to EDO RAM in the PC advert refers to a technology that helps to optimise the transmission of signals to and fro - in other words it speeds things up once again. DRAM and SRAM (and other variants) are special types of RAM.

2.23 The RAM on a typical business PC is likely to have a capacity of **16 to 64 megabytes** (most usually 32 Mb). The size of the RAM is **extremely** important. A computer with a

200 MHz clock speed but only 8 Mb of RAM will not be as efficient as a 100 MHz PC with 32 Mb of RAM.

Question 1

When you start up a program on a typical modern PC you generally hear a crackling noise and a little light flickers on the front of the base unit.

Answer

The program is being read from the PC's hard disk into its RAM. There will be more crackling and flickering if you open an existing document or if you wish to use a part of the program that is not automatically loaded when the program starts.

(For instance, start up Microsoft Word and then click on Format ... Paragraph, or Tools... Spelling. You will hear and see the hard drive talking to the RAM.)

Cache

2.24   The **cache** (or primary cache) is a small capacity but **extremely fast** memory chip which saves a second copy of the pieces of data most recently read from or written to main memory. When the cache is full, older entries are 'flushed out' to make room for new ones. Primary cache is often part of the same chip as the CPU.

2.25   The principle is that if a piece of data is accessed once it is highly likely that it will be accessed again soon afterwards, and so keeping it readily to hand will speed up processing.

2.26   **Secondary cache** is a larger, slower cache between the primary cache and the main memory. You may also see the term **pipeline burst cache** in PC ads. 'Pipeline burst' refers to an extremely efficient method of handling data in memory.

ROM

KEY TERM

ROM (read-only memory) is a memory chip into which fixed data is written permanently at the time of its manufacture. New data cannot be written into the memory, and so the data on the memory chip is unchangeable and irremovable.

2.27   ROM is '**non-volatile**' memory, which means that its contents do not disappear when the computer's power source is switched off. A computer's **start-up program**, known as a 'bootstrap' program, is always held in a form of a ROM. 'Booting up' means running this program.

2.28   When you turn on a PC you will usually see a reference to **BIOS** (basic input/output system). This is part of the ROM chip containing all the programs needed to control the keyboard, screen, disk drives and so on.

3   INPUT DEVICES

3.1   Input is a **labour-intensive** process, typically involving the keying in of data using a keyboard. In many cases, transcription, the process of inputting data by keyboard so that it can be converted into the electronic pulses on which the computer circuitry operates, is avoided by a process of **data capture**, where data is recorded in such a way as to be directly convertible into a machine-sensible form without any human intervention. In many situations, data capture or transcription occur far away from the main computer, and data has to be **transmitted** to where it is to be processed.

The keyboard

3.2   You will already be familiar with the basic QWERTY typewriter keyboard which includes the **alphabet, numbers** 0 - 9 and some basic **punctuation**, together with other keys (for example a space bar and a shift key, which allows a second set of key features to be used, including the upper case alphabet keys). Computer keyboards are derived from this standard keyboard.

Question 2

A typical computer keyboard has 102 or 105 keys and is a development of the QWERTY design. What types of keys does it have?

Solution

A basic keyboard includes the following.

(a)   Ordinary **typing keys** used to enter data or text.

(b)   A separate **numeric key pad** for use with the built-in calculator.

(c)   **Cursor control** keys, basically up/down/left/right **arrow** keys to move the cursor.

(d)   Additional **cursor keys**, such as Home, End, Pg Up and Pg Dn, for rapid movement through documents/files.

(e)   A number of **function keys** (usually 12) for use by the system and application software. Each represents a particular command or string of commands.

(f)   **Return** or **Enter** key. All commands direct to the system must be 'entered' with this key.

(g)   **Esc**ape key. This key can be used to exit from a procedure.

(h)   Control (**Ctrl**) key and Alternate (**Alt**) key. These tell the machine that a command is about to be entered.

(i)   A **Windows 95** keyboard has three extra keys which operate the **'Start'** button where the Windows 95 operating system is being used.

The VDU

3.3   A VDU (visual display unit) or 'monitor' displays text and graphics. The screen's **resolution** is the number of pixels that are lit up. A **pixel** is a picture element -a 'dot' on the screen, as it were. The fewer the pixels on screen, the larger they will be: the resolution of any picture will be low. More and smaller pixels enable detailed high-resolution display.

3.4   Older PCs often have a resolution of 640 × 480, the resolution offered by IBM's VGA standard. Higher resolution requires more processing power. Super VGA, or SVGA, is the standard for newer monitors and offers resolutions up to 1,280 × 1,024. Monitors are controlled by circuitry within the base unit called **video cards**, graphics cards and so on A **graphics accelerator** is circuitry that performs tasks such as plotting lines, shading and so on.

Exam focus point

Again, this explanation is more techy than anything than you would get in an exam, but may be useful if you are buying a PC.

However, you may get questions on **screen design** – the way in which things are laid out on the screen. There is more on this in **Chapter 14**.

3.5   The user must 'scroll' up, down or sideways across the screen when he or she wants to view a different piece of text. Alternatively two or more bits of text which are in different places in the overall layout (or even in different documents) can be viewed on screen at the same time by making use of 'windows'.

3.6   The screen is used in conjunction with a keyboard to display text to allow the operator to carry out a **visual check** on what he or she has keyed in, to help the operator to input data by displaying 'forms' for filling in, and to display **output**, for example answers to file enquiries.

3.7   In addition, the screen can be used to give messages to the operator, and the operator can respond to messages by keying in new instructions. Touch-sensitive screens have been developed but they are expensive and not widely used.

Mouse

3.8   A mouse is often used in conjunction with a keyboard, particularly in Windows-based systems. A mouse is a handheld device with a rubber or metal ball protruding from a small hole in its base. The **mouse is moved** over a flat surface, usually a special mouse mat which is designed to possess enough friction to prevent the ball slipping, and as it moves, internal sensors pick up the motion and convert it into electronic signals which instruct the **cursor on screen to move** in the same direction.

3.9   The mouse has (usually) two or three **buttons** which can be pressed (**clicked**) to send specific signals. For example, a 'click' on the left hand button can be used to send the cursor to a new cell in a spreadsheet and a 'double click' can select a particular application from a Windows menu. The latest variety also have a **wheel** to facilitate scrolling up and down a screen display.

3.10   Similar to the mouse is the **trackball**. This is prevalent on notebook computers, where there is not always space to place a mouse mat on a flat surface next to the computer. It operates in a similar way, except that the casing is fixed to the computer and a ball, which protrudes upwards, is manipulated by hand. Some mobile computers use a touch sensitive pad for mouse functions; others have a tiny joystick (called a '**nipple**') in the centre of the keys on the keyboard.

Document reading methods

3.11   Copying manually-prepared data into a computer-sensible form such as disk or tape is costly in terms of manpower, time and accuracy. Document reading methods **reduce human 'intrusion'** into data capture and cut out the need to transcribe manually-prepared data on to a computer-sensible input medium. This **saves time and money** and also **reduces errors** because it cuts out all data preparation errors and also, in the case of **pre-printed documents** such as cheques, many data recording errors too.

Magnetic ink character recognition

3.12 MICR is the recognition by a machine of special formatted characters printed in **magnetic ink**. Using ink which contains a metallic powder, highly stylised characters (such as those as on a **cheque**) are encoded on to documents by means of special typewriters. The document must be **passed through a magnetic field** before the characters can be detected by a suitable reading device.

3.13 The main advantage of MICR is its **accuracy**, but MICR documents are **expensive** to produce, and so MICR has only limited application in practice. A large MICR reader in the banking system can scan up to 2,000 documents per minute.

Optical character recognition

3.14 OCR is a method of input involving a machine that is able to read characters by **optical detection** of the **shape** of those characters. Optical (or laser) scanners can read **printed documents** at up to 300 pages per hour. They recognise the characters, convert them into machine code and record them.

3.15 The advantage of OCR over MICR is that the computer can read **ordinary** typed or printed text, provided that the quality of the input document is satisfactory. In practice the difficulty of distinguishing between O and 0, and I and 1, means that OCR applications are limited.

3.16 The technology now exists for computers to recognise **handwriting** and devices that allow the user to 'write' on the screen and have this writing automatically converted into computer sensible form are becoming quite widely used in applications such as police work, where fairly standard details need to be noted quickly and accurately while **on the scene** of an incident. Commercial applications include warehousing and stock control.

Optical mark reading

3.17 Optical mark reading is generally used for **numeric** characters. Values are denoted by a line or cross in an appropriate box, whose **position** represents a value, on the preprinted source document (or card). The card is then read by a device which senses the mark in each box using an **electric current** and translates it into machine code. A computer program written specifically for the application interprets each marks as appropriate.

3.18 Applications in which OMR is used are the recording of gas and electricity meter readings on to preprinted documents, **National Lottery** entry forms, and answer sheets for **multiple choice questions**. Once the readings are made, the documents are input to the computer using an OMR reading system.

Turnaround documents

3.19 OCR and OMR methods of character recognition can make use of a turnaround document. A turnaround document is a document that is initially **produced by computer**. It is then used to collect more data and then **re-input to the computer** for processing of the additional data. The main drawback to turnaround documents is their limited application. There are not many situations where an organisation can produce a document which can then be used for subsequent data input. Examples of turnround documents are as follows.

(a) Credit card companies, for example Visa and Mastercard, include a **payment counterfoil** with their computer-produced bill, which is returned with payment and then used for inputting payment data to a computer.

(b) An examining body that stores multiple choice questions on a computer file can produce **examination answer sheets** by computer. Candidates are then asked to tick the correct answer, and the position of the answer mark will be detectable by an OMR reader, and so the examination paper can be marked by computer.

Exam focus point

The question on document reading devices that appeared in **June 1996** concerned an examining body.

Bar coding and EPOS

3.20 A bar code reader is a device which reads bar codes, which are groups of marks which, by their **spacing and thickness**, indicate specific codes or values. Look at the back cover of this book for an example of a bar code.

3.21 Such devices are now commonly used as an input medium for **point of sale systems** in **supermarkets** - nearly all food and drink products now carry bar coding on their labels. When a customer buys bar coded items and takes them to the checkout to pay, the shop assistant will use a bar code reader which transmits the bar coded data to a central processor in the store. The computer then provides the price of the item being purchased (from a price list held on the stock file) and this is output to the cashier's check-out point.

3.22 At the same time, the data about the purchases that have been read into the computer from the bar codes can be used to **update the stock file** and **record the sales data** for management information purposes.

3.23 More and more large retail stores are introducing **Electronic Point of Sale (EPOS)** devices, using bar coding, which act both as cash registers and as terminals connected to a main computer. This enables the computer to produce **useful management information** such as sales details and analysis and stock control information **very quickly**. The provision of immediate sales information (for example, which products sell quickly), perhaps analysed on a branch basis, permits great speed and flexibility in **decision-making** (certainly of a short-term nature), as consumer wishes can be responded to quickly.

Card reading devices

Magnetic stripe cards

3.24 The standard magnetic stripe card is rectangular in shape, measuring about 8.5cm by 5.4 cm. One face of the card contains the name of the **issuer**, the **payments system** the card applies to (for example VISA), and often a **hologram image** (for example a bird on VISA cards) for security purposes. The customer's **name**, the card **number** and the card **expiry date** also appear (in embossed form, so that the details can be printed on to credit card payment slips).

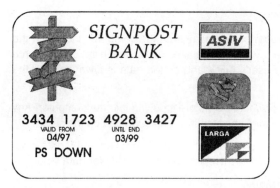

3.25 However, none of this surface information is strictly necessary for data input to a computer system. All the machine-sensible data is contained on the back, on a **magnetic stripe**, which is a thin strip of magnetic recording tape, about 1.2cm wide, stuck to the back of the card. The magnetic card reader converts this information into directly computer-sensible form.

3.26 The widest application of magnetic stripe cards is as bank credit or service cards, for use in **automated teller machines** (ATMs) and bank payment systems. Many retailers have now introduced systems for the **Electronic Funds Transfer at the Point Of Sale** (EFTPOS) (see the next chapter).

Smart cards

3.27 Smart cards are similar to magnetic stripe cards in that information is held on a plastic card for the customer to use at will. However, the technology by which this is achieved is quite different. Smart cards are much **more versatile** than magnetic stripe cards. They are currently most widely used in France. A smart card is a plastic card in which is embedded a **microprocessor chip**.

3.28 Besides basic account data, a smart card would typically contain a **memory** and a **processing capability**. The smart card is used in a similar way to magnetic stripe cards for money transmission. One of the principal economic advantages of smart cards over magnetic stripe cards is that they are much **harder to duplicate**, and so are more secure. On the other hand, the technology is **more expensive** to produce.

Voice recognition

3.29 Computer software has been developed that can **convert speech** into computer sensible form: the input device needed in this case is simply a **microphone**. At present, affordable versions of the software (ranging from less than £100 to about £500) require users to speak very slowly, dictating one word at a time, and at best they are **not much more than 90% accurate**. However the technology is improving. A voice-enabled version of the Sage Line 50 (formerly Sage Sterling) accounting package is planned for release soon.

Question 3

What are the advantages and disadvantages of keyboard input?

Answer

By far the most significant **advantage** of direct input via keyboard is that a computer user can have **interactive processing** using a keyboard and VDU. Interactive processing is when data can be input to a computer, output information received quickly, and where appropriate further input keyed in and output received. The computer user gets the information he or she wants 'instantly'.

The other advantages of keyboard input are as follows.

(a) The person keying in the data can be in a **location far away** from the computer itself, with the keyboard terminal linked to the computer by telephone link or private wire. The source document never has to leave the computer user's office and so the data is always under the user's own control.

(b) The person keying in the data can **check it on the VDU** before inputting it to the computer. Any keying errors, or even errors in the data itself, might be identified and corrected on the spot.

(c) Keyboard input is convenient for **small volumes** of data when the time taken up by data input is only short. Most microcomputer systems in offices use keyboard and VDU for data input.

Direct keyboard input has a number of **disadvantages**.

(a) It is unsuitable for **large volumes** of transaction data. Keying in takes a long time (in computer terms), and when a keyboard terminal is on-line to a computer, the CPU is idle for much of the time. Input via tape or disk makes much better use of the computer's processing capabilities, and processing is much faster as a result.

(b) Keyboard input is likely to be **error-prone** because the only data verification that can be done is a visual check of the data on the VDU screen before input.

(c) There might be **security problems**. Keyboard terminals are less 'secure' than a computer centre, and there is a possibility that unauthorised users can gain access to a keyboard terminal in an office (or that unauthorised people can gain access from their own personal terminal to someone else's computer).

4   OUTPUT DEVICES

4.1   The commonest methods of computer output are printers and screen display although it is also possible to output onto **microfilm** or microfiche and onto transparencies for **overhead projection**. Many home computers also produce **sound** output through **speakers**. It will usually be clear which method is suited to a particular application, as the characteristics of each are very different, particularly in respect of their transience and their suitability for presenting differing volumes of information.

The choice of output medium

4.2   Choosing a suitable output medium depends on a number of factors.

Factor	Comment
Hard copy	Is a hard copy of the output required; in other words, is a printed version of the output needed? If so, what quality must the output be?
Volume	The **volume** of information produced may affect the choice. For example, a VDU screen can hold a certain amount of data, but it becomes more difficult to read when information goes 'off-screen' and can only be read a 'page' at a time.
Speed	The **speed** at which output is required may critical. For example, to print a large volume of data, a high speed printer might be most suitable to finish the work more quickly (and release the CPU for other jobs). If a single enquiry is required, it may be quicker to make notes from a VDU display.
Suitability for further use	The **suitability** of the output medium to the purpose for which the output is needed. Output on to a magnetic disk or tape would be appropriate if the data is for further processing. Large volumes of reference data for human users to hold in a library might be held on microfilm or microfiche, and so output in these forms would be appropriate.

Factor	Comment
Cost	Some output devices would not be worth having because their advantages would not justify their **cost**, and so another output medium should be chosen as 'second best'.

Exam focus point

It is more likely that you would be asked to say which sort of output device was suitable for what circumstances than that you would actually have to describe, say, the characteristics of a laser printer.

Printers

4.3 A **line printer** prints a complete line in a single operation, usually printing between 600 and 1,000 lines per minute. They offer the operational speeds necessary for the **bulk printing requirements** of many systems.

4.4 **Character printers** print a single character at a time. Examples include daisy-wheel printers, dot matrix printers.

 (a) Daisy wheel printers are **slow and noisy**, but produce print of a **high quality**. Companies are unlikely to buy new daisy wheel printers today because other types printers are more versatile.

 (b) Dot matrix printers are quite widely used in accounting departments. Their main drawback is the **low-resolution** of their printed characters, which is unsuitable for many forms of printed output. They are also relatively **slow** and rather **noisy**. Prices start at under £100.

4.5 **Bubblejet** and **inkjet** printers are small and prices start at under £100, making them popular where a 'private' output device is required, for example in a director's office. They work by sending a jet of ink on to the paper to produce the required characters. They are fairly **quiet and fast**, but they may produce **smudged** output if the paper is not handled carefully.

4.6 **Laser printers** print a whole page at a time, rather than line by line. Unlike daisywheel and dot matrix printers, they print on to individual **sheets of paper** (in the same way as photocopiers do) and so they do not use 'tractor fed' continuous computer stationery.

4.7 The resolution of printed characters and diagrams with laser printers is **very high** - up to 600 dots per inch - and this high-quality resolution makes laser printing output good enough to be used for commercial printing.

4.8 Typically, a desk-top laser printer will print about 4 to 24 A4 pages per minute. **High speed** laser printers print up to 500 pages per minute. Laser printers are a microprocessor in their own right, with **RAM memory** for storing data prior to printing.

4.9 Laser printers are **more expensive** than other types - a good one will cost about £700 - but it is quite possible that several users will be able to **share** a single laser printer.

4.10 There are several distinct **advantages** of laser printers.

 (a) They can be used to combine different **fonts**, for example italics or bold characters, and a wide range of characters, including mathematical symbols and Greek letters.

(b) They can be used to produce **graphics** and logos as well as characters. A firm can therefore produce letter-heads as well as the letters themselves on to blank paper using a laser printer.

(c) They are **quiet**, because unlike daisy wheel and dot matrix printers, laser printers are not impact printers which rely on the striking of hammers or pins.

The VDU

4.11 Screens were described earlier in this chapter, as they are used together with computer keyboards for **input**. It should also be clear that they can be used as an **output** medium, primarily where the output **volume is low** (for example a single enquiry) and **no permanent output** is required (for example the current balance on an account).

5   STORAGE DEVICES

> ### Exam focus point
> Once again you are not likely to get a question simply asking you to describe the various storage devices available, but this information is relevant background knowledge for a number of highly examinable issues, for example **systems design** and **security and back-up** of data.

Disks

5.1 Disks are the predominant form of backing storage medium nowadays because they offer **direct access** to data, an extremely important feature. It is essential for **real-time** systems, **interactive** processing, and **database** systems.

5.2 Disks are covered on both sides with a **magnetic** material. Data is held on a number of circular, concentric **tracks** on the surfaces of the disk, and is read or written by rotating the disk past read/write heads, which can write data from the CPU's memory on to disk, or can read data from the disk for input to the CPU's memory. The mechanism that causes the disk to rotate is called a **disk drive**. The data on a disk is located by its **sector**, as each track and sector has a unique identification number.

Hard disks

5.3 A modern business PC invariably has an **internal hard disk**, but external disks may be used too. At the time of writing the average new **PC** has a hard disk size of around **1 Gigabyte** (2^{30} bytes), but 2 Gb disks are not uncommon. The standard size has increased dramatically over recent years as ever more Windows-based software which is hungry for hard disk space is released.

5.4 In larger computer systems **removable disk packs** are commonly used.

5.5 **IDE** (Integrated Drive Electronics) and Extended IDE (**EIDE**) are hard disk technologies common on PCs. More powerful and flexible (but currently more expensive) are **SCSI** (Small Computer System Interface, pronounced 'scuzzy') and 'Firewire (1394)'. The differences between these systems lies in the way that data is transmitted between the hard disk and the processor, but you need not concern yourself with the details.

5.6 A **Zip Drive** is a disk drive made by the Iomega Corporation. It is a **removable** 100 megabyte hard disk for PCs. The drive is suitable for back-up, mass storage or for moving files between computers. A Zip drive costs about £100, and disks cost about £10. The company also makes a larger Jaz drive, which takes 1Gb and 2Gb disks.

Floppy disks

5.7 Modern PCs will also have one or two floppy disk drives. The floppy disk provides a **cost-effective** means of on-line storage for small business computer systems.

5.8 A 'floppy' disk is an **exchangeable** circular, flexible disk (typically $3^1/_2$ inches in diameter) which is held permanently in a plastic case. The case can bear an identification label for recognising the disk. A $3^1/_2$" disk can hold up to **1.44 Mb** of data and costs about £0.25.

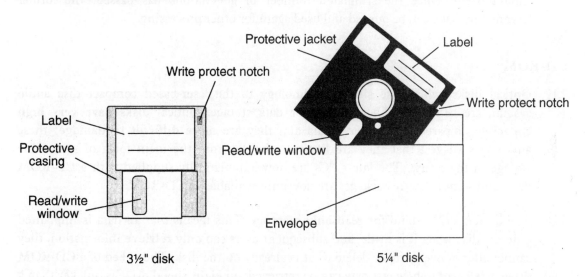

Protective jacket — Label

Write protect notch

Label

Protective casing

Read/write window

Read/write window — Write protect notch

Envelope

3½" disk 5¼" disk

5.9 Floppy disks do not require special storage conditions, and indeed, they are often stored or filed in open trays. However, data on them can be **easily corrupted**. In particular, they are subject to **physical wear**, because the read/write head actually comes into contact with the disk surface during operation. This is not the case with other types of disk.

5.10 Because they can be left lying around an office, they are also prone to **physical damage**, such as having cups of coffee spilled over them. As the disks tend to be less reliable than hard disks administrative procedures should be instituted to protect them (for example the use of steel filing cabinets and careful handling).

Tape storage

5.11 Like an audio or video cassette, data has to be recorded **along the length** of a computer tape and so it is **more difficult to access** (compare the time it takes to find your favourite record on an audiocassette compared with the time it takes with a vinyl record or CD).

5.12 In using tapes, it is not practical to read from and then write on to a single piece of tape. **Reading and writing are separate operations**, using separate heads, and so two drives are necessary for the two operations.

5.13 It follows that magnetic tape as a file storage medium is only practical when **every record** on the file will be **processed in turn**. For example a supermarket's stock records might have movements in every item of stock every day, and so tape would be a suitable for **backing up** at the end of the day.

5.14   Tape cartridges have a **larger capacity** than floppy disks and they are still widely used as a **backing storage** medium. Some are similar to but larger in size than a normal audio cassette, some are larger and some are about the size of a dictaphone mini-cassette. They are generally measured in terms of tape width and length. For instance an 8mm tape that is 112m long can store up to **5Gb** of data; a tape like this costs about £12. Fast tapes which can be used to create a back-up file very quickly are known as **tape streamers**.

5.15   Tapes can only be **updated** by producing a completely new carried forward tape, and this provides an automatic means of **data security**. The brought forward tapes can be kept for two or three 'generations' to safeguard against the loss of data on a current file.

5.16   This **'grandfather-father-son' technique** allows for files to be reconstructed if a disaster should occur. Once the stipulated number of generations has passed, the former 'grandfather' tape can be purged and used again for other processing.

CD-ROM

5.17   Optical disks, which use similar technology to the laser-based compact disc audio system, are being used increasingly for data storage. Optical disks have **very high capacity** compared with other media and they are **more difficult to damage**: these advantages suggest that they are likely to develop into the main form of removable storage in the future. The latest PCs are now automatically supplied with a CD-ROM drive and some software packages are now only available on CD-ROM.

5.18   The initials ROM stand for **read-only memory**. This means that all data is implanted onto the disc when it is made, and subsequent users can only **retrieve** information, they cannot alter or overwrite or delete what is already on the disk. The **speed** of a CD-ROM drive is relevant to how fast data can be retrieved: an **eight speed** drive is quicker than a **four speed** drive.

Question 4

Why do PCs currently need both CD-ROM drives and floppy disk drives?

Answer

See the next paragraph

5.19   CD recorders are now available for general business use with blank CDs (CD-R), but this does not alter the fact that, until recently CDs have not been reusable in the way that floppy disks are. This is why PCs invariably have floppy disk drives as well as CD-ROM drives. However, **a rewritable disk** (CD-RW) is now available. A CD can hold up to **650 Mb** of data. CD-Rs cost £2 to £3 each; CD-RWs cost about £15.

5.20   In a few years time the CD format is likely to be entirely superseded by DVD. Read the case example below.

Case example: DVD

The time when multimedia CD-Roms were the cutting edge of new media has long gone. Now the focus is on trying to integrate the various media - with a keen focus on the Internet and online links.

With their 600 megabytes of data storage, CD-Roms were, not too long ago considered the holy grail for 'content' developers. But it soon became evident that this amount of storage was puny. Multimedia files with their rich graphics, video and audio content quickly soaked up the available storage space and the slow speeds of CD-Rom drives and the limited graphics capabilities of Windows systems, plus the compatibility problems with that platform left many frustrated users.

CD-Roms are rapidly becoming obsolete as far as new media are concerned. The replacement is Digital Versatile Disk (DVD) Rom technology which can store **almost 5 gigabytes** of data with excellent access speeds, and Internet-based technologies which promise three-dimensional worlds, CD-quality sound, and video.

DVD will take a couple of years to become established as a standard, and in the meantime, CD-Rom titles combining Internet links will fill the gap. Local CD-Rom or DVD-Rom disks will provide PC users with much of the graphics and audio content since sending such large files over the Internet will remain a slow process, at least for the next few years until faster communications technologies become available.

Technologies such as Intel's MMX multimedia microprocessor, plus media co-processors from a host of companies, will help PCs display high quality graphics, video and surround sound audio.

DVD has a key advantage in that it will be **backward compatible** with current CD-ROMs which will protect the user's current investment in CD-ROM titles while adding the superior capabilities of DVD.

Financial Times, December 1996

Document image processing

5.21 Document image processing is an electronic form of filing. In a DIP system, a document is passed through a **scanner**, translated into **digital form** and a digitised image is then stored on a storage device (perhaps an **optical disk**). (This can then be retrieved at will and shown on a computer screen. The image of the document can include handwriting and printed text.)

5.22 Some DIP systems not only store the electronic image of a document, but allow the stored documents to be used in other office systems. It might be possible to display, on the VDU, both the scanned document, and **keyed-in text commentary** (which can be stored with a file, for example notes of a subsequent phone conversation about a dispute referred to in a letter).

5.23 The **advantages** of DIP are as follows.

(a) **Reduced space** needed for files.
(b) The same file can be viewed by **different users** simultaneously.
(c) Files **cannot be 'lost'** as the original image is on disk.
(d) **Faster retrieval** of files than with a manual system.

5.24 One optical disk could contain **60,000 pages of A4** (this could range from 60,000 single page letters to over 1,000 sets of accounts.) The main cost savings of using DIP over paper are in storage and retrieval, as the time taken to hunt for a file is eliminated. In order for these savings to be achieved, documents must be scanned as soon as they are received by the mail room, for computer usage.

5.25 Applications of DIP include **electronic data interchange, desktop publishing** (by enabling photographs, for example, or other images to be stored) and management of **accounting transactions** - all the documentation relating to an accounting transaction can be referenced to the ledger record: an entry in the sales ledger for example could be accompanied by images of all the related paperwork.

6   THE OPERATING SYSTEM

6.1   An **operating system** is like a 'silent partner' for the computer user, providing the interface between the computer hardware and both the user (via keyboard) and the other software.

> **KEY TERM**
>
> An operating system or operating software can be defined as a program or suite of programs which provide the 'bridge' between **applications** software (such as word processing packages, spreadsheets or accounting packages) and the **hardware**.
>
> For example, access to data files held on disk during the processing of a business application would be managed by the operating system.

6.2   An operating system will typically perform the following tasks.

   (a)   Initial **set-up** of the computer once it has booted up.

   (b)   Checking that the **hardware** (including peripheral devices such as printers) is functioning properly.

   (c)   Calling up of program files and data files from disk storage into **memory**.

   (d)   **Opening and closing** of files, checking of file labels etc.

   (e)   Maintenance of **directories** in disk storage.

   (f)   Controlling **input and output** devices, including the interaction with the user.

   (g)   Controlling system **security** (for example monitoring the use of passwords).

   (h)   Handling of **interruptions** (for example program abnormalities or machine failure).

   (i)   Managing **multitasking**.

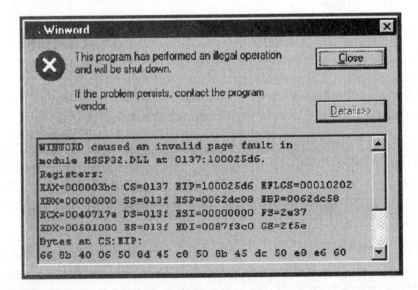

6.3   **Multitasking** means what it says: doing a lot of tasks at once, for example printing out a document you have just finished while you get on with working on the next one. With a large number of programs and peripheral units, the CPU can be kept occupied for almost all of the time.

6.4   This needs a suitable operating system and sufficient memory to hold all programs and the data which is to be processed by each program. One program must not be allowed to overlap into store allocated to another, and **priority ratings** must be allocated for each program. The highest priority program is allowed to use the CPU whenever it requires to do so. When the program can no longer use the CPU, the operating system allocates processing time to the next program in line.

UNIX

6.5   The UNIX operating system was developed as a **non-proprietary** (ie not specific to one manufacturer) **multitasking** operating system that could be portable to different computer architectures. By the 1980s it had been developed far enough for commercial users to take an interest in it.

6.6   UNIX works equally well in a PC network environment as in a mainframe system. Particular areas where UNIX has demonstrated its capabilities are **communications**, where the ability to accommodate PC operating systems in the UNIX environment supports the use of electronic mail, and **engineering**, where UNIX's capabilities are suited to driving high-resolution graphics systems.

6.7   There are two main versions of UNIX, one called **System V**, the other **BSD**. Unix also comes in **'flavours'**, depending who is selling it. For instance IBM have a version for PCs known as AIX; Hewlett Packard's Unix is called HP-UX. SCO is another well-known variety.

PC operating systems

6.8   In the PC market there is a sort of **de facto** open systems arrangement, given that there are so many 'clones' of the PC originally developed by IBM, all of which use versions of a Microsoft operating system, **Windows** or, on older machines, **MS-DOS**.

Windows

6.9   Early incarnations of Windows, culminating in **Windows 3.1** and **Windows for Workgroups 3.11**, were not genuine operating systems in their own right, but were really an operating environment for an older Microsoft system called **MS-DOS**. This meant that MS-DOS, which is very hostile to beginners, was always running underneath any applications and users were therefore still constrained by, for example, **eight-character file names** and various problems relating to the conventional memory of a PC.

6.10   In 1993, Microsoft launched **Windows NT**, a complete operating system in its own right, designed for **networks**, and now providing strong competition for other network operating systems like Novell Netware.

For PCs and smaller networks there is now **Windows 95**, also a complete operating system in its own right, though it still includes MS-DOS. A new version, Windows 98, was about to be launched at the time of publication of this Text.

> **Exam focus point**
> The choice of operating system is a key consideration in **systems design**. It also dictates, to some extent what **hardware** is chosen. For instance if you suggest that an organisation uses Windows 95, bear in mind that Windows 95 will not run comfortably on much less than a Pentium PC with 16Mb of RAM. It takes up at least 40Mb of hard disk space, before any other programs are loaded.

Windows 95 and Windows NT

6.11   Features of Windows 95 include the following (see also the illustrations in various places in this Text).

(a)   A '**desktop**', from which everything in the system branches out. Disk drives, folders (directories), applications and files can all be placed on the desktop.

(b)   A '**taskbar**' which is always on top and which includes a **Start** button (featured in advertising around the time of the release) and buttons representing every open application.

(c)   **Long file names** are supported (up to 256 characters).

(d)   There is a **Recycle Bin** for easy deletion of files.

(e)   Easy integration with widely used **networking** software is possible.

(f)   **Multitasking** is available. It is described as 'true' or pre-emptive multitasking, under which each program is allocated a time slice and tasks switch whenever the operating system dictates.

6.12   Although it has bugs and irritations for the experienced user, Microsoft Windows provides a **comprehensive working environment**, managing programs specifically written for it by other software companies (WordPerfect for Windows, Lotus 1-2-3 for Windows etc) as well as older versions which were written for MS-DOS. This makes it **easier for beginners** to learn how to use PCs, as most new applications tend to look and 'feel' the same as existing ones.

Windows 98

6.13   Windows 98 is due to be launched in mid-1998. New features and benefits fall into six key areas. (Many of these are already available to users who use the browser Microsoft Internet Explorer 4 in conjunction with Windows 95.)

Area	Comments
Easier to use	User interface enhancements include easier navigation, such as **single-click launching** of applications, icon highlighting, forward/backward buttons, and an easy to customise Start Menu. (See the next section of this chapter for more on the 'user interface'.)
Greater reliability	Many refinements and improvements over Windows 95 are planned, including the following.
	(a) **Windows Update,** an Internet-based resource site, allowing users of Windows 98 to keep their PCs up-to-date by continually providing the latest drivers and operating system files.
	(b) Windows 98 will regularly **test** the user's hard disk, system files, and configuration information to increase the system reliability, and in many cases fix problems automatically.
	(c) Enhanced **backup** and **restore** functions.

Area	Comments
Greater reliability	Many refinements and improvements over Windows 95 are planned, including the following.
	(a) **Windows Update**, an Internet-based resource site, allowing users of Windows 98 to keep their PCs up-to-date by continually providing the latest drivers and operating system files.
	(b) Windows 98 will regularly **test** the user's hard disk, system files, and configuration information to increase the system reliability, and in many cases fix problems automatically.
	(c) Enhanced **backup** and **restore** functions.
Faster	**Application loading, system startup**, and **shut down** time are **faster**. A technology called 'OnNow' will simply 'suspend' the computer when it is not needed, avoiding the normal shut down and boot up procedures, which can often be time consuming, especially if the computer has to link up to network resources. A **Tune-Up Wizard** will help the PC to maintain itself automatically and provide the best possible performance. File storage will be more efficient, freeing up hard drive space.
Web integration	There will be a variety of features designed to enhance **Internet access** and use of Internet facilities and technologies, and integrate them with the users system. For instance it will be possible to access a website directly from the 'Explorer' file management system (see Chapter 2).
More entertaining	Windows 98 has better **graphics** and **video capabilities** and better support for **games** hardware such as joysticks. It will support **digital video disks** (DVD) and technologies connected with **digital television** (also to be launched in the UK in 1998). Much to the dismay of many employers, users will be able to watch TV on their PCs (provided the PC is fitted with a TV card, but this is likely to become standard in new PCs). There is even to be a built in program guide!
More manageable for businesses	Tools such as Dr. Watson and System Information Utility will make it easier for IT support staff to **diagnose and correct problems**. An Upgrade Wizard is designed to make it easy for businesses to **migrate** from Windows 95 and Windows 3.x-based systems.

Apple Macs

6.14   There is still a minority of microcomputer users, particularly those working in design and graphics, who prefer the Apple Macintosh system, claiming that Windows 95 merely does what 'Apple Macs' have done for years. For an organisation that already has many Apple Macs and many staff familiar with them the best option may be to continue to use them.

6.15   The majority of Apple users have an operating system called System 7, which does indeed pre-date Windows 95 and to which Windows 95 bears a striking resemblance. A new version, System 8, was released in 1997.

Other operating systems

6.16 Other competitors to Windows exist, such as **IBM's OS/2** but, since the majority of PC manufacturers send out their products with Windows 95 pre-loaded, this is the system that is likely to predominate.

7 DATA PROCESSING WITH A COMPUTER

7.1 In commercial data processing, a data **file** is a collection of **records** with similar characteristics. Examples of data files include the sales ledger, the purchase ledger and the nominal ledger.

7.2 A **record** in a file consists of data relating to one logically definable unit of business information. A collection of similar records makes up a file. For example, the records for a sales ledger file consist of customer records (or 'customer accounts').

7.3 Records in files consist of **fields** of information. A field of information is an item of data relating to a record. For example, a customer record on the sales ledger file will include name, address, customer reference number, balance owing, and credit limit. Within the file the records, or fields within records, may be of fixed or variable length.

 (a) **Fixed length records** will all contain the same number of characters and each record will have fields of fixed lengths too. Account numbers are fixed length records.

 (b) In a file with **variable length records**, each record may contain a different number of fields and corresponding fields may have a different number of characters. An example would be customer addresses.

Key fields

7.4 Records on a file should contain at least one key field. This is an item of data within the record by which it can be uniquely identified.

 (a) The key field in a transaction record is the item of data which will be used to identify the master file record with which it should be associated.

 (b) The key field in a master file record is the item of data by which the record in the file is sequenced or indexed, for retrieval purposes.

Exam focus point
This information abut files, records and fields is particularly important for exam questions that deal with database design. These come up very regularly.

Types of file

7.5 Files are conventionally classified into **transaction** files, and **master** files. These distinctions are particularly relevant in batch processing applications.

Transaction files

7.6 A transaction file is a file containing records that relate to **individual transactions** that occur from day to day. For instance, as you know, when a company sells its goods day by day, the accounts staff might record the sales in a **sales day book**, which lists the sales made on that day, for which invoices have been issued. Eventually these transactions in the sales day book will be transferred ('**posted**') to the personal accounts of the individual customers in the sales ledger.

7.7   The sales day book entries are examples of **transaction records** in a **transactions file**.

Master files

7.8   A master file in such a system is a file containing **reference data**, which is normally altered (updated) infrequently and also **cumulative transactions data**.

7.9   For example, in a purchase ledger system, the master file is the **purchase ledger** itself. This is a file consisting of:

(a)   '**standing**' **reference data** for each supplier (supplier name and address, reference number, amount currently owed etc) and

(b)   **transaction data for each supplier**, itemising purchases, purchase returns and payments to the supplier. This transaction data is built up over time.

Old hat?

7.10   The terms transaction file and master file are not used much in modern processing, which prefers to talk in terms of '**databases**'. This is why we have not designated them as KEY TERMS.

Data processing operations

7.11   Files are used to **store** data and information that will be needed again at some future time (eg next week, next month, next year) or to **provide** data or information for current use. The main types of data processing operations involving files are file **updating**, file **maintenance** and file enquiry or file **interrogation**

7.12   Computers, input, files and output can be brought together in a variety of different ways to provide a computer system. So how do we set about designing a computer system to do a particular job of data processing? Both manual and computer data processing can be divided into two broad types: batch processing and real-time processing.

Batch processing

> ### KEY TERM
> **Batch processing** is the processing **as a group** of a number of transactions of a similar kind which have been entered over a period of time to a computer system.

7.13   For example the **payroll** work for salaried staff is done in one operation once a month. To help with organising the work, the payroll office might deal with **each department separately,** and do the salaries for department 1, then the salaries for department 2, and then department 3, and so on. If this is the case, then the batch processing would be carried out by dividing the transaction records into smaller batches eg **one batch per department**.

7.14   Transactions will be collected up over a period of time, perhaps in a transaction file, and will then be dealt with all at the same time. Some **delay** in processing the transactions must therefore be acceptable- ie in a payroll system, employees must agree to regular weekly or monthly payment.

7.15   Batch input allows for good **control** over the input data, because data can be grouped into **numbered batches**. The batches are dispatched for processing and processed in these batches, and printed output **listings** of the processed transactions are usually organised in **batch order**.

7.16   If any records go missing - for example get lost in transit - it is possible to locate the batch in which the missing record should belong. **Errors** in transaction records can be located more quickly by identifying its **batch number**. A check can be made to ensure that every batch of data sent off for processing is eventually received back from processing, so that entire batches of records do not go missing.

7.17   Bulk volume processing in batch mode allows the **processing** to be divided into separate stages, where each stage of processing is performed by a **separate computer programs**. (Long complex programs are more prone to error and take up more space in the CPU's internal store.)

Exam focus point
Batch processing featured in some of the Pilot Paper questions set by the **old examiner**, but has not reappeared specifically since.

7.18   EXAMPLE: BATCH PROCESSING OF SALES LEDGER APPLICATION
A company operates a computer based sales ledger. The main stages of processing are as follows.

Step 1.   The **sales invoices** are prepared manually and one copy of each is retained. At the end of the day all the invoices are clipped together and a **batch control** slip is attached. The sales clerk allocates the **next unused batch number** in the batch control book. He or she enters the batch number on the control slip, together with the **total number of documents** and the **total value of the invoices**. The control details are also entered in the control book.

Step 2.   The batch of invoices is then passed to the data processing department. The data control clerk records the batch as having been received.

Step 3.   The invoice and control details are **encoded, verified, and input** to the computer. The first program is a **validation** program which performs various checks on the data and produces a listing of all valid invoices together with some **control totals**. It also produces **rejection listings** (exception reports).

Step 4.   The data control clerk **reconciles the totals** on the batch control slip with the totals for valid and rejected data.

Step 5.   The **ledger update program** is run to process the invoice data.

Step 6.   Among the information, the computer prints out the **total of invoices** posted to the ledger and the data control clerk again **reconciles** this to the batch totals, before despatching all the output documents to the sales department.

Step 7.   All **rejected** transaction records are carefully **investigated** and followed up, usually to be re-input with the next processing run.

Real-time processing

> **KEY TERM**
>
> **Real-time processing** is the continual receiving and rapid processing of data so as to be able, more or less instantly, to feed back the results of that input to the source of the data.

7.19   Real-time processing uses an **'on-line'** computer system (see below) to interrogate or update files as requested rather than batching such requests together for subsequent processing.

7.20   Transactions for processing might arise infrequently, and so it would take too long to build up a batch for processing at the same time. Instead, each transaction would be **processed individually** as it arises.

7.21   Alternatively, the information user might want to process a transaction **immediately**, and would not be prepared to accept the delay implicit in batch processing.

7.22   As each transaction is processed immediately on input (rather than in batches), all the batch processing stages of input, validation of data, updating and output are applied to that one transaction by a **single computer program**.

7.23   Real time systems are practically the norm in modern business. **Examples** include the following.

    (a)   As a sale is made in a department store or a supermarket and details are keyed in on the **point of sale terminal**, the stock records are updated in real-time. Any customer wishing to buy a product can be informed as to whether the item is available or not (if not, an alternative might be offered).

        Although the stock files are maintained in real time, other files (for example sales analysis or debtors) may be batch processed at a later stage with the accumulated sales details (for example stored on magnetic tape) from each point of sale terminal.

    (b)   In **banking and credit card** systems whereby customer details are maintained in a real-time environment. There can be immediate access to customer balances, credit position etc and authorisation for withdrawals (or use of a credit card).

    (c)   **Travel agents, airlines** and **theatre ticket** agencies all have to use real-time systems. Once a hotel room, plane seat or theatre seat is booked up everybody on the system must know about it immediately so that they do not sell the same holiday or seat to two (or more) different customers.

On-line

7.24   On-line refers to a machine which is under the **direct control** of the principal **central processor** for that hardware configuration. A terminal is said to be on-line when it communicates interactively with the central processor. Modern computers such as PCs are on-line by definition (they have their own processor), but mainframe-based systems may not be.

KEY TERM

Response times are a significant feature of on-line processing. This is the time that elapses between initiating an on-line enquiry or transaction and receiving back the output result.

7.25　Computer users generally prefer **fast** response times, to **avoid the idle time** of the operator spent waiting for the response to come. Broadly speaking, response times can be grouped into four categories.

Category	Comment
Immediate response	This is a response time measured in microseconds. Such rapid response times are only needed in systems where a computer is controlling a technical process (for example acting in a timing device or measuring device).
Conventional response time for terminal users.	In many on-line systems the average response time (or maximum response time) might be 5 seconds or less.
Response time when starting or closing a procedure.	When a terminal user is starting a new procedure, and is instructing the computer about what procedure is required, a slower response time of, perhaps, up to 15 seconds might be regarded as 'conventional' and acceptable.
Response time at the computer's convenience.	In some situations, it might be sufficient to expect the computer to produce a response as soon as it can, but at the convenience of its processing operations, so that the response time might vary from several seconds to several minutes.

Chapter roundup

- A **computer** may be defined as a device which will accept input data, process it according to programmed logical and arithmetic rules, store and output data and/or calculate results. Computers have traditionally been be classified as supercomputers, mainframes, minicomputers and microcomputers, but the distinctions are vague nowadays.

- The **processor** is at the heart of any computer. It consists of an arithmetic and logic unit, a control unit and a memory. Important concepts are clock speed (MHz) and RAM.

- Data for **input** may originally be recorded *manually* on a keyboard. Alternatively, data for input may originally be recorded in computer-sensible form, for example via a document reading device. The ideal method of data input in a given application is one which minimises input time, cost, errors and the period before receipt of output.

- **Output** might be human-sensible, which means that it can be recognised and understood by humans (**printed, visual or sound** output) and uses a printer, the VDU or speakers, or computer-sensible, with output stored for later processing or for processing by another computer.

- The most common types of **storage** are magnetic disk and magnetic tape, though optical storage on **CD** is becoming more common. **Document image processing** systems allow documents to be scanned and then filed in electronic form.

- Software which supervises the running of other programs, providing a 'bridge' between applications software and the hardware, is known as **operating systems** software.

- Computer **files** consist of **records**, which are themselves made up of **fields** and **characters**. Records are identified by **key fields**. Files are conventionally referred to as transaction files or master files for the purposes of processing.

- In **batch processing**, input transactions are collected in batches, before processing. It is suitable for large volumes of routine data, for which output is not required instantly. Batch processing helps with the control of data.

- In **real-time processing**, transactions are processed as they arise. It is suitable for processing data that arises irregularly and for which output is required very quickly. It is becoming the norm.

Quick quiz

1 Describe the features and uses of a mainframe. (see paras 1.9 - 1.12)

2 What types of medium and small business computers are there? (1.13 - 1.22)

3 What is the difference between MegaHertz and megabytes? (2.8, 2.16 - 2.18)

4 Define RAM and ROM. (2.17, 2.27)

5 List ten input devices. (3.1 - 3.29)

6 What five factors affect the choice of output medium? (4.2)

7 What are the advantages of DIP? (5.23)

8 What does an operating system do? (6.2)

9 What is a key field? (7.4)

10 What is batch processing? (7.13)

11 What is real-time processing? (7.19)

12 What does the term 'response time' mean? (7.24)

Question to try	Level	Marks	Time
5	Exam standard	15	27 mins

Chapter 5

OFFICE AUTOMATION

Chapter topic list	Syllabus reference
1 Manual systems	1(b)
2 Spreadsheets	1(b)
3 Word processing, DTP and graphics	1(b)
4 Communications	1(b)
5 Conferencing and data interchange	1(b)
6 The Internet	1(b)
7 Office automation and its effect on business	1(b)

Introduction

Office work is generally a matter of information handling and information processing. In spite of the widespread use of the telephone, and even the early developments in computer technology, office work has long been associated with paperwork, and office workers thought of as paper pushers.

The twin advances of **computer** technology and **communications** technology (the foundations of **information technology**) have brought nearer the coming of the **electronic office**, a term used to describe the way in which the modern office is developing. Computer technology has developed to the point where an office might have a computer terminal (keyboard and screen) on every desk, with data processed and transmitted by terminal link-up to a computer rather than by means of paper and internal mail.

1   MANUAL SYSTEMS

1.1 **People like manual methods** of working and often find it more convenient to jot down notes with pen and paper or tap out a few figures with a calculator than to use a computer. This is especially true of people who have not been brought up with computers: at present in the UK this means almost everybody over the age of about 25, the bulk of the working population.

1.2 People also prefer **communicating face to face** with their colleagues, not just to fulfil their social needs but also because it is the most effective means of communication for many everyday tasks.

1.3 Computers can **waste time**, especially if the user is not properly trained or if the system has deficiencies such as limited access to printers.

Manual systems v computerised systems

1.4 However, there are a number of reasons why manual office systems are **less beneficial** than computerised systems.

(a) Labour **productivity** is usually lower, particularly in routine and operational applications.

(b) Processing is **slower** where large volumes of data need to be dealt with.

(c) Besides taking up more time and requiring more staff, slower processing means that **information that could be provided**, such as statistical analyses of data or lists (of customers or products or whatever) categorised in a variety of ways, **will not be provided** at all, because there is not time.

(d) The **risk of errors** is greater, especially in repetitive work like payroll calculations.

(e) Information is generally **less accessible**. Unless there is a great deal of duplication of records access to information is restricted to one user at a time. Paper files can easily be mislaid or buried in in-trays, in which case the information they contain is not available at all. This can mean inconvenience and wasted time internally and may prevent the organisation from providing its services to customers.

(f) It is difficult to make **corrections or alterations**. If a document contains errors or needs updating it is often necessary to recreate the **whole** document from scratch, rather than just a new version with the relevant details changed. If several copies of a paper record are stored in different places each of them will need to be changed: this can easily be overlooked and so some parts of the system will be using out of date or inaccurate data. Unless changes are dated, it may not be clear which is the correct version.

(g) **Quality of output** is less consistent and not as high as well-designed computer output. At worst, handwritten records may be illegible and so completely useless. Badly presented information may fail to communicate because key points will not have their intended impact.

(h) Paper based systems are generally very **bulky** both to handle and to store, and office space is expensive.

Exam focus point
The scenario question in the **June 1995** exam asked about the problems arising at a health centre as a result of relying on manual systems.

Question 1

(a) Work through the list of points above (perhaps using the ACCURATE acronym) and see how likely it is that a manual system will produce *good* information.

(b) In the exam you would be expected to **apply** these points to a specific scenario. Explain how each point would apply in businesses with which you are familiar, such as your employer, a large shop, a hospital, a bank, or whatever.

2 SPREADSHEETS

> ### KEY TERM
>
> A **spreadsheet** is a general purpose software package for **modelling**, 'spreadsheet' being a term loosely derived from the application's likeness to a 'spreadsheet of paper' divided into **rows** and **columns**. Modern spreadsheets have added a **third dimension** to columns and rows so that separate **sheets** can be manipulated together and linked to one another.

2.1 The spreadsheet was one of the software products which made a success of the PC in the business environment. While originally used as an aid to accountants or financial specialists, it is now a ubiquitous feature of many organisations' computer systems.

2.2 There are many spreadsheet packages available. The most widely used are **Lotus 1-2-3** and **Microsoft Excel**. You almost certainly use one of these packages yourself in your day to day work.

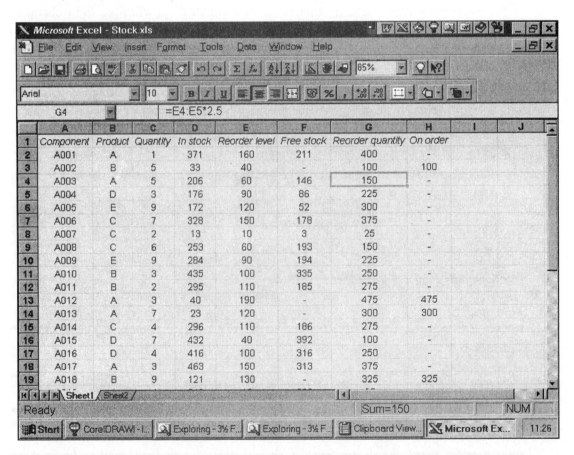

2.3 The spreadsheet user generally constructs a model, in rows and columns format, by doing the following.

   (a) Identifying what data goes into each row and column, by **inserting text**, for example column headings and row identifications.

   (b) Specifying how the **numerical data** in the model should be **derived**.

   Numerical data might be generated in different ways.

   (i) It might be inserted into the model via **keyboard input**.

   (ii) It might be **calculated** from other data in the model by means of a formula specified within the model itself. In the example shown above the first cell

(F2) in the column headed *Free stock* has the formula =IF(D2-E2>0, (D2-E2), "-"). (The '=' sign tells the computer that what follows is a formula).

(iii)   It might be obtained from data from **another application program**. For example a Microsoft Excel spreadsheet might be **dynamically linked** to a Microsoft Word word processing document or a Microsoft Access database table. If the user changes the document or table the spreadsheet is automatically changed, too.

Question 2

Explain the meaning of the formula in the *Free stock* column in the above illustration and suggest what the formula in the *On order* column might be.

Commands and facilities

2.4   Spreadsheets are **versatile** tools that can be used for a wide variety of tasks and calculations. The only pre-ordained structure imposed on the end user is the grid of rows and columns. The absence of imposed formats or contents gives the spreadsheet great flexibility and it is this that users find so valuable in **decision making**.

2.5   Different spreadsheets will offer different **facilities**, but some of the more basic ones which should feature in all spreadsheet programs are as follows. As you are probably aware from experience, this list is far from exhaustive! Look at the illustration above as you read through.

Facility	Explanation
File commands	Opening, naming, saving, printing and closing the spreadsheet file are the key tasks.
Editing	Data (cells rows or columns) can easily be copied or moved from one part of the spreadsheet to another using a mouse and 'cut and paste' and 'drag and drop' facilities. Data entry is facilitated by intelligent software that can guess, for example, that if you type *Jan 2000* in the first cell you are likely to want *Feb 2000*, *Mar 2000* and so on in the cells below.
Facilities to rearrange the spreadsheet	You can insert a column or row at a desired spot. For example, you might wish to split 'cash receipts' into 'trade' and 'other'. The insert command facilitates this, and the formulae in the spreadsheet are adjusted automatically.
Format	This command controls the way in which headings and data are shown, for example by altering column widths, 'justifying' text and numbers (to indent or have a right-hand justification, etc), changing the number of decimal places displayed, or the font used. You can format the whole spreadsheet, or a specified range of cells.
Protect facilities	A protect facility ensures that the contents of a specified range of cells (for example the text titles, or a column of base data) cannot be tampered with.
Sorting	Data can be sorted alphabetically or numerically.

Facility	Explanation
Graphics facility	Most spreadsheets also contain a graphics facility which enables the presentation of tables of data as graphs or pie charts for example.
Macros	Many spreadsheets provide a macro facility. This allows the user to automate a sequence of actions or commands, executing them with the depression of just two pre-defined keys.

Exam focus point

A question in the **December 1996** exam included spreadsheets as one of a number of technologies that students were invited to explain.

You also had to explain their effect on the way people work, for which you would need to draw on Sections 1 and 7 of this chapter.

Who uses spreadsheets?

2.6 Spreadsheets are particularly useful at **tactical** level.

(a) At **operational** level, decisions are more structured and routine and therefore more suited to specific application packages.

(b) At **strategic** level, decisions are less structured and relevant factors are less likely to be able to be incorporated into a computer package.

(c) Much tactical management, however, involves the **analysis and interpretation** of operational information. The **'what if?'** manipulation of data, for example, is probably the most important facility in a spreadsheet package.

As a simple illustration, a manager planning activities for the next six months might want to know how his department's cash flow would be affected if interest rates changed. It is a simple matter to set up a spreadsheet so that the interest rate is entered in a separate cell and treated as a variable in the cash flow calculations. The value in this cell can then be changed at will to see **what** happens to cash flow **if** the rate is 5%, 6%, 7% and so on.

Exam focus point

A question in the **December 1995** exam asked why spreadsheets were appropriate for tactical decisions and about problems arising from the extensive use of spreadsheets.

Potential drawbacks

2.7 Spreadsheets are immensely popular and can be used for a very wide range of modelling tasks. However, because they are essentially **single-user packages** and because each one is **designed from scratch**, there are risks in their use.

(a) Although users are sometimes trained in how to use a spreadsheet, they are rarely trained in **spreadsheet discipline** or **best practice**. This means that spreadsheets may be **badly designed**, increasing the risk of errors or inefficiency.

(i)   For example, a user may put a second large table of data immediately below a first, rather than diagonally offset. If he or she then deletes a column of data from the first table, then data may be **unintentionally lost** from the second one as well.

(ii)   Another common error is to set up data *en bloc* rather than having a **separate 'input' section, 'calculation' section and 'output' section**. This makes it very difficult to use the spreadsheet to analyse different scenarios. A fresh sheet has to be constructed whenever the variables change.

(b)   Users are unlikely to **document** the workings of their spreadsheet, as they consider it 'obvious'. This makes it difficult for other staff (temporary replacement or permanent successor) to understand, use or modify the model.

(c)   The '**macro**' is an important feature of all but the simplest spreadsheets. Macros can be **difficult to write and to understand** and are not as conducive to tight control as the use of a programming language.

(d)   The **lack of a proper audit trail** can be a disadvantage. Because the user works with a spreadsheet in memory (RAM), only saving it at certain intervals, it is unlikely that a record of the intermediate stages will be maintained, even if output from the intermediate stages is important. Even when a spreadsheet is saved, the previous version is usually overwritten.

3   WORD PROCESSING, DTP AND GRAPHICS

> **KEY TERM**
>
> **Word processing** is the **processing of text information**. Typically, word processing software may be used for the production of standard letters and for the drafting and redrafting of documents.

3.1   Word processing enables the person preparing the text to check the input visually on the VDU as it is being keyed in, and to **correct errors immediately**. Instead of having to erase typing mistakes with a manual eraser or Tipp-Ex, the WP operator can quickly key in the corrections and print a fresh corrected version of the text.

3.2   It is a straightforward matter to **make amendments** to the original text. If the contents of the text are discussed and as a result of these discussions, changes are agreed, the changes can be made quickly and simply. For example, a company might hold its rules and procedures books, or its price lists, on a WP file and update them just before they are to be reprinted.

Word processing hardware

3.3   Modern word processors are essentially PCs with a **word processing software** package.

3.4   **Laser printers** are widely used with word processors, as they offer the high quality required for many letters and documents.

3.5   The WYSIWYG (What You See Is What You Get) facility is another helpful feature for users who wish to see on screen exactly the **format and typeface** (italics, bold etc) they will get on paper.

3.6   The word processor screen is given **all the characteristics of a sheet of paper**. The operator is able to specify the width and length of the area (s)he wishes the text to cover on the page, taking into account desired **margins** when the text is printed on to paper. If the text area is larger than the screen can accommodate, the operator has the facility, rather like a movie cameraman, to **scroll up and down** or to **pan from side to side** in order to view and edit a page.

Software features

3.7   Once the text in its basic form has been keyed in, the **editing** facilities of the software come into their own. The functions of **deletion, correction, insertion** that used to have to be done by hand in updating or reorganising printed material are all available on screen with the word processor. Blocks of text can be **moved or duplicated**. Text can be **justified automatically** within preset margins.

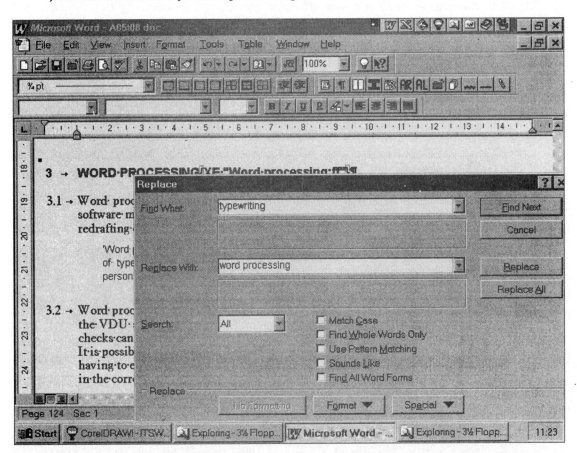

3.8   Examples of other valuable aids in producing documents include the following.

Aid	Comment
Headers	*Page headers* (chapter titles) are keyed in only once, but inserted by the program at the top of each page of the chapter.
Page numbers	An 'input' point may be inserted so that the appropriate page number within the document will be printed automatically.
Spell checking	A *spell-checker* program which checks a specified word, page or file against its own dictionary and calls attention to any word it cannot recognise: the operator then has the choice of ignoring the word (if it is unfamiliar to the machine, but correctly spelt), adding it to the dictionary (if it is unfamiliar, correctly spelt and much used), or correcting the error (by substituting a word offered by the machine from its dictionaries, or by typing afresh).

Aid	Comment
Presentation	*Typescript* variations are available, for emphasis or presentation. For example <u>underlining</u>, *italics* or **emboldening.**
Styles	*Style sheets* enable a selected typeface/font style/justification to be given a name and stored for later use.
Mail merge	*Mail merge* is a process where the typist need only enter names and addresses, and calls up a proforma letter, for a number of standard letters to be printed, for example reminders to debtors.
Importing	*Importing* data from other programs such as spreadsheets or databases (or exporting data to them) is very easy with modern packages like Word and Wordperfect.
Compatibility	Major packages are now very similar and highly *compatible*. For example, it is possible to open a Wordperfect document with Word, edit it, and save it, either in Word or Wordperfect format.

Question 3

What are the advantages of word processing over a manual or simple electronic typewriter for producing text?

Answer

The advantages of word processing for producing text include the following.

(a) The ability to produce personalised letters of a standard type.
(b) The ability to amend, correct or update text on screen easily.
(c) A low error rate in the text.
(d) Speed of keying in text, and corrections.
(e) Easy formatting of text.
(f) Quality is improved.
(g) Security may be enhanced.

Exam focus point

Word processing was another of the techniques that featured in the **December 1996** question asking for a description and notes on the impact on working methods.

Desktop publishing (DTP)

KEY TERM

Desktop publishing (DTP) is the use of office computers to implement computerised typesetting and composition systems.

3.9   Some DTP packages are suitable for the general PC user producing an occasional document. Others are appropriate for full-time in-house publishing departments, producing **brochures, price lists, bulletins and company reports and advertisements,** with sophisticated photography and artwork for output onto professional typesetting printers.

3.10   DTP systems pull **graphics and text** together from other programs and it enables the page, both graphics and text, to be seen as the 'artwork' image for editing and production. A space for a picture can be moved around the page, like 'cut and paste' artwork. This **cuts out the intermediate stage in publishing** or sending material to a phototypesetter to make up pages for printing.

Question 4

Give examples of how a business organisation can use DTP.

Answer

(a)   Design of management reports

(b)   Design and preparation of the annual report

(c)   Design of external documentation, such as press releases and mailshots

(d)   Design of advertisements

(e)   Publication of in-house magazine

(f)   Design of an organisation's standard documentation (for example order forms and quality assurance manuals)

Computer graphics

3.11   Another use of computers is the production of information in the form of **pictures, diagrams or graphs**. A widely used 'office' package is Coreldraw (examples include all of the illustrations in this book).

3.12   **Spreadsheets** and **word processing packages** also commonly incorporate **graphics facilities**.

Question 5

Some programs with a graphics facility allow the user to display data in a simple graphical form. What types of graph or diagram might you wish to prepare using a graphics package?

Answer

(a)   Line graphs (for example a time series graph, showing sales and profits over a period of time).
(b)   Bar charts.
(c)   Pie charts.
(d)   Scattergraphs which plot the value of pairs of data.
(e)   Maps (in two or three dimensions).
(f)   Architectural drawings.
(g)   Organisation charts.

In fact, (a) to (e) can easily be done with a spreadsheet package rather than special graphics software.

Presentation graphics

3.13   Programs for presentation graphics are programs which allow the user to build up a series of graphical displays or images which can be used for presentation. With additional hardware, this type of software can be used to produce **35 mm slides** for an on-screen slideshow or storyboard (which can be synchronised with a sound track). The slides that your lecturer uses on the **overhead projector** may well be produced by similar means using, for example, the **Microsoft PowerPoint** package.

Scanners

3.14   Computers can **read words and pictures** from a 'hard-copy' page, using a scanner. A scanner looks at a whole printed page of input or a photograph or illustration, and records and stores a pattern of dots. The image will be fed in to the computer, where it can be enlarged or reduced, and 'cut and pasted' into position alongside printed text on a page.

3.15   Another use of scanning is to 'read' a book and store the text on a complete file. This might be useful where the **original** book or document was **not produced by computerised methods**, but there is now a requirement to computerise the production of future editions.

4   COMMUNICATIONS

4.1   Some people have referred to the 1990s as the **'telecoms revolution'** in the same way as the 1980s were regarded as the computer revolution.

> **KEY TERMS**
>
> **Digital** means 'of digits or numbers'. Digital information is information in a coded (binary) form.
>
> Information in **analogue** form uses continuously variable signals.
>
> It is enough for you to appreciate that there is a distinction between the two and that digital methods are more advanced.

Modems and digital transmission

4.2   New technologies require **transmission systems** capable of delivering substantial quantities of data at great speed.

4.3   For data transmission through the existing 'analogue' telephone network to be possible, there has to be a device at each end of the telephone line that can convert (MOdulate) the data from digital form to analogue form, and (DEModulate) from analogue form to digital form, depending on whether the data is being sent out or received along the telephone line. This conversion of data is done by devices called **modems**. There must be a modem at each end of the telephone line.

Integrated Systems Digital Networks (ISDN)

4.4   An important development in the 1990s is the introduction, by both British Telecom and Mercury, of *Integrated Systems Digital Networks (ISDN)*, which in effect will make the entire telephone network **digital** – it will therefore be possible to send **voice, data, video and fax** communications from a single desktop computer system over the telecommunication link, without using a modem.

4.5   There are various **other new technologies** associated with companies need to send or receive large amounts of data, often in short bursts or on an occasional basis which would make the installation of a high capacity line uneconomic. As the demand for sending and receiving large graphics files, video, voice and other multimedia data services increases these will become increasingly important.

(a) **Synchronous Digital Hierarchy (SDH)** offers data speeds from 155 megabits per second (Mbps) to as much as 10 gigabits per second, and it can carry ATM and frame relay (see below) too.

(b) **Asynchronous Transfer Mode (ATM)** is capable of sending data at speeds of 155 Mbps or more.

(c) However, at present most companies find a speed of about 1.5 Mbps perfectly adequate: **frame relay switching** is a slower but cheaper technology than ATM that can cope with such requirements.

Exam focus point

These issues are becoming increasingly important **in practice**, which is why we include them. **Exams** have not yet caught up!

Mobile communications

4.6 **Radio networks** for portable telephone communications, also known as 'cellular phones', started up in the late 1980s and have boomed in developed countries in the 1990s, as you are no doubt aware from the deluge of advertising on television and radio.

4.7 Again, **digital networks** are being installed and likely to supersede the early transmission systems in the not-too-distant future. These are better able to support data transmission then the older analogue networks, with **higher transmission speeds** and **less likelihood of data corruption**.

4.8 This means that a salesperson out on the road, say, can send or receive a fax or e-mail simply by plugging a lap-top PC into a mobile handset. A combined palmtop computer and cellular phone is already on the market.

4.9 In theory it is now possible to do any kind of 'office' activity outside on the move, although **limitations in battery power** (a technology lagging far behind others described here) impose restrictions.

4.10 The mobile services available are increasing all the time. Here are some examples.

(a) **Messaging services** such as: voice mail; short message service (SMS) which allows messages of up to 160 characters to be transmitted over a standard digital phone; and paging services

(b) **Call handling services** such as: call barring, conference calls and call divert

(c) **Corporate services** such as: integrated numbering, so that people have a single contact number for both the phone on their desk and for their mobile; and virtual private networks that incorporate mobile phones as well as conventional desktop phones, so that users can dial internal extension numbers directly.

(d) **Internet access** is possible, although the speed of transmission when downloading information is relatively slow at present.

(e) **Dual mode handsets** are due to be released shortly which allow users to use both cheap cordless technology when in the office and cellular technology when outside.

(f) There are several **satellite projects** in progress which by about 2000 will mean that business people can contact each other at a modest cost using a mobile phone from virtually any point on Earth.

Case example: Mobile telecoms

Tesco, the UK's leading supermarket chain, has equipped staff at its Southampton depot with cordless telephones to improve internal and external communications. ... In older depots Tesco uses the more conventional radio and public address communications systems but has found that they are inefficient. When people are called over a public system they have to find the nearest phone extension and wait for the incoming call to be diverted to it. This takes too much time and the call can be lost before it is picked up, which in turn causes unnecessary waste of time and the extra expense of calling back. With the new cordless system staff can now be contacted easily anywhere within the depot by head office, local stores or business partners.

Source: Financial Times, June 1996

Telex

4.11 Telex is a service which enables users to transmit and receive printed messages over a telephone line. Users have to be telex subscribers, with their own telex equipment and code number, in order to send or receive messages.

4.12 The telex service started in the 1930s, and from the mid-1970s it developed significantly as an international message transmission system. Advances in telex technology made it possible for a telex user to connect PCs to the telex system.

4.13 However **data transmission speeds are very slow** compared with other methods of telecommunication and only a restricted set of characters can be used in messages.

4.14 Telex is still used, but Fax and e-mail are likely to **replace it entirely**, in time.

Fax

> **KEY TERM**
>
> **Fax** (or **facsimile transmission**) involves the transmission by data link of exact duplicate copies of documents. The original is fed into the fax machine, which 'reads' it and converts it into electronic form so it can be transmitted over the telephone. It is printed by the recipient's fax machine.

4.15 As mentioned, fax has largely **superseded** systems such as telex and the computerised equivalent 'teletex' (not to be confused with 'teletext').

4.16 The latest fax machines can also be used as **scanners** to scan data into a PC, as **printers** for PC output and as **photocopiers**. Faster machines are being developed that will cut down the time to send an A4 sheet from six seconds to one to two seconds.

4.17 Alternatively a PC can be fitted with a **fax modem**, allowing data to be transmitted directly from the PC without going through a separate fax machine.

4.18 However, users of PCs fitted with fax modems may easily forget that when they switch off their machine at the end of the day it will **not be able to receive fax messages**, unlike a stand-alone machine, which tends to be left on-line 24 hours.

Electronic mail (E-mail)

4.19   The term 'electronic mail', or **e-mail**, is used to describe various systems of sending data or messages electronically via a telephone or data network and a central computer, without the need to post letters or place memos in pigeon-holes or despatch documents by courier.

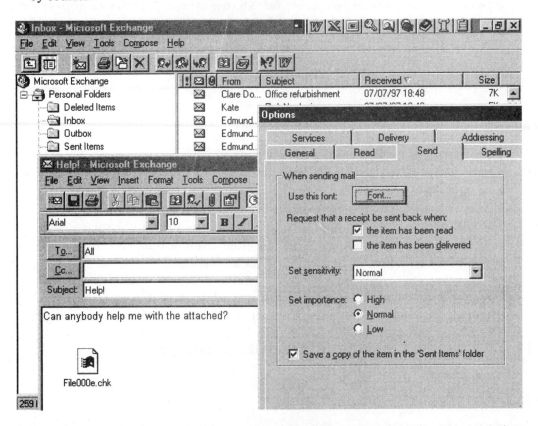

Exam focus point

E-mail was another of the technologies that featured in the **December 1996** question.

4.20   E-mail has the following **advantages**.

(a)   **Speed** (transmission, being electronic, is almost instantaneous). E-mail is far faster than post or fax. It is a particular time-saver when communicating with people overseas.

(b)   **Economy** (no need for stamps etc). E-mail is reckoned to be 20 times cheaper than fax.

(c)   **Efficiency** (a message is prepared once but can be sent to thousands of employees at the touch of a button).

(d)   **Security** (access can be restricted by the use of passwords).

(e)   Documents can be retrieved from **word-processing** and graphics packages.

(f)   Electronic **delivery and read receipts** can be requested.

(g)   E-mail can be used to send **documents and reports** as well as short memos, for instance by 'attaching' a file.

4.21   Typically information is 'posted' by the sender to a central computer which allocates disk storage as a **'mailbox'** for each user. The information is subsequently 'collected' by the receiver from the mailbox.

(a) Senders of information thus have **documentary evidence** that they have given a piece of information to the recipient and that the recipient has picked up the message.

(b) Receivers are **not disturbed** by the information when it is sent (as they would be by face-to-face meetings or phone calls), but collect it later at their convenience.

4.22 Each user will typically have **password protected access** to his own inbox, outbox and filing system. He can prepare and edit text and other documents using a **word processing** function, and send mail using **standard headers and identifiers** to an individual or a group of people on a prepared **distribution list**.

4.23 E-mail systems may serve one department or the whole organisation. It is also possible to connect an e-mail system to outside organisations.

4.24 E-mail is currently more popular **within organisations** than between them, but the Internet, discussed in detail later in this chapter, is changing this.

Voice mail

4.25 Voice mail (or v-mail) systems enable the **caller's message to be recorded** at the recipient's voice mail box (similar to a mail box in an e-mail system).

4.26 The main **advantage** of the system is that it only requires a telephone to be used. No typing or keying in is necessary. A voice mail message is basically a **spoken memo**: for the person sending the message it is much more convenient than typing it or having it typed and then faxing it.

4.27 Voice mail can be used for different situations.

(a) To contact sales representatives **'in the field'**.
(b) To **leave messages** in departments in different time zones.
(c) In organisations where employees might be **working away** at a client's premises.

Voice messaging

4.28 This is a kind of **switchboard answerphone** that takes the place of a human receptionist, or at least relieves the receptionist of the burden of dealing with common, straightforward calls.

4.29 Typically, when a call is answered a **recorded message** tells the caller to dial the extension they want if they know it, or to hold if they want to speak to the operator. Sometimes other options are offered, such as 'press 2 if you want to know about X service and 3 if you want to know about Y'.

4.30 Such systems **work well** if callers frequently have **similar needs** and these can be accurately anticipated.

4.31 They can be **frustrating** for callers with **non-standard enquiries**, however, and many people find the impersonality of responding to an answerphone unappealing. Badly set up systems can result in the caller being bounced about from one recorded message to another and never getting through to the person they want to deal with.

Case example: Interactive voice response (IVR)

Several pharmaceutical companies have installed sophisticated interactive voice response systems to deal with enquiries from doctors, chemists or patients. For example some allow the caller to press a number on their handset and have details of possible side effects sent back to them by fax.

Computer Telephony Integration (CTI)

4.32 Computer Telephony Integration (CTI) systems **gather information about callers** such as their telephone number and customer account number or demographic information (age, income, interests etc). This is stored on a customer database and can be **called up and sent to the screen** of the person dealing with the call, perhaps before the call has even been put through.

4.33 Thus sales staff dealing with hundreds of calls every day might **appear to remember individual callers** personally and know in advance what they are likely to order. Order forms with key details entered already can be displayed on screen automatically, saving time for both the sales staff and the caller.

4.34 Alternatively a busy manager might note that an **unwelcome call** is coming in on the 'screen pop' that appears on her PC and choose to direct it to her voice mail box rather than dealing with it at once.

4.35 As another example, a bank might use CTI to **prompt sales people** with changes in share prices and with the details of the investors they should call to offer dealing advice.

5   CONFERENCING AND DATA INTERCHANGE

Computer conferencing and bulletin boards

5.1 A computer conferencing system is similar to e-mail but more expensive, in that there is a huge central mailbox on the system where all persons connected to the system can **deposit messages** for everyone to see, and, in turn, **read what other people have left** in the system.

5.2 Computer conferencing can be appropriate for a team of individuals at different locations to compare notes. It becomes a way of keeping track of progress on a **project** between routine team meetings.

5.3 Computer conferencing systems can become **organisation-wide bulletin boards**, where members can leave messages of general import. A bulletin board system can be a way of re-establishing some of the social ties of office life which are alleged to have suffered from computerisation.

Exam focus point
Teleconferencing featured in the **December 1996** question already mentioned several times in this chapter.

Videoconferencing

5.4 Videoconferencing is the use of computer and communications technology to **conduct meetings** in which several participants, perhaps in different parts of the world, are linked up via **computer and a video system**. (Conference calls on a **telephone system**, where several people can converse at the same time, are a precursor of teleconferencing.)

5.5 Videoconferencing has become increasingly common as the ready availability of chips capable of processing video images has brought the service to desktop PCs at reasonable cost. More expensive systems feature a **separate room with several video screens**, which show the images of those participating in a meeting.

5.6 Even if the technology used is expensive, it is far **cheaper** when compared to the cost in management time and air fares of business **travel**.

Electronic data interchange

5.7 Electronic data interchange (EDI) is a form of computer-to-computer **data** interchange, and so another form of electronic mail. Instead of sending each other reams of paper in the form of invoices, statements and so on, details of inter-company transactions are sent via telecoms links, **avoiding the need for output** and paper at the sending end, and **for re-keying of data** at the receiving end.

5.8 The general concept of having one computer talk directly to another might seem straightforward enough in principle, but in practice there are two major **difficulties**.

   (a) Each business wants to produce documents (and hold records on file) to its own **individual requirements** and structure. Thus a computer of X Ltd could not transmit data to a computer of Y Ltd because the records/data transmitted **would not be in a format or structure** to suit Y Ltd.

   (b) Businesses may work to differing **time schedules**, especially when they are engaged in international trade. If a London company's computer wants to send a message to a computer in San Francisco, the San Francisco computer might not be switched on or otherwise able to receive the message.

5.9 Until recently different makes of computer could not easily 'talk' to each other. The problem of **compatibility** between different makes of computer was a serious one, and some form of interface between the computers had to be devised to enable data interchange to take place. This is less and less of a problem as businesses adopt common standards and set up sites on the **Internet**.

5.10 Joining an **EDI network** (there are several) is quite **expensive**, but many smaller companies are encouraged to do so by their **suppliers and/or customers**. Many of Marks and Spencer's suppliers have been converted to EDI.

Electronic Funds Transfer

5.11 Electronic Funds Transfer (EFT) describes a system whereby a computer user can use his computer system to **transfer funds** - for example make payments to a **supplier**, or pay salaries into **employees'** bank accounts, or transfer funds from one bank account to another account by sending electronic data to his bank. Since businesses keep most of their cash in bank accounts, electronic funds transfer must involve the **banks** themselves.

SWIFT

5.12 A system for the electronic transfer of funds **internationally between banks** themselves is known as SWIFT (the Society for Worldwide Interbank Financial

Telecommunications). If X Ltd in the UK wishes to make a payment to a company in, say, Germany, and if his UK bank and the German company's bank are members of the SWIFT network (all the UK clearing banks are members), the settlement between the banks themselves can be made through the SWIFT system.

CHAPS and BACS

5.13   Interbank settlements by the clearing banks **within the UK** are also made by electronic funds transfer, using the CHAPS system (Clearing House Automated Payments System).

5.14   Many large companies now pay the salaries of employees by providing computer data to their bank, using the **BACS (Bankers' Automated Clearing Services)** or BACSTEL service. It has been estimated that switching to BACS can save 90% on transaction charges.

6   THE INTERNET

6.1   The **Internet** is the name given to the technology that allows any computer with a telecommunications link to exchange information with any other suitably equipped computer.

6.2   Terms such as 'the net', 'the information superhighway', 'cyberspace', and the 'World Wide Web (www)' are used fairly interchangeably, although technically the **'web'** is what makes the 'net' **user-friendly** (rather like Windows did for MS-DOS).

Case example: How world-wide is the web?

Overall about 100m people in 150 countries already have access to the Internet and this figure is expected to reach 250m by the end of the century.

Two out of three major European firms are currently using the Internet for business, and one in five reports higher sales as a result, according to a Gallup survey commissioned by the Wall Street Journal and IBM.

While the survey indicates that web usage is still immature (most companies are using the web to gather information and communicate with customers), 37 per cent of wired companies are actually conducting electronic commerce over the net. The Internet has even influenced some companies to change their corporate strategies.

When broken down by country, the survey documents clear disparities in web usage by Europe's three biggest economies. Germany has the most net-connected companies with 74 per cent of the companies contacted saying they were using the Net for business, compared to 70 per cent in Britain and 55 per cent in France.

Access to the Internet will become easier and easier: most new PCs now come pre-loaded with the necessary software, cheaper Internet devices are about to hit the market, and developments in telecommunications networks will eventually render modems unnecessary. The UK is in the forefront of all of these developments.

Websites

6.3   As you are no doubt aware, most companies of any size now have a **'site'** on the Net. A site is a collection of screens providing information in text and graphic form, any of which can be viewed simply by clicking the appropriate button, word or image on the screen.

6.4   The user generally starts at the site's **'home page'**, which sets out the contents of the site. For instance, **here is Microsoft's home page.**

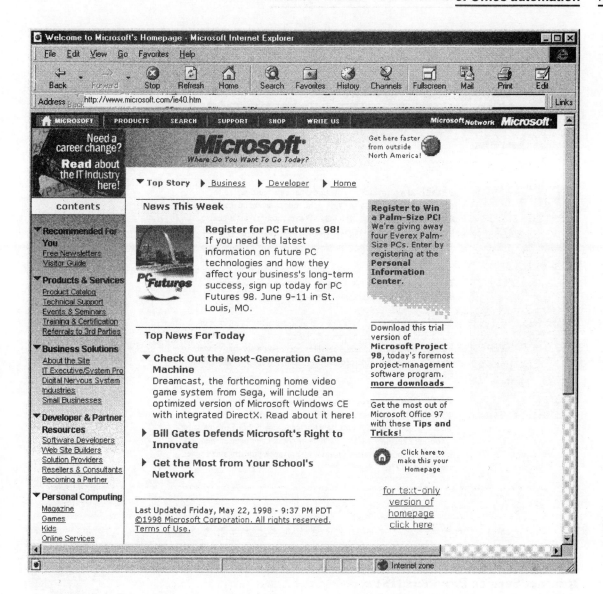

6.5   The main part of the page offers **news** about what is happening at the company. The buttons in the black bar across the top of the page take the user to other pages where they can:

(a)   find out more details about individual Microsoft **products**;

(b)   carry out a **Search** of the whole site to find Microsoft web pages connected with the information they are looking for;

(c)   consult pages that offer technical **Support** for Microsoft products, perhaps including **FAQs** (frequently asked questions and their answers) and files to **download** such as **free demonstrations** of products or **fixes** for problems with Microsoft software.

(d)   order products directly (**Shop**) or find out the names of re-sellers in their local area;

(e)   contact Microsoft directly (**Write Us**) to ask questions or make comments about Microsoft and its products.

A further set of **links** is provided in the frame on the left of the page. These are fairly self-explanatory.

6.6   As another, more financially-oriented, example here is an illustration of a **page** from **Reuters** site on the Internet.

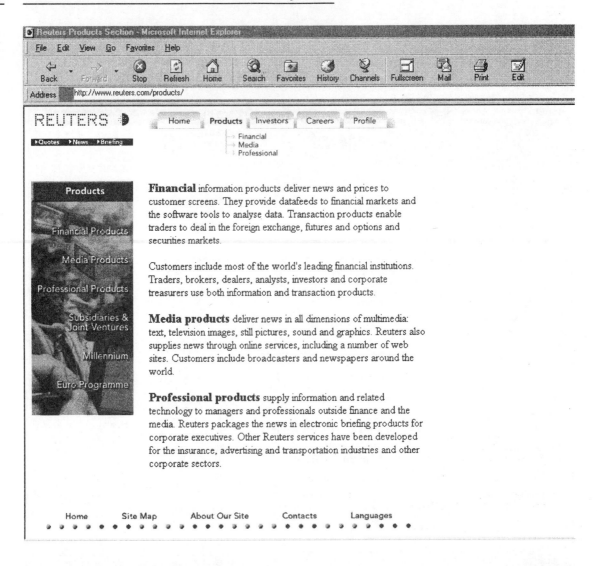

Internet Service Providers (ISPs)

6.7 Connection (if not available through a user's organisation) is made via an Internet Service Provider (ISP). The user is registered as an Internet subscriber and pays a small monthly fee together with **local telephone call charges,** even if contacting other users on the other side of the world.

6.8 ISPs such as **CompuServe, America Online (AOL)** and **Microsoft Network** provide their own services, in addition to Internet access and e-mail capability. For instance, AOL also offers a main menu with options such as Life, Travel, Entertainment, Sport, Kids. It is rather like a quality Sunday newspaper, except that the sections are updated at least daily, and it provides **much larger information resources** (one option in the travel section, for instance, is to find out about train and plane timetables throughout the UK or worldwide).

6.9 Other ISPs in the UK include **Demon** and **UUNet,** who have a strong presence in the **business** market.

Browsers and search engines

6.10 Most people use the Net through interface programs called **browsers** that make it more user-friendly and accessible. The best known are **Netscape Navigator** and Microsoft **Internet Explorer**.

6.11 Surfing the Net is done using a **search engine** such as Yahoo!, Excite or AltaVista. These guide users to destinations throughout the world: the user simply types in a word or phrase like 'beer' to find a list of thousands of websites that contain something connected with beer.

6.12 Companies like Yahoo! make money by **selling advertising space**. For instance if you type in 'beer', an advertisement for Miller Genuine Draft will appear, as well as your list of beer-related sites. If you click on the advertisement you are taken to the advertiser's website, perhaps just to be told more about the product, perhaps to be favourably influenced by the entertainment provided by the site, or perhaps even to buy some of the product.

6.13 The advertiser may get you to **register your interest** in the product so that you can be directly targeted in future. At the very least advertisers know exactly how many people have viewed their message and how many were interested enough in it to click on it to find out more.

6.14 An Internet development that has created a good deal of excitement is known as '**push**' **technology**, because instead of having to search for individual pieces of information the user simply accesses a '**channel**' and watches as information is sent down the line.

   (a) For instance **PointCast** has attracted more than 1m regular viewers to its Web news channel, which automatically delivers content from newspapers and magazines at regular intervals. It retrieves information from selected sources on the net and presents it, with advertisements, headlines and stock prices, on a screen saver.

   (b) **Marimba** allows users to download a 'tuner' and select content channels, very much like switching channels on TV.

6.15 Browser software packages provide a facility to **store Internet addresses** so that users can access frequently-visited sites without having to go through a long search process. Thus in business use, workers who **regularly need up-to-date information**, say, on stock market movements, or new government legislation, or the activities of a competitor, can simply click on the appropriate entry in a personal 'favourites' directory and be taken straight to the relevant site.

Going directly to an Internet address (URLs)

6.16 You may know the precise address of an Internet site that you wish to visit, perhaps because you have seen or heard it on TV or radio or read it in a newspaper or magazine. Typically the format is something like '**http://www.bbc.co.uk**'.

6.17   The address is called a **URL** or **Uniform Resource Locator**

URL element	Explanation
http://	**Hypertext Transfer Protocol**, the protocol (see Chapter 15) used on the World-Wide Web for the exchange of documents produced in what is known as 'hypertext mark-up language' (HTML). A common alternative to **http** is **ftp** (file transfer protocol) explained briefly later. The two forward slashes after the colon introduce a 'host name' such as **www**.
www	This stands for **World Wide Web**. As noted before, to put it simply the web (via its use of HTML), is what makes the Internet user-friendly
bbc	This is the **domain name** of the organisation or individual whose site is located at this URL
co	This part of the URL indicates the type of organisation concerned. The Internet actually spans many different physical networks around the world including commercial (**com** or **co**), university (**ac** or **edu**) and other research networks (**org, net**), military (**mil**) networks, and government (**gov**) networks.
uk	As you can probably guess, this indicates that the organisation is located in the UK

Internal communication: intranets

6.18   The idea behind an 'intranet' is that companies set up their own mini version of the Internet, using a combination of the company's own networked computers and Internet technology. Each employee has a browser and a server computer distributes corporate information on a wide variety of topics, and also offers access to the global Net.

6.19   Potential applications include daily company newspapers, induction material, online procedure and policy manuals, employee web pages where individuals post up details of their activities and progress, and internal databases of the corporate information store.

6.20   Most of the **cost** of an intranet is the staff time required to set up the system, which is often quite small. The **benefits** of intranets are diverse.

(a)   A considerable amount of money can be saved from the **elimination of storage, printing and distribution of documents** that can be made available to employees on-line.

(b)   Documents on-line are **more widely used** than those that are kept on shelves, especially if the document is bulky (for instance company information handbooks, finance manuals and procedures manuals) and needs to be searched. This means that there are **improvements in productivity and efficiency**.

(c)   It is much **easier to update** information in electronic form.

(d)   Wider access to corporate information should open the way to **more flexible working** patterns. For instance if bulky reference materials are available on-line then there is little need to be in the office at all.

Case example: Groupware and intranets

The original idea of a 'personal' computer was to allow people to work together and share information across a network through a mainframe computer'. However, users became so frustrated at their inability to get what they wanted from mainframe systems that they welcomed the IBM PC, used in stand-alone mode, with open arms.

This meant in turn that groupware (software designed to let users work together and share information through computers) had to be invented. (Examples are Lotus Notes (now Lotus Domino), Novell Groupwise, and Microsoft Exchange.) Groupware technology has been widely used to enable people to communicate, to share information, to work together and, most importantly, to carry out business processes and execute transactions, often using unstructured data.

The current fashion for intranets has given new impetus to these ideas, and all of the major products have now adopted Internet-type standards. Such products may have an advantage over intranets built from scratch because they recognise and address the problems of bringing about the *cultural* changes needed to get better business processes and generate competitive advantage.

Case example: Swiss Bank Corporation

'One of the biggest users of intranets is Swiss Bank Corporation. In fact it has so many - around 100 - that it has just appointed a head of intranets to co-ordinate them all.

At Swiss Bank Corporation intranets are used for:

    Corporate accounting and credit information
    Publishing research internally, and to a select group of 50 external clients
    Trading information
    Ordering information technology equipment
    IT project management
    Informing staff of regulatory changes

The job of Marie Adee, the company's new head of intranets, is to unify the disparate sites so that employees can find information easily. The sites will also be given a common look and feel. All the company's sites can be searched using the Netscape Navigator Web browser, but the company is also standardising on Lotus Domino software.

This software will sit on the server computers that store the intranet information. Domino incorporates Lotus Notes information sharing software. So employees will be able to input information to Web sites either through Notes or through their Web browsers. It will also be possible for SBC to set up workflow applications - which control the flow of work between users in a team.

Other Internet services

6.21   Here are three other terms that you are likely to encounter frequently in connection with the Internet.

   (a)   **File Transfer Protocol (FTP)** is the facility on the Internet that allows users to **copy files from one computer to another across the network.** Using an FTP program, information and applications residing on distant computers can be accessed and retrieved. A wide range of files are available via system called 'Anonymous FTP'. This lets users connect to a remote computer and **download files** from a public area of its disk. Many companies maintain such a site to allow customers to download new versions of software and product information.

   (b)   **Telnet** is an application that allows a user to establish a connection to a **remote computer,** perhaps on the other side of the world, as if it were on the next desk. Once connected the telnet software acts as an intermediary, translating the user's keyboard strokes so that the distant computer can understand them and interpret the information the distant computer sends back. In effect, it is as if a **keyboard and screen** on this side of the world were **directly connected** to the computer on the other side of the world.

(c) **Usenet** is short for User's Network, a series of open conferences or **discussion groups** on a multitude of topics. People who register with a Usenet newsgroup receive copies of all messages and articles posted by other members of the group. For instance there is a Usenet group called **uk.finance**.

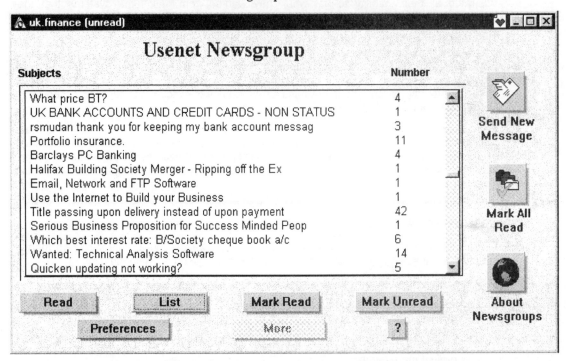

Commercial use of the Internet

Marketing

6.22 Besides its usefulness for tapping into worldwide information resources businesses are also using it to **provide information** about their own products and services. Customers are often reluctant to phone a company or ask to see a sales person to ask basic questions because they do not know who they should speak to, they are not quite sure what they want to know, and they are conscious of appearing to waste the provider's time.

6.23 The Internet offers a **speedy and impersonal** way of getting to know the basics (or even the details) of the services that a company provides. For businesses the advantage is that it is **much cheaper** to provide the information in electronic form than it would be to employ staff to man the phones on an enquiry desk, and much **more effective** than sending out mailshots that people would either throw away or forget about when they needed the information.

6.24 Thus business use of the Internet is set to grow for any product or service about which **customers** are liable to engage in **information seeking**; in other words for most **intermittent**, relatively **high value purchases** such as washing machines, hi-fi and TVs, motor cars and the like.

Question 6

(a) Beg, steal or borrow a PC with Internet access and experience these things for yourself.

(b) If you have Internet access at work, how does it help you (or your colleagues) to do a better job?

Sales

6.25   Interactive **electronic purchasing**, however, is **relatively rare** at present. Somewhat illogically, people are very reluctant to supply their credit card details to a computer, although they will very gladly do so in a one-to-one transaction in a shop or over the telephone, and happily transcribe the details onto a bill that they are paying by post. Logical or not, customers need to be **reassured** about security before interactive purchasing takes off.

6.26   Further **technological developments** will provide whatever reassurance is needed, and once people are used to this method of buying it is likely to become the **norm** for many transactions that are presently conducted by post, fax or phone.

Distribution

6.27   The Internet can be used to get certain products directly into people's homes. Anything that can be converted into **digital form** can simply be uploaded onto the seller's site and then **downloaded** onto the customer's PC at home. The Internet thus offers huge opportunities to producers of **text, graphics/video, and sound-based products**. Much computer software is now distributed in this way.

Problems with the Internet

6.28   To a large extent the Internet has grown organically **without any formal organisation.** There are specific communication rules, but it is **not owned** by any one body and there are no clear guidelines on how it should develop.

6.29   **Cost** is a major issue. Although the minimum hardware requirements can now be obtained very cheaply — a 386 plus a cheap modem would probably do — for **effective** use a more powerful PC is needed: ideally a Pentium with a clock speed of over 100MHz, at least 16 Mb RAM and at least a 28,000 bits per second (bps) modem.

6.30   Even then data only downloads onto the user's PC at the speed of the slowest. telecommunications link, as at present downloading data can sometimes be a **painfully slow** and time-wasting procedure. It has been likened to 'wading through toffee' or 'driving a Ferrari across a ploughed field'. However, future developments will mean that speeds will improve: most crucially, telecoms links that can carry voice, video TV and the Internet need to become the norm rather than the exception.

6.31   So much data is available on the Net that employers worry that their staff will **spend too much time** browsing, possibly through irrelevant or non-work-related websites. The quality of much of the information on the Internet leaves much to be desired.

6.32   **Security** is perhaps the biggest worry of all. Security aspects of the Internet are discussed in Chapter 15.

7   OFFICE AUTOMATION AND ITS EFFECT ON BUSINESS

7.1   Office automation has an enormous effect on business, in a variety of ways.

Routine processing

7.2 The processing of routine data can be done in **bigger volumes**, at **greater speed** and with **greater accuracy** than with non-automated, manual systems.

The paperless office

7.3 There might be **less paper** in the office (but not necessarily so) with more data-processing done by keyboard. Data handling is likely to shift from moving and storing paper to moving and storing data electronically.

Management information

7.4 The nature and **quality of management information** will change.

   (a) Managers are likely to have **access to more information** - for example from a database. Information is also likely to be **more accurate, reliable and up to date**. The range of **management reports** is likely to be wider and their content more comprehensive.

   (b) **Planning activities** should be more thorough, with the use of **models** (eg spreadsheets for budgeting) and **sensitivity analysis**.

   (c) Information for **control** should be more readily available. For example, a computerised sales ledger system should provide prompt reminder letters for late payers, and might incorporate other credit control routines. Stock systems, especially for companies with stocks distributed around several different warehouses, should provide better stock control.

   (d) **Decision making** by managers can be helped by **decision support systems**.

Organisation structure

7.5 The **organisation structure** might change. PC networks give local office managers a means of setting up a good **local management information system**, and **localised data processing** while retaining access to **centrally-held databases** and programs. Office automation can therefore encourage a tendency towards **decentralisation** of authority within an organisation.

7.6 On the other hand, such systems help **head office** to **keep in touch** with what is going on in local offices. Head office can therefore readily monitor and control the activities of individual departments, and retain a co-ordinating influence.

Customer service

7.7 Office automation, in some organisations, results in **better customer service**. When an organisation receives large numbers of telephone enquiries from customers, the staff who take the calls should be able to provide a prompt and helpful service if they have **on-line access** to the organisation's data files.

Staff issues

7.8   The **behavioural or 'human' aspects** of installing a computer system are potentially fairly complex, but broadly speaking the following should be considered.

    (a)   Office staff must show a **greater computer awareness**, especially in areas of the office where computerisation is most likely to occur first - typically the accounts department.

    (b)   Staff must **learn new habits,** such as the care of floppy disks and VDUs, how to use keyboards, and remembering to make back-up copies of files for data security purposes.

Homeworking

7.9   Advances in communications technology have, for some tasks, **reduced the need for the actual presence of an individual in the office.** This is particularly true of tasks involving computers.

- The worker can, for example, do **'keying in'** tasks at home.
- The keyed-in data can be **sent over a telecommunications link** to head office.

7.10   The **advantages to the organisation** of homeworking are as follows.

    (a)   **Cost savings on space.** Office rental costs and other charges can be very expensive. If firms can move some of their employees on to a homeworking basis, money can be saved.

    (b)   A **larger pool of labour.** The possibility of working at home might attract more applicants for clerical positions, especially from people who have other demands on their time (eg going to and from school) which cannot be fitted round standard office hours.

    (c)   If the homeworkers are **freelances,** then the organisation **avoids the need to pay them** when there is insufficient work, when they are sick, on holiday etc.

7.11   The **advantages to the individual** of homeworking are as follows.

    (a)   **No time is wasted commuting** to the office. Perhaps commuting time is more a problem of the congested metropolis of London than in some other areas, but commuting can often take up over two hours a day.

    (b)   The **work can be organised flexibly** around the individual's domestic commitments (eg school trips).

    (c)   **Jobs which require concentration** can sometimes be done better at home without the disruption of the office.

7.12   The **problems for the organisation** are chiefly problems of **control.** Managers who practise close supervision will perhaps feels a worrying loss of control. Managers might view homeworking as an opportunity for laziness and slack work (more 'tele' than work!)

7.13   Other **'problems'** for the organisation might be as follows.

    (a)   **Co-ordination** of the work of different homeworkers. The job design should ensure that homeworkers perform to the required standard.

    (b)   **Training.** If a homeworker needs a lot of help on a task, this implies that the task has not been properly explained.

(c) **Culture**. A homeworker is relatively isolated from the office and therefore, it might be assumed, from the firm. However, questions of loyalty and commitment do not apply for an organisation's sales force, whose members are rarely in the office.

7.14 **Problems for homeworkers** are as follows.

(a) **Isolation**. Work provides people with a social life, and many people might miss the sense of community if they are forced to work at home.

(b) **Intrusions**. A homeworker is vulnerable, by definition, to other interruptions (eg from members of his or her family forgetting that the worker is *working* at home, in time that the employer is paying for).

(c) **Adequate space**. It is not always possible to obtain a quiet space at home in which to work.

(d) In practice many homeworkers, especially if they are freelances, have **fewer employment rights**. They are not entitled to sick pay or holiday pay. They have limited security, as the firm can dispense with their services at whim.

Chapter roundup

- **Computerised** systems offer advantages such as higher productivity, faster processing, greater information access, greater accuracy, ease of correction, higher quality output and less bulk.

- **Spreadsheets** are versatile tools that can be used for a wide variety of tasks, especially at tactical level. There are potential drawbacks due to overuse and poor practice.

- **Word processing** is probably the most widespread feature of the electronic office. It uses a computer system to produce and edit typed letters and documents and store them on magnetic storage media.

- **Computer graphics** allows information to be presented easily in the form of charts or diagrams. **Presentation graphics** software enable the transfer of computer graphics to 35 mm transparencies or overhead projector slides.

- **Desktop publishing** software is used to implement computerised typesetting and composition. A DTP package pulls together **text and graphics** from other programs and is used to 'cut and paste' text and images as required.

- The electronic office may allow **communications** by a number of media including telex, teletex, fax, e-mail, voice mail, computer **conferencing** and teleconferencing.

- **Electronic data interchange** allows the electronic transfer between businesses not just of messages but of trading and commercial documents. In certain sectors, suppliers and customers are adopting EDI to deal with each other.

- The **Internet** connects millions of computers worldwide and is having a major impact on ways of communicating and doing business. Companies are setting up their own **intranets** using the same technology.

- Office automation has **affected business** in a number of ways. Automation has an impact on office staff and their working practices, and the overall organisation structure might change. The nature and quality of management information is changing, with more up-to-date information being available.

Quick quiz

1   Why are manually based systems less beneficial than computerised ones? (see para 1.3)

2   What are the drawbacks of spreadsheets? (2.7)

3   List six features commonly found in a word processing package. (3.8)

4   What is a fax modem? (4.17)

5   What are the advantages of e-mail? (4.20)

6   What are advantages of teleconferencing? (5.1 - 5.6)

7   Describe EDI. (5.7)

8   What is a website? (6.3)

9   What is an intranet? (6.18)

10   What is ftp? (6.21)

11   How might management information change in the electronic office? (7.4)

12   What problems might be caused by homeworking? (7.12 - 7.14)

Question to try	Level	Marks	Time
6	Exam standard	15	27 mins

Part B

Information systems environment

Chapter 6

INFORMATION SYSTEMS STRATEGY AND ORGANISATION

Chapter topic list	Syllabus reference
1 Information strategy	2(b), 4(b), 4(c)
2 Systems development	2(b), 4(b), 4(c)
3 IT expenditure and funding	2(b), 4(b), 4(c)
4 Outsourcing the IS function	2(b), 4(b), 4(c)
5 Centralisation and decentralisation	2(b), 4(b), 4(c)
6 Multi-user and distributed systems	2(b), 4(b), 4(c)
7 LANs, WANs and client-server computing	2(b), 4(b), 4(c)
8 Interoperability and open systems	2(b), 4(b), 4(c)

Introduction

According to the examiner, strategic issues in Paper 5 centre around how IT should be **organised** within a business rather than with how IT complements the overall strategy of a business.

Accordingly, this chapter looks at a variety of information systems issues that all businesses have to face as they grow larger. It is likely to be particularly useful for answering Section A questions based on a scenario.

1   INFORMATION STRATEGY

Information management

1.1   Information must be managed just like any other organisational resource. Information management entails the following tasks.

- Identifying current and future information **needs**

- Identifying information **sources**

- **Collecting** the information

- **Storing** the information

- Facilitating existing methods of **using** information and identifying new ways of using it

- Ensuring that information is **communicated** to those who need it, but **kept secure** from those who are *not* entitled to see it.

1.2   Technology has provided new **sources** of information, new ways of **collecting** it, **storing** it and **processing** it, and new methods of **communicating** it. This in turn has meant that information needs have changed and will continue to change as new technologies become available.

Information strategy

1.3   An information strategy deals with the integration of an organisation's information requirements and information systems planning with its **long-term overall goals** (customer service etc).

> ### KEY TERM
>
> A **strategy** is a general statement of long-term **objectives** and goals and the ways by which these will be achieved.

1.4   Here are some reasons justifying the case for a strategy for information systems (IS) and information technology (IT).

(a)   Information systems involve **high costs**.

(b)   Information systems are **critical to the success** of many organisations.

(c)   Information systems are now used as part of the **commercial strategy** in the battle for competitive advantage.

(d)   Information systems involve many **stakeholders**, not just management, and not just within the organisation.

A high cost activity

1.5   Many organisations invest large amounts of money in IS, but not always wisely. The importance is not how much is spent but **how well** the funds are spent.

1.6   The problem is made more acute because **individual components** of an information system are now **not particularly expensive**. A very powerful PC can be bought for less than £1,000, and much software can be downloaded for free or at very little cost from the Internet.

1.7   However, the **unmanaged proliferation** of IT is likely to lead to **chaos**: no two users would have the same equipment or use the same processing methods or software, and the two key benefits of IT - the ability to **share** information and the **avoidance of duplication -** would be lost.

1.8   All IT expenditure therefore needs **rigorous scrutiny** to ensure that it enhances rather than detracts from the overall information management strategy.

Critical to the success of many organisations

1.9   In developing a strategy a firm should assess **how important IT actually is** in the provision of products and services. IT may be any of the following.

(a)   **A support activity** (for example providing ad hoc responses to queries) which is useful but not critical to organisational success.

(b)   A 'factory' activity where information systems are **crucial to current operations** and their management but **not at the heart** of the company's **strategic** development.

(c) A **turnround** activity in which IT is seen as crucial to a firm's business development, and is used to **open up new opportunities** (for example information technology acquired to enhance flexibility of marketing and production of consumer goods).

(d) A **strategic** activity, where without IT the firm **could not function at all** (for example many financial services companies depend on computers, telecommunications and databases, just like a manufacturing company depends on raw materials or a transport company depends on vehicles).

A strategic weapon

1.10 IT can be used as a strategic weapon in the following ways.

(a) IT can be used to **develop new businesses** (for example Reuters created an electronic market place where subscribers could trade via Reuters terminals).

(b) IT is a potential supplier of **competitive advantage** to an organisation.

Competitive advantage

1.11 An organisation can employ three basic strategies to obtain competitive advantage.

Strategy	Comment
Overall cost leadership	This involves becoming the most cost efficient producer. IT can reduce costs by: • reducing labour costs (for example production control systems, clerical work); • reducing manufacturing costs by efficient scheduling etc (for example computer integrated manufacturing, better monitoring of raw materials usage to reduce wastage).
Product differentiation	This involves making a unique product or a product which appears different from your competitors', and hence more attractive. Information technology can be used to: • design new products speedily (Computer Aided Design); • enable customisation of a product to a customer's particular specification (Computer Integrated Manufacturing); • differentiate the product by using IT-based components to make it unique (for example, one travel company has introduced multimedia booths so customers can get a better idea of different holiday destinations).
Focus on a market niche.	A market niche is a group of consumers who have particular needs. • Use sales data to identify customer preferences and spot unusual trends. • Use IT to analyse market research and statistical information.

Question 1

Think about the role of Information Technology in securing an advantage over competitors. Try to think of an example of each of the following.

(a) The use of IT to 'lock out' competitors.

(b)   The use of IT to commit customers to investment, reducing the likelihood of their changing suppliers.

(c)   The use of IT to secure a straightforward performance advantage.

(d)   The use of IT to generate a new product or service.

Answer

(a)   An example is an airline booking service. Let's take a fictitious airline: British Transatlantic Airways (BTA). A passenger wishes to fly BTA from the UK to New York, and then from New York to Minneapolis. BTA is not allowed to make internal flights in the USA. However, several American airlines fly from New York to Minneapolis. BTA's booking system is interlinked with that of one American airline, whose flights are always chosen for connections by the BTA booking system. The IT system is thus a barrier to competition, as alternative flights from New York to Minneapolis are not offered by BTA.

(b)   Once a bank customer has gone to the effort and expense of installing a home banking system, he or she is unlikely to make a decision to change banks (which requires a switch to another system).

(c)   Efficient stock control systems (for example just-in-time) might make an organisation more dependent on efficient suppliers, resulting in its stopping trading with less efficient companies which hamper its own ability to deliver.

(d)   An outstandingly successful example in the financial services sector is simple insurance policies approved over the telephone (using expert systems).

Stakeholders

1.12   A stakeholder is a person or organisation that has an interest in an enterprise. An organisation must take steps to manage these external stakeholders. Parties interested in an organisation's use of IS are as follows.

(a)   **Other businesses** for example, for common standards for **electronic data interchange**. These can form into lobbying groups for a particular industry.

(b)   **Governments** (for example, data protection regulation).

(c)   **Consumers** (for example in testing technology-based products such as teleshopping).

(d)   **Employees** and internal users (as IS affect work practices).

2   SYSTEMS DEVELOPMENT

2.1   Managing information systems **development** is a major operation involving large parts of an organisation and elements of its environment.

2.2   Two approaches to the description of the development process can be distinguished.

(a)   A **model** is a framework which identifies the various stages through which the organisation or department passes. It is intended to be predictive and to be of value to management in developing techniques to deal with each stage.

(b)   A **methodology** is a structured approach to the management of IS development. It is a collection of tools, techniques and procedures used by systems development staff in implementing a new information system.

2.3   Two **models** will be introduced here. Part C of this text is concerned with methodologies.

The stage hypothesis

2.4 Richard Nolan developed a model to reflect the acquisition and use of computers in the organisation. His **stage hypothesis** can be used as a planning tool for the future development of systems. The six stages include phases where progress is made and phases of consolidation.

Stage	Comment
Initiation	This stage covers the organisation's first steps in computerisation. Systems are selected because the more technically-minded staff are keen to acquire them, not because they are necessarily cost effective.
Contagion	The wider benefits of computerisation are perceived by a range of potential users, and the organisation is committed to large-scale investment, not necessarily in a co-ordinated manner. End-users begin to influence the development process.
Control	Following the contagion stage, there is user dissatisfaction with systems and it becomes apparent that the organisation's resources are finite. This may be the point at which it is realised that investment in computers should not be undertaken solely for financial reasons. Controls may be introduced in the form of steering committees, project management teams and the introduction of development controls.
Integration	The role of the controls which have been implemented becomes clear. User involvement in development and IT issues generally increases.
Data administration	It becomes apparent that data is an important resource of the organisation. Even if there is no corporate database, data management becomes an important concept. A database administrator may be appointed.
Maturity	Information flows in the organisation mirror the real-world requirements of the organisation. Data resources are flexible, permitting their use in any application. It is acknowledged that this final stage may not be reached in practice.

2.5 An organisation will **never be at a single point in this process**. It is far more likely that different departments will be at different points of development at the same time. The stage hypothesis helps management to identify the stage which a department or operating unit has reached, so that development activities can be **monitored and controlled.**

The systems development lifecycle

2.6 The systems development lifecycle was developed in the 1960s by the National Computing Centre.

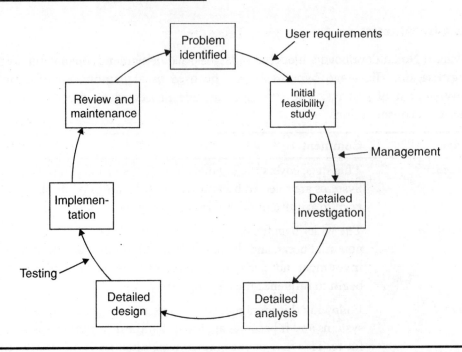

Stage	Comment
Identification of a problem	In the case of the development of a new information system, this stage will involve an analysis of the organisation's information requirements. Such an analysis should be carried out in conjunction with users, so that their *actual* requirements can be identified, rather than their *likely* requirements.
Feasibility study	This involves a brief review of the existing system and the identification of a range of possible alternative solutions. One will usually be recommended on the basis of its costs and benefits, although it is possible for a decision not to proceed to result.
Systems investigation	This is a fact finding exercise which investigates the existing system to assess its problems and requirements and to obtain details of data volumes, response times and other key indicators.
Systems analysis	Once the workings of the existing system have been documented, they can be analysed. This process examines why current methods are used, what alternatives might achieve the same, or better, results, what restricts the effectiveness of the system and what performance criteria are required from a system.
Systems design	This is a technical phase which considers both computerised and manual procedures, addressing, in particular, inputs, outputs, program design, file design and security. A detailed specification of the new system is produced.
Systems implementation	This stage carries development through from design to operations. It involves acquisition (or writing) of software, program testing, file conversion or set-up, acquisition and installation of hardware and 'going live'.
Review and maintenance	This is an ongoing process which ensures that the system meets the objectives set during the feasibility study, that it is accepted by users and that its performance is satisfactory.

Criticisms of the systems development lifecycle

2.7   The systems development lifecycle approach to systems development was adopted by many organisations. While it has some advantages, it has a number of **drawbacks** if incorrectly applied.

(a)   The information needs of **middle and senior management** could be ignored if computerisation is just seen as a means of speeding up high-volume routine transaction processing, not providing information for decision-making.

(b)   When computer systems are first introduced, they may be modelled after the manual systems they were replacing. If the computerisation is ambitious, it might lead to a potentially beneficial **rethink** of the way the organisation carries out its activities.

(c)   **User requirements** may be poorly defined and so new systems do not live up to users' expectations.

(d)   System **documentation** may be written for programmers and specialists and be more of a technical manual than a guide for the user. Problems could also occur, if inadequately documented modifications lead to 'bugs' elsewhere in the system.

(e)   Routine transaction processing systems may not be able to cope with **unusual situations,** and so some complicated processing will still be performed manually.

3   IT EXPENDITURE AND FUNDING

3.1   As information systems support a wide variety of functions in an organisation, and information systems incur significant capital and revenue costs, it is not surprising that many organisations should seek to develop costing systems so that **user departments pay for their usage** of information systems.

3.2   There are three broad possibilities. Information management (IM) can be treated as a central administrative **overhead**, it can be **charged out 'at cost'**, or it can be **charged out at market rates**, generating a profit (or loss) for the information systems (IS) department.

Exam focus point
Funding of IT came up in the **December 1994** and **December 1995** exams.

Information technology as a corporate overhead

3.3   Under this system IM expense is treated as a general administrative expense, and is **not allocated** to user departments. User departments do not have to 'pay' for IM services.

3.4   **Advantages** of this approach are as follows.

(a)   It is **simple** and **cheap to administer,** as there is no chargeout system to administrate, forms to be filled out and so forth.

(b)   Arguably, it encourages **innovation** and **experimentation** by the information systems department which user departments might be unwilling to pay for. (However, the existence of a unit for research and development within the IS department should be sufficient for this purpose.)

(c) There is **minimal conflict**, over costs at least, between the IS department and user departments.

3.5   This approach also has a number of **disadvantages**.

(a)   The IS department has **no incentive to control costs** or use available resources efficiently, other than the enthusiasm of management: the IS budget will have been determined at the beginning of the year.

(b)   It does not encourage **responsible use** of the IS resource by user departments, who do not have the cost information to prioritise their requirements. Also, IS department management are not given the right cost information to choose between competing projects.

Information technology charged out on a cost basis

3.6   A cost-based chargeout means that users are **charged a proportion** of the costs of the IS department according to some measure, preferably reflecting actual use. Cost-based chargeout systems should motivate users to employ computer resources efficiently. The following measures can help with this.

(a)   Chargeout rates should be based on a tangible service which the user can **understand**. Examples are: cost per transaction processed; cost per page; cost per hour of programmer's and/or analyst's time; cost per number of terminals/workstations; cost per unit of CPU time.

(b)   **Standard costing** systems should be used. This is so that:

(i)   user departments are not penalised for **inefficiencies** in the IS department;

(ii)   the **IS department is not penalised** with variances caused by user departments' increased usage;

(iii)   user departments are not charged with those **long term fixed costs** of the IS department itself (eg its building), over which they have **no control**.

3.7   The **advantages** of the cost based chargeout system are as follows.

(a)   It is conceptually **simple**.

(b)   It **motivates user departments** to consider the cost of their usage of IT services and to regulate it efficiently.

(c)   It ties in with costing systems which use **responsibility accounting** as a means of controlling costs.

3.8   **Disadvantages** exist, too.

(a)   Unless precautions are taken, **inefficiencies** in the IS department are merely **passed on** to users. Programmers could actually design programmes to take lots of CPU time so that the IT department made more money.

(b)   Although simple in concept, it is **complex** in practice.

(c)   It is often difficult to determine an **appropriate cost unit** on which to base the chargeout system (eg how easy is it to assess the cost of a single transaction? How easily can indirect but variable costs be allocated?)

(d)   There might be no comparison. Users are faced, effectively, with a **monopoly supplier**.

(e)   Overhead costs of the department **have to be met,** even if the IT services are not used.

Market-based chargeout methods

3.9   These methods are used where the IS department acts as a **profit centre.** It sets its own prices and charges for its services to make a profit, perhaps as a separate business unit or subsidiary. This is only workable in situations where there is an external market for the same services.

3.10   The **advantages** of the market-based chargeout method are as follows.

(a)   **External standards** of service and price are available.
(b)   It supposedly encourages an **entrepreneurial** attitude.
(c)   Prices are **negotiable.**

3.11   **Disadvantages** are as follows.

(a)   There may be **no comparable service** outside the organisation where services of the type and intensity that users require can be purchased.

(b)   It is difficult to implement where **common or shared resources** are concerned.

(c)   It may not be in the organisation's strategic interest for user departments to buy from outsiders: the IS function's fixed costs still have to be covered, and there may result an **under-use of resources** available within the organisation.

(d)   There may be a **lack of appropriate management skills** in the department. Running a company is likely to be much more challenging than running a department.

> ### Exam focus point
> The **December 1996** exam's scenario question featured a hospital that was considering developing its own recruitment system and then selling it to other hospitals. Some of the hospital's management regarded this as a **risky** strategy. Points raised in the preceding section would have been relevant to a discussion of the risks.

4   OUTSOURCING THE IS FUNCTION

4.1   Many organisations do not employ **specialist IS staff** because they cannot justify the costs of full time professionals. Other organisations might employ some specialist staff but not enough for all their requirements. In some cases, organisations will not even possess the **equipment** to do their own computerised processing.

4.2   If an organisation does not wish (or cannot afford) to have its own in-house IS management it may prefer to use **external resources**.

Outsourcing

4.3   Outsourcing, also referred to as **facilities management (FM),** is not a concept which is limited to the arena of computing. Any company which contracts out necessary services to a third party is using **facilities management (FM)** in one form or another.

4.4   **Buying in services** is seen as a better way of managing resources and of obtaining access to specialists in particular fields. The practice has been firmly established for years in such activities as sandwich-making, laundry services and office cleaning.

4.5   As the significance of IT grew through the 1980s, it became clear that a large proportion of many companies' workforces were engaged in IT activities and that IT expenditure was frequently in excess of budget. This experience clashed with the belief held by many executives that IT should be a **critical but subordinate function** of the core business, whether operating in international financial markets or running a UK county council.

4.6   Outsourcing has enabled many organisations simply to pick a supplier, draw up a contract and **hand over the entire responsibility** for running the organisation's IT function.

4.7   The third party supplier, or FM company, usually takes over the **employment contracts** of the organisation's IT staff. Their terms and conditions of employment are protected by legislation in the form of the Transfer of Undertakings (Protection of Employment) Regulations, or TUPE. It may also take over the organisation's **computer centre**.

4.8   FM companies operating in the UK include Andersens, Cap Gemini, EDS and CFM.

Case example: Sears

The retailer Sears recently outsourced the management of its vast information technology and accounting functions to Andersen Consulting (*The Times,* February 1996). It is estimated that *savings* will grow from £5 million per annum in 1998-99 to £14 million in the following year, and thereafter. This is clearly considerable, although re-organisation costs relating to redundancies, relocation and asset write-offs are thought to be in the region of £35 million. About 900 staff are involved: under the transfer of undertakings regulations (which protect employees when part or all of a company changes hands), Andersen is obliged to take on the existing Sears staff. This appears to mean new opportunities for the staff who are moving, while those whom Sears are retaining are free to concentrate on strategy, development and management direction.

Advantages of outsourcing arrangements

4.9   The **advantages** of facilities management are as follows.

(a)   Facilities management is an effective form of **cost control**, as there is often a long-term contract where services are specified in advance for a **fixed price**. If the computing services are inefficient, the costs will be borne by the FM company. This is also an incentive to the FM company to provide a high quality service, of course.

(b)   **Long-term contracts** (maybe up to ten years) allow much greater certainty in **planning for the future**.

(c)   A facilities management company has **economies of scale**. Several organisations will employ the same FM company, and so the FM company's research into new products on the market or new technologies will be shared between them.

(d)   **Skills and knowledge are retained.** Many organisations do not have a sufficiently well developed IT department to offer existing staff good opportunities for personal development. They find that talented staff leave to pursue their careers elsewhere, taking their skill and knowledge (much of which may have been acquired at the expense of the original organisation) with them. An FM company that takes over the contracts of existing employees will be able to offer them the advancement they are looking for.

(e) **New skills and knowledge become available.** An FM company can **share** staff with **specific expertise** (such as programming in HTML to produce Web pages) between several clients. This means that the outsourcing company can take advantage of new developments without the need to recruit new people or re-train existing staff, and without the cost.

(f) **Resources employed can be scaled up or down** depending upon demand. For instance, during a major changeover from one system to another the number of IT staff needed may be twice as large as it will be once the new system is working satisfactorily. This is likely to be difficult to manage and to cause morale problems in an in-house IT facility.

An outsourcing organisation, however, is likely to arrange its work on a **project** basis, whereby some staff will expect to be moved periodically from one project to the next.

Disadvantages of outsourcing arrangements

4.10   The **drawbacks**, however, can be quite considerable.

(a) It is arguable that information and its provision is **an inherent part of the business and of management**. Unlike office cleaning, or catering, an organisation's IS services may be too important to be contracted out. Information is at the heart of management.

(b) A company may have highly **confidential information** and to let outsiders handle it could be seen as highly **risky** in commercial and/or legal terms.

(c) Information strategy can be used to gain **competitive advantage**. Opportunities may be missed if a third party is handling IS services, because there is no onus upon internal management to keep up with new developments and have new ideas. If the FM company has a good new idea there is nothing to prevent it from selling it to more than one company.

(d) Once an organisation has handed over its computing to an FM company, it is **locked in** to the contract. The decision may be very difficult to reverse. If the FM company supplies unsatisfactory levels of service for whatever reason (takeover, financial difficulties etc), then the effort and expense the organisation would have to incur to rebuild its own computing function and expertise would be enormous.

(e) The use of FM does not encourage a **proper awareness of the potential costs and benefits** of IT amongst managers. If managers cannot manage in-house IT resources effectively, then it could be argued that they will not be able to manage an IT outsourcing arrangement effectively either.

The contract

4.11   As indicated above (under both advantages and disadvantages), a vital aspect of any FM contract is the **service level contract** (SLC). This should specify clearly minimum levels of service to be provided. It should also contain arrangements for an exit route, addressing what happens if the contract is handed over to another contractor or brought in-house. The responsibilities of the outgoing FM company should be clearly specified.

4.12   Some companies have found that aspects of information systems management that they believed would be included in their FM contract have turned out to be **extras**, for which considerable **extra fees** are payable. It is probably not possible to draw up a contract that covers every eventuality, particularly as some eventualities, such as new technologies, may not even be imaginable at the time when the contract is first drawn up.

Other organisations

Computer bureaux

4.13   Computer bureaux are organisations which provide **computing facilities** to their clients, usually in the area of **basic data processing**. The range of services offered by computer bureaux is considerable, with some offering a complete service while others specialise in particular areas, such as **payroll**.

Software houses

4.14   Software houses concentrate on the provision of services including feasibility studies, systems analysis and design, development of operating systems software, provision of application program packages, 'tailor-made' application programming, specialist systems advice, and so on.

Consultancy firms

4.15   The use of consultancy services enables management to **learn directly or indirectly from the experience of others**. The success of an individual consultancy project will depend largely on the expertise of the firm approached and more particularly on the individual consultant or consultants employed. Many larger consultancies are owned by big international **accountancy firms**; smaller consultancies may consist of one or two person outfits with a high level of **specialist experience** in one area.

Computer manufacturers

4.16   Computer manufacturers or their designated suppliers will provide the **equipment** necessary for a system. They will also provide, under a **maintenance contract**, engineers who will deal with any routine servicing and with any breakdown of the equipment. In addition they may supply the **operating systems software** and very often **application** programs. They may also undertake to '**tailor**' the application programs to fit into the client's system. On supplying the equipment and software, the manufacturer will normally offer a **training** course for the client's staff, the cost of which may be included in the total price, or may be charged separately.

5   CENTRALISATION AND DECENTRALISATION

5.1   An important IS organisation issue is whether the IS function ought to be centralised or decentralised.

Centralised processing

5.2   Centralised processing means having the data/information processing done in a central place, such as a computer centre at head office. Data will be collected at 'remote' (ie geographically separate) offices and other locations and sent in to the central location, by post, by courier or by telecommunications link. Processing could be in either batch processing mode or on-line.

5.3   At the central location there will be:

   (a)   a central computer, probably a large mainframe computer;

   (b)   central files, containing all the files needed for the system.

Question 2

Think of examples of types of business that have 'remote' offices/locations.

Answer

You should have had no difficulty with this. Obvious examples include banks and building societies, chains of supermarkets, high street chains, hotel chains, pubs ... in fact it is hard to think of a business type that does not have remote offices or locations.

5.4   The **advantages** of centralised processing are as follows.

   (a)   There is **one set of files**. Everyone uses the same data and information.

   (b)   It gives **better security/control** over data and files. It is easier to enforce standards.

   (c)   **Head office** is in a better position to know what is going on.

   (d)   An organisation might be able to afford a **very large central computer,** with extensive processing capabilities that smaller 'local' computers could not carry out.

   (e)   There are **economies of scale** available in purchasing computer equipment and supplies.

   (f)   Computer staff are in a single location, and **more expert staff** are likely to be employed. Career paths may be more clearly defined.

5.5   The **disadvantages** of centralised processing are as follows.

   (a)   Local offices might have to **wait** for data to be processed centrally, especially if processing is done by batches.

   (b)   **Reliance on head office**. Local offices have to rely on the central processing unit to provide the information they need.

   (c)   If the central computer **breaks down,** or the software develops a fault, the entire system goes out of operation.

Decentralised processing

5.6   Decentralised processing means having the data/information processing carried out at several different locations, away from the 'centre' or 'head office'. Sometimes this is referred to as **distributed** processing. Each region, department or office will have its own processing systems, and so:

   (a)   there will be several different and **unconnected computers** in the various offices;

   (b)   each computer will operate with its own **programs** and its own **files**.

5.7   The **advantages** of decentralised processing are set out below.

(a)   Each office can introduce an information system specially **tailored** for its individual needs. Local changes in business requirements can be taken into account.

(b)   If data **originates locally** it might make sense to process it locally too.

(c)   Each office has **control over its own** data.

(d)   There is likely to be easy/quick **access to information** when it is needed.

(e)   Any **breakdowns** in the system are **restricted** to just one part of the system.

(f)   It fits in with the organisation **structure**, and **responsibility accounting** systems (profit centres).

(g)   It allows staff to concentrate on **business objectives** rather than being constrained by IT objectives.

5.8   The **disadvantages** of decentralised processing are set out below.

(a)   Many different and **unco-ordinated information systems** will be introduced.

(b)   Decentralisation encourages **lack of co-ordination between departments**.

(c)   One office might be **unable to obtain information** from the information system of another office.

(d)   There might be a **duplication of data**, with different offices holding the same data on their own separate files.

Question 3

You should have studied organisation structure in detail as part of your work for Paper 4, *The Organisational Framework,* so we are not going to go over familiar ground in any detail here. You should be able to explain all of the following terms.

(a)   Scalar chain
(b)   Span of control
(c)   Tall and flat organisations
(d)   Functional structure
(e)   Matrix organisation

Answer

(a)   The scalar chain is the formal management hierarchy, from the most junior up to the most senior for example constable, sergeant, inspector and so on.

(b)   The span of control is the number of people a manager has working for him. If you have a wide span of control you are in charge of a lot of people.

(c)   A tall organisation is one with narrow spans of control and many management levels. A flat organisation is the opposite.

(d)   An organisation with a functional structure is divided into departments on the basis of the work done, for example, sales, production, finance. Other possible bases for division are: by product (cars division/lorries division), by customer type, and by geographical region.

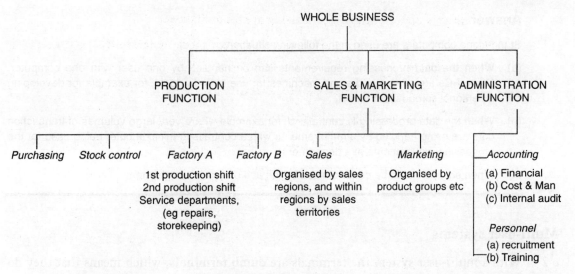

(e) A matrix structure is one where teams are managed by two bosses, for example a functional manager and a regional manager.

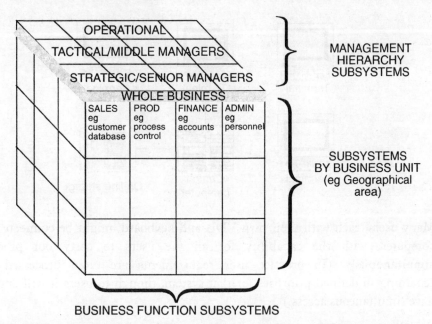

If you struggled with any of these questions you need to revise your earlier study material.

6   MULTI-USER AND DISTRIBUTED SYSTEMS

6.1   In practice, information systems do not have to be entirely centralised or entirely decentralised, and these days a suitable **mixture of centralisation and decentralisation** will normally be used.

(a) Local offices can have their own **local systems,** perhaps on PC, and also input some data to a centralised processing system.

(b) Computer systems can be **networked,** and there might be:

(i) a **multi-user system;** or

(ii) a **'distributed'** data processing system.

Question 4

When would you expect a **stand-alone** computer to be used?

Answer

Stand-alone computers are used in the following situations.

(a) When the data processing requirements can be handled by one user with one computer. Office PCs are often stand-alone machines for use by individuals, for example for developing a personal spreadsheet model.

(b) When the data processing is centralised, for example where very large volumes of transaction data are being handled by a mainframe, or with a centralised minicomputer being used for the processing requirements of a department.

(c) When security could be compromised by the use of a multi-user system.

Multi-user systems

6.2 With a multi-user system the terminals are **dumb terminals**, which means that they do not include a CPU and so **cannot do independent data processing**. A dumb terminal relies on the central computer for its data processing power.

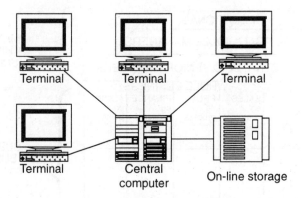

6.3 Many users, each with their own VDU and keyboard, might be connected to the same computer, with the capability for all the users to carry out processing work **simultaneously**. (In practice user requirements are often processed successively, according to defined priorities for that system, though to users it will appear that they have simultaneous access.)

6.4 The terminals in a multi-user system might be sited in the **same room** or building as the central computer, or may be **geographically distant** from the central computer, connected by an external data link. Terminals can be used:

(a) for **interactive computing** with the central computer; or
(b) to **input data** ('transactions' data) into the computer from a remote location.

KEY TERMS

Remote access describes access to a central computer installation from a terminal which is physically 'distant'.

The term **remote job entry** is used to describe a method of processing in which the computer user inputs his data to the computer from a remote terminal.

Advantages

6.5 The **benefits** of multi-user systems are as follows.

(a) More departments or sections can have **access** to the computer, its data files and its programs. This improves the data processing capabilities of 'local' offices.

(b) By giving departments more computing power and access to centralised information files, multi-user systems also make it easier for an organisation to **decentralise authority** from head office to local managers.

(c) The **speed of processing,** for both local offices and head office, is very fast.

(d) Local offices **retain their input documents,** and do not have to send them to a remote computer centre for processing.

Distributed processing

6.6 Distributed processing links several computers together. A typical system might consist of a mainframe computer with PCs as **intelligent terminals**, with a range of peripheral equipment and with files either held centrally or at dispersed sites.

> **KEY TERM**
>
> A **distributed system** is a combination of processing hardware located at a central place, eg a mainframe computer, with other, usually smaller, computers located at various sites within the organisation. The central and dispersed computers are linked by a communications network.
>
> (CIMA, *Computing Terminology*)

6.7 The key features of distributed processing are as follows.

(a) Computers distributed or spread over a **wide geographical area**.

(b) A computer can **access** the information files of **other computers** in the system.

(c) The ability for computers within the system to **process data 'jointly'** or **'interactively'**.

(d) **Processing** is **either** carried out centrally, or at dispersed locations.

(e) **Files** are held **either** centrally or at local sites.

(f) **Authority is decentralised** as processing can be performed autonomously by local computers.

(g) **End-users** of computing facilities are given responsibility for, and control over, their own data.

6.8 One form of distributed data processing system is illustrated below.

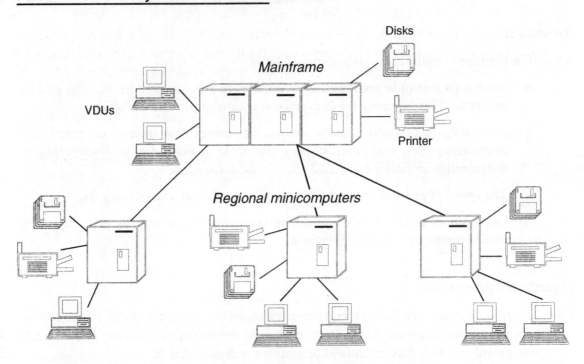

Advantages and disadvantages of distributed processing

6.9 The **advantages** of using a distributed processing system compared with having a stand-alone centralised mainframe computer are as follows.

(a) There is **greater flexibility** in system design. The system can cater for both the specific needs of each local user of an individual computer and also for the needs of the organisation as a whole, by providing communications between different local computers in the system.

(b) Since data files can be held locally, **data transmission is restricted** because each computer maintains its own data files which provide most of the data it will need. This reduces the costs and security risks in data transmission.

(c) **Speed of processing** for both local branches and also for the central (head office) branch.

(d) There is a possibility of a **distributed database**. Data is held in a number of locations, but any user can access all of it for a global view.

(e) The effect of **breakdowns** is **minimised**, because a fault in one computer will not affect other computers in the system. With a centralised processing system, a fault in the mainframe computer would put the entire system out of service.

(f) The fact that it is possible to acquire powerful PCs at a 'cheap' price enables an organisation to dedicate them to particular applications. This in turn means that the computer system can be more readily **tailored** to the organisation's systems, rather than forcing the organisation to change its systems to satisfy the requirements for a mainframe computer.

(g) Decentralisation allows for **better localised control** over the physical and procedural aspects of the system.

(h) Decentralised processing may facilitate **greater user involvement** and increase familiarity with the use of computer technology. The end user must accept responsibility for the accuracy of locally-held files and local data processing.

6.10 Distributed processing has certain **disadvantages,** some of which might be overcome by future technological developments.

(a) Minicomputers and PCs have **not had a large storage capacity** in the past, and the high-level language programs needed for distributed processing have used up much of the storage capacity available. This disadvantage is now being eliminated by the development of more powerful small machines.

(b) There may be a **duplication of data** on the files of different computers. If this is the case, there may be some unnecessary storage costs incurred.

(c) A distributed network can be more **difficult to administer** and to **maintain** with service engineers.

(d) The items of equipment used in the system must, of course, be **compatible** with each other.

Networks

> ### KEY TERM
>
> A **network** is an interconnected collection of **autonomous** processors. (Strictly, in a 'distributed' system, the user should be unaware that the system has more than one processor.)

6.11 There are two main types of network, a **local area network** (LAN) and a **wide area network** (WAN).

6.12 The key idea of a network is that users need **equal access to resources** such as data, but they do not necessarily have to have equal computing power.

6.13 LANs, WANs and this **'client-server'** concept are so important in modern computing that they deserve a section to themselves.

> ### Exam focus point
>
> The scenario in the June 1996 exam included a proposal by a consultant that a system of stand-alone PCs should be networked.

7   LANS, WANS AND CLIENT-SERVER COMPUTING

Local area networks (LANs)

7.1 A *local area network* (LAN) is a network of computers located in a single building or on a **single site**. The parts of the network are linked by **computer cable** rather than via telecommunications lines. This means that a LAN does not need modems.

Network topologies

7.2 Network topology means the physical arrangement of **nodes** in a network. A node is any device connected to a network: it can be a computer, or a peripheral device such as a printer.

7.3 There are several types of LAN system configuration. For example, in a **bus structure** (shown below), messages are sent out from one point along a single communication channel, and the messages are received by other connected machines.

7.4   Each device can **communicate with every other device** and communication is quick and reliable. Nodes can be **added or unplugged** very easily. Locating cable faults is also relatively simple.

Bus system

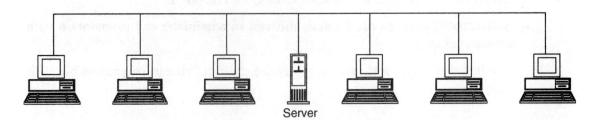

Server

7.5   Local area networks have been **successful** for a number of reasons. First of all, personal computers of sufficient **power** and related software (for example Unix) were developed, so that network applications became possible. Networks have been made available to computer users at a fairly **low price**. Some computer users who could not afford a mainframe or minicomputer with terminal links have been able to afford a LAN with personal computers and software packages.

Wide area networks (WANs)

7.6   **Wide area networks** (WANs) are networks on a number of sites, perhaps on a wide geographical scale. WANs often use minicomputers or mainframes as the 'pumps' that keep the data messages circulating, whereas shorter-distance LANs normally use PCs for this task.

7.7   A wide area network is similar to a local area network in concept, but the key differences are as follows.

(a)   The **geographical area** covered by the network is greater, not being limited to a single building or site.

(b)   WANs will send data over **telecommunications links,** and so will need modems. LANs, in contrast, will use direct cables only for transmitting data.

(c)   WANs will often use a **larger computer** as a file server.

(d)   WANs will often be larger than LANs, with **more terminals or computers** linked to the network.

(e)   A WAN can link two or more LANs, using **gateways**.

(i)   Connections may be **leased**. This is the preferred option where there is a **high** volume of inter-office communication.

(ii)   Connections may be made over the **public telephone network**. Standard call charges will apply, so this is beneficial where communication levels are relatively low.

Client-server computing

7.8   The term client-server computing has gained widespread usage in the mid 1990s. This is a way of describing the relationship between the devices in a network. With client-server computing, the tasks that need to be carried out are distributed among the various machines on the network.

KEY TERMS

A **client** is a machine which requests a service, for example a PC running a spreadsheet application which the user wishes to print out.

A **server** is a machine which is dedicated to providing a particular function or service requested by a client. Servers include file servers (see below), print servers, e-mail servers and fax servers.

7.9 A client-server system allows **computer power** to be distributed to where it is most needed. The **client**, or user, will use a powerful personal workstation with local processing capability. The **server** provides services such as shared printers, communications links, special-purpose processing and database storage.

7.10 This approach has a number of benefits.

(a) It reduces network **communications** costs.

(b) It allows the central computer to be used for **administrative** tasks such as network management.

(c) The technological flexibility of this type of system allows the use of **sophisticated applications** such as multimedia and DIP.

7.11 A server computer (or file server) may be a powerful PC or a minicomputer. As its name implies, it **serves** the rest of the network offering a generally-accessible hard disk file for all the other processors in the system and sometimes offering other resources, such as a **shared printer** for the network.

7.12 Clients on a network generally have their **own hard disk** storage capability. The server's hard disk can also be **partitioned** into separate drives for use by each node, and **programs** or data (eg a database) for **common use** can be stored on the file server. Accounting packages written for small businesses are usually available in a multi-user version for this purpose.

File servers

7.13 File servers must be powerful enough to handle **multiple user requests** and provide **adequate storage**. File servers are typically classified as 'low end' or 'high end'.

(a) A **low end file server** might be used in a network of around six users running WP software and a database. A low end server might be a dedicated machine or might be a highly specified standard PC. Once it is asked to support more than 10 users, it will probably need replacing and can be 'demoted' for use as a desktop PC.

(b) It might be replaced by a **'mid range server'**. A mid range server might support 20-30 users.

(c) A **high end file server** might be used in a large department network of about 50-100 users handling transaction processing and an accounting system. High end servers have now been joined by **superservers** and **'enterprise servers'** (effectively, mainframes). These are either departmental or organisation-wide, running sophisticated mission-critical systems and offering fault tolerance features. They might support upwards of 250 users.

Network operating systems

7.14 To carry out the administrative tasks connected with operating a network a special operating system is required. This establishes the links between the nodes of the network, monitors the operation of the network and controls recovery processes when the system or part of it breaks down. The main examples are **Novell Netware** and Microsoft **Windows NT**, both of which are able to work in conjunction with the DOS and Windows 95 operating systems on individual PCs. **Unix** is also used on larger systems.

The advantages of client/server computing

7.15 The advantages of the network approach using the client/server model are as follows.

Advantage	Comment
Greater resilience	*Processing is spread* over several computers, so client/server systems are more resilient. If one server breaks down, other locations can carry on processing.
Scalability	They are highly *scalable.* In other words instead of having to buy computing power in large quantities you can buy just the amount of power you need to do the job. When you need more you simply add another server.
Shared programs and data	*Program and data files* held on a file server can be *shared* by all the PCs in the network. With stand-alone PCs, each computer would have its own data files, and there might be unnecessary duplication of data.
	A system where everyone uses the same data will help to improve data processing and decision making. The value of some information increases with its availability.
Shared work-loads	Each PC in a network can do the *same work.*
	If there were separate stand-alone PCs, A might do job 1, B might do job 2, C might do job 3 and so on. In a network, any PC, (A, B or C) could do any job (1, 2 or 3). This provides flexibility in sharing work-loads. In a peak period for job 1, say, two or more people can share the work without having to leave their own desk.
Shared peripherals	*Peripheral* equipment can be *shared.* For example, in a LAN, five PCs might share a single on-line printer, whereas if there were stand-alone PCs, each might be given its own separate printer. If resources are scarce (for example fast laser printers) this is a significant benefit.
Communication and time management	LANs can be linked up to the office *communications network*, thus adding to the processing capabilities in an office. Electronic mail can be used to send messages, memos and electronic letters from node to node. Electronic calendar and diary facilities can also be used.
Compatibility	Client/server systems are more likely than centralised systems to have Windows *interfaces*, making it easier to move information between applications such as spreadsheets and accounting systems.

Advantage	Comment
Ad hoc enquiries	They enable information to be moved to a separate server, allowing managers to make *ad hoc* enquiries without disrupting the main system.

The disadvantages of client/server computing

7.16 Not everybody is convinced of the value of the client/server approach.

(a) **Mainframes** are better at dealing with **very large volumes** of transactions.

(b) It is easier to **control** and **maintain** a system centrally. In particular it is easier to keep data **secure**.

(c) It may be **cheaper** to 'tweak' an existing mainframe system rather than throwing it away and starting from scratch: for example it may be possible to give it a graphical user interface and to make data exchangeable between Windows and non-Windows based applications.

Network computers: thin clients

7.17 A widespread criticism at present is that there is now far **more computing power** on the desktop than is really necessary and a compromise is needed to control costs and simplify computing for end-users.

7.18 The **Network Computer (NC)** is being developed by rivals to Microsoft and Intel such as Oracle and Sun Microsystems. An NC is intended to be used for similar purposes to the PC but it **does not have a hard disk** (hence the name 'thin client'): its **applications are downloaded** when needed from powerful ('fat') servers on the organisation's own network or from a public network such as the Internet.

7.19 This saves greatly on both **hardware costs**, because the machine itself is less packed with expensive electronics, and on **software and support costs**, because there is no need to buy and install a separate copy of each application for each machine every time there is a new upgrade.

7.20 The main example to date is the **JavaStation** launched by Sun in 1996. Microsoft are said to be planning their own 'NetPCs'.

8 INTEROPERABILITY AND OPEN SYSTEMS

8.1 In this section we describe a number of key 1990s issues in organisational IT strategy. All of them are **linked**: for instance interoperability can be achieved if everyone adopts, say, the latest version of Windows NT.

Interoperability

> ### KEY TERM
>
> **Interoperability** means that any company, individual or institution can readily share and exchange information and facilities with any other company, individual or institution. Moreover, they can do so without having to use the same service provider as the other party, without having to use the same technology platform, or even know what technology platform is used by the other party. They need have only a minimum of concern about data structures, and there is a minimum need for new skills when using new applications and technologies.

Backward compatibility

8.2   A new version of a **program** is said to be backward compatible if it can use files and data created with an **older version** of the same program. Computer **hardware** is said to be backward compatible if it can run the same software as **previous models**.

8.3   Backward compatibility is important because it **eliminates the need to start afresh** when upgrading to a newer product. A backward-compatible word processor, for instance, allows users to edit documents created with a previous version of the program. In general, manufacturers try to keep their products backward compatible. Sometimes, however, it is necessary to **sacrifice** backward compatibility to take advantage of a **new technology**. (Microsoft intends to sacrifice compatibility with old Windows and DOS based programs: Windows 98 is the last operating system they will release that offers this feature.)

Legacy system

8.4   A legacy system is a computer system or application program which **continues to be used** because of the **prohibitive cost of replacing or redesigning it** and often despite its poor competitiveness and compatibility with modern equivalents. The implication is that the system is **large, monolithic and difficult to modify**.

8.5   Legacy **software** may only run on antiquated **hardware**, and the cost of maintaining this may eventually outweigh the cost of replacing both the software and hardware.

Open systems

8.6   Organisations develop computerised systems over a period of time, perhaps focusing on different functions at different times, and a number of consequences are likely to become apparent.

  (a) They may have networks or other equipment supplied by a **range of manufacturers**.
  (b) **Data is duplicated** in different areas of the business.
  (c) **Software** may have become **inefficient and out of date**.

8.7   **Open systems** aim to ensure compatibility between different makes of equipment, enabling users to choose on the basis of price and performance. An open systems approach has a number of characteristics. The first is **vendor independence**. Applications can be 'ported' from one system to another. An open systems infrastructure supports **organisation-wide functions** and allows interoperability of networks and systems. Authorised users would be able to access applications and data from any part of the system.

Case example: Pure Java v Microsoft Java

Depending on who you talk to, Java is three things. Firstly, it is a programming language: a scaled down version, some would even argue a derivative, of C++. Java has the benefit of being a write-once-run-anywhere language, or so its creators claim.

Secondly, Java is a platform all of its own. It runs on any computer that has a Java Virtual machine - embedded code that recognises and reads Java code as it is downloaded onto the machine. Java is a single unifying platform for organisations with heterogeneous computing environments, which is most companies. Finally, Java has assumed the role as the ultimate IT panacea, 'Java-as-lifestyle'.

[A number of] industry heavyweights are jostling for position in their attempts to dominate the Java field. First up, naturally, is Sun. Creator and progenitor of Java, Sun appears to be betting the company jewels on Java. Definitely belonging to the 'Java-as-lifestyle' element, Sun has even committed itself to a '100% Pure Java' initiative, a bid to get programmers to write for and in native Java without calling on any local machine code, such as Windows APIs, for extra functionality.

Behind the Java evangelists are the two companies with most to gain from Java as a platform: IBM and Oracle. Although IBM has publicly chided Microsoft for not supporting the 100% Pure Java initiative, it is the Java as middleware idea that would appear to drive IBM's interest. Firstly, it has many different platforms to unify. Vendors are also increasingly wary of committing to proprietary security, messaging and transaction software from IBM, because they have been burned in the past and because they now demand the inter-operability and openness that the Internet exemplifies. ...

And then there is Microsoft, both contrary and dominant simultaneously. Microsoft has been anything but slow in developing Java. Its own Java VM is the fastest available. Yet Microsoft insists that Java is just a language. And to demonstrate its ambivalent attitude towards Java, it will make its breakaway move whilst attempting to win plaudits for development the fastest Java VM. ... This sort of commitment to developing Java tools and code for its other products, but endless re-iteration of how Java itself is only a poor rival to C++, is why so many of Microsoft's opponents accuse it of hypocrisy.

Microsoft came under more scrutiny when UK manager Jeremy Gittins commented on the likelihood of Microsoft splitting from the Java standard. Although Microsoft has yet to endorse these comments, it seems that the company is gearing itself up for a split. Microsoft claims publicly that the Sun standard for Java will only run on 42 per cent of systems before making calls to the operating system, and that the cross-platform Java claim is simply not true except for trivial applets. So, the 'Java-as-extension-of-Windows' model is one that Microsoft appears committed to follow.

Source: *Information Week,* September 1997

Network operating systems

8.8 To carry out the administrative tasks connected with operating a network a special operating system is required. This **establishes the links** between the nodes of the network, **monitors the operation** of the network and **controls recovery processes** when the system or part of it breaks down. The main examples are Novell Netware, Microsoft Windows NT, and UNIX .

Case example: UNIX v NT

From small businesses to large multinationals, companies are ditching their UNIX and Novell NetWare and buying into a Microsoft idea of one 'total solution' - NT across the enterprise. One indication of the rise of NT has been the sudden increase in membership of the Windows NT User Forum over the last six months. According to Grant Pearson, managing director of the Forum: 'Among the people that are signing up for the User Forum are those who have been using Windows 3.11 and never really trusted Windows 95 for their workstations. NT seems to have come of age and users are bypassing 95 and installing NT.'

Pearson notes, however, that very few NT users are opting for total NT solutions. According to Forum figures, almost a third are still running UNIX, and another third use NetWare alongside NT, because many users don't totally believe Microsoft's marketing message, and are installing NT only in areas where there are sound technology reasons.

'There is no doubt that NT is a good operating system, but it is just as good as anything else. UNIX handles applications better and NetWare has a better file and print system, for example,' he says.

NT's success stems from Microsoft's marketing machine, which has managed to convince users that it is more compatible with the rest of its software, according to Pearson. 'If your company was using Exchange or Office, then the Microsoft marketing machine would convince you that NT would bring the whole thing together.'

Microsoft's marketing has certainly convinced users that it is more appealing than its rivals. 'NT is forcing its way into the corporate market on the basis of its sex appeal. NT looks like 95 for users who are Windows-comfortable. But UNIX does not look as friendly and NetWare is not as pretty.'

But Pearson feels that UNIX will hold its ground among customers, because it has a solid following among IT staff. 'Certainly on application servers it is a lot more powerful than NT,' Pearson says.

(Source: *Information Week,* October 1997)

Chapter roundup

- A **strategy** is needed for information management because IT involves **high costs**, it is **critical to the success** of many organisations, it can be used as a **strategic weapon** and it affects **stakeholders** in the organisation.

- Two models of how systems develop are Nolan's **stage hypothesis** and the **systems development lifecycle.**

- Information systems **costs** should be rigorously controlled. Some organisations develop costing systems so that instead of treating the expenditure as a central overhead, the costs are passed on to **user** departments. This has the advantage of improving local **responsibility,** but it can be **complex and divisive.**

- **Outsourcing** or **facilities management** entails contracting out the management of information systems to a third party. This is an increasingly common trend.

- An important issue in systems development is the question of **centralisation** or **decentralisation.** Centralisation allows the use of a single set of files and offers better security and control. Disadvantages include the extent of local office reliance on head office and the risk of delays in processing.

- A **multi-user system** is a system that appears to serve more than one user at one time. A multi-user system normally has one central computer and set of files which are accessed by a number of dumb terminals.

- **Distributed data processing** is processing done by a distributed system, a system containing a number of separate but connected processors, in which some centralised processing is possible.

- A **local area network** is a system of interconnected PCs (and other devices, such as printers and disks) which are connected by special cable. LANs can have a server computer holding files used by more than one computer, and providing storage capacity to the other computers in the network. In a LAN, data processing tasks can be shared between a number of PCs, and single items of peripheral equipment can be accessed by all of them.

- A **wide area network** is a network of computers which are dispersed on a wider geographical scale than LANs. They are connected over the public telecommunications network. A WAN will normally use minicomputers or powerful PCs.

- **Client-server** computing is a configuration in which desktop PCs are regarded as 'clients' that request access to the services available on a more powerful server PC, such as access to a file, e-mail, or printing facilities.

- **Interoperability** means that it is possible to share and exchange information and facilities with others without having to use the same service provider or technology platform and with a minimum of concern about data structures, and a minimum need for new skills. A key issue in the **open systems** debate at present is the choice of **UNIX or Windows NT** as an operating system.

Quick quiz

1   What tasks does information management involve? (see para 1.1)

2   How can IT help a business to win competitive advantage? (1.11)

3   Explain the stages of the systems development lifecycle. (2.6)

4   What are the disadvantages of cost-based chargeout systems for IT expenditure? (3.8)

5   What are the advantages and disadvantages of facilities management? (4.9-4.12)

6   What are the advantages of decentralised processing? (5.7)

7   What are the differences between a LAN and a WAN? (7.7)

8   What are the advantages of the client/server approach? (7.15)

9   What does interoperability mean? (8.1)

10 What is a legacy system? (8.4)

Question to try	Level	Marks	Time
7	Exam standard	15	27 mins

Chapter 7

IDENTIFYING IS PROJECTS

Chapter topic list	Syllabus reference
1 Identifying IS projects	
2 The feasibility study	3(c), 3(d)
3 Areas of feasibility	3(c)
4 Costs and benefits	3(c)
5 Cost-benefit analysis	3(c)
6 The feasibility study report	3(c), 3(d)

Introduction

This chapter is concerned with the first stage of the systems development lifecycle, the **feasibility study,** the purpose of which is to identify viable IS projects that an organisation might pursue.

Some of the techniques introduced in very general terms here will be explained in much more detail in Chapters 12 and 16.

1   IDENTIFYING IS PROJECTS

Exam focus point

A question set by the old examiner in **June 1995** asked what steps an organisation might take to facilitate identification and selection of computer projects and ensure a planned approach.

The following suggestions introduce topics that will be developed throughout the rest of this book and provide a very useful summary of what you have seen so far and is to come.

A planned approach

1.1   A planned approach is needed when identifying and selecting new computer projects. The following actions should be considered.

(a)   IT is critical to the success of many organisations. This means that an **IT strategy** should form a **core part of the overall corporate strategy** and should be developed/updated whenever the organisation's strategy is reviewed or as otherwise necessary. IT needs can then be identified in the context of **overall business needs**.

(b)   Because IT is critical, it requires adequate **representation at senior management level.** It is no longer suitable for IT to be under the control of the MD, FD or computer centre manager. It really needs a separate Board level person responsible, such as an **Information Director** or an **IS director**. This will help to ensure that IT is given adequate consideration at strategic level.

(c) The IT development can no longer function as a subsystem of accounting, administration or finance. Its importance means that it should be given **separate departmental or functional status** in the organisation with its own reporting lines and responsibilities. It is no longer simply an organ of the accounts department: as more departments use IT, there is less reason for it to be organised by one department.

(d) Once the IT department has been set up, its **funding** must be considered. A simplistic approach would be to treat it as an overhead; this is simple but inefficient. There are various approaches possible to the recovery of IT costs from user departments, and the IT department may even operate as a commercial concern providing services to third parties at a profit.

(e) **A strategic plan for the use of IT** should be developed. This should take in separate elements such as information technology and information systems. It should also acknowledge the importance of the organisation's information resource.

(f) If new computer systems are to be introduced regularly, the organisation may set up a **steering committee** to oversee **systems development**. A steering committee can also be set up for a one-off project. The role of the steering committee includes approving or rejecting individual projects and where appropriate submitting projects to the Board for approval. The composition and determination of terms of reference for the steering committee must be agreed.

(g) The **approach** of the organisation to individual projects must be decided. Will it follow the traditional **life cycle** or will it use a **methodology**? Commercial methodologies impose discipline and have a number of advantages.

(h) Procedures for **evaluating and monitoring performance** both during and after a project need to be put in place. Many methodologies require formal sign-off of each stage, but this does not obviate the need for good project management or for post-implementation evaluation.

(i) Details of the **systems development procedures** must be agreed. If a commercial methodology is used, much of this will be pre-determined, but, for example, decisions must be made on the approach to **feasibility studies**, methods of **cost-benefit analysis**, **design specifications** and conventions, **tools and techniques** which will be used, **reporting** lines, contents of standard **invitations to tender**, drawing up of **supplier conditions** and procedures for **testing and implementation**.

2   THE FEASIBILITY STUDY

2.1   The feasibility study is the first stage of systems development in the systems development lifecycle.

KEY TERM

A **feasibility study** is a formal study to decide what type of system can be developed which meets the needs of the organisation.

2.2   Some of the work performed at the feasibility study stage may be similar to work performed later on in the development of the project. This is because some of the information necessary to decide whether to go ahead with a project or trying to define a problem is common to both phases. Amongst factors which may be considered as part of the feasibility study which might also feature in a later stage in the systems development are **investigation and analysis work**, a **cost-benefit analysis** and the identification of **user requirements**, at least in outline.

2.3 Among the reasons for having a feasibility study are that new systems can **cost** a great deal to develop, be very **disruptive** during development and implementation in terms of the opportunity cost of management time, and have far reaching consequences in a way an organisation conducts its business or is structured.

2.4 **Project management** skills are necessary from an early stage. Project management is considered in Chapter 16.

Terms of reference

2.5 The terms of reference for a feasibility study group must be set out by a steering committee, the information director or the board of directors, and might consist of the following items.

   (a) To **investigate** and report on an **existing system**, its procedures and costs.
   (b) To define the **systems requirements**.
   (c) To establish whether these requirements are being met by the **existing** system.
   (d) To establish whether they could be met by an **alternative** system.
   (e) To specify **performance criteria** for the system.
   (f) To recommend the **most suitable system** to meet the system's objectives.
   (g) To prepare a detailed **cost budget**, within a specified budget limit.
   (h) To prepare a draft **plan for implementation** within a specified timescale.
   (i) To establish whether the hoped-for **benefits** could be realised.
   (j) To establish a detailed design, implementation and operating **budget**.
   (k) To **compare** the detailed budget with the costs of the current system.
   (l) To set the **date** by which the study group must **report back**.
   (m) To decide which **operational managers** should be approached by the study group.

2.6 The remit of a feasibility study may be narrow or quite wide. The feasibility study team must engage in a substantial effort of fact finding. These facts may include matters relevant to the project which are not necessarily of a data processing nature.

Problem definition

2.7 In some circumstances the 'problem' (for example the necessity for a real-time as opposed to a batch processed application) may be quite **exact**, in others it may be characterised as 'soft' (related to people and the way they behave).

2.8 The problem definition stage should result in the production of a set of documents which define the problem.

   (a) A set of **diagrams** representing, in overview:

      (i) the current physical flows of data in the organisation (**documents**); and
      (ii) the activities underlying them (**data flows**).

   (b) A description of all the people, jobs, activities and so on (**entities**) that make up the system, and their relationship to one another.

   (c) The **problems/requirements** list established from the terms of reference and after consultation with users.

The problems/requirements list

2.9   The problems/requirements list or catalogue can cover, amongst other things, the following areas.

(a)   The data **input** to the current system.

(b)   The nature of the **output** information (contents, timing etc).

(c)   Methods of **processing**.

(d)   The expected **growth** of the organisation and so **future volumes** of processing.

(e)   The systems **control** in operation.

(f)   **Staffing** arrangements and organisational **structure**.

(g)   The **operational costs** of the system.

(h)   **Type of system** (batch, on-line).

(i)   **Response times**.

(j)   Current organisational **problems**.

Project identification

2.10   This stage involves suggesting a number of **options** for a new system, evaluating them and recommending one for adoption. It concludes with a final **feasibility study report**.

Step 1   Create the **base constraints** in terms of expenditure, implementation and design time, and system requirements, which any system should satisfy.

- **Operations** (for example faster processing, larger volumes, greater security, greater accuracy, better quality, real-time as opposed to other forms of processing).

- Information **output** (quality, frequency, presentation, eg GUIs, database for managers, EIS facilities).

- **Volume of processing**.

- **General system requirements** (eg accuracy, security and controls, audit trail, flexibility, adaptability).

- **Compatibility/integration** with existing systems.

Step 2   Create outlines of **project options**, describing, in brief, each option. The number will vary depending on the complexity of the problem, or the size of the application, but is typically between three and six.

Step 3   Assess the **impact** each proposal has on the work of the relevant user department and/or the organisation as a whole.

Step 4   **Review** these proposals with users, who should indicate those options they favour for further analysis.

System justification

2.11   A new system should not be recommended unless it can be justified. The justification for a new system would have to come from:

(a)   an evaluation of the **costs and benefits** of the proposed system; and/or

(b)   other **performance criteria**.

3   AREAS OF FEASIBILITY

3.1   There are four key areas in which a project must be feasible if it is to be selected.

- Technical feasibility
- Operational feasibility
- Social feasibility
- Economic feasibility

Technical feasibility

3.2   The requirements, as defined in the feasibility study, must be technically achievable. This means that any proposed solution must be capable of being implemented using available **hardware, software and other equipment**. The type of requirement which might depend for success on technical feasibility might be one of the following.

- **Volume** of transactions which can be processed within a given time
- **Capacity** to hold files or records of a certain size
- **Response times** (how quickly the computer does what you ask it to)
- **Number of users** which can be supported without deterioration in the other criteria

Operational feasibility

3.3   Operational feasibility is a key concern. If a solution makes technical sense but **conflicts with the way the organisation does business,** the solution is not feasible. Thus an organisation might reject a solution because it forces a change in management responsibilities, status and chains of command, or does not suit regional reporting structures, or because the costs of redundancies, retraining and reorganisation are considered too high.

Social feasibility

3.4   An assessment of social feasibility will address a number of areas, including the following.

(a) **Personnel** policies
(b) Redrawing of **job specifications**
(c) Threats to **industrial relations**
(d) Expected **skills requirements**
(e) **Motivation**

Economic feasibility

3.5   A system which satisfies all the above criteria must still be economically feasible. This means that it must be a 'good investment'. This has two strands.

(a) The project selected must be the 'best' of the **computerisation** projects under consideration.

(b) The project selected **must compete with other projects in other areas** of the business for funds. Even if it is projected to produce a positive return and satisfies all relevant criteria, it may not be chosen because a **new warehouse** is needed or the head office is to be relocated, and available funds are allocated to these projects instead.

Exam focus point

A question set in **June 1996** asked about operational feasibility and economic feasibility in the context of a specific scenario.

4   COSTS AND BENEFITS

The costs of a proposed system

4.1   In general the best cost estimates will be obtained for systems bought from an **outside vendor** who provides a cost quotation against a specification. Less concrete cost estimates are generally found with development projects where the work is performed by the organisation's own employees.

4.2   The costs of a new system will include costs in a number of different categories.

Cost	Example
Equipment costs	• Computer and peripherals • Ancillary equipment • The initial system supplies (disks, tapes, paper etc)
Installation costs	• New buildings (if necessary) • The computer room (wiring, air-conditioning if necessary)
Development costs	These include costs of measuring and analysing the existing system and costs of looking at the new system. They include software/consultancy work and systems analysis and programming. Changeover costs, particularly file conversion, may be very considerable.
Personnel costs	• Staff training • Staff recruitment/relocation • Staff salaries and pensions • Redundancy payments • Overheads
Operating costs	• Consumable materials (tapes, disks, stationery etc) • Maintenance • Accommodation costs • Heating/power/insurance/telephone • Standby arrangements, in case the system breaks down

Capital and revenue costs

4.3   The distinction between capital costs and revenue costs is important.

   (a)   To establish the **cash** outflows arising from the system, the costs/benefit analysis of a system ought to be based on **cash flows and DCF**.

   (b)   The annual charge against **profits** shown in the financial accounts is of interest to **stakeholders**.

4.4 **Capital** items will be capitalised and depreciated, and revenue items will be expensed as incurred as a regular annual cost.

4.5 Items treated as **one-off revenue costs** are costs which would usually fall to be treated as revenue which, by virtue of being incurred during the period of development only and in connection with the development are one-off.

4.6 In practice, **accounting treatment** of such items may **vary widely** between organisations depending on their accounting policies and on agreement with their auditors.

Question 1

Draw up a table with three headings: capital cost items, one-off revenue cost items and regular annual costs. Identify at least three items to be included under each heading. You may wish to refer back to the preceding paragraphs for examples of costs.

Answer

Capital cost items	*'One-off' revenue cost items*	*Regular annual costs*
Hardware purchase costs	Consultancy fees	Operating staff salaries/wages
Software purchase costs	Systems analysts' and programmers' salaries	Data transmission costs
Purchase of accommo-dation (if needed)	Costs of testing the system (staff costs, consumables)	Consumable materials
Installation costs (new desks, cables, physical storage etc)	Costs of converting the files for the new system	Power
		Maintenance costs
	Staff recruitment fees	Cost of standby arrange-ments
		Ongoing staff training

The benefits of a proposed system

4.7 The benefits from a proposed new system must also be evaluated. These ought to consist of benefits of several types.

(a) **Savings** because the **old system** will no longer be operated. The savings should include:

    (i)   savings in **staff costs**;

    (ii)   savings in **other operating costs,** such as consumable materials.

(b) Extra **savings** or revenue benefits because of the improvements or enhancements that the **new system** should bring:

    (i)   possibly **more sales revenue** and so additional contribution;

    (ii)   **better stock control** (with a new stock control system) and so fewer stock losses from obsolescence and deterioration;

    (iii) further savings in **staff time**, resulting perhaps in reduced future staff growth.

(c) Possibly, some one-off revenue benefits from the **sale of equipment** which the existing system uses, but which will no longer be required. Second-hand computer equipment does not have a high value, however! It is also possible that the new system will use **less office space**, and so there will be benefits from selling or renting the spare accommodation.

4.8 Some benefits might be **intangible**, or impossible to give a money value to.

(a) Greater **customer satisfaction**, arising from a more prompt service (eg because of a computerised sales and delivery service).

(b) Improved **staff morale** from working with a 'better' system.

(c) **Better decision making** is hard to quantify, but may result from better MIS, DSS or EIS.

5 COST-BENEFIT ANALYSIS

5.1 There are three principal methods of evaluating a capital project.

Method	Comment
Payback period	This method of investment appraisal calculates the length of time a project will take to recoup the initial investment; in other words how long a project will take to pay for itself. The method is based on **cash flows**.
Accounting rate of return	This method, also called **return on investment**, calculates the profits that will be earned by a project and expresses this as a percentage of the capital invested in the project. The higher the rate of return, the higher a project is ranked. This method is based on **accounting** results rather than cash flows.
Discounted cash flow (DCF)	This is a method which may be sub-divided into two approaches. (a) **Net present value (NPV)**, which considers all relevant cash flows associated with a project over the whole of its life and adjusts those occurring in future years to 'present value' by discounting at a rate called the 'cost of capital'. (b) **Internal rate of return (IRR)**, which involves comparing the rate of return expected from the project calculated on a discounted cash flow basis with the rate used as the cost of capital. Projects with an IRR higher than the cost of capital are worth undertaking.

Cash flow forecasting

5.2 Before looking at each of these methods in turn it is worth considering one **problem** common to all of them, that of **estimating future cash flows**. Cash flow forecasting is never easy, but in capital budgeting the problems are particularly acute. This is because the period under consideration may not be merely a year or two, but five or even ten years.

5.3 It is therefore important that decision makers should consider how **variations** in the estimates **might affect their decision**. For the time being, it is assumed that future cash flows are known with certainty.

The payback method

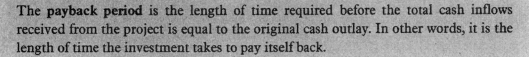

KEY TERM

The **payback period** is the length of time required before the total cash inflows received from the project is equal to the original cash outlay. In other words, it is the length of time the investment takes to pay itself back.

5.4 EXAMPLE: PAYBACK

The payback method has obvious disadvantages. Consider the case of two projects for which the following information is available.

	Project P £	Project Q £
Cost	100,000	100,000
Cash savings		
Year 1	10,000	50,000
2	20,000	50,000
3	60,000	10,000
4	70,000	5,000
5	80,000	5,000
	240,000	120,000

5.5 SOLUTION

Project Q pays back at the end of year two and Project P not until early in year four. Using the payback method Project Q is to be preferred, but this ignores the fact that the total profitability of Project P (£240,000) is double that of Q.

5.6 Despite the disadvantages of the payback method it is **widely used in practice**, though often only as a **supplement** to more sophisticated methods.

5.7 Besides being simple to calculate and understand, the argument in its favour is that its use will tend to **minimise** the effects of **risk** and **help liquidity**. This is because greater weight is given to **earlier cash flows** which can probably be **predicted more accurately** than distant cash flows.

Exam focus point

You are more likely to have to explain the advantages and disadvantages of different approaches to cost-benefit analysis than to do calculations. Such a written question came up in **June 1996**.

Accounting rate of return

5.8 A project may be assessed by calculating the accounting rate of return (ARR) and comparing it with a pre-determined target level. Various formulae are used, but the important thing is to be **consistent** once a method has been selected. A formula for ARR which is common in practice is:

5.9   EXAMPLE: ARR

Caddick Limited is contemplating a computerisation project and has two alternatives. Based on the ARR method which of the two projects would be recommended?

	Project X	Project Y
Hardware cost	£100,000	£120,000
Estimated residual value	10,000	£15,000
Estimated life	5 years	5 years
Estimated future cost savings per annum before depreciation	£28,000	£32,500

5.10   SOLUTION

It is first necessary to calculate the average profits (net savings) and average investment.

	Project X £	Project Y £
Total savings before depreciation	140,000	162,500
Total depreciation	90,000	105,000
Total savings after depreciation	50,000	57,500
Average savings	10,000	11,500
Value of investment initially	100,000	120,000
Eventual scrap value	10,000	15,000
	110,000	135,000
Average investment	55,000	67,500

5.11   The accounting rates of return are as follows. Project X would therefore be chosen.

$$\text{Project X} = \frac{£10,000}{£55,000} = 18.1\%$$

$$\text{Project Y} = \frac{£11,500}{£67,500} = 17.0\%$$

5.12   The return on investment is a measure of (accounting) profitability and its major **advantages** that it can be obtained from **readily available accounting data** and that its meaning is **widely understood**.

5.13   Its major **shortcomings** are that it is based on accounting profits rather than cash flows and that it fails to take account of the **timing** of cash inflows and outflows. For example, in the problem above cash savings in each year were assumed to be the same, whereas management might favour higher cash inflows in the **early years**. Early cash flows are less risky and they improve liquidity. This might lead them to choose a project with a lower ARR.

> **KEY TERM**
>
> **Discounted cash flow** or DCF is a technique of evaluating capital investment projects, using **discounting arithmetic** to determine whether or not they will provide a satisfactory return.

5.14 A typical investment project involves a payment of capital for fixed assets at the **start** of the project and then there will be profits coming in from the investment over a number of years. When the system goes live, there will be **running costs** as well. The benefits of the system should exceed the running costs, to give net annual benefits.

5.15 DCF recognises that there is a **'time value'** or interest cost and **risk** cost to investing money, so that the expected benefits from a project should not only pay back the costs, but should also yield a satisfactory return. Only **relevant** costs are recognised: accounting conventions like depreciation, which is not a real cash flow, are ignored.

5.16 £1 is now worth more than £1 in a year's time, because £1 now could be used to earn interest by the end of year 1. Money has a lower and lower value, the further from 'now' that it will be earned or paid. With DCF, this time value on money is allowed for by converting cash flows in future years to a smaller, **present value**, equivalent.

5.17 EXAMPLE: NPV

A DCF evaluation, using NPV analysis, of a proposed computer project might be as follows.

Project: new network system for administration department

Development and hardware purchase costs (all incurred over a short time)	£150,000
Operating costs of new system, expressed as cash outflows per annum	£55,000
Annual savings from new system, expressed as cash inflow	£115,000
Annual net savings (net cash inflows)	£60,000
Expected system life 4 years	
Required return on investment 15% pa	

5.18 SOLUTION

The calculation of NPV is performed as follows.

Year	Cost/Savings	Discount factor at 15%	Present value at 15%
	£		£
0	(150,000)	1.000	(150,000)
1	60,000	0.870	52,200
2	60,000	0.756	45,360
3	60,000	0.658	39,480
4	60,000	0.572	34,320
		Net present value of the project	21,360

5.19 In this example, the present value of the expected benefits of the project exceed the present value of its costs, all discounted at 15% pa, and so the project is financially justifiable because it would be expected to earn a yield greater than the minimum target return of 15%. Payback of the development costs and hardware costs of £150,000 would occur after 2½ years.

5.20 One disadvantage of the NPV method is that it involves complicated maths and this might make it **difficult to understand** for some people. More seriously, it is difficult in practice to determine the true **cost of capital.**

Internal rate of return

5.21 The internal rate of return(IRR) methods of DCF involves two steps.

(a) Calculating the **rate of return** which is expected from a project.
(b) **Comparing** the rate of return with the **cost of capital**.

5.22 If a project earns a higher rate of return than the cost of capital, it will be worth undertaking (and its NPV would be positive). If it earns a lower rate of return, it is not worthwhile (and its NPV would be negative). If a project earns a return which is exactly equal to the cost of capital, its NPV will be 0 and it will only just be worthwhile.

5.23 The manual method of calculating the rate of return is sometimes considered to be rather 'messy' and unsatisfactory because it involves some guesswork and approximation, but **spreadsheets** can do it with speed and precision.

Question 2

Draw up a table which identifies, for each of payback, ARR and NPV, two advantages and two disadvantages.

Answer

Method	Advantages	Disadvantages
Payback	(1) Easy to calculate (2) Favours projects that offer quick returns	(1) Ignores cash flows after payback period (2) Only a crude measure of timing of a project's cash flows.
ARR	(1) Easy to calculate (2) Easy to understand	(1) Doesn't allow for timing of inflows/outflows of cash (2) Subject to accounting conventions.
NPV	(1) Uses relevant cost approach by concentrating on cash flows (2) Represents increase to company's wealth, expressed in present day terms	(1) Not easily understood by laymen. (2) Cost of capital may be difficult to calculate.

6   THE FEASIBILITY STUDY REPORT

6.1 Once the outline project specifications are prepared, these are presented to **users** who, with the assistance of technical staff will evaluate each option and make a **final choice**. This stage is much more intensive than when the original options were first examined. All the systems specified in the project specifications are feasible and it is simply a matter of **weighing up the advantages and disadvantages** of each.

6.2 One option may be to **carry on with the existing system** as it is, with no development option being chosen. If the feasibility study has been quite a lengthy one, circumstances beyond the control of the study teams may render any systems development inappropriate. For example, interest rates may rise increasing the organisation's cost of capital, and in this context the cost/benefit analysis might render the proposed system uneconomic.

6.3 This is the final step of the feasibility phase. A number of projects were mooted. A few favoured ones were examined and specified in more detail, and a choice made after evaluation. The results of these deliberations are included in a **feasibility study report**. This should contain the following points.

(a) The **introduction** will contain the study's terms of reference and details as to how and when the study was carried out.

(b) The **problem definition** will contain material from the problem definition stage, as outlined earlier.

(c) **Outline project specifications** are summaries of the detailed project specifications prepared for a number of project options.

(d) **Reasons for selection of preferred project option** may include cost/benefit analyses, or any of the non-economic criteria noted above.

(e) **Specification of selected project option** will include:

   (i)   outline **data flow diagrams** and processes of the new system;
   (ii)   a description of the **entity model**;
   (iii)   an updated **problems/requirements list**;
   (iv)   a brief description of the system's **physical implementation**.

6.4 We shall explain what data flow diagrams and entity models are in Chapter 12.

Exam focus point

A question set in **June 1994** (by the old examiner) asked about the contents of a feasibility study report.

Question 3

You are the member of a feasibility study group with responsibility for preparing the first draft of the report so that this can be circulated to the other group members for their comments before your next meeting. List the sections of the report.

Answer

A typical report might include:

(a)   terms of reference;
(b)   description of existing system;
(c)   system requirements;
(d)   details of the proposed system;
(e)   cost/benefit analysis;
(f)   development and implementation plans; and
(g)   recommendations as to the preferred option.

Chapter roundup

- The feasibility study is the **first stage of systems development** in the systems development lifecycle. Some of the work undertaken may overlap with elements of the systems investigation and system analysis stages.

- The **feasibility study** is a formal study to decide what type of system can be developed which meets the needs of the organisation.

- Work carried out includes the production of **diagrams** showing **data and document flows**, a description of all the **entities** in the system (people, activities etc) and a **problems/requirements list**. This is the problem definition phase.

- The second phase of the study is project identification, during which a number of options for a new system are evaluated and one recommended.

- There are four key areas in which a project must be feasible if it is to be selected. It must be justifiable on **technical, operational, social** and **economic** grounds.

- One of the most important elements of the feasibility study is the **cost-benefit analysis**.

  o **Costs** may be analysed in different ways, but include equipment costs, installation costs, development costs, personnel costs and running costs.

  o **Benefits** are usually somewhat more intangible, but include cost savings, revenue benefits and qualitative benefits.

- There are three principal methods of evaluating a capital project.

  o **Payback period** calculates the length of time a project will take to cover the initial investment in cashflow terms.

  o **Accounting rate of return** calculates the profits which will be generated and expresses this return as a percentage of the capital invested.

  o **DCF techniques** are also cash flow based; two approaches are net present value calculations and the internal rate of return.

- The feasibility study culminates with a **feasibility study report**, reflecting all of the above analysis and recommending and giving a specification for the selected option.

Quick quiz

1 Suggest four actions that might be considered to ensure a planned approach to IS projects. (see para 1.1)

2 Define a feasibility study. (2.1)

3 What might be covered in a problems/requirements list? (2.9)

4 Suggest four steps in project identification. (2.10)

5 What is meant by technical feasibility and social feasibility? (3.2, 3.4)

6 What sort of costs might a new system have? (4.2)

7 What benefits might a new system have? (4.7, 4.8)

8 Describe the contents of a feasibility study report. (6.3)

Question to try	Level	Marks	Time
8	Exam standard	10	18 mins

Chapter 8

ACQUISITION PROCEDURES

Chapter topic list	Syllabus reference
1 Vendor hardware and software proposals	4(a), 4(b), 4(d)
2 Financing methods	4(a), 4(b), 4(d)
3 Evaluation of vendor proposals	4(a), 4(b), 4(d)
4 Choosing hardware and software	4(a), 4(b), 4(d)
5 Software contracts	4(a), 4(b), 4(d)

Introduction

In this chapter we look at the various procedures that an organisation might adopt when acquiring hardware and software for information systems, and the many matters that have to be considered. Most of these have appeared in exam questions.

This develops material in Chapter 6 on the importance of rigorous control of costs.

1 VENDOR HARDWARE AND SOFTWARE PROPOSALS

1.1 A computer user might buy hardware and software direct from a manufacturer, or through an intermediate supplier. Given that the expense is often considerable, the purchasing procedure must be carefully controlled.

Invitation to tender (ITT)

1.2 An organisation may issue an **invitation to tender (ITT)** to a range of suppliers.

> **KEY TERM**
>
> An **invitation to tender** sets out the specification for the required system, explaining how it is to be used and setting out the timescale for implementation. It will set the performance criteria required of the new system.

1.3 The invitation to tender would give some **background information** about the company, together with an indication of the **purpose of the system** and with the details of requirements such as:

(a) the **volume of data** to be processed;

(b) the **complexity of processing** requirements (including interfaces with other systems);

(c) the **number of offices** or individual **people** who will want to access the computer system, and whether access needs to be instant or not;

(d) the **speed of processing** required, eg response times;

(e) **inputs and outputs** desired;

(f) the type of **file processing** needed (ie whether the company require a real-time system);

(g) estimated **life** of the system;

(h) possible **upgrades** or expansion anticipated.

1.4 Details about the company should relate to its present **organisation structure**, the nature and **size** of its business and its plans for **future expansion**.

1.5 The invitation should also give details of such general matters as:

- **contact** within company
- any overall **financial constraints**
- **form** that submissions are to take
- **closing date** for submission of tenders
- **address** to which tenders should be sent

1.6 **Responses** to an invitation to tender may vary from the sending of standard **brochures** and **price lists,** not tailored in any way to the organisation's needs, to offers to **visit** the organisation's site and provide a free **demonstration** of equipment and its capabilities.

Exam focus point
A question in **June 1995** asked about the contents of an ITT.

2   FINANCING METHODS

2.1 The financing decision can be an important consideration in the choice of hardware or software. Failure to make the right choice can lead to serious consequences financially and operationally.

2.2 There are various financing options.

- Purchase
- Leasing
- Rental

A fourth option is to pay someone else for the use of their hardware and software. Outsourcing, or facilities management is covered in Chapter 6.

Exam focus point
Questions in **December 1994** and **June 1995** asked about financing methods.

Purchase

2.3 An outright purchase may be funded from one of three sources.

- **Cash or working capital** from within the organisation
- A new **loan** or other borrowing
- **Credit** from a finance house, in the form of a **hire-purchase** agreement.

2.4 It is arguable particularly that **PCs** give a **good return on investment**, in that old PCs can still perform useful work in an office environment, even though they are not 'state of the art'. PCs can still be used long after they are fully depreciated.

2.5 Purchase of more expensive equipment may involve a **gamble on second-hand values** (perhaps better left to leasing companies) and will create a **drain on liquidity** or **increase gearing**. A **depreciation charge** will also need to be posted, and this may be substantial.

2.6 Important matters related to **software** support, maintenance and warranties can be dealt with in the purchase arrangement. It is particularly important to establish when title passes, as the owner will be responsible for any risk of loss, and so **insurance cover** should not be neglected.

Leasing

2.7 A leasing arrangement means that the lessee uses the equipment for a defined period of time, for the payment of a fee to the lessor. It **remains the property of the lessor**, usually a specialist leasing company which has purchased the equipment from the manufacturer. A typical lease agreement may be five, seven or ten years in length, certain agreements recently offering the user an opportunity to 'upgrade' at various points, albeit with the imposition of higher interest charges.

2.8 In a so-called **finance lease** arrangement, in many cases you will pay the bulk of what you owe over the first few years of the lease. In effect you are **buying** the equipment over time, by repaying the value of the equipment to the lessor. For practical purposes, the assets are the possessions of lessees, although the lessor retains title to them. However you generally pay the capital cost of the equipment to the lessor.

2.9 **Operating leases** are much simpler **rental** arrangements, usually for a short term. The lessor (ie the owner of the equipment) does not expect to recover the capital cost of the equipment. In effect you are paying a rent. They tend to offer extra benefits over finance leases, and might be **more flexible**. Many offer **upgrading** facilities.

2.10 Finance and operating leases do have an effect on the reporting of a company's profits and the **published financial statements** and require comprehensive disclosure.

2.11 Compared with purchasing, leasing has the following features.

(a) **Payment spread over time**, rather than required 'up-front' in one lump sum. This is kinder, in the short term, to cash flow.

(b) **Maintenance costs**, and the costs of rectifying faulty equipment are generally **included** under operating leases.

(c) The **interest** payment on a lease is **fixed** in advance. This might be a disadvantage if interest rates are falling, so making bank loans or overdrafts cheaper.

(d) The lessor owns the asset, and can **repossess** it if payments are not made. As they own the equipment.

(e) A lessor's **criteria for lending** may be less strict than other lenders.

(f) An operating lease may permit the lessee to **terminate the contract**, which might be useful when changes in software require more powerful equipment.

Renting

2.12 Renting usually involves a **fixed charge** payable over a set period, perhaps five years. Renting is **relatively expensive** and there is **no ownership** of the equipment at any stage. However, this latter point may well be seen as an advantage.

2.13 Other advantages are that rental payments are simply charged against profit as incurred and allow **certainty** in financial planning, and obsolescence is not a concern.

2.14 Compared with leasing, renting has the following features.

(a) It is likely to be **more expensive**.

(b) **Maintenance** is more likely to need to be arranged **separately** under a leasing agreement.

(c) **Accounting** requirements are simpler.

(d) There is **less risk of being tied** into a long agreement with out-of-date equipment as technology changes.

2.15 In all cases, however, it is necessary to carry out a sensible **costing exercise** (eg using discounted cash flow techniques), and to **read the small print** of the contract.

3 EVALUATION OF VENDOR PROPOSALS

3.1 Once vendor proposals have been obtained, they must be evaluated. Evaluation becomes very complicated if there is any doubt about system's **performance**, as this may necessitate a **test of the system**. The variety of responses may make a direct **comparison** of different tenders difficult.

3.2 The vendor will usually try to match the customer's profile with that of an **existing customer** to demonstrate that the system can handle such a workload. However, if the application is unusual or new, this will not be possible, and so a formal evaluation using **benchmarking** or **simulation tests** will be necessary.

Benchmark tests

3.3 Since there are several factors involved in measuring a computer's power, it is not an easy job to **compare the power** of one machine against the power of another similar machine, made perhaps by a rival manufacturer.

3.4 One way of comparing power is to conduct **benchmark tests**.

KEY TERM

Benchmark tests test how long it takes a machine to run through a particular set of programs. More powerful machines will do the processing more quickly.

3.5 There is some concern that some benchmark tests created by **manufacturers** are designed to give the most **favourable** result to their products. Also, it may be hard to say that one computer performs better than another, as it may depend on the **application** used.

3.6   Benchmark tests are carried out to compare the performance of a piece of hardware or software against **pre-set criteria**. Typical criteria which may be used as benchmarks include **speed of performance** of a particular operation, acceptable volumes before a degradation in **response times** is apparent and the general **user-friendliness** of equipment. Benchmarks do not have to be objective, though clearly with subjective tests, such as user-friendliness, it may be harder to reach definitive conclusions.

Case example: Winstone 97

Winstone 97 is Ziff Davis' benchmark suite for PCs running Windows 95 or NT. Winstone 97 measures overall PC performance by running commercially available Windows applications and performing the kind of tasks that are carried out in everyday use.

The applications used are selected on the basis of market research into which applications are most commonly used in the real world. In Business Winstone 97, these include Adobe PageMaker 6.0, CorelDraw 6.0, Microsoft PowerPoint 7.0, Borland Paradox 7.0, Microsoft Access 7.0, Microsoft Word 7.0, Microsoft Excel 7.0 and Lotus Word Pro 96.

Winstone 97 comes up with an overall system performance figure by timing how long a PC takes to complete a set of real-world tasks for each of the applications. The tests are then compared to timings of tests on a basic reference machine, a Gateway 2000 PC with 16 Mb Ram and a 66Mhz 486 DX2 processor, running at a screen resolution of 1024×768 pixels.

The relative scores are used to calculate a weighted average score for each category, which are used to calculate a harmonic weighted average mean for the overall Winstone 97 score. Bigger scores are better; a machine with a score of 20.0 is twice as fast as one that scores 10.0

3.7   **Software** can, of course, also be benchmarked. In this case the organisation might try out a series of different packages on its own existing hardware to see which performed the best according to various predefined criteria such as **speed** of response, ability to process different **volumes** of transactions, **reporting** capabilities and so on.

Simulation tests

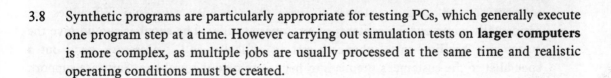

KEY TERM

Simulation testing uses *synthetic programs* written specifically for testing purposes and incorporating routines designed to test a variety of situations.

3.8   Synthetic programs are particularly appropriate for testing PCs, which generally execute one program step at a time. However carrying out simulation tests on **larger computers** is more complex, as multiple jobs are usually processed at the same time and realistic operating conditions must be created.

Other factors

3.9   Once the performance of the system has been evaluated, the acquiring organisation should consider other features of the proposal.

Supplier reliability

3.10   Reliability of suppliers should be considered in terms of **financial stability** (their help with the system they provide may be needed for many years to come), and **track record**.

3.11   If the supplier is a **major world player** such as Microsoft or Dell then there need be little doubt as to their reliability.

3.12   Suppliers of more specialised software or equipment may be much **smaller** and their products are necessarily **less well tested** because they have a much smaller number of users. If the buyer is asking for a unique item, it is the **only** guinea pig.

Cost

3.13   Cost is obviously an important factor. By **shopping around**, a customer might be able to negotiate quite a large **discount** on the price from a supplier.

Utility software

3.14   A hardware supplier should supply a range of utility software and software tools with the hardware. It might be worth checking what these are, and whether they vary between different suppliers.

Warranty and maintenance

3.15   All hardware comes with a warranty, but the **warranty period** might vary from just a few months to well over a year. One year is quite a common warranty period. Obviously, the longer the better.

3.16   As part of the warranty cover, there will be arrangements for **maintenance** in the event of a breakdown. The terms of the maintenance support can be important.

   (a)   They will specify **how quickly** the supplier promises to have a repair engineer out to visit the customer.

   (b)   If the hardware has to be taken away for repair, the supplier might promise to provide **back-up** - eg a replacement PC to stand in for the one being repaired.

3.17   The customer might want a maintenance contract **after** the warranty period expires. Will the supplier sign a maintenance contract? If so, what would the contract **cost** the customer, and what would be the other **terms**?

Software support

3.18   In a similar way to hardware maintenance, a software vendor should be prepared to offer software support to the customer, in case the customer runs into difficulties (eg accidentally wipes out the contents of an important file). The supplier should give the customer a 'hot-line' to telephone in case of difficulty, and if necessary, **send out a specialist** to the customer's premises to help to resolve the problem. Software support, like hardware maintenance support, might be 'free' for a short time, and then be provided at a cost. There is more on this in **Chapter 18.**

Training

3.19   Another element in the purchase deal could be **training** of the customer's staff. There might be an agreement by the supplier to provide training for a specified number of the customer's employees (probably on the supplier's own premises unless the customer is buying a mainframe or a large software system) for a specified period of time.

   (a)   **How many** will be trained?
   (b)   **How long** will they be trained for?

Keeping the package up-to-date

3.20 New improved versions of popular software packages are frequently brought on to the market. Occasionally, errors in existing packages are discovered and corrected. The vendor proposal for a software package should specify what **arrangements** there will be, if any, for the software supplier to provide the customer with any **changes or enhancements** to the software as they occur.

Key factors

3.21 The company might identify a number of **key factors** such as cost, security, support available and so on and **weight them** in order of importance.

3.22 Thus if **cost** were a factor a ideal score might be 100 and different tenders might score 60, 90 or 130 (or whatever), depending on how their cost compared to the ideal (130 would be cheaper than anticipated); if **security** were an issue an ideal might be 50 ('totally secure') in which case it is unlikely that a maximum ideal score would be achieved by any of the tenders.

3.23 The tender with the **highest overall score** would then be the first candidate for consideration, although there would no doubt still be certain qualitative issues to be taken into account.

4   CHOOSING HARDWARE AND SOFTWARE

Hardware

4.1 In general terms, the choice of computer hardware will depend on the following factors.

Factor	Comment
User requirements	The ease with which the computer configuration fits in with the *user's requirements* (eg direct access facilities, hard-copy output in given quantities).
Power	The *power* of the computer must be sufficient for current and foreseeable requirements. This is measured by: • Processor type (Pentium, Pentium II etc) • RAM in Mb • Clock speed in MHz • Hard disk size in Mb or Gb
Reliability	There should be a low expected 'break-down' rate. There should be back-up facilities, and in the case of a microcomputer, this might mean being able to resort temporarily back to a manual system when the computer is down.
Simplicity	Simple systems are probably best for small organisations.
Ease of communication	The system (hardware and software) should be able to communicate well with the user. Software is referred to as 'user-friendly' or 'user-unfriendly' but similar considerations apply to hardware (eg not all terminals are of standard screen size; the number and accessibility of terminals might also have a bearing on how well the user is able to put data into the computer or extract information).

Factor	Comment
Flexibility	The hardware should be able to meet new requirements as they emerge. More powerful CPUs tend to be more flexible.
Security	Keeping out 'hackers' and other unauthorised users is easier with more powerful systems, although security can be a major problem for any computer system.
Cost	
Changeover	Whether the choice of hardware will help with a smooth *changeover* from the old to the new system.
Networking	*Networking* capacity, if a PC has been purchased.
Software	The hardware must obviously be capable of running whatever software has been chosen.

Software

4.2   There is a long checklist of points to consider when choosing a suitable package.

Factor	Comment
User requirements	Does the package fit the user's particular *requirements*? This should cover such matters as report production, anticipated volume of data, data validation routines and any omissions which the user might compromise on.
	If the package requires substantial changes to the user's *organisation*, it might be rejected as unacceptable. The package should ideally be suited to the user and the user might rightly object to having to adjust his organisation to the dictates of the software.
Processing times	Are the *processing times* fast enough? If response times to enquiries, for example, are fairly slow, the user might consider the package unacceptable because of the time wastage.
Documentation	Is there full and clear *documentation* for the user? User manuals can be full of jargon and hard for a non-technical person to understand. They shouldn't be.
User-friendliness	Is the package easy to use? Is the software *user friendly* with menus and clear on-screen prompts for the keyboard operator? A user-friendly package will provide prompts and will be menu-driven, giving the operator a clear choice of what to do next. Some packages also provide extensive on-screen 'help' facilities for when the operator runs into difficulties and doesn't know what to do next.
Controls	What *controls* are included in the package (eg passwords, data validation checks, spelling checks, standard accounting controls and reconciliations, an audit trail facility etc)?
Up-to-dateness	How will the package be kept *up-to-date*? (eg what if a fault is discovered in the program by the software manufacturer? In an accounting package, what if the rate of VAT alters? etc).

Factor	Comment
Modification	Can the package be *modified* by the user - eg allowing the user to insert amendments to the format of reports or screen displays etc? Or will the software supplier agree to write a few tailor-made amendments to the software?
Other users	How many *other users* have bought the package, and how long has it been on the market? New packages might offer enhanced facilities, whereas well-established (but regularly updated) packages are more likely to be error-free.
Compatibility	Will the package *run* on the user's computer? Will additional peripheral equipment have to be bought - eg does the package need more hard disk space than is available?
	Also, does the software use file formats, field lengths and so on that are compatible with existing systems that will remain in use?
Support and maintenance	What *support* and *maintenance* service will the software supplier provide, in the event that the user has difficulty with the package?
Cost	*Comparative costs* of different packages should be a low priority. Off-the-shelf packages are fairly cheap on the whole, and a company should really buy what it needs for efficient operations rather than the least-cost package available. The savings in purchase price would not be worth the trouble caused by trying to use an unsuitable package for a business application. However, the package must not cost so much that the costs are greater than the benefits of having it.

Bespoke or off-the-shelf?

4.3 A key question regarding software is whether to develop a system specially or buy what is already available.

> **KEY TERM**
>
> A **bespoke package** is one designed and written either 'in-house' by the IS department or externally by a software house.
>
> An **off-the shelf package** is one like Microsoft Word or Sage Sterling, that is sold to lots of users and intended to handle the most common user requirements.

Bespoke software

4.4 **Advantages** of having software specially written include the following.

(a) The company **owns** the software and may be able to **sell it** to other potential users.

(b) Alternatively, the company may be able to do things with its software that **competitors** cannot do with theirs. In other words it is a source of competitive advantage.

(c) The software will be able to **do everything** that the company requires it to do, both now and (with further enhancements in the face of changing business needs) in the future.

4.5   However, only **large organisations** are likely to have sufficiently complex processing requirements to justify employing full time computer programmers. Key **disadvantages** are as follows.

   (a)   The software may **not work** at all.

   (b)   There may be a **long delay** before the software is ready.

   (c)   The **cost** is considerable, compared with a ready-made package (the latter can be sold to lots of different users, not just one).

Exam focus point

A question in the **December 1997** exam painted a scenario in which there was a proposal to develop a bespoke system using COBOL (a programming language: see Chapter 14). The advantage in the context of the question was that the in-house team had experience of COBOL already. The disadvantages were that development in COBOL is slower than more modern methods and lends itself far less easily to Windows-like user interfaces.

Off-the shelf packages

4.6   The **advantages** of using an off-the-shelf package as opposed to designing a system from scratch are as follows.

   (a)   It is **available now** and ready for use.

   (b)   It is almost certainly **cheaper** than a specially commissioned product because it is 'mass-produced', and there is no need for specialist in-house staff..

   (c)   It should have been written by software specialists and so should be of a **high quality**.

   (d)   A successful package will be **continually updated** by the software manufacturer, and so the version that a customer buys should be up-to-date.

   (e)   **Other users** will have used the package already, and a well established package should be **error-free** and well-suited to the general needs of users.

   (f)   Good packages are **well-documented**, with easy to follow user manuals. Good documentation is a key feature of successful software development.

   (g)   Some standard packages can be **customised** to the user's specific needs (but see below).

4.7   The **disadvantages** of ready-made packages are as follows.

   (a)   The computer user gets a **standardised solution** to a data processing task. A standard solution may not be well suited to the individual user's particular needs.

   (b)   The user is **dependent on the supplier** for maintenance of the package - ie updating the package, providing assistance in the event of problems for the user or even program errors cropping up. This is especially true if the general package is tailored in any way.

   (c)   Competitors may well use the same package and so there is **no competitive edge** from having a system that can do something that other systems don't allow competitors to do.

Customised versions of standard packages

4.8   Standard packages can be **customised** so that they fit an organisation's specific requirements. This can either be done by **purchasing the source code** of the package and making modifications in-house or by paying the maker of the package to customise it.

4.9   **Advantages** of customisation are similar to those of producing a bespoke system, with the additional advantages that:

(a)   development time should be much **quicker**, given that most of the system will be written already;

(b)   if the work is done in-house the organisation gains considerable **knowledge of how the software works** and may be able to 'tune' it so that it works more efficiently with the company's hardware.

4.10   **Disadvantages** of customising a standard package include the following.

(a)   It may prove more **costly** than expected, because **new** versions of the standard package will **also** have to be customised. For instance upgrades to Sage Sterling, the most popular off-the-shelf package for small and medium sized businesses in the UK, are released at least twice a year. Each new version would have to be customised, too.

(b)   Customisation may **delay delivery** of the software.

(c)   Customisation may introduce **bugs** that do not exist in the standard version.

(d)   If done **in-house**, the in-house team may have to **learn new skills**.

(e)   If done by the **original manufacturer** disadvantages such as those for off-the-shelf packages may arise.

Add-ons and programming tools

4.11   Two other ways of trying to give a computer user more flexibility with packages are:

(a)   the sale of **'add-ons'** to a basic package, which the user can buy if they suit his particular needs;

(b)   the provision of **programming tools**, such as fourth generation languages, with a package, which allows a computer user to write his own amendments to the package software (without having to be a programming expert).

> **Exam focus point**
> The question of whether to buy bespoke or off-the-shelf software has featured several times in exam questions. It featured in the **Pilot Case Study**, where it was necessary to decide what the best option was in a specific scenario, and also in questions in **June 1996**, and **December 1997**.

5   SOFTWARE CONTRACTS

5.1   We have already mentioned many of the matters that might typically be included in a software contract, such as the following.

•   **Cost** and what it does and does not include

•   **Duration**

- **Warranty** terms

- **Support** available

- Arrangements for **upgrades**

- **Maintenance** arrangements (software maintenance is discussed in more detail in Chapter 18)

5.2   If the software is being **specially written** there are likely to will be clauses about when the software is to be **delivered**, and who has **ownership** of the software and its source code once it has been delivered. **Performance criteria** (what the software will and will not do, how fast, for how many users etc) may also be specified.

5.3   Packaged software generally has a **licence,** the terms of which users are deemed to have agreed to the moment the package is unwrapped or a seal is broken.

5.4   A licence typically covers matters such as:

- **how many people** can install the software on their computer

- whether the software can be **copied**

- whether it can be **modified** without the manufacturer's consent

- in what circumstances the licence is **terminated**

- a limitation of **liability** (the writer of an accounting package, for instance, does not wish to be held liable if a user commits a computer fraud)

- the obligation to correct errors or **bugs** if they exist

Have you broken the law?

5.5   Shown below is a typical licence for an off-the-shelf package. **There is no need to sit down and learn this** (!), but if you have ever installed a software package yourself you have almost certainly agreed to abide by such a licence, so it will certainly not hurt you to read one now. See how many of the items noted above you can spot.

Case example: Licence for off-the-shelf package

1.   **PROGRAM & LICENCE**

(i)   The "Program" means the licensed software programs as stored on the computer disks or compact disks included in this box.

(ii)   This Licence permits you to install the Program on a single personal computer (or single network, where you have purchased this version) and install data onto the Program for a single set of data at any one time (unless, and to the extent that, you have purchased the relevant licence for multiple users and/or multiple sets of data from X Co Ltd), whether for a company, partnership, group, person or otherwise, in the course of which you may make one copy of the Program in any computer readable format for back-up purposes. The copyright design right and any other intellectual property rights in the source and object codes of this Program vest exclusively in X Co Ltd ("X Co Ltd").

(iii)   The Program may not be copied without the express consent in writing of X Co Ltd under such terms as it shall determine. In particular, the Program shall not be installed onto any additional network (where you have purchased such version) or onto any additional personal computer including any lap-top or portable computer without an additional user licence, available at separate cost from X Co Ltd.

(iv)   THIS LICENCE IS PERSONAL TO YOU. YOU MAY NOT TRANSFER OR PART WITH POSSESSION OF THE PROGRAMS OR SEEK TO SUB-LICENSE OR ASSIGN THIS LICENCE OR YOUR RIGHTS UNDER IT.

YOU MUST NOT MODIFY OR MERGE (EXCEPT BY A X CO LTD APPROVED DEALER, OR OTHERWISE WITH THE WRITTEN CONSENT OF X CO LTD), REVERSE ENGINEER OR DECOMPILE THE PROGRAM. YOU MUST NOT COPY THE PROGRAM EXCEPT AS EXPRESSLY PROVIDED IN (II) ABOVE. ANY BREACH OF THIS SUB-CLAUSE (IV) WILL AUTOMATICALLY TERMINATE YOUR LICENCE.

(v)   X CO LTD DOES NOT WARRANT OR GUARANTEE THAT THE PROGRAM PERFORMS ANY PARTICULAR FUNCTION OR OPERATION WHICH MAY BE SUITABLE FOR YOUR REQUIREMENTS OTHER THAN MAY BE DISCLOSED IN RELEVANT DOCUMENTATION PUBLISHED BY X CO LTD.

2.   TERMINATION

(i)   X Co Ltd may at its sole and absolute discretion terminate the Licence, in which event X Co Ltd shall refund to you the cost of the Program.

(ii)   This Licence may be terminated by X Co Ltd without refund if you fail to make payment after 7 days notice of any sums due to X Co Ltd under this or any other contract with X Co Ltd.

(iii)   Within 14 days of termination of this Licence, you will return to X Co Ltd the original and all copies and part copies of the Program or furnish to X Co Ltd a letter attesting to the destruction of the original and any copies. You may terminate this Licence at any time by returning all copies or furnishing such confirmation.

3.   DISCLAIMER OF WARRANTY

(i)   X Co Ltd makes no warranties with respect to the Program other than to guarantee the original disk(s) against faulty materials or workmanship for the relevant FREE X CO LTD MAINTENANCE period as is shown on your Program's X CO LTD MAINTENANCE registration form from the date on which you register the Licence by telephoning X Co Ltd, provided that registration is made within fourteen days of receiving the Program and that upon the date you receive the Program the said disk(s) is/are immediately backed up as instructed in the documentation included with the Program.

(ii)   During that FREE X CO LTD MAINTENANCE period, X Co Ltd will provide during business hours telephone technical advice assistance and support and/or replace any Program not meeting the above guarantee. In the event of any errors in the Program, X Co Ltd may at its sole discretion correct the same by "patching" or by new versions. Should X Co Ltd be unable to rectify any defect in the Program, X Co Ltd shall terminate this Licence by refunding your money together with the cost of postage after receipt of the Program and any copy from yourself. X Co Ltd does not warrant or guarantee you uninterrupted or error free service.

(iii)   THE ABOVE WARRANTY EXCLUDES DEFECTS CAUSED BY ACCIDENTS, ABUSE, POOR STORAGE OR HANDLING OR ANY ACT REFERRED TO IN SUB-CLAUSE 1(iv) ABOVE.

(iv)   X CO LTD RESERVES THE RIGHT TO WITHHOLD SUPPORT UNDER YOUR FREE X CO LTD MAINTENANCE WHERE PROGRAMS HAVE BEEN MODIFIED OR MERGED BY PERSONS OTHER THAN X CO LTD, NOTWITHSTANDING THAT SUCH PERSONS MAY BE X CO LTD APPROVED DEALERS.

4.   LIMITATION OF LIABILITY

(i)   EXCEPT AS PROVIDED ABOVE, OR AS EXPRESSED BY STATUTE TO BE INCAPABLE OF EXCLUSION OR LIMITATION, NO OTHER REPRESENTATIONS, WARRANTIES, CONDITIONS AND GUARANTEES, EXPRESS OR IMPLIED, INCLUDING BUT NOT LIMITED TO THE IMPLIED WARRANTIES OF FITNESS FOR PURPOSE AND SATISFACTORY QUALITY, ARE MADE WITH RESPECT TO THE PROGRAM BY X CO LTD.

(ii)   X CO LTD SHALL NOT BE LIABLE FOR ANY DIRECT INDIRECT OR CONSEQUENTIAL LOSS DAMAGE OR EXPENSE (INCLUDING BUT NOT LIMITED TO LOSS OF DATA, USE, SAVINGS OR PROFITS) SUFFERED OR ARISING IN ANY MANNER WHATSOEVER OUT OF OR IN CONNECTION WITH THE USE OF THIS PROGRAM OR X Co Ltd's TERMINATION OF THIS LICENCE FOR ANY REASON WHATSOEVER.

(iii)   IN NO EVENT SHALL THE TOTAL LIABILITY OF X CO LTD (HOWSOEVER ARISING) UNDER THIS LICENCE EXCEED THE AMOUNT PAID BY YOU FOR THE PROGRAM.

5.   **GENERAL**

(i)   This Licence does not affect or prejudice your statutory rights nor seek to limit or restrict X Co Ltd's liability in negligence for death or personal injury. If any of the above provisions or portions thereof are invalid or unenforceable by any judicial or statutory authority, this shall not nullify the remaining provisions of this Licence which shall remain in full force and effect.

(ii)   ANY RE-SELLER, DISTRIBUTOR OR DEALER (INCLUDING ANY X CO LTD APPROVED DEALER) FROM WHOM YOU PURCHASED THE PROGRAM IS NOT APPOINTED OR AUTHORISED BY X CO LTD AS ITS SERVANT OR AGENT. Such persons have no authority (either express or implied) to enter into a contract or grant any licence or provide any representation, warranty, condition or guarantee with or to you on behalf of X Co Ltd, or thereby bind X Co Ltd. X Co Ltd cannot be responsible for any modifications or mergers made to the Program by such persons.

(iii)   Failure by X Co Ltd to enforce any of the terms and conditions of this Agreement shall not be construed as a waiver of its rights. X Co Ltd shall not be under liability to you in respect of any circumstance beyond its reasonable control.

(iv)   This Licence constitutes the entire agreement between the parties relating to the Program and its licensing, and shall be governed and construed in accordance with the laws of England and any dispute under this Agreement or the Program shall be submitted to the exclusive jurisdiction of the English Courts, save where X Co Ltd otherwise agree. No variation, amendment of or addition to this Licence shall be effective unless X Co Ltd's prior agreement in writing shall have been obtained. In the event that any provision of these Conditions are held to be void or unenforceable, that shall not affect the remaining provisions which shall remain in full force and effect.

Chapter roundup

- When acquiring hardware and software an organisation may issue an **invitation to tender** giving potential suppliers details about the proposed system.

- The main **financing methods** are outright purchase, leasing and renting, each of which have advantages and disadvantages.

- Suppliers' proposals need to be evaluated using **benchmark tests** and **simulation tests,** and also on the basis of factors such as **reliability**, **warranty**, **support** and **training**.

- **Choice of hardware** depends on factors such as user requirements, power, security and the software to be run.

- **Choice of software** depends on factors such as user requirements, user-friendliness, controls, compatibility and cost.

- A key question is whether software should be **specially written** (bespoke) or whether an **off-the-shelf** package will do.

- **Software contracts** include provisions relating to matters such as warranty, support and maintenance, ownership, liability and so on.

Quick quiz

1   What are the contents of a typical ITT? (see paras 1.3 - 1.5)

2   What are the features of leasing? (2.11)

3   How is a benchmark test conducted? (3.6)

4   What factors should be borne in mind when considering supplier reliability? (3.10 - 3.12)

5   List ten factors to consider when choosing hardware. (4.1)

6   List eleven factors to consider when choosing software. (4.2)

7   What are the advantages of an off-the-shelf package? (4.6)

8   What sort of matters are typically covered in a software licence? (5.4)

Question to try	Level	Marks	Time
9	Exam standard	15	27 mins

Chapter 9

SECURITY AND PRIVACY REQUIREMENTS

Chapter topic list	Syllabus reference
1 Security	3(a), 3(b), 4(c)
2 Physical threats	4(c)
3 Physical access control	4(c)
4 Privacy and data protection	3(b), 4(c)
5 The Computer Misuse Act	4(c)

Introduction

This chapter deals with **security** from the point of view of how the information systems **environment** may endanger it - essentially in the form of physical threats to data. (The way in which the **system itself** is operated also has security implications: these are covered in Part C of this Text.)

We also look at how information systems may **threaten** the environment - by abusing personal **privacy** rights - and at legislation to prevent this.

1   SECURITY

The responsibilities of ownership

1.1   If you own **something that you value** – a nice watch, say, or a pet dog – you **look after it**. You keep it somewhere safe, you regularly check to see that it is in good condition (wind it, feed it, take it to the jewellers or the vet if it is not well), and you **don't allow it to upset others** (tell them the wrong time, bleep or bark too loudly, or bite them).

1.2   **Information** is a valuable possession and it deserves similar care.

KEY TERM

Security, in information management terms, means the **protection of data** from accidental or deliberate threats which might cause unauthorised modification, disclosure or destruction of data, and the **protection of the information system** from the degradation or non-availability of services.

1.3   Security covers a wide managerial remit, as it refers to **technical** issues related to the computer system, psychological and **behavioural** factors in the organisation and its employees, and protection against the unpredictable occurrences of the **natural world**.

1.4   Security can be subdivided into a number of aspects.

(a)   **Prevention**. It is in practice impossible to prevent all threats cost-effectively.

(b)   **Detection**. Detection techniques are often combined with prevention techniques: a log can be maintained of unauthorised attempts to gain access to a computer system.

(c)   **Deterrence**. As an example, computer misuse by personnel can be made grounds for dismissal.

(d)   **Recovery procedures**. If the threat occurs, its consequences can be contained (for example checkpoint programs).

(e)   **Correction procedures**. These ensure the vulnerability is dealt with (for example, by instituting stricter controls).

(f)   **Threat avoidance**. This might mean changing the design of the system.

Exam focus point

The topic of **physical security** has been rather neglected by examiners in Paper 5 in recent years, and is possibly **overdue** to feature heavily in a question.

2   PHYSICAL THREATS

2.1   The **physical environment** quite obviously has a major effect on information system security, and so planning it properly is an important precondition of an adequate security plan.

Fire

2.2   Fire is the **most serious hazard** to computer systems. Destruction of data can be even more costly than the destruction of hardware.

2.3   A proper fire safety plan is an essential feature of security procedures, in order to prevent fire, detect fire and put out the fire. Fire safety includes:

(a)   **site preparation** (for example, appropriate building **materials**, fire doors);

(b)   **detection** (for example, **smoke detectors**);

(c)   **extinguishing** (for example, **sprinklers**);

(d)   training for staff in observing **fire safety procedures** (for example, **no smoking** in computer room).

Water

2.4   Water is a serious hazard. **Flooding** and water damage are often encountered following **firefighting** activities elsewhere in a building.

2.5   This problem can be countered by the use of **waterproof ceilings and floors** together with the provision of **adequate drainage**.

2.6   In some areas **flooding** is a natural risk, for example in parts of central London and many other towns and cities near rivers or coasts. **Basements** are therefore generally not regarded as appropriate sites for computer installation!

Weather

2.7 The weather may be a threat. Wind, rain and storms can all cause substantial **damage to buildings**. In certain areas the risks are greater, for example the risk of typhoons in parts of the Far East. Many organisations make heavy use of **prefabricated** and portable offices, which are particularly vulnerable.

2.8 **Cutbacks in maintenance** expenditure may lead to leaking roofs or dripping pipes, which can invite problems of this type, and maintenance should be kept up if at all possible.

Lightning

2.9 Lightning and electrical storms pose an additional threat, as they can play havoc with **power supplies**, causing power **failures** coupled with power **surges** as services are restored. Minute adjustments in power supplies may be enough to affect computer processing operations (characterised by lights which dim as the country's population turns on electric kettles following a popular television program).

2.10 One way of combating this is by the use of **uninterrupted (protected) power supplies.** This will protect equipment from fluctuations in the supply. Power failure can be protected against by the use of a **separate generator**.

Terrorist activity

2.11 The threat of bombs planted by **political terrorists** has beset UK organisations for many years. Other parts of the world such as the Middle East, central Europe and the US have been equally or worse afflicted. Political terrorism is the main risk, but there are also threats from groups such as **animal rights** activists and from individuals with **grudges.**

2.12 In some cases there is very little that an organisation can do: its buildings may just happen to **be in the wrong place** and bear the brunt of an attack aimed at another organisation or intended to cause general disruption.

2.13 There are some avoidance measures that should be taken, however.

(a) **Physical access** to buildings should be controlled (see the next section).

(b) Activities likely to give rise to terrorism such as **exploitation** of workers or **cruelty** to animals should be stopped.

(c) The organisation should consult with police and fire authorities about potential risks, and **co-operate** with their efforts to avoid them.

Accidental damage

2.14 **People** are a physical threat to computer installations because they are **careless and clumsy**: there can be few of us who have not at some time spilt a cup of coffee over a desk covered with papers, or tripped and fallen doing some damage to ourselves or to an item of office equipment.

2.15 Combating accidental damage is a matter of:

- sensible **attitudes** to office behaviour
- good office **layout**

Question 1

You are the financial controller of your organisation. The company is in the process of installing a mainframe computer, and because your department will be the primary user, you have been co-opted onto the project team with responsibility for systems installation. You have a meeting at which the office services manager will be present, and you realise that no-one has yet mentioned the risks of fire or flooding in the discussions about site selection. Make a note of the issues which you would like to raise under these headings.

Answer

(a) **Fire**. Fire security measures can usefully be categorised as preventative, detective and corrective. Preventative measures include siting of the computer in a building constructed of suitable materials and the use of a site which is not affected by the storage of inflammable materials (eg stationery, chemicals). Detective measures involve the use of smoke detectors. Corrective measures may include installation of a sprinkler system (water-based or possibly gas-based to avoid electrical problems), training of fire officers and good siting of exit signs and fire extinguishers.

(b) **Flooding**. Water damage may result from flooding or from fire recovery procedures. The golden rule is to avoid siting the computer in a basement.

3   PHYSICAL ACCESS CONTROL

3.1   Access control aims to prevent intruders getting near the computer equipment or storage media. Methods of controlling human access range from:

- **personnel** (security guards);
- **mechanical devices** (eg keys, whose issue is recorded);
- **electronic identification devices** (eg card-swipe systems).

3.2   Obviously, the best form of access control would be one which **recognised** individuals immediately, without the need for personnel, who can be assaulted, or cards, which can be stolen. However, machines which can identify a person's fingerprints or scan the pattern of a retina are too **expensive** for many organisations.

3.3   It may not be cost effective or convenient to have the same type of access controls around the whole building all of the time. Instead, the various **security requirements of different departments** should be estimated, and appropriate boundaries drawn. Some areas will be very restricted, whereas others will be relatively open.

3.4   Guidelines for security against physical threats which should be applied **within the office** are as follows.

(a) **Fireproof cabinets** should be used to store files, or **lockable metal boxes** for floppy disks. If files contain confidential data, they should be kept in a safe.

(b) Computers with **lockable keyboards** are sometimes used. Computer terminals should be **sited carefully**, to minimise the risk of unauthorised use.

(c) If computer printout is likely to include confidential data, it should be **shredded** before it is eventually thrown away after use.

(d) **Disks** should not be left lying around an office. They can get lost or stolen. More likely still, they can get damaged, by spilling **tea or coffee** over them, or allowing the disks to gather **dust**, which can make them unreadable.

(e) The computer's **environment** (humidity, temperature, dust) should be properly controlled. This is not so important with PC systems as for mainframes. Even so, the computer's environment, and the environment of the files, should **not be excessively hot**.

3.5   Measures that can be **designed** into programs such as **password controls** and automatic **back-up,** will be discussed in the **Systems Development** part of this text (Chapter 15).

PINs

3.6   In some systems, the user might have a special personal identification number, or PIN, which identifies him or her to the system. According to what the user's PIN is, the user will be **allowed** access to certain data and parts of the system, but **forbidden** access to other parts.

Door locks

3.7   Conventional door locks are of value in certain circumstances, particularly where users are only required to pass through the door a **couple of times a day**. If the number of people using the door increases and the frequency of use is high, it will be difficult to persuade staff to lock a door every time they pass through it.

3.8   If this approach is adopted, a 'good' lock must be accompanied by a **strong door,** otherwise an intruder may simply bypass the lock. Similarly, other points of entry into the room/complex must be as well protected, otherwise the intruder will simply use a **window** to gain access.

3.9   One difficulty with conventional locks is the matter of **key control**. Inevitably, each person authorised to use the door will have a key and there will also be a master key maintained by security. Cleaners and other contractors might be issued with keys. Practices such as lending out keys or taking duplicate keys may be difficult to prevent.

3.10   One approach to this is the installation of **combination locks,** where a numbered keypad is located outside the door and access allowed only after the correct 'code', or sequence of digits has been entered. This will only be fully effective if users keep the combination **secret** and the combination is **changed** frequently.

Card entry systems

3.11   There is a range of card entry systems available. This is a more sophisticated means of control than the use of locks, as **cards can be programmed** to allow access to certain parts of a building only, between certain times.

3.12   These allow a high degree of monitoring of staff movements; they can for example be used instead of clock cards to record details of time spent on site. Such cards can be incorporated into **identity cards**, which also carry the photograph and signature of the user and which must be 'displayed' at all times.

Computer theft

3.13   A problem which is related to the problem of physical access control is that of equipment theft. As computer equipment becomes **smaller** and **more portable**, it can be 'smuggled' out of buildings with greater ease. Indeed much equipment is specifically **designed for use off-site** (for example laptops, notebooks, handhelds, bubblejet printers) and so control is not simply a question of ensuring that all equipment stays on site.

3.14   A **log of all equipment** should be maintained. This may already exist in basic form as a part of the fixed asset register. The log should include the **make, model** and **serial number** of each item, together with some other organisation-generated code which identifies the **department** which owns the item, the **individual** responsible for the item and its **location**. Anyone taking any equipment off-site should book it out and book it back in.

3.15   Computer theft may be carried out by persons who have official access to equipment. It may equally be carried out by those who do not. **Burglar alarms** should be installed.

3.16   **Smaller items** of equipment, such as laptop computers and floppy disks, should always be **locked securely away**. Larger items cannot be moved with ease and one approach adopted is the use of **bolts** to secure them to desks. This discourages 'opportunity' thieves. Larger organisations may also employ site security guards and install closed circuit camera systems.

Question 2

You are the chief accountant at your company. Your department, located in an open-plan office, has five networked desktop PCs, a laser printer and a dot matrix printer.

You have just read an article suggesting that the best form of security is to lock hardware away in fireproof cabinets, but you feel that this is impracticable. Make a note of any alternative security measures which you could adopt to protect the hardware.

Answer

(a)   'Postcode' all pieces of hardware. Invisible ink postcoding is popular, but visible marking is a better deterrent. Soldering irons are ideal for writing on plastic casing.

(b)   Mark the equipment in other ways. Some organisations spray their hardware with permanent paint, perhaps in a particular colour (bright red is popular) or using stencilled shapes.

(c)   Hardware can be bolted to desks. If bolts are passed through the desk and through the bottom of the hardware casing, the equipment can be rendered immobile.

(d)   Ensure that the organisation's standard security procedures (magnetic passes, keypad access to offices, signing in of visitors etc) are followed.

---

4   PRIVACY AND DATA PROTECTION

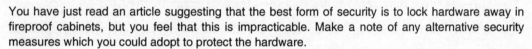

KEY TERM

Privacy is the right of the individual to control the user of information about him or her, including information on financial status, health and lifestyle (ie prevent unauthorised disclosure).

Why is privacy an important issue?

4.1   In recent years, there has been a growing popular fear that **information** about individuals which was stored on computer files and processed by computer could be **misused**.

4.2   In particular, it was felt that an individual could easily be harmed by the existence of computerised data about him or her which was inaccurate or misleading and which could be **transferred to unauthorised third parties** at high speed and little cost.

4.3   In the UK the legislation current at the time of preparation of this text is the **Data Protection Act 1984**. This is due to be replaced by the **Data Protection Act 1998**, which must become law by 24 October 1998, although the new requirements may be phased in over a longer period.

Exam focus point

The new Data Protection Act will **not be examinable** in December 1998 (because it will not pass into law before the ACCA deadline of 1 June 1998), but it will certainly **not harm your chances** if you mentioned some of the forthcoming changes (described later in this chapter) in any answer you may have to write about data protection issues.

It will be examinable from **June 1999** onwards.

The Data Protection Act 1984

4.4   The Data Protection Act 1984 is an attempt to protect the **individual**. The terms of the Act cover data about individuals - **not corporate bodies** - and data which is **processed mechanically**, ie by 'equipment operated automatically in response to the instructions given for that purpose'. This is important.

(a)   **Manual data records** are **excluded** from coverage by the Act.

(b)   Data records that are covered include data processed by any **equipment** which processes personal data automatically, not just computers.

Exam focus point

A question in the **December 1996** exam asked students to identify four basic principles of data protection (see the next page) but then to apply that knowledge and **explain their relevance** in a particular scenario and suggest some **controls** that the organisation described could put in place to ensure adherence to the principles. We shall return to the question of controls in Section C of this Text.

Note that the present examiner recognises that the **details** of UK legislation do not apply for overseas students, but the **reasoning** behind the legislation (people's rights and how they might be abused) are relevant no matter what country you live in.

Definitions of terms used in the Act

4.5   In order to understand the Act it is necessary to know some of the technical terms used in it.

KEY TERMS

Personal data is information about a living individual, including expressions of opinion about him or her. Data about other organisations (eg supplier or customer companies) is not personal data, unless it contains data about individuals who belong to those other organisations.

Data users are organisations or individuals who control the contents of files of personal data and the use of personal data which is processed (or intended to be processed) automatically - ie who use personal data which is covered by the terms of the Act.

A computer bureau is an organisation (or individual) which processes personal data for data users, or allows data users to process personal data on its equipment. An organisation or an individual may be classified as a computer bureau under the Act even though not actually in business as a computer bureau.

A data subject is an individual who is the subject of personal data.

The data protection principles

4.6 There are certain Data Protection Principles which registered data users must comply with.

DATA PROTECTION PRINCIPLES (1984 ACT)

Personal data held by data users

(1) The information to be contained in personal data shall be obtained, and personal data shall be processed, fairly and lawfully. Processing means amending, adding to, deleting or re- arranging the data, or extracting the information that forms the data.

(2) Personal data shall be held only for one or more specified (ie registered) and lawful purposes.

(3) Personal data held for any purpose or purposes shall not be used or disclosed in any manner incompatible with that purpose or those purposes.

(4) Personal data held for any purpose or purposes shall be adequate, relevant and not excessive in relation to that purpose or those purposes.

(5) Personal data shall be accurate and, where necessary, kept up to date. 'Accurate' means correct and not misleading as to any matter of fact. An opinion cannot be challenged on the grounds of inaccuracy and breach of the fifth Data Protection Principle.

(6) Personal data held for any purpose or purposes shall not be kept for longer than is necessary for that purpose or those purposes. Data users should therefore review their personal data regularly, and delete any data which no longer serves a purpose.

(7) An individual shall be entitled:

    (a) at reasonable intervals, and without undue delay or expense to be informed by any data user whether he holds personal data of which that individual is the subject and to access to any such data held by a data user; and

    (b) where appropriate, to have such data corrected or erased.

Personal data held by data users or in respect of which services are provided by persons carrying on computer bureaux

(8) Appropriate security measures shall be taken against unauthorised access to, or alteration, disclosure or destruction of, personal data and against accidental loss or destruction of personal data. The prime responsibility for creating and putting into practice a security policy rests with the data user.   *(Data Protection Act 1984)*

The coverage of the Act

4.7 Key points of the Act can be summarised as follows.

(a) With certain exceptions, all **data users** and all computer bureaux have had to **register** under the Act with the **Data Protection Registrar**.

(b) **Individuals** (data subjects) are awarded certain **legal rights**.

(c) **Data users** and computer bureaux must adhere to the **data protection principles**.

Registration under the Act

4.8 The Data Protection Registrar keeps a Register of all data users. Each entry in the Register relates to a data user or computer bureau. Unless a data user has an entry in the Register he may not hold personal data. Even if the data user is registered, he must only hold data and use data for the **purposes** which are registered. A data user must apply to be registered.

The rights of data subjects

4.9 The Act establishes the following rights for data subjects.

(a) A data subject may seek **compensation** through the courts for damage and any associated distress caused by the **loss**, **destruction** or **unauthorised disclosure** of data about himself or herself or by **inaccurate data** about himself or herself.

(b) A data subject may apply to the courts for **inaccurate data** to be **put right** or even **wiped off** the data user's files altogether. Such applications may also be made to the Registrar.

(c) A data subject may obtain **access** to personal data of which he is the subject. (This is known as the 'subject access' provision.) In other words, a data subject can ask to see his or her personal data that the data user is holding.

(d) A data subject can **sue** a data user (or bureau) for any **damage or distress** caused to him by personal data about him which is **incorrect** or **misleading** as to matter of **fact** (rather than opinion).

Case example

In July 1997 the Data Protection Registrar issued an enforcement notice to **British Gas Trading Limited**. The notice sought to restrain BGTL from using personal data held in connection with the supply of gas to domestic customers, or derived from that data, for the promotion of non-gas related products or services without the consent of customers. British Gas appealed against the notice to the **Data Protection Tribunal**, but lost the case in **May 1998**.

BGTL sent out a leaflet to existing customers inviting them to opt-out of disclosure of data. However, the tribunal took the view that it was **unfair** of BGTL to assume that those customers who **failed to respond** to the leaflet were silently consenting to disclosure of their personal data to other companies or to the use of their personal data for marketing non-energy related products or services.

The Data Protection Bill 1998

4.10 The Data Protection Act was brought in originally to bring the UK's laws into line with the minimum requirements laid down by the European Union (EU). In July 1995, however, the European Parliament adopted a new **Directive on Data Protection**, with two main purposes.

(a) To protect **individual privacy**. Current UK law only applies to **computer-based** information. The directive applies to **all personal data, in any form.**

(b) To **harmonise data protection legislation** so that, in the interests of improving the operation of the single European market, there can be a **free flow of personal data** between the member states of the EU.

The directive has wide implications. A new **Data Protection Bill** in the UK was issued in January 1998. A new Act must be in force by **24 October 1998**.

4.11 Some important features of the new legislation are likely to be as follows.

(a) It will spell out the **conditions under which processing is lawful**. This is not at all clear under the current Act.

(b) Everyone will have the right to go to court to seek redress for **any breach** of data protection law, rather than just for certain aspects of it, as at present.

(c) Filing systems that are structured so as to facilitate access to information about a particular person will fall within the legislation. This includes systems that are **paper-based** or on **microfilm** or **microfiche**. Personnel records, in particular, are likely to be caught by the Act in future.

(d) Processing of personal data will be **forbidden** except in the following circumstances.

   (i) With the **consent** of the subject. Consent cannot be implied: it must be by freely given, specific and informed agreement

   (ii) As a result of a **contractual arrangement**

   (iii) Because of a **legal obligation**

   (iv) To **protect the vital interests** of the subject

   (v) Where processing is in the **public interest**

   (vi) Where processing is required to exercise **official authority**

(e) The processing of 'sensitive data' is forbidden, unless express consent has been obtained or there are conflicting obligations under employment law. Sensitive data includes data relating to **racial origin, political opinions, religious beliefs**, physical or mental **health, sexual proclivities** and **trade union** membership.

(f) If data about a data subject is **obtained from a third party** the data subject will have to be given the following information.

   (i) The identity of the **controller** of the data
   (ii) The **purposes** for which the data are being processed
   (iii) **What data** will be disclosed and **to whom**
   (iv) The existence of a right of subject **access** to the data

(g) Data subjects will have a right not only to have a **copy of data** held about them but also the right to know **why** the data are being processed and **what is the logic** behind the processing.

DATA PROTECTION PRINCIPLES (1998 BILL)
Schedule 1 of the Bill contains the revised data protection principles.

1   Personal data shall be processed fairly and lawfully and, in particular, shall not be processed unless:

    (a)   at least one of the conditions in Schedule 2 is met (see item (d) above), and

    (b)   in the case of sensitive personal data, at least one of the conditions in Schedule 3 is also met (see item (e) above).

2   Personal data shall be obtained only for one or more specified and lawful purposes, and shall not be further processed in any manner incompatible with that purpose or those purposes.

3   Personal data shall be adequate, relevant and not excessive in relation to the purpose or purposes for which they are processed.

4   Personal data shall be accurate and, where necessary, kept up to date.

5   Personal data processed for any purpose or purposes shall not be kept for longer than is necessary for that purpose or those purposes.

6   Personal data shall be processed in accordance with the rights of data subjects under this Act.

7   Appropriate technical and organisational measures shall be taken against unauthorised or unlawful processing of personal data and against accidental loss or destruction of, or damage to, personal data.

8   Personal data shall not be transferred to a country or territory outside the European Economic Area unless that country or territory ensures an adequate level of protection for the rights and freedoms of data subjects in relation to the processing of personal data.

Question 3

(a)   Your MD has asked you to recommend measures that your company, which is based in the UK, could take *now* to prepare for changes in data protection legislation. Suggest what measures should be taken.

(b)   Watch the newspapers and the *ACCA Students' Newsletter* for details of further developments in data protection legislation.

Answer

(a)   Measures could include the following.

- Obtain consent from individuals to hold any sensitive personal data you need

- Supply individuals with a copy of any manual files you have about them if so requested

- Consider if you may need to obtain consent to process personal data, on computer, paper or microfiche

- Consider how you will be able to meet the notification requirements of the Directive in situations where you obtain personal data about individuals from third parties

(b)   This is an ongoing exercise, because the law is likely to change within the lifetime of this Study Text.

Protection of data

4.12   The *Copyright and Rights in Databases Regulations* 1997 came into force on 1 January 1998.

(a)   Databases are defined as a collection of independent works, data or other materials arranged in a systematic or methodical way and individually accessible by electronic or other means.

(b) Databases include literary, artistic and manual collections, and also other collections of data such as texts, sounds, images, numbers and facts. The 'protected' part is the headings or categories or structure of the database, not the information itself (which may be copyright works in their own right).

4.13 Most organisations operate databases that fall within these criteria (a list of customers would seem to fit the description), but usually such databases are for internal use only and so copyright will not be an issue. It only becomes an issue if the owner of the database tries to exploit it for profit.

4.14 On the other hand, it is increasingly likely that organisations will be opening up a database of some sort to the public because of the commercial need to have a presence on the Internet.

5   THE COMPUTER MISUSE ACT

5.1 The Computer Misuse Act 1990 was enacted to respond to the growing threat of hacking to computer systems and data. Hacking means obtaining unauthorised access, usually through telecommunications links (see Chapter 15).

Crime	Explanation
Unauthorised access	This means that a hacker, who, knowing he or she is unauthorised, tries to gain access to another computer system. It is the **attempt** which is the crime: the hacker's success or failure is irrelevant.
Unauthorised access with the **intention** of committing another offence	This results in **stricter penalties** than unauthorised access alone. However, it might be a suitable charge if a hacker had been caught in the early stages of a fraud.
Unauthorised **modification** of data or programs	In effect this makes the deliberate introduction of computer **viruses** into a system a criminal offence. However, this does not apply to the simple addition of data, just its corruption or destruction. Guilt is based on the **intention to impair** the operation of a computer or program, or prevent or **hinder access** to data.

Chapter roundup

- **Security** is the protection of data from accidental or deliberate threats and the protection of an information system from such threats.

- **Physical threats** to security may be natural or man made. They include fire, flooding, weather, lightning, terrorist activity and accidental damage.

- **Physical access control** attempts to stop **intruders** or other unauthorised persons getting near to computer equipment or storage media.

- Important aspects of physical access of control are **door locks** and **card entry systems**. Computer theft is becoming more prevalent as equipment becomes smaller and more portable. All computer equipment should be tagged and registered, and portable items should be logged in and out.

- **Privacy** is the right of the individual not to have information about him or her disclosed in an unauthorised manner.

- The **Data Protection Act 1984** is a piece of UK legislation which protects individuals about whom data is held on computer.

    o Data users must register with the Data Protection Registrar and announce the uses to which the data will be put.

    o The Act contains eight data protection principles, to which all data users must adhere.

- A **new Data Protection Act** must be passed in the UK by 24 October 1998. Amongst a number of significant changes this gives **new and extended rights** to individuals and covers **manual records** as well as computerised ones.

- The **Computer Misuse Act 1990** was enacted in the UK to respond to the growing threat to computer systems and data from hacking. While it cannot *prevent* hacking, it recognises a number of offences and provides certain punishments.

Quick quiz

1 List six aspects of security. (see para 1.4)

2 How can fire be guarded against? (2.3)

3 How can problems caused by lightning be combated? (2.10)

4 What physical threats exist besides fire? (2.4 - 2.15)

5 Why are door locks not necessarily an adequate means of controlling physical access? (3.7 - 3.10)

6 Define privacy. (4.1)

7 What is a data user? (4.5)

8 What are eight data protection principles? (4.6)

9 What are the two main purposes of the forthcoming UK legislation on Data Protection? (4.10)

10 What are the three crimes under the Computer Misuse Act? (5.1)

Question to try	Level	Marks	Time
10	Introductory	n/a	20 mins

Chapter 10

SYSTEMS OPERATION AND CONTROL

Chapter topic list	Syllabus reference
1 The role of the auditor	4(c), 5(d)
2 Auditing systems development	4(c), 5(d)
3 Personnel security planning	4(c), 5(d)
4 Disaster recovery strategies	4(c), 5(d)
5 Computer audit	4(c), 5(d)

Introduction

The final chapter in this Part of the text on the systems **environment** looks at a variety of controls over information systems that operate **independently** of the system itself. In particular this means the **people** whose job it is to ensure that systems are operating properly and the **issues** that they will be particularly interested in.

Auditing is covered in more depth in **Paper 6,** so if you are currently studying for that too, concentrate on sections 2, 3 and 4 of this chapter. **Section 2** is particularly important.

1   THE ROLE OF THE AUDITOR

External auditors

> **KEY TERM**
>
> An **external auditor** is an independent person brought in from outside an organisation to review the accounts prepared by management, or to review and report on some other aspect of the business.

1.1   Businesses that operate as companies with **limited liability** are required to produce accounts that indicate how successfully they are performing.

1.2   An independent examination or **audit** of the accounts is needed so that the **owners** of the business can assess how well **management** have discharged their stewardship.

1.3   An **independent** auditor is needed because there is often a **division of interests** between those who carry out the day-to-day management of the undertaking and those who provide the necessary finance but do not participate in management (shareholders).

1.4   The **external** auditor is from **outside** the enterprise, and certain statutory and professional rules seek to ensure his **independence**.

1.5   External auditors may also be engaged by an organisation to perform a range of other tasks. Examples are given below.

    (a)   Summaries of sales in support of a statement of **royalties** payable where goods are sold under licence.

    (b)   The **circulation** figures of a newspaper, for advertising purposes.

    (c)   **Investigations** into specific aspects of an organisation's operations, for example a systems breakdown or the results of a particular branch operation.

Internal auditors

> ### KEY TERM
>
> An **internal auditor** is an employee of an organisation whose function is to monitor and report on all aspects of the running of the company's operations.

1.6   The management of an organisation will wish to establish systems to ensure that business activities are carried out efficiently. They will institute clerical, administrative and financial **controls**.

1.7   **Internal audit** staff are an example of this kind of control.

1.8   Although some of the work carried out by internal auditors is similar to that performed by external auditors, there are important **distinctions** between the nature of the two functions.

External	Internal
Independent of the organisation	Responsible to the management
Responsibility fixed by statute	Responsibilities are decided by management
Reports to the members	Reports to the management (directors)
Primarily concerned to express an opinion on the truth and fairness of the accounts	Work ranges over many areas and activities, both operational and financial, as determined by management

> ### Exam focus point
>
> Naturally, these points are covered in much more depth in **Paper 6**. Auditing has not featured significantly in any Paper 5 question set under the new syllabus except as **background** to questions on other topics.
>
> A question in the original **Pilot Paper** asked what **controls** an internal auditor might be looking for. A question in **June 1994** asked about **documentation** that might be kept. Controls and documentation are covered elsewhere in this text.

Auditing and information systems

1.9   An **external auditor** needs to be assured that the computer and related systems function well enough to produce **financial statements** which can be relied on to be true and fair.

1.10 The **internal auditor** needs the same assurance, but for a **wide range of reasons** connected with the efficient running of the business.

1.11 Extensive guidelines on internal audit and computerised systems have been issued by the **Institute of Internal Auditors**. These are **not** part of the ACCA syllabus.

1.12 For external auditors the only relevant guideline is one issued in the early 1980s on the audit of computer based systems. This says that the auditor needs to check two sorts of controls: **general** controls; and **application** controls.

KEY TERM

General controls are controls, other than application controls which 'relate to the **environment** within which computer-based systems are **developed, maintained** and **operated** and are generally applicable to all the applications.'

General control area	Example of general controls
Environment	• Personnel **recruitment** policies
	• **Segregation of duties** between different types of job
	• Proper **training**
	• **Physical security** of hardware and software.
Development	• **Authorisation** procedures for development projects
	• Proper system **justification** in cost and operational terms.
	• Proper **control** over the actual process of system development, using various **project management** techniques.
	• Regular **review** of work on a project completed to date.
	• Use of a systems development **methodology**
	• Controls to ensure all systems are **tested** before implementation.
	• Controls over **changes** to systems (eg approval, documentation).
Maintenance	• Controls to ensure regular **reviews** of system **performance**,
	• **Authorisation** procedures for program **amendments** and **testing**.
Operation	• Basic **physical security** against natural disasters or thefts.
	• **Back-up** procedures
	• Controls over **access** to the system (eg passwords to log on).
	• Controls over **hardware** usage
	• **Segregation** of **program** files and **data** files.
	• Measures to prevent unauthorised access (eg by a **hacker**).
	• Controls to ensure that the computing **resources** are used **efficiently**.

KEY TERM

Application controls are those specific to each 'application' (ie to individual programs).

Application control	Example
Controls over **input**	Verification, batch control totals, validation and data vet routines, review of input data.
Controls over **processing**	Checkpoint programs, recovery procedures, file identification checks, regular review of master file data.
Controls over **output**	Distribution, actioning of error reports, maintenance of audit trail.
Controls over **data**	A coding system.

Exam focus point

You will cover the above in more depth for **Paper 6**. However the checklists above might be useful for **Paper 5** questions on **security and control in general**, whether or not the question specifically mentions auditing.

2   AUDITING SYSTEMS DEVELOPMENT

2.1   Because of the **time** spent on systems development, the **cost** of it, and the probable **complexity** and **volume of detail** involved, it is essential to lay down high standards of control over system design, development and testing.

2.2   This section considers the areas that internal and external auditors are likely to examine.

Systems development controls

2.3   Systems development controls have the following objectives.

(a)   To ensure that new computer systems are developed only if they appear to be **beneficial**. System justification should be on the grounds of favourable **cost benefit analysis** or other performance criteria.

(b)   To ensure that each system under development has **clear, specified objectives**.

(c)   To control the **scheduling** of development work.

(d)   To ensure that suitable **operational and administrative controls** are built into the system design when it is being developed.

(e)   To ensure that **users** acquire an understanding of the new system.

(f)   To ensure that the system is properly **tested**.

(g)   To establish a basis for **management review** of the system.

(h)   To ensure that systems and programs are **maintained** when the system goes operational.

(i)   To ensure that proper and complete **documentation** of the system is created and maintained.

2.4   One of the purposes of systems development **methodologies** is to exercise control over the development of systems. We shall look at methodologies in Part C of this Text.

Controls of costs, progress and system design amendments

2.5   Costs, progress and planning amendments must be reviewed at each phase of the development to ensure tight control.

2.6   Control of **costs** can be achieved in three ways, all of which should be used.

(a)   Control over system development costs, using **budgets** and **budgetary control variance reporting**. If actual development costs exceed the budget, the manager responsible for the over-spending will be required to take control action, or justify the higher spending to his superiors.

(b)   Monitoring **changes in the expected future costs and benefits** of the system. Costs already incurred in development work to date should be ignored, and the future development costs, expected system running costs and expected benefits should be the factors which determine whether it is worthwhile continuing with the system development.

(c)   The **post-implementation review** of a project should study the actual development costs, system running costs and system benefits, to determine:

(i)   whether the system is **currently justifiable**, or should be abandoned even at this late stage;

(ii)   whether the **original decision** to develop the system was a good one, with the benefit of hindsight;

(iii)   by how much actual costs and benefits **differed from expectation**, the reasons for these differences, and whether there are any lessons to be learned for the future.

2.7   Controls should be exercised over **amendments**, so that if any amendments are proposed which are not included in the system specification, they must be **authorised** at a suitable managerial level (for example by the steering committee) and the authorisation and details of the amendment should be included in the amendments section of the system **specification**.

Project management reporting stages

2.8   One of the important controls is that **senior management** on the steering committee or board of directors, and managers in the **user department**, are given the opportunity at several stages in the development work to satisfy themselves that the project is developing as required.

2.9   There are several formal reporting stages, which you might like to compare with the stages of the **systems development life cycle**.

- Initial project selection
- Feasibility study report
- Analysis and design
- Completion of system tests and acceptance tests
- Post-implementation review

2.10   The **authorisation** of each stage in development must be **documented**.

(a)   The authorisation of the feasibility study recommendation should be recorded in the **minutes** of the meeting of the steering committee and/or board of directors where the authorisation is given.

(b) **Users** formally authorise the specification of requirements.

(c) The authorisation of the system specification is recorded in the **specification** itself.

Structured walkthroughs

KEY TERM

Structured walkthroughs are a technique used by those responsible for the design of some aspect of a system (particularly analysts and programmers) to present their design to interested user groups. Structured walkthroughs are formal meetings, in which the documentation produced during development is reviewed and checked for errors or omissions.

2.11 These presentations are used both to **introduce and explain** the new systems to users and also to offer the users the opportunity of making **constructive criticism** of the proposed systems, and suggestions for further **amendments/improvements**, before the final systems specification is agreed.

2.12 **Users** are involved in structured walkthroughs because their knowledge of the desired system is more extensive than that of the systems development personnel. Walkthroughs are sometimes referred to as **user validation**.

The importance of signing off work

2.13 At the end of **each stage** of development, the resulting output is presented to users for their approval. There must be a **formal sign-off** of each completed stage before work on the next stage begins.

2.14 This **minimises reworking**, as if work does not meet user requirements, only the immediately preceding stage must be revisited. More importantly, it clarifies responsibilities and leaves little room for later **disputes**.

(a) If the **systems developers fail** to deliver something that both parties formally agreed to, it is the developers' responsibility to put it right, at their own expense, and compensate the user for the delay.

(b) If **users ask for something extra or different**, that was not formally agreed to, the developers cannot be blamed and the user must pay for further amendments and be prepared to accept some delay.

Exam focus point

This point about signing off is an important one that has been examined in a number of contexts.

Personnel involved in structured walkthroughs

2.15 Although the number and types of staff who attend a walkthrough may change, there are several **roles** which have become fairly standardised.

(a) **Chairperson**

The chairperson will control the **overall direction** of the walkthrough, ensuring that the agenda is adhered to.

He or she will also have **overall responsibility for administrative matters** such as inviting various representatives to the meeting.

The chairperson needs to be highly **technically competent** and thoroughly familiar with the particular **project** and the business's **requirements**.

The chairperson is also likely to responsible for formally **signing off** the project.

(b) **Author**

The author is the person who has **created** the system under discussion.

The role of the author is to **present and explain** the material which is being walked through.

(c) **Recorder**

The **recorder** ensures that all agreed action points are noted and follows them up. The author might fulfil this role.

(d) **User representatives**

Users will obviously be present because their **knowledge of the desired system** is more extensive than that of the systems development personnel.

Their chief responsibility is to **approve** the system when they are satisfied that they **understand** it and that it **will do what they want it to do**.

Users will include not only people who will actually be **operators** of the system in their day-to-day work, but also those interested its output, such as **internal or external auditors**, and **senior management** who will want to ensure that their organisation's money is being well spent, and that **their** information needs will be met.

(e) **Reviewers**

These people get an **advance working model** of the material being walked through (or detailed **documentation** of the system that is about to be built) and their role, in essence, is to try and break it!

They are expected to have worked through the proposed system, checking it against a **list of criteria** and noting any respects in which it is likely to **fall short** of the required quality.

Reviews will be completed and passed to those leading the meeting (notably the author and chairperson) in advance of the actual meeting, but reviewers will also attend the meeting, in case any points need **clarification**, and to learn about how the problems they identified are going to be **dealt with** (as a basis for their *next* review).

Question 1

What, besides identification of mistakes (errors, omission, inconsistencies etc), would you expect the benefits of a walkthrough to be?

Answer

(a) Users become involved in the systems analysis process. Since this process is a critical appraisal of their work, they should have the opportunity to provide feedback on the appraisal itself.

(b) The output from the development is shown to people who are not systems development personnel. This encourages its originators to prepare it to a higher quality and in user-friendly form.

(c) Because the onus is on users to approve design, they are more likely to become committed to the new system and less likely to 'rubbish' it.

(d) The process focuses on quality of and good practice in operations generally.

(e) It avoids disputes about who is responsible for what.

3   PERSONNEL SECURITY PLANNING

3.1   The establishment and maintenance of a security framework should be made the responsibility of a **security officer,** who should be a member of the senior management team.

3.2   The role of a computer security officer is less concerned with investigation and more with **prevention**. The officer will be responsible for creating and monitoring a secure computing environment.

(a) Employees should be made aware, and reminded at regular intervals, of their **responsibilities.**

(b) Employees should realise that the environment is conducive to **fraud detection** and that any perpetrator is likely to be discovered.

Personnel

3.3   Certain employees will always be placed in a **position of trust,** for example senior systems analysts, the database administrator and the computer security officer.

3.4   If they wish to, such individuals can compromise the security of the organisation.

3.5   The types of measure which can be used to control these people as follows.

- Careful recruitment
- Job rotation
- Supervision and observation by a superior
- Review of computer usage (for example via systems logs)
- Enforced vacations

3.6   The key is that security should depend on the **minimum** possible number of personnel; although this is a weakness, it is also a strength.

Job sensitivity analysis

> **KEY TERM**
>
> **Job sensitivity analysis** is a system of review by the security and personnel functions, which seeks to identify risks by performing an analysis of each job and the potential for fraudulent behaviour inherent in the design of that job.

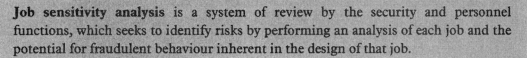

3.7 Every individual in an organisation has some **opportunity to commit fraud**. The potential which they will have to do so depends on a number of factors.

- Ability to gain **access** to critical resources
- **Time** available to plan and carry out fraudulent activities
- **Skill**
- **Motivation**

3.8 Job security analysis involves identification of valuable **assets**, for example portable **computers**, **payments** made to customers or postings to **suspense accounts**, and considers all those **staff** who might have an opportunity to cause loss.

3.9 There are a number of indications, or **warning signs**, which may suggest that an employee's behaviour should be investigated more closely. Many can be contained under the heading of evidence of **unduly lavish lifestyles**.

(a) Unexplained **wealth**, enabling for example purchase of a new car or house.

(b) Higher than usual **spending patterns**, on holiday entertainment, gambling etc.

(c) Liaisons with **staff from rival businesses**.

(d) **Lack of respect** for the organisation, for example poor timekeeping, expressions of disaffection or insubordination.

(e) Regular **working 'after hours'** even when this does not seem necessary.

3.10 There may of course be perfectly rational explanations for any of these indicators. The key is that any suspicions should be handled with utmost **sensitivity**. Unfounded accusations of dishonesty can at best ruin the individual's career, and a loss of staff morale is also likely.

3.11 At the same time, a 'softly softly' approach may **warn the fraudster** that he or she has been placed under suspicion. Absolute **secrecy** should be maintained while investigators set to work.

4   DISASTER RECOVERY STRATEGIES

Risk and risk management

4.1 With so much more data being held in computerised form, and much higher investment in IT, all organisations should attempt to identify **threats** to its information systems, ie potential dangers which, if realised, would destroy or alter the working of an information system and the **vulnerability** in the information system (ie its weak points).

4.2 The best way of dealing with such risks is to **avoid** them completely, in other words to modify the system so that it is not vulnerable to risk. Failing this, risk must be **managed**.

4.3   Organisations and their environment change constantly and so risk management is an **ongoing process,** not a one-off exercise. A regularly reviewed **security policy** is needed, not simply a collection of measures adopted ad hoc.

4.4   Risk management involves three stages.

(a)   **Risk assessment**

(i)   **Identification** of risks

(ii)   **Quantification** of risks

(iii)   Placing risks in order of **potential loss**

The importance of some attempt to **quantify** potential loss in financial terms is that this is a measure against which the cost of safeguards can be assessed.

(b)   **Risk minimisation**

(i)   **Identification** of counter-measures

(ii)   **Costing** of counter-measures

(iii)   **Selection** of counter-measures. Insignificant risks may not justify the cost of setting up and operating controls.

(iv)   **Implementation** of counter-measures

(v)   Draw up **contingency plans** in case all counter-measures are ineffective

Scenario analysis is a technique whereby descriptions of a number of possible loss-causing events are circulated to the relevant functional managers who assess which are the most probable. Security measures are taken against any events which are thought likely to result in loss.

(c)   **Risk transfer (insurance)**

It is impossible to eliminate all risk. Risks that cannot be covered by security measures should be **insured against**, so that at least the financial consequences are not too severe.

Contingency planning

> **KEY TERM**
>
> A **contingency** is an unscheduled interruption of computing services that requires measures outside the day-to-day routine operating procedures.

4.5   The preparation of a contingency plan is one of the stages in the development of an organisation-wide security policy. A contingency plan is necessary in case of some terrible **disaster** occurring to the system, or if some of the **security measures** discussed elsewhere **fail.**

4.6   A **disaster** occurs where the system for some reason breaks down, leading to potential **losses** of equipment, data or funds. The victim, however, cannot simply wait before continuing operations. The system **must recover as soon as possible** so that further losses are not incurred, and current losses can be rectified.

Question 2

What actions or events might lead to a systems breakdown?

Answer

System breakdowns can occur in a variety of circumstances, for example:

(a) fire destroying data files and equipment;

(b) flooding (so it is best not to site the computer room in a basement);

(c) a computer virus completely destroying a data or program file;

(d) a technical fault in the equipment;

(e) accidental destruction of telecommunications links (eg builders severing a cable);

(f) terrorist attack;

(g) system failure caused by software bugs which were not discovered at the design stage;

(h) internal sabotage (eg logic bombs built into the software).

4.7   Any contingency plan must therefore provide for:

(a) **standby procedures** so that some operations can be performed while normal services are disrupted;

(b) **recovery procedures** once the cause of the breakdown has been discovered or corrected;

(c) the **personnel management** policies to ensure that (a) and (b) above are implemented properly.

Contents of a contingency plan

4.8   The contents of a contingency plan will include the following.

Section	Comment
Definition of responsibilities	It is important that somebody (a manager or co-ordinator) is designated to take control in a crisis. This individual can then delegate specific tasks or responsibilities to other designated personnel.
Priorities	Limited resources may be available for processing. Some tasks are more important than others. These must be established in advance. Similarly, the recovery program may indicate that certain areas must be tackled first.
Backup and standby arrangements	These may be with other installations, with a company (eg a computer bureau) that provides such services; or manual procedures.
Communication with staff	The problems of a disaster can be confounded by poor communication between members of staff.
Public relations	If the disaster has a public impact, the recovery team may come under pressure from the public or from the media.
Risk assessment	Some way must be found of assessing the requirements of the problem, if it is contained, with the continued operation of the organisation as a whole.

Standby facilities

4.9   Standby facilities which can be used for disaster recovery include the following.

(a) **Computer bureaux** can agree to make their own systems available in the event of an emergency. Such an arrangement has to be specified in advance, as there might be other demands on a bureau's resources.

(b) **Co-operating with other organisations** in the locality, through a mutual aid agreement, may be a way of pooling resources. However, these other organisations themselves might not, in the event, be able to spare the computer time.

(c) **Disaster standby companies** offer office premises with desks, telephones and storage space which are equipped with hardware and possibly software of the same type as that used by their customers.

(d) **Hardware duplication.** The provision of back-up computers is obviously costly if these systems have no other function. However, many organisations use several smaller computer systems rather than a single, large one, and find that a significant level of protection against system faults can be provided by shifting operations to one of the systems still functioning.

5   COMPUTER AUDIT

Exam focus point

Computer audit has barely featured in Paper 5 questions to date, although it comes up invariably in **Paper 6.** Just **skim** this section if you are also studying for Paper 6 at present; refer to your BPP Study Text for Paper 6 for more detail.

Audit of computer systems

5.1   The obvious problem with auditing a computer system is that processing operations **cannot be seen**, and the results of processing might be stored on disk.

Audit trails

5.2   The original concept of an **audit trail** was to print out data at all stages of processing so that a manager or auditor could follow transactions stage-by-stage through a system to ensure that they had been processed correctly. The intention is:

(a)   to **identify errors,** perhaps with a view to redesigning the system or ensuring that users of the system are properly trained;

(b)   to **detect fraud.**

5.3   Modern computer methods have now cut out much of the laborious, time-consuming stage-by-stage working of older systems, but there should still be some **means of identifying individual records** and the **input and output documents** associated with the processing of any individual transaction.

KEY TERM

An **audit trail** allows auditors to investigate errors that they have discovered in more detail. Ideally the audit trail should make it possible to trace all the reports and other information items that have been affected by the error, and to trace the cause of the error.

5.4   An audit trail should be provided so that every transaction on a file contains a **unique reference** back to the **original source** of the input (eg a sales system transaction record should hold a reference to the customer order, delivery note and invoice).

Question 3

What cross-checks might you carry out on the records in an audit trail?

Answer

You would check that records were consistent with one another. For instance, if there is a customer order, is there a delivery note, and do the details agree? For any given invoice is there any evidence that the invoiced item was delivered? And so on.

This may seem self-evident, but it is all too easy to forget to raise these questions in exam answers, and also (as some auditors have found to their cost) in real life!

5.5 When file records are updated from **several sources,** the provision of a satisfactory audit trail is difficult but some attempt should nevertheless be made to provide one. Typical contents, perhaps gathered from several sources, include the following items.

(a) A **transaction number** and **type**

(b) Full **transaction details** (see the illustration below) such as net and gross amount, customer ID and so on

(c) The identity of the **person who entered the transaction** and/or the **PC or terminal** used to enter it

(d) The **date** and perhaps the **time** of the entry

(e) Reference to **related transactions** such as journal entries, reversals, credit notes and the like

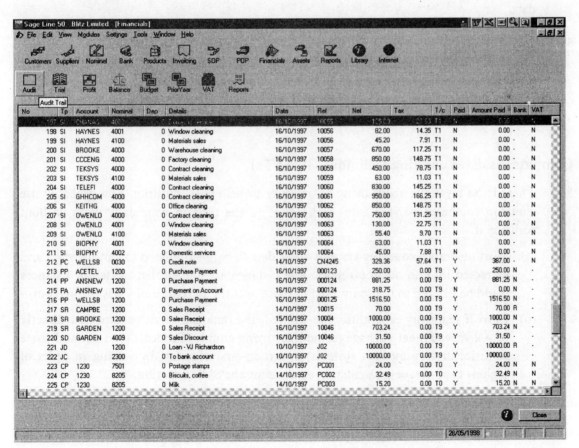

Round the computer and through the computer audits

5.6   Some years ago, it was widely considered that an accountant could discharge his duties as an auditor in a company with computer based systems without having any detailed knowledge of computers.

5.7   The auditor would audit '**round the computer**' by ignoring the procedures which take place within the computer programs and concentrating solely on the **input** and corresponding **output**. Audit procedures would include checking authorisation, coding and control totals of input and checking the output with source documents and clerical control tests.

5.8   This view is now frowned upon and it is recognised that one of the principal problems facing the internal auditor is that of acquiring an understanding of the workings of the computer system itself.

5.9   It is now customary for auditors to audit '**through the computer**'. This involves an examination of the detailed **processing** routines of the computer to determine whether the **controls** in the system are adequate to ensure complete and correct processing of all data.

5.10 One of the major reasons why the 'round the computer' audit approach is no longer considered adequate is that as the complexity of computer systems has increased there has been a corresponding **loss of audit trail**. One way the auditor can try to overcome the difficulties of lost audit trails is by employing **computer aided audit techniques** (CAATs).

Computer assisted auditing techniques (CAATs)

5.11 There is no mystique about using a computer to help with auditing. You probably use common computer assisted audit techniques all the time in your daily work without realising it.

(a) Most modern accounting systems allow data to be manipulated in various ways and extracted into an **ad hoc report**. For instance a complete list of debtor balances could be **filtered** so that only a list of those over their credit limits was printed out.

(b) Even if reporting capabilities are limited, the data can often be exported directly into a **spreadsheet** package (sometimes using simple Windows-type cut and paste facilities in very modern systems) and then analysed, say, by sorting in order of highest balances, or recalculating totals using the SUM function.

(c) Most systems have **searching** facilities that are much quicker to use than searching through print-outs by hand. This offsets the so-called 'loss of audit trail' to a significant extent. The trail is still there, even though it may have to be followed through in electronic form.

5.12 There are a variety of packages specially designed either to ease the auditing task itself (for example selecting records to investigate, based on various statistical **sampling** techniques or calculating **audit risk**), or to carry out **audit interrogations** of computerised data automatically. There are also a variety of ways of testing the processing that is carried out.

Using the right files

5.13   Before any audit software is run, the auditors should check the **identity and version of the data files and programs used**, whether they are taken from the company's records and systems or supplied by themselves. This will normally involve checking with external evidence, such as control totals, and looking at file lengths, dates, times or other file properties.

Audit interrogation software

5.14   Interrogation software performs the sort of checks on data that auditors might otherwise have to perform by hand.

(a)   Programs may have to be **written specially**, in which case the internal auditor must take care not to rely to too great an extent on the IT staff whose systems and processing are being examined.

(b)   **Packages** such as WinIdea and ACL for Windows are available commercially from a variety of software suppliers and also from firms of external auditors.

5.15   Here are some of the uses of audit packages.

- Identify **trends**, pinpoint **exceptions** and potential **areas of concern**

- Locate **errors** and **potential fraud** by comparing and analysing files according to end user criteria

- **Recalculate** and verify balances

- Identify control issues and ensure **compliance with standards**

- **Age and analyse** accounts receivable, payables or any other time-sensitive transactions

- Recover expenses or lost revenues by testing for **duplicate** payments, **gaps** in invoice numbers or **unbilled** services

- Test for **unauthorised** employee/supplier relationships

- **Automate repetitive tasks** by creating custom applications or batches

5.16   Audit interrogation software is particularly appropriate during **substantive testing** of transactions and especially balances. By using audit software, the auditors may scrutinise **large volumes** of data and concentrate skilled manual resources on the **investigation** of results, rather than on the **extraction** of information.

Test data

5.17   An obvious way of seeing whether a system is **processing** data in the way that it should be is to input some test data and see what happens. The **expected results** can be calculated in advance and then compared with the **results that actually arise**.

5.18   The problem with test data is that any resulting corruption of the data files has to be corrected. This is difficult with modern real-time systems, which often have built in (and highly desirable) controls to ensure that data entered *cannot* easily be removed without leaving a mark. Consequently test data is **used less and less** as a CAAT.

Advanced audit facilities

5.19 The results of using **test data** would, in any case, be completely distorted if the **programs** used to process it were **not the ones normally used for processing**. For example a fraudulent member of the IT department might substitute a version of the program that gave the correct results, purely for the duration of the test, and then replace it with a version that siphoned off the company's funds into his own bank account.

5.20 To allow a **continuous** review of the data recorded and the manner in which it is treated by the system, it may be possible to use CAATs referred to as 'embedded audit facilities'.

5.21 An **embedded facility** consists of audit modules that are incorporated into the computer element of the enterprise's accounting system. Two frequently encountered examples are Integrated Test Facility (ITF) and Systems Control and Review File (SCARF).

Integrated test facility

5.22 Integrated Test Facility involves the creation of a **fictitious entity** (for example a department or a customer) within the framework of the regular application. Transactions are then posted to the fictitious entity along with the regular transactions. The results produced by the normal processing cycle are compared with what should have been produced, which is predetermined by other means.

Systems Control and Review File (SCARF)

5.23 To operate *SCARF* each account record in a system is given two **'auditor's' fields**: a **Yes/No field** indicating whether or not SCARF applies to this account; and a monetary value which is a **threshold amount** set by the auditors.

5.24 Subsequently all transactions posted to a SCARF account which had a value in excess of the threshold amount would also be **written to a separate 'SCARF' file**. This technique thus enables the auditors to monitor **material transactions** or **sensitive accounts** with ease and provides an assurance that all such transactions are under scrutiny.

Other techniques

Simulation

5.25 Simulation (or 'parallel simulation)' entails the preparation of a separate program that **simulates the processing of the organisation's real system**. Real data can then be passed not only through the system proper but also through the simulated program. For example the simulation program may be used to re-perform controls such as those used to identify any missing items from a sequence.

Program logic and coding

5.26 Two further types of CAATs worth mentioning are:

(a) **logical path analysis**, which will draw flowcharts of the program logic; and

(b) **code comparison programs**, which compare the original specified program to the current program to detect unauthorised amendments.

Knowledge-based systems

5.27 **Decision support systems** and **expert systems** can be used to assist with the auditors' own judgement and decisions. This is likely to save time and money as such methods increase the efficiency of the audit procedures used, and the maintenance of audit records. Other cost savings include the reduction in the number of staff required, and the fact that routine tasks can be assigned to technicians, who are helped by the expert system.

Chapter roundup

- **External auditors** are independent of the organisation. Their main concern is to review the financial statements of a business and the accounting systems underlying them.

- **Internal auditors** are appointed by management to monitor and report on all aspects of the running of the company's operations.

- External auditors will look at **general** controls over the system environment and **application** controls, specific to individual programs.

- **System development controls** aim to ensure that projects are justified, properly scheduled and properly documented and particularly that they stay within budget.

- **Structured walkthroughs** are a technique whereby systems developers present their design to interested user groups.

- Some **personnel** will always be placed in a position of trust and can compromise the security of an organisation.

- **Job sensitivity analysis** seeks to identify the risks inherent in jobs and the potential for fraud.

- Organisations should develop **contingency plans** to be activated in the event of major or long-term systems problems. **Standby facilities** include computer bureaux and co-operation with other organisations.

- Auditors should audit **through the computer.** Computer Assisted Audit Techniques include audit interrogation software and test data.

Quick quiz

1 What are the distinctions between external and internal audit? (see para 1.8)

2 Give ten examples of general controls. (1.12)

3 How can control of costs be achieved? (2.6)

4 Why is it important that development work is signed off by users? (2.13, 2.14)

5 What personnel might be involved in a structured walkthrough? (2.15)

6 What warning signs might suggest that an employee is perpetrating a fraud? (3.9)

7 What are the three stages of risk management? (4.4)

8 What should a contingency plan contain? (4.8)

9 What is the purpose of an audit trail? (5.2 - 5.5)

10 What uses might an audit interrogation package have? (5.15)

Question to try	Level	Marks	Time
11	Exam standard	15	27 mins
12	Introductory	n/a	20 mins

Part C
Systems development

Chapter 11

SYSTEMS ANALYSIS

Chapter topic list	Syllabus reference
1 Methodologies	3(c), 3(d), 3(f)
2 Structured Systems Analysis and Design Methodology (SSADM)	3(d), (e)
3 Other methodologies	3(f)
4 Systems investigation	3(d)

Introduction

In this chapter, we consider formal approaches to systems development, known as **methodologies,** and look at the first main stage of development after the feasibility study, which is the fact-finding process of systems **investigation** - interviews, questionnaires and so on.

You will undoubtedly find the overview of the main methodology - SSADM - quite **scary** when you first read it! This is only because it refers to complex-sounding techniques such as 'entity relationship modelling' which are actually **very easy.** You will see for yourself in the chapter that follows this one.

1   METHODOLOGIES

1.1   We referred to methodologies in Chapter 6 when discussing the **systems development lifecycle.**

KEY TERM

A systems development **'methodology'** is a collection of procedures, techniques, tools and documentation aids which will help systems developers in their efforts to implement a new information system.

Characteristics of methodologies

1.2   Many methodologies work on the assumptions that the **logical design** is to be distinguished from the **physical design** of a system, and is carried out first. That is to say, there is no use in buying a computer and then trying to find a system that will be compatible with it if the system does not meet the needs of users.

1.3   Rather, **what** a system is supposed to do, and the **data items** it deals with, should be defined first, and the physical implementation made subject to these requirements. The system is described in terms of **what** it is to do, rather than **how** this can be done.

1.4   **Hardware and software** are therefore acquired **for the system,** rather than a system acquired to fit in with the purchased hardware and software. On the other hand, **technological constraints** cannot be ignored.

1.5   A second theme in many methodologies is that the **type of data** an organisation needs is **less likely to change** than either the **processes** which operate on it or the output information required of it.

1.6   Thirdly, within the organisation, the **needs of users** as expressed in the **outputs** or potential outputs required of the system are considered prior to hunting for input data. The user's information requirements and potential requirements should determine the type of data collected or captured by the system.

Comparing and evaluating methodologies

1.7   Jayaratna (*Understanding and Evaluating Methodologies*, 1994) estimates that there are **over 1,000 brand named methodologies** in use in the world. Clearly this book cannot cover all of them. The aim is to illustrate some general principles that may **help you to hold your own** if you ever come into contact with systems analysts and designers.

1.8   Before going into further detail, however, it will be useful to review some of the main conclusions reached by Jayaratna about methodologies.

(a)   All methodologies **evolve** over time as their creators and users use them in practice and revise them as appropriate.

(b)   All methodologies are underpinned by a set of **philosophical beliefs**. For instance, some are based on the belief that systems development is based on unchangeable and **objective facts,** while others take the view that the 'facts' may be **interpreted** differently depending on one's viewpoint. A sales target may be simply a figure, or it may be 'part of a political process which negotiates between sales personnel, management and directors', possibly with 'far reaching implications relating to people's lives, remuneration, job satisfaction' etc (Avison and Fitzgerald, *Information Systems Development*).

The point is that if you don't subscribe to the philosophy behind a methodology there is a good chance that you will not get the system that you want. Methodologies measure **success** in terms of their underlying philosophy.

(c)   Different methodologies emphasise different aspects of the development process. For example, 'soft systems methodology' concentrates on the **problem formulation** stage, while structured methodologies such as SSADM emphasise the design of **solutions**.

1.9   All methodologies seek to facilitate the **'best' solution**. But 'best' may be interpreted in a number of ways, such as **most rapid** or **least cost** systems. Some methodologies are highly **prescriptive** and require rigid adherence to stages whilst others are highly **adaptive** allowing for creative use of their components. The former may be viewed as following a recipe and the latter as selecting suitable tools from a toolkit.

1.10   In choosing the **most appropriate methodology,** an organisation must consider the following questions. (Unfamiliar terms will be described in subsequent chapters.)

(a)   How **open** is the system?
(b)   To what extent does it facilitate **participation**?
(c)   Does it generate **alternative solutions**?
(d)   Is it **well documented, tried, tested and proven** to work?
(e)   Can component **'tools'** be selected and used as required?
(f)   Will it benefit from **CASE** tools and **prototyping**?

1.11   It is **not** necessary to be **restricted** to the tools offered by **just one methodology**. For instance soft systems methodology may be useful at the outset, to get a system well-defined, and subsequently to review its performance. Elements of 'harder' techniques such as SSADM and possibly prototyping might usefully be employed during development.

1.12   Ultimately it is important to remember that whilst methodologies may be valuable in the development their use is a matter of **great skill and experience**. They do not, by themselves, produce good systems solutions.

Question 1

Why does it matter how 'open' a system is?

Solution

An open system is much affected by unpredictable and rapidly changing environmental factors (a hospital admissions system, for instance) and it needs an approach that takes account of 'soft' (people-related) problems. A highly stable system, such as a payroll system, simply needs to follow predefined rules (payroll rules change, but even the changes are relatively predictable) and may have less need for 'soft' thinking.

Advantages and disadvantages

1.13   The advantages of using a **standard** approach such as a methodology are as follows.

   (a)   The **documentation requirements** are rigorous.

   (b)   Standard methods allow less qualified staff to carry out some of the analysis work, thus **cutting the cost** of the exercise.

   (c)   Using a standard development process leads to improved system **specifications**.

   (d)   Systems developed in this way are easier to **maintain and improve**.

   (e)   **Users are involved** with development work from an early stage and are required to **sign off** each stage (see the previous chapter).

   (e)   The emphasis on **diagramming** makes it easier for relevant parties, including users, to understand the system than if purely narrative descriptions were used.

   (f)   The **structured framework** of a methodology **helps with planning**. It defines the tasks to be performed and sets out when they should be done. Each step has an identifiable end product. This allows control by reference to actual achievements rather than to estimates of progress.

   (g)   A **logical design** is produced that is **independent of hardware and software**. This logical design can then be given a physical design using whatever computer equipment and implementation language is required.

   (h)   Techniques such as dataflow diagrams, logical data structures and entity life histories allow information to be **cross-checked** between diagrams and ensure that the system delivered is **what was wanted**. These techniques are explained in the next chapter.

1.14   The use of a methodology in systems development also has some **disadvantages**.

   (a)   Methodologies are generally tailored to **large, complex organisations**. Only recently, as in Micro-SSADM, are they being adapted for PC-based systems.

(b) It has been argued that methodologies are **ideal** for analysing and documenting **processes** and **data items** are operational level, but are perhaps **inappropriate** for information of a **strategic nature** that is collected on an ad hoc basis.

(c) Some are a little **too limited in scope**, being too concerned with systems design, and not with their impact on actual **work processes** or **social context** of the system.

(d) The **conceptual basis** of some is **not properly thought out**. Many methodologies grew out of diagramming conventions.

(e) Arguably methodologies are just as happy documenting a **bad design** as a good one.

Exam focus point
A question in **June 1995** asked what is meant by 'structured methodologies' (see below) and how a methodology might help to deal with some specific problems that were described in a scenario.

2   STRUCTURED SYSTEMS ANALYSIS AND DESIGN METHODOLOGY (SSADM)

Structured methods

2.1   Structured methodologies represent an approach to systems analysis and design which:

(a) emphasises the **logical** design of a system (what types of data item there are, the relationships between them, what processing operations they undergo and so on) before **physical** implementation (before programs are written, hardware specified);

(b) proceeds **from the general to the particular** via a series of modules, stages and steps (so the system **as a whole** is designed before individual applications or programs);

(c) is **heavily documented** in a standard way using techniques to show the links between data, processes, functions, customers etc such as **dataflow diagrams** (DFDs) and **entity relationship models** (see the next chapter).

2.2   There are a number of methodologies based around the principles of structured analysis. **Structured Systems Analysis and Design Methodology (SSADM)** was developed in conjunction with the UK government's Central Computer and Telecommunications Agency, and it is revised regularly to take account of new developments.

SSADM

2.3   SSADM is a widely used methodology, and the structure it supplies forms the basis of much discussion of systems analysis and design. SSADM has several features.

(a) It describes **how** a system is to be developed.

(b) It reduces development into **stages,** and each stage contains a number of steps. The work done in one stage is refined and developed in the next.

(c) It is **self-checking**, and can be **tailored** to a number of applications.

2.4   The **structure** of SSADM in a system development lifecycle is outlined below. This structure is the one used in SSADM Version 4. (The latest version at the time of publication is SSADM 4+ Version 4.3, published in October 1996 to address the issue of Graphical User Interfaces.)

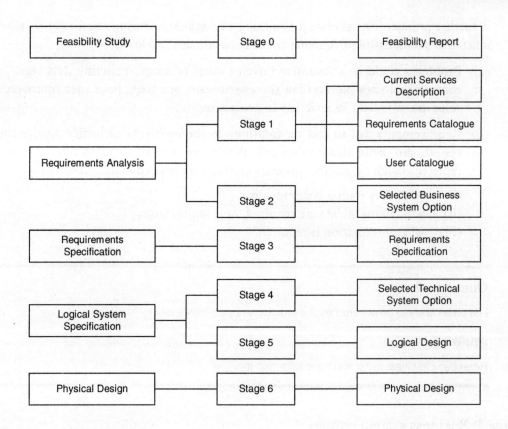

Stage 0: Feasibility study

2.5   This stage, although not mandatory in many SSADM projects, is to examine the 'case' for undertaking a particular project in terms of its social, technical, operational and economic feasibility. This was discussed in some detail in Chapter 7.

2.6   As we have seen, this stage is divided into four steps.

(a)   **Prepare for the feasibility study**, taking a preliminary view and setting out plans for the rest of the study.

(b)   **Define the problem**, where a problem (some deficiency in the system as it is now running, or an anticipated future deficiency) is identified. Information about it is gathered and the new requirements are set out in a **Problem Definition Statement**.

(c)   **Select feasibility options**: a series of options are identified for solving, or at least coping with the problems defined. Each potential project identified will have an outline specification and will be costed.

(d)   The results of this stage are formalised into a **feasibility study report**, which should also contain costings for the next phase.

Stage 1: Investigation of current environment

2.7   In this stage the current system is **investigated**, described and analysed using the techniques of observation, questionnaires, document description forms and so forth (see later in this chapter). Some of the work may have been done already during the feasibility study.

2.8   A major requirement of this phase is that the current system is properly documented in **dataflow diagrams** and the **logical data structure** (entity-relationship model) is described.

2.9 A further product from this stage (building on work done during the feasibility study) is a detailed **problems/requirements** list or requirements catalogue.

(a) **Problems** could be encountered over a range of areas, including data input, poor controls, volumes higher than the system can cope with, poor user interface, slow response times and inflexibility in processing.

(b) **Requirements** can in fact be **solutions** to the problems identified in the current system, but could also imply a completely **new way** of doing things, (for example replacing batch by on-line processing). Users are invited to describe:

    (i) what they want a system to do;

    (ii) what items of data are required for it to deal with;

    (iii) what information is required.

Question 2

List areas likely to be covered by the problems/requirements list.

Answer

Refer back to Chapter 7 if you have forgotten this.

Stage 2: Business system options

2.10 This involves the specification of the requirements of the new system, where **what users actually require** is laid down in detail. Any solution offered must satisfy these requirements. There will normally be a number of possible solutions and those considered the best will be put forward to users as Business System Options.

(a) Six **options**, say, are suggested, from which a shortlist is created. For each option on the shortlist there is drawn up a level-1 DFD, function descriptions (the basic processes that transform data), a logical data structure (entity model), a cost/benefit analysis (in brief) and an assessment of the impact of the proposed system.

(b) Users are then asked to make a **choice**.

Stage 3: Requirements specification

2.11 At this stage, the team takes the results of the previous stage, and arrives at a **requirements specification**. This stage has several steps. (Terms like normalisation and entity life history are, again, explained in depth in the next chapter.)

(a) The chosen option is **defined more precisely**.

Detailed DFDs etc are drawn up, and the **required** system matched with the **current** system to ensure that all necessary processing has been performed. The DFDs are modified by the solutions to the problems/requirements identified earlier.

(b) Specifications for **input** and **output** from the chosen system are prepared.

These input/output descriptions detail what appears on screen, or on a document. An input/output description of a sales statement will list what should appear on the statement (eg customer number, name, address, statement date, transaction type, transaction data, balance brought forward).

(c) A relational data analysis (**normalisation**) is performed on the input and output descriptions.

This is to identify any entities that might not have been noticed, or drawn in enough detail, in the existing **logical data structure** (entity model). Whereas production of the logical data structure is a **top down** view, the analysis carried out here is a **bottom up** complement to it.

(d) **Entity life histories** are drawn up.

What has been missing so far is a means of **matching** the DFDs (which show flows of data through the system and what happens to it), with the logical data structure (which denotes the building blocks of the system). An **entity life history** is a technique which indicates what happens to an entity ie what functions (processes) it is subjected to, and so forth.

Stage 4: Technical system options

2.12 At this point users are asked to make choices concerning the means by which they would like the system to be **implemented**: there might be a number of ways of implementing a system physically. These can include:

(a) **hardware configuration** (for example mainframe, mini, PC; centralised or distributed processing); and

(b) **software** (use of a database or a conventional file structure).

Some of the technical options may have been outlined in brief at the feasibility study stage.

2.13 Users are presented with the various options outlined, and the implications of each are stated, so that the decision is an informed one. Once this is achieved, these details are incorporated into the required logical system design. Performance objectives are then specified in detail so that these can be followed in the actual design of the system.

Stage 5: Logical design

2.14 In this stage, the data and file structures for the entire new system are designed. The input to this stage are the descriptions of input and output from stage 3, and functions 'and processes that act upon or use data items are specified.

- **Update** is a function which alters in some way the contents of a file.
- **Enquiry** is simply accessing a record to see what it is.

2.15 This stage includes the development of **output formats**, and specifying the type of **dialogue** that users will have with the system, to ensure that it is consistent with what has been prepared so far.

Question 3

What does 'dialogue' mean?

Answer

This term refers to the messages that appear on screen (such as 'Are you sure you want to delete this file?') and the responses that the user makes - often just clicking on OK or Cancel. See Chapter 14 for more on this aspect of design.

Stage 6: Physical design

2.16 Physical design involves the following tasks.

(a) **Initial physical design** (obtaining the design rules from the chosen database, and applying them to the logical data design drawn up in the previous stages).

(b) Further define the **processing** required. For instance requirements for audit, security and control are considered. Briefly, these can include:

(i) **controls over access** to the system;

(ii) controls **incorporated within programs** (eg data validation, error handling);

(iii) **recovery procedures**, in case processing is interrupted.

(c) **Program specifications** are created. These provide in detail exactly what a particular program is supposed to achieve. **Structured English** may be used. Each process may be designated batch or on-line.

(d) Program specifications are assessed for their **performance** when implemented. For example, it should be possible to make some estimate of the times that some programs will take to run. These may initially fall below the targets originally set, and so there may have to be some changes to the specifications or users may have to accept some deficiencies in required performance, or the equipment may have to be changed.

(e) **File and database specifications** are designed in detail, and will contain, typically:

- name;
- contents;
- record size, types, fields per record etc.

(f) **Operating instructions** are drawn up (user documentation). These will include such items as error correction and detailed instructions for operators and users (eg the sort of screen format that will appear).

Systems Development Template

2.17 SSADM 4+ includes a framework called the **Systems Development Template (SDT)**. This is used to determine user requirements, analyse information needs and then design and specify systems.

2.18 The SSADM user establishes **which parts** of the **SDT** are important and then **adapts the components of SSADM** to suit the specific project.

Question 4

(a) Glance forward to Chapters 12 and 13 and get a rough idea of what is meant by the terms dataflow diagram, entity relationship model, entity life history, normalisation and Structured English.

Then find each of the above terms in the summary of SSADM given above.

(b) What is meant by logical design?

Answer

(a) Either do this now, or else come back to this section after you have studied Chapters 12 and 13. You will find it makes a lot more sense.

(b) See paragraphs 1.2 to 1.3.

Assessment of SSADM

2.19   Organisations may wish to adopt SSADM for the following reasons.

(a)   It incorporates **clear stages** with instructions as to how to proceed from one stage to the next.

(b)   **Standard methods** make it **cheaper and quicker to train staff** and consequently save project costs.

(c)   All stages are rigorously **defined** and fully **documented**, making systems **easier to maintain and improve**.

2.20   However, too great a rigidity in the application of the methodology may lead to **disregard for the social and organisational context of the system**. This may produce systems which are technically satisfactory but do not satisfy the users. They reduce the need for creative thinking and this could affect staff well-being and motivation.

2.21   Users may be **reluctant** to be involved with what they may regard as complex methods - they may be **unfamiliar** with techniques such as DFDs, and possibly **suspicious** of the procedures.

2.22.   SSADM should therefore be used in a highly **open and participative manner** if it is to help an organisation to produce a widely accepted and valued system.

3   OTHER METHODOLOGIES

> ### Exam focus point
> A general awareness of the existence of other methodologies may be useful, but exam questions so far have always been answerable using the ideas and conventions of **SSADM,** which is also the principle basis of the current **examiner's own books** on the subject.

Data-driven methodologies

3.1   Whilst structured analysis emphasises **processes**, which are broken down into logically defined segments of a system, other approaches to system design emphasise the **data** used by a system. Even if applications change, the data already collected may still be relevant. This, in many respects, is the approach behind **database design**.

Information Engineering

3.2   Information Engineering is an information systems development methodology which starts with a **strategic planning** exercise, to identify important information systems required by the business, and then develops chosen priority systems through **successively detailed** analysis and design, through to implementation.

(a)   **Strategic management planning** uses any **existing** strategic or tactical statements that may exist and/or a management questionnaire to gather information about business strategy. It then goes on to identify and define **potential goals** (critical success factors) and issues, and defines strategies to deal with each. This part of the process concludes with the creation of the strategic agenda and formal documentation of strategic decisions, rationale, assumptions, conclusions and alternatives.

(b)   **Information strategy planning** documents the business objectives in terms of information required. The key document produced is the information system development strategy, looking at the current information requirements and analysing business functions, data types, technical support for systems.

(c) **Business area analysis** further analyses areas of the business in terms of data used and the relationships between different types of data (entity analysis), and functions and processes.

(d) **Business system design** is the logical design of the new system and will include how the data in the database will be structured, the use of data flow diagrams to map the processes of a business and planning for technical design (for example screen dialogue, reports).

(e) **Implementation** is technology dependent, and is carried out using suitable CASE and other development tools (see Chapter 14).

3.3 Information engineering has a **strong strategic perspective** at the outset, but in later stages it suffers from many of the problems identified at the end of the previous section with structured methodologies such as SSADM. For instance it could be said to be too **limited in scope**, too **concerned with systems design** and not with the impact of systems on **actual work processes** or the **social context of the system**.

User-driven methodologies

3.4 One of the principle characteristics of organisational systems is that they incorporate, and depend on, some element of human behaviour. They are 'people' oriented. The presence of people means that systems cannot be guaranteed to behave in a predictable manner. **User-driven development** focuses on the **behavioural aspects** of information systems design.

Soft Systems Methodology

3.5 Soft Systems Methodology (SSM) is a problem-solving approach developed to help solve **ill-defined problem situations**. It is intended as an aid for managing complex organisational issues in a **participative** process that is **self-determined by the people** holding stakes in it.

3.6 The purpose of SSM is to enhance understanding of **human** situations that are perceived as problematic and, as a consequence, where improvements are aimed at. Typically in any organisation there will be many divergent perspectives on the issues to be dealt with, and each of these needs to be taken into account.

3.7 SSM involves a process of enquiry which leads to action, but this action is **not ever regarded as an end point** unless the participants in the process choose to make it one. SSM recognises that taking action changes the problem situation: this means that the enquiry is a **continual learning process** that remains open for new findings.

3.8 The learning process of SSM therefore cycles between **learning and action** and follows a set of seven stages.

Stage 1   In the first stage the **problematical situation is entered into**. This very step is viewed as an intervention (being itself problematic and as such analysable).

Stage 2   Secondly, the problem situation is expressed in three analytical steps (**intervention, prevalent culture**, and **power relationships**).

Stage 3   The third stage involves a representation of these findings in a set of '**root definitions**', in other words systems thought to be relevant to a deeper exploration of the problem situation which will lead to action in order to improve it.

Stage 4   **Conceptual models** are built in stage four where the verbal concepts previously defined are logically structured by use of arrows to form relevant combinations of an operational and a monitoring and control system.

Stage 5   By **comparing models and reality** (real-world actions) stage five aims at inducing learning steps in the participating group which in general leads to a reiteration of the preceding stages.

Stage 6   The purpose of the sixth stage is then to achieve a common understanding regarding **possible changes of the real-world situation** which could improve it.

Stage 7   The last stage of SSM is concerned with **taking action** and putting the changes in place – thus changing the problem situation itself and restarting the cycle.

3.9   However, soft systems methodology has many **critics**.

(a)   **Technically oriented** critics complain that SSM doesn't actually tell you how to build a system, that **there is no real 'method'**, though proponents would reply that what is really needed is a way of securing commitment and taking into account a variety of interests.

(b)   **Management oriented** critics worry that the **open ended** nature of SSM makes it **impossible to manage**.

(c)   **Radical (and traditional socialist) critics** say that SSM assumes that all members of the enterprise have equal choice. SSM **ignores issues of power**.

(d)   Critics also argue that SSM imposes values of openness and 'niceness' which are **more suitable to middle class academics** than to managers or workers. These criticisms suggest that SSM has a fairly simple understanding of society.

Business process re-engineering

3.10   BPR claims to align organisation change (and IT development) with business strategy. BPR is intended to **improve (re-engineer) business processes which are of primary strategic importance**, such as getting goods to customers, a process which cuts across each of the sales administration, production and distribution functions.

3.11   The thinking on BPR has been **developed by a number of different consultants** each of whom is promoting their firm's proprietary methodology, so each version uses different terminology. The following account therefore merges elements from a number of different versions of BPR.

3.12   Usually re-engineering concentrates on a **small number of processes** which are **most critical** to the organisation's strategy. The assumption is that, provided the processes chosen are complete (not parts of processes) and the re-engineering is thorough, a flow-on effect will probably mean that unsatisfactory neighbouring processes will soon become candidates for redesign.

3.13   Processes with **obvious problems** are clear candidates for reengineering. Obvious problems include **customer complaints**, multiple buffers and **long delays** between steps in the process. A process which is both 'sick' and strategically important can have a serious effect on any organisation.

3.14   Like SSM, BPR assesses the **culture and politics** of the organisational units performing activities within the process, and how these units are viewed in wider organisational politics and culture, recognising that successful re-engineering ultimately depends on the co-operation of those performing the process.

3.15   Some proponents of BPR advocate starting with a **'clean slate'** but most recommend that time is spent studying **existing processes**. There are a number of reasons for this.

(1)   People in the organisations (and customers) will use **language** based on the existing processes.

(2)   When implementing the new processes it is necessary to plan **change from the current situation** - the existing processes.

(3)   The existing processes may be causing **problems** which **could easily be repeated** if they are not understood. Existing processes may also contain activities for avoiding problems which might not be anticipated when designing the new system.

(4)   The existing processes are the base from which improvement is **measured**.

3.16   The next step is to judge whether there are **sufficient resources** available to proceed with the project by asking questions such as: is the organisation **used to change**? Are people **willing to learn**? Is **appropriate technology** available to support the new processes?

3.17   Design and implementation of the new processes can use any suitable methodology, but **prototyping** (see Chapter 14) tends to be favoured, particularly because BPR is performance oriented and the methodology must be able to predict performance during design, and because BPR projects are meant to be done **quickly**.

3.18   The main problem with BPR is that it was so **strongly hyped** in the early 1990s that it was taken up by many organisations and consultants who didn't understand the full picture and tended to use it as merely as an **excuse to cut staff numbers**.

3.19   **Prototyping** is **frowned upon** by some systems developers who argue that it lacks rigour, and produces shoddy, inefficient programs.

4   SYSTEMS INVESTIGATION

Fact finding

4.1   The systems investigation is a detailed **fact finding** exercise about the areas under consideration.

- The project team has to determine the inputs, outputs, processing methods and volumes of the current system.

- It also examines controls, staffing and costs and reviews the organisational structure.

- It should also consider the expected growth of the organisation and its future requirements.

4.2   The stages involved in this phase of systems development are as follows.

(a)   **Fact finding** by means of questionnaires, interviews, observation, reading handbooks, manuals, organisation charts, or from the knowledge and experience of members of the study team.

(b)   **Fact recording** using flowcharts, decision tables, narrative descriptions, organisation and responsibility charts.

(c) **Evaluation,** assessing the strengths and weaknesses of the existing system.

Interviews

4.3 Interviews with members of staff are undoubtedly the **most effective method** of fact finding. If properly conducted, an interview should enable the analyst (investigator) to **overcome the fears and resistance** to change that may be felt by the employee, in addition to finding out facts about his work.

4.4 There are some helpful **guidelines** as to the approach and attitude to be adopted by the investigator who is conducting a fact finding interview.

(a) The interviewer must appreciate that he is dealing with many different individuals with different attitudes and personalities. He must be able to **adapt his approach** to suit the individual interviewee, rather than follow a standard routine.

(b) The interviewer should be **fully prepared** for the interview, having details of the interviewee's name and job position, and a plan of questions to ask.

(c) Employees ought to be informed before the interview that a systems investigation is taking place, and its **purpose explained.**

(d) The interviewer must ask questions at the **level appropriate** to the employee's position within the organisation (for example top management will be concerned with policy, supervisors with functional problems).

(e) The interview should **not be too formal** a question and answer session, but should be allowed to develop into a **conversation** whereby the interviewee offers his opinions and suggestions.

(f) The interviewer must **not jump to conclusions** or confuse opinions with facts. He should accept what the interviewee has to say (for the moment) and refrain from interrupting or propounding his own opinions.

(g) The interviewer should **gain the interviewee's confidence** by explaining in full what is going on and not giving the impression that he is there solely to find fault. This confidence can also be obtained by allowing the interview to take place on the interviewee's 'home ground' (desk or office) and by ensuring that the interviewee has no objection to notes being taken.

(h) The interviewer should arrange interviews so that he **moves progressively** through the system, for example from input clerk to supervisor to manager.

(i) The interviewer should refrain from making **off the record** comments during the course of the interview, for example about what he is going to recommend.

(j) The interview should be **long enough** for the interviewer to obtain the information he requires and to ensure that he understands the system but **short enough** to ensure that concentration does not wander.

(k) The interview should be **concluded** by a résumé of its main points (so that the interviewee can confirm that the interviewer has obtained what he should have done) and the interviewer should thank the interviewee for his time and trouble.

Question 5

Draw up a checklist of do's and don'ts for conducting fact finding interviews.

Answer

A useful checklist for guidance in conducting interviews is suggested by Daniels and Yeates in *Basic Training in Systems Analysis* as follows:

Do	Don't
Plan	Be late
Make appointments	Be too formal or too casual
Ask questions at the right level	Interrupt
Listen	Use technical jargon
Use the local terminology	Confuse opinion with fact
Accept ideas and hints	Jump to conclusions
Hear both sides	Argue
Collect documents and forms	Criticise
Check the facts back	Suggest
Part pleasantly	

4.5   Interviews can be **time consuming** for the analyst, who may have several to conduct, and therefore expensive.

4.6   If conducted effectively, however, they allow the interviewer to **provide information** as well as obtain it. In an interview, **nuances and attitudes** not apparent from other sources may be obtained, and **immediate follow up** to unsatisfactory/**ambiguous replies** is possible. Interviews are particularly appropriate for **senior management**, as other approaches may not be appropriate at executive levels.

Questionnaires

4.7   The use of questionnaires may be useful whenever a **limited amount of information** is required from a **large number of individuals**, or where the organisation is decentralised with many 'separate entity' locations.

4.8   Questionnaires may be used **in advance of an interview** to save the analyst's and employee's time, but it should be remembered that they must be properly introduced.

(a)   Employees ought to be informed before receiving the questionnaire that a systems investigation is to take place, and its **purpose** explained.

(b)   **Questions** must be designed to **obtain exactly the information necessary** for the study. This is a very difficult task.

4.9   It must be stressed that questionnaires, by themselves, are an **inadequate** means of fact finding, and should usually be followed up by an **interview** or **observation**.

4.10   Whenever possible, questionnaires should be **designed** with the following in mind.

(a)   They should **not contain too many questions** (people tend to lose interest quickly and become less accurate in their answers).

(b)   They should be **organised in a logical sequence**.

(c)   They should include an occasional **question** the answer to which **corroborates the answers** to previous questions.

(d)   Ideally, they should be designed so that each question can be answered by either **'yes' or 'no' or a 'tick'** rather than sentences or paragraphs.

(e)   They should be **tested independently** before being issued to the actual individuals. The test answers should enable the systems analyst to establish the effectiveness of his questions and help determine the level of subsequent interviews and observations.

(f)   They should take into account the **sensitivity of individuals** in respect of their job security, change of job definition etc. Staff may prefer **anonymity,** but this prevents follow-up of 'interesting' responses.

Question 6

Next time you receive a questionnaire of any sort, study it carefully to see how well it adheres to these design principles.

Observation

4.11   Once the analyst has some understanding of the methods and procedures used in the organisation, he should be able to **verify** his findings and **clarify** any problem areas by an observation of operations.

4.12   Observation is a useful way of **cross-checking** with the facts obtained by interview or questionnaire. Different methods of recording facts ought to produce the same information, but it is not inconceivable that staff do their work in one way, whilst management believe that they do something different.

4.13   It should be noted that staff **may act differently from normal** if they know that they are being observed: whereas there might normally be a lack of adherence to procedures laid down in manuals, these might be rigorously followed in the presence of a systems analyst.

Document review

4.14   The systems analyst must investigate the **documents** that are used in the system. This may be a wide ranging investigation, using for example organisation charts, procedures manuals and standard operational forms.

4.15   One way of recording facts about document usage is the **document description form**. This is simply a standard form which the analyst can use to describe a document. It includes certain details about any document.

(a)   A list of **all the items** on the document.

(b)   The **size** of each data item (fixed length or variable length field).

(c)   The **format** of the item, in terms of alphabetic, numeric or other characters, eg:

A(15)   means 15 alphabetic characters
ANN   means a letter followed by two numbers

(d)   The **person responsible for entering the data item** on the document.

(e)   **Source** and **destination** of each copy of the document.

(f)   **Purpose** of the document.

(g) **Name** of the document.

(h) Space for the system analyst to make any **further notes** (for example price or discount allowed on a sales invoice, whether the completed document is checked and authorised by a supervisor etc).

4.16 The overriding risk is that staff do not follow documented policies and procedures or that these documents have not been properly updated, so this method is **best used in tandem with one or more other techniques**.

Question 7

How would you investigate an existing operational system in a company which operates through a network of regional branches controlled from a centrally located head office?

Answer

Because the company operates through a network of regional branches controlled from a centrally located head office, it may be appropriate for the systems analysis team to visit head office and a single representative branch. Interviews will be used with key head office staff and on the branch visit, where document analysis and observation can be used for corroborative purposes. Questionnaires can then be designed for use at other branches and, if necessary, followed up if the results do not appear compatible with those obtained by direct contact/observation at the branch visited.

Chapter roundup

- A **methodology** is a collection of procedures, techniques, tools and documentation aids which are designed to help systems developers in their efforts to implement a new system. Methodologies are usually broken down into phases.

- The **advantages** of methodologies are that they standardise the development process and impose rigorous documentation requirements. There are a number of disadvantages too.

- **Structured methodologies** emphasise the **logical** design of a system before its physical implementation. They proceed from the general to the particular, designing the system **as a whole** before individual parts of it. They are heavily documented.

- **SSADM** is a widely used example. It breaks development into stages, steps and tasks. The main stages are feasibility study, investigation of current environment, business system options, requirements specification, technical system options, logical design and physical design.

- **Data-driven methodologies** emphasise the data used by a system. The steps involved in database design usually follow this type of approach. Information engineering is an example of a data-driven methodology. Data needs are identified before processing options.

- **User-driven** methodologies focus on **people** and the behavioural aspects of systems design.

- The first main phase of development is **investigation** of the current environment. This may be done by a variety of methods (a combination is best).

  o **Interviews**
  o **Questionnaires**
  o **Observation**
  o **Document review**

Quick quiz

1   What is the difference between logical design and physical design? (see paras 1.2 - 1.4)

2   What questions might you ask when choosing an appropriate methodology? (1.10)

3   What are the advantages of using a standard approach to systems development? (1.13)

4   List the stages of SSADM. (2.4)

5   What are the steps of the requirements specification stage? (2.11)

6   Distinguish between structured methodologies, data-driven methodologies and user-driven methodologies. (3.1, 3.4)

7   Suggest four guidelines for the conduct of interviews. (4.4)

8   When is it useful to use a questionnaire? (4.7)

9   What is the value of observation? (4.11, 4.12)

10   Why is document review not adequate on its own? (4.16)

Question to try	Level	Marks	Time
13	Exam standard	15	27 mins

Chapter 12

SYSTEMS DEVELOPMENT TECHNIQUES

Chapter topic list	Syllabus reference
1 Data flow diagrams	3(f)
2 Entity relationship models	3(c), 3(f)
3 Entity life histories	3(e), 3(f)
4 Normalisation	3(e), 3(f)
5 Looking forward ...	-

Introduction

This is the first of two chapters in which we examine some of the techniques and tools used in systems analysis and design. We are mostly concerned with **data** analysis in this chapter, whereas in the next chapter we are more concerned with the **logic** of processes.

The topics in this chapter feature regularly in **exam questions**. You are more likely to have to **interpret** a diagram or table ready-provided than to have to draw one up yourself, but the best way of learning how to interpret something is to understand how it was actually constructed in the first place.

1   DATA FLOW DIAGRAMS

1.1   A useful way of recording the ways in which data is processed, without bothering with the equipment used, is a data flow diagram. The production of a data flow diagram is often the first step in a structured systems analysis, because it provides a **basic understanding of how the system works**.

Four symbols are used in data flow diagrams. They should *not* be confused with any type of flowcharting symbols that you have learned for other subjects.

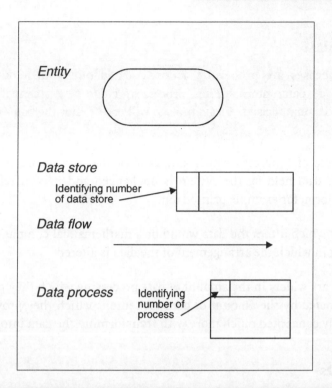

KEY TERM

An **entity** is a **source** or **destination** of data which is considered **external to the system** (not necessarily external to the organisation). It may be people or groups who provide data or input information or who receive data or output information. An example would be a customer.

KEY TERM

A **data store** is a point which holds data, and receives a data flow. Examples of data stores are transaction records, data files, reports and documents.

1.2   Data stores are not restricted as to their **form**, and might be held in a computer's memory, in the form of various magnetic media, or in the form of documents in a filing cabinet, or microfiche.

KEY TERM

A **data flow** represents the movement or transfer of data from one point in the system to another. A data flow could be 'physically' anything - for example a letter, a telephone call, a fax message, a link between computers, or a verbal statement.

1.3   A data flow may involve a document transfer or it may simply involve a notification that some event has occurred without any detailed information being passed.

When a data flow occurs a copy of the data transferred may also be retained at the transmitting point.

> **KEY TERM**
>
> **Data processes** are processing actions carried out from a data store, or which produce a data store. The processes could be manual, mechanised or automated/computerised. A data process will use or alter the data in some way.

1.4   An example of a process which simply **uses** the data would be an output operation, where the data held by the system is unchanged and it is merely made available in a different form, for example printed out.

1.5   A process which **alters** the data would be a mathematical computation or a process such as sorting in which the arrangement of the data is altered.

1.6   Systems vary widely in the amount of data processing which they perform. Some systems are dominated by the amount of data **movement** which they provide, whilst others are intensively concerned much more with **transforming** the data into a more useful form.

Levelled DFDs

1.7   The complexity of business systems means that it is impossible to represent the operations of any system by means of a **single** diagram.

1.8   At the top level, an overview of the different systems in an organisation can be given, or alternatively the position of a single system in the organisation shown. This might be achieved by means of a **context diagram**.

1.9   This is in turn 'exploded' by means of a more detailed data flow diagram, known as a Level-1 DFD. Further detail can be represented on a Level-2 DFD, and so on until all individual entities, stores, flows and processes are shown.

1.10   The diagram below illustrates how levels of DFDs are built up.

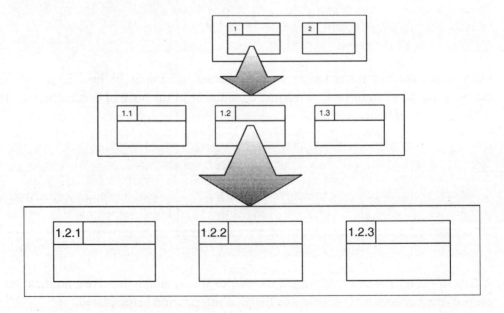

1.11   EXAMPLE: DATA FLOW DIAGRAM

The example used here is a system used for purchasing in a manufacturing company. Three data flow diagrams are shown; each is prepared to record a certain level of detail.

Level-0 DFD (context diagram)

1.12   A Level-0 DFD or **context diagram** summarises the inputs and outputs to the system at a high level.

1.13   The central box represents the system as a whole and (for simplicity in this case) one external entity is shown. (Usually the box would be *surrounded* by external entities, such as different types of suppliers who are dealt with in different ways by the system, and the diagram would look like a spider.)

1.14   Note that we are only showing **flows of data**. The physical resources (the goods supplied) *can* be shown (by means of broad arrows ⇨), but this tends to overcomplicate the diagram. Also no data stores are shown on the context diagram.

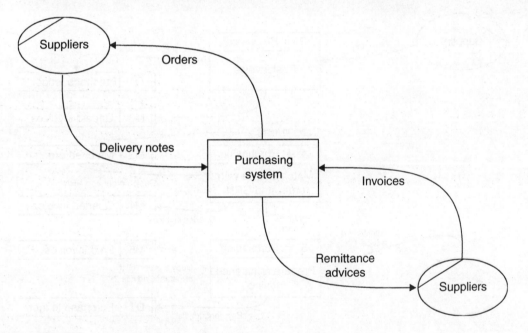

Level 1 DFDs

1.15   Within the purchasing system as a whole in this organisation there are two **subsystems**: the **Stores department** places requests for purchases and accepts delivery of the goods themselves; the **Purchasing department** places orders, and receives and pays invoices.

1.16   On the next page is shown a Level-1 DFD for the **purchasing department**.

1.17   This is not meant to depict an **ideal** system, if there is any such thing. You may be able to detect flaws or inefficiencies in the system shown on the next page. This is **irrelevant** at this stage since we are only trying to **describe** the system as it currently exists.

1.18   Also, for the sake of simplicity, we are only showing **purchasing department activities**. The supplier would send delivery notes to the Stores department who would carry out their own checks, prepare GRNs, and have other data flows with other subsystems.

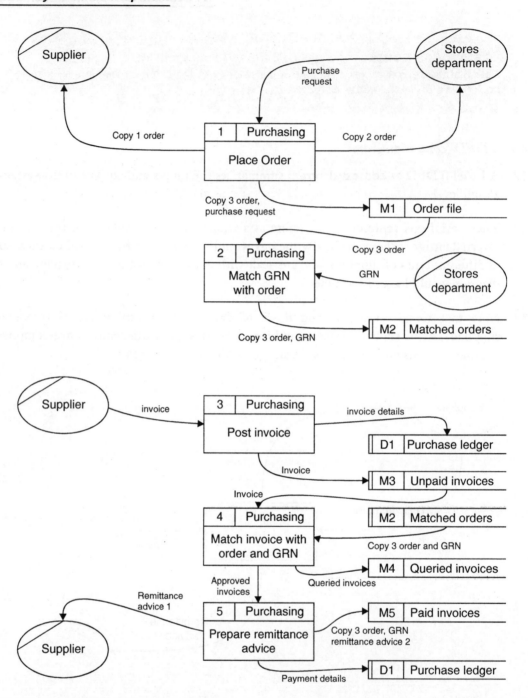

1.19   Note the following **important** points.

(a)   Each process is **numbered,** but this is only for ease of identification: the numbers are **not** meant to show the **strict sequence of events**.

(b)   The process box also has a heading showing where the process is carried out or who does it. The **description** of the process should be a **clear verb** like 'prepare', 'calculate', 'check' (**not** 'process', which is too vague).

(c)   Arrows must **always** finish at or start from a **process**. (If you simply remember that data **cannot move** without intervention (processing) you should never get this wrong.)

(d)   Rather than having data flow arrows criss-crossing all over the place it is often simpler to show a symbol **more than once** on the same diagram, wherever it is needed. When this is done **an additional line** is put within the symbol. The **supplier** entity and several of the **data stores** have extra lines for this reason.

(e)   Data stores are given a reference number (again sequence is not important).

This is preceded by an M if it is a **manual** store and a D if it is a **computer** store.

(f) There may be **little reason to label arrows** that go **in and out of data stores,** because it will be clear enough from the description of the process. (See, for example, process 3 in the example DFD shown: is it really necessary to label the arrows 'invoice', 'invoice details', especially at this level?)

Exam focus point

In the **December 1996** exam candidates were asked to criticise a DFD with the important note 'In this style of data flow diagrams, data flows in and out of data stores do not have to be named'. Non-naming of data flows in and out of data stores was therefore not a valid criticism!

Level-2 DFDs

1.20   A separate DFD (Level-2) would then be prepared for **each of the numbered processes**.

1.21   This is known as **decomposing** a process. The diagram below, for example, shows the data flows for process 1, placing the order.

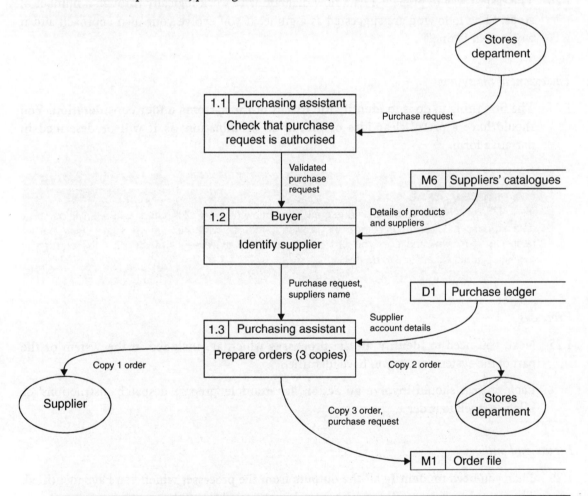

Question 1

Compare this diagram with the Level-1 DFD and note how it is possible to trace the same data flows from one level to the next.

1.22   In turn box 1.1 could be **further decomposed** in a Level-3 DFD, with processes 1.1.1, 1.1.2 and so on, and box 1.2 could be decomposed into processes 1.2.1, 1.2.2 etc. In theory there is no limit to the number of lower levels, but **three levels is usually enough**.

Question 2

Study these diagrams carefully and then try to 'decompose' some of the other processes in the Level-1 DFD into Level-2 DFDs. For example try process 4 and show what might happen if an invoice does *not* match the GRN. You might also like to try to construct a Level-1 DFD for the Stores department.

Answer

There are no right answers, because we have not given you full details of the system: you will **need to make assumptions** based on your knowledge and experience of typical accounting systems. This is to encourage you to have a go without being scared of making mistakes. (Experienced and highly paid systems analysts are likely to make mistakes when they first try to get a system down in DFD form: they will only get it right after discussion and agreement with **users**, which is the whole point of the exercise.)

Drawing data flow diagrams

1.23 The easiest way to prepare a data flow diagram is to work logically through a number of **steps**. (The following are suggested as a guide; if you evolve your own approach and it works, that is fine!)

The extent of the system

1.24 The first thing to do is to **identify the extent of the systems under consideration**. You should have a pretty clear idea of this in an examination, as it will be described in narrative form.

Processes

1.25 Next, you need to **identify all the processes** which are included in the system or the part of the system which you have identified.

Each process should **involve an action**, for example 'prepare despatch instructions' or 'allocate stock to order'.

Inputs and outputs

1.26 Then you need to **identify all the outputs** from the processes which you have identified. These are data flows, each of which must be connected to another symbol.

1.27 You also need to **identify the input or inputs** to each process. The arrow representing each data flow should lead into the process and should start at a point of origin (for which the options are the same as those available for output destinations).

1.28 As already mentioned **some connections are not allowed,** as summarised in the following table.

	Entity	Process	Store
Entity	No	**Yes**	No
Process	**Yes**	**Yes**	**Yes**
Store	No	**Yes**	No

Question 3

What are the *four* destinations to which a data flow leading from a process might lead?

Answer

It can lead to any of the following.

(a)   Another process on the same DFD.
(b)   A process on another DFD.
(c)   An external entity.
(d)   A data store.

Entities

1.29   In identifying outputs and inputs, you should also have **identified all the external entities**, as these will be sources or destinations of data flows (sometimes referred to as 'sources and sinks').

Drawing the diagram

1.30   Note the following points for exams.

(a)   Use **plenty of space** on the paper.

(b)   If possible **use a stencil** which includes suitable shapes.

(c)   Use a **ruler** or other straight edge for boxes.

(d)   **Data flow arrows** look nicer as **curved** lines, as shown above. (They somehow make the system look more human and realistic, less 'techy'.) If you can't do this *neatly*, however, your hand-drawn diagrams will look *very* messy: straight lines drawn with a ruler are better than mess.

(e)   Lastly, it should go without saying that you should **write legibly**.

> **Exam focus point**
> With any luck, you will be **given** a DFD and asked to explain it, say how it could be improved and so on. However, you will not be able to do this without some practical experience of drawing your own. Practice with as many question as you can.

2   ENTITY RELATIONSHIP MODELS

Entities, attributes and relationships

2.1   An **entity**, as we have seen, is an item (a person, a job, a business, an activity, a product or stores item etc) about which information is stored.

- In a sales ledger system a **customer** is an entity.
- In a payroll system an **employee** is an entity.

2.2   An **attribute** is a characteristic or property of an entity. For a customer, attributes include customer name and address, amounts owing, date of invoices sent and payments received, credit limit etc.

2.3   For any entity we can identify **relationships** between attributes and relationships between entities. Here are some simple examples. (The diagrams are sometimes called **Bachmann diagrams**.)

No relationship

2.4   There are **no relationships** in a printout of customer names. This is simply a list of records. Each address is an attribute.

One-to-one relationship

2.5   The relationship **employs** exists between *company* and *finance director*. There is one company which can only employ one finance director.

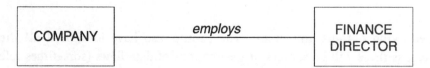

One-to-many relationship

2.6   The relationship **employs** also exists between *company* and *director*. The company employs more than one director.

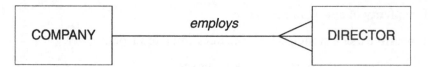

Many-to-one relationship

2.7   This is really the same as the previous example, but **viewed from the opposite direction**. For example, many *sales managers* report to one *sales director*.

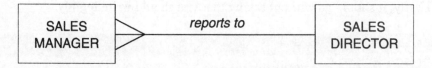

Many-to-many relationship

2.8   The relationship between *product* and *part* is **many-to-many**. A product is composed of many parts, and a part might be used in many products.

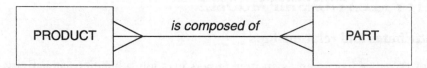

Breaking down relationships

2.9   Many-to-many relationships **cause difficulties** when designing the software to search for items and they should if possible be broken down so that they are eliminated.

2.10 The relationship depicted above could be amended by the insertion of a **new entity** called 'job sheet'. Thus a product is manufactured to job sheets and job sheets specify a part.

Entity relationship models

> **KEY TERM**
>
> An entity relationship model (ERM) (also known as an **entity model** or a **logical data structure**) provides an understanding of the logical data requirements of a system independently of the system's organisation and processes.

2.11 An **entity relationship model (ERM)** uses one-to-one, one-to-many and many-to-many relationships. These relationships can also be described by the notations: *1:1*, *1:n* and *m:n* respectively.

2.12 The correct classification of relationships is important. If the one-to-many relationship **customer order contains part numbers** is incorrectly described as one-to-one, the system designed on the basis of this ERM might allow an order to be entered with one item and one item only, thus necessitating the creation of a separate order for each part.

2.13 EXAMPLE: ERM

An example of a diagram relevant to a warehousing and despatch system is given below. This indicates that:

- a **customer** may make **many orders**

- that an **order form** can contain **several order lines**

- that each **line** on the order form can only detail **one product**, but that one product can appear on several lines of the order.

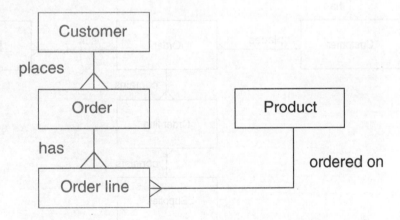

2.14 Another example of an entity model is given below. Note the structure of the accompanying narrative.

> **Exam focus point**
>
> An exam question might give you an ERM and ask you to provide the narrative or find flaws in the diagram. Such a question came up in **June 1996**.

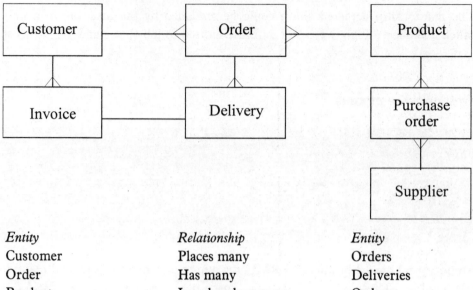

Entity	Relationship	Entity
Customer	Places many	Orders
Order	Has many	Deliveries
Product	Is ordered on many	Orders
Supplier	Supplies many	Products
Product	Is ordered on many	Purchase orders
Supplier	Receives many	Purchase orders
Invoice	Is for one	Deliveries
Customer	Receives many	Invoices

Question 4

Customers send orders in to your company. The company send supplies to customers as soon as the order, or part of the order, can be fulfilled. An invoice is raised for each delivery. Draw an entity relationship model to show these procedures.

Answer

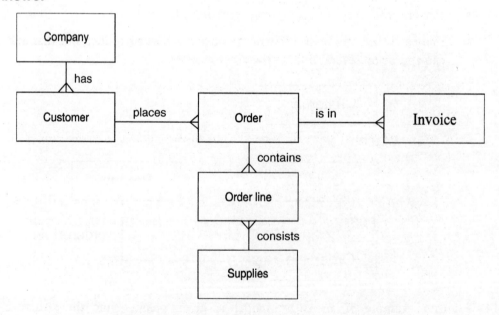

---

3 ENTITY LIFE HISTORIES

3.1 Don't confuse **entity life histories** (logical data structures) with **entity relationship models** which take a **static** view of the data.

KEY TERM

An **entity life history** (ELH) is a diagram of the *processes* that happen to an *entity*. Data items do not remain unchanged at all times, they may come into existence by a specific operation and be destroyed by another. For example, a customer order forms part of a number of processes, and is affected by a number of different events. An entity life history gives a **dynamic** view of the data.

3.2   At its simplest, an entity life history displays the following structure.

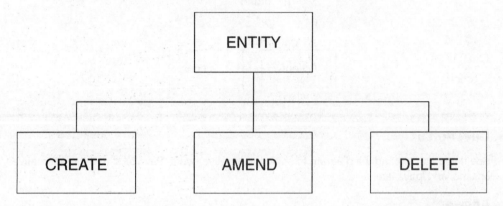

3.3   Entity life histories identify the various states that an entity can legitimately be in. It is really the **functions and events** which cause the state of the entity to change that are being analysed, rather than the entity itself. The ELH diagram provides a pictorial way of communication that enables users to validate easily the accuracy (or otherwise) of the analysis.

3.4   The following conventions for ELHs are used in SSADM and in the examiner's book on systems analysis.

  (a)   **Three** symbols are used. The main one is a **rectangular** box. Within this may be placed an **asterisk** or a **small circle**. as explained below.

  (b)   At the top level the first box (the **'root node'**) shows the **entity** itself.

  (c)   At lower levels the boxes represent **events** that affect the life of the entity.

  (d)   The second level is most commonly some form of **'create, amend, delete'**, as shown above (or birth, life, death if you prefer). The boxes are read **in sequence** from left to right.

  (e)   If an event may affect an entity many times (**iteration**) this is shown by an asterisk in the top right hand corner of the box. A customer account, for example, will be updated many times.

  (f)   If events are alternatives (for example accept large order or reject large order) (**selection**) a small circle is placed in the top right hand corner.

3.5   Note the three types of process logic:

  •   **Sequence**
  •   **Iteration**
  •   **Selection**

3.6   Here is a very simple example.

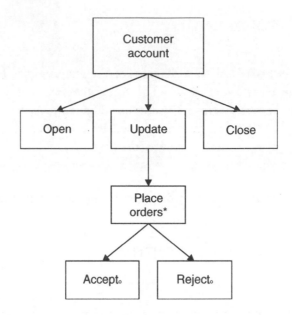

Question 5

See if you can expand the diagram to show the iterative event 'Pays bills' and the alternatives 'pays on time' and 'pays late'

Answer

Your diagram should be along the following lines: another (iteration) box coming out of the update box called something like 'Pays'; two selection boxes coming out of the 'Pays' box for 'On time' and 'Late'.

---

4   NORMALISATION

4.1   When thinking about how data should be organised in a computer system two features are particularly desirable.

 (a)   **Links** between items of data that are related, such as **customer name** and **customer address,** should be preserved.

 (b)   **Duplication** of data items should be avoided, so that as **little space** is taken up as possible, and so that there is as little chance as possible of **inconsistencies** between examples of the same data stored in different places.

4.2   **Normalisation** is a way of achieving this.

> ### KEY TERM
>
> **Normalisation** is a step-by-step process in which a set of related data fields are refined into new sets having progressively simpler and more regular structure.
>
> Normalisation is also called **relational data analysis**.

4.3   Normalisation is a useful technique for designing 'relational' databases, as we shall see in Chapter 14. You may find it particularly valuable if you are ever expected to use a package such as Microsoft Access at work.

4.4 EXAMPLE: NORMALISATION

An organisation has the following table of data showing which customers are interested in which products. You are required to convert it to 'Third Normal Form'

Product Code	Product Name	Customer code	Customer name	Customer Since	Sales Rep Code	Sales Rep name	Credit Status	Discount %
A005	Large	A071	Agassi	02/02/95	145	Singh	A	10
		L015	Laver	05/04/96	145	Singh	C	5
		W006	Wade	31/10/96	172	Michaels	D	5
		B104	Becker	25/11/94	145	Singh	F	0
		W015	Wade	13/07/93	172	Michaels	B	7
A006	Medium	L015	Laver	05/04/96	175	Hempel	E	0
		F094	Frentzen	06/08/95	175	Hempel	B	7
		D149	Dumali	02/03/97	175	Hempel	C	5
A007	Small	F094	Frentzen	06/08/95	175	Hempel	A	10
		W015	Wade	13/07/93	144	Calder	B	7
		S022	Scholes	17/09/96	144	Calder	E	0
		H053	Henman	19/05/97	175	Hempel	C	5

4.5 SOLUTION

In normalisation a row of data is called a **row** (!), and a column is called a **field**. The **column headings** are the names of the fields.

Step 1. Identify the **key field.**

This is a term worth highlighting again, although you have met it before.

> ### KEY TERM
>
> The **key field** is the item of data within a row by which the row can be uniquely identified.

- Choose a **code** rather than a text field, if possible
- Choose a field that is **not determined** by any other field or combination of fields

In this case, **product code** seems the obvious choice. (In theory it does not matter what you choose: normalisation will always give the same end-result. However, a good choice at the start saves work.)

Step 2. Convert to **First Normal Form** by **removing repeating groups**

A **repeating group** is a field or set of fields which have data in them more than once for a single value of the key field.

This is easy to see in our example. Each product code has a related product name field that has data in it only once, while each of the other fields have several different data items. There is repeating group of data about customers.

The original table is therefore split into two. The repeating data has the key field appended to it to **preserve the link** between all data items.

Product Code	Product Name
A005	Large
A006	Medium
A007	Small

Product Code	Customer Code	Customer Name	Customer Since	Sales Rep Code	Sales Rep Name	Credit Status	Discount %
A005	A071	Agassi	02/02/95	145	Singh	A	10
A005	L015	Laver	05/04/96	145	Singh	C	5
A005	W006	Wade	31/10/96	172	Michaels	D	5
A005	B104	Becker	25/11/94	145	Singh	F	0
A005	W015	Wade	13/07/93	172	Michaels	B	7
A006	L015	Laver	05/04/96	175	Hempel	E	0
A006	F094	Frentzen	06/08/95	175	Hempel	B	7
A006	D149	Dumali	02/03/97	175	Hempel	C	5
A007	F094	Frentzen	06/08/95	175	Hempel	A	10
A007	W015	Wade	13/07/93	144	Calder	B	7
A007	S022	Scholes	17/09/96	144	Calder	E	0
A007	H053	Henman	19/05/97	175	Hempel	C	5

Step 3. **Identify key fields** for the new tables

The Product Code table's key field will clearly be Product Code

However, there are a number of rows in the second table with the same Product Code. A better choice would be **Customer Code,** but this does not uniquely identify a row. For instance two rows have the code L015.

In this case we use a **compound key** which is made up of two or more fields which together uniquely identify a row. In this case we can use **Product Code and Customer Code.**

A simpler way of presenting the story so far is as follows. The **key field(s)** are shown in **bold**.

PRODUCT   **Product Code,** Product Name

PRODUCT/CUSTOMER   **Product Code, Customer Code,** Customer Name, Customer Since, Sales Rep Code, Sales Rep Name, Credit Status, Discount %

Exam focus point
A question in June 1997 presents partially normalised data in this way, and the examiner also uses this style in his book on Systems Analysis.

Step 4. Convert to **Second Normal Form** by ensuring that **EITHER**:

- The key is a single item **OR**

- Fields that are not key are **fully dependent** on **all of the fields that are key,** not just **part** of them

In our example the PRODUCT table's key is a single item, so it is already in second normal form.

In the PRODUCT/CUSTOMER table, however, some of the non-key items do not depend on both of the key fields.

- Customer name and Customer Since could be determined from (in other words they depend on) Customer Code

- However Sales Rep Code, Sales Rep Name, Credit Status and Discount % can only be determined by referring to both Product Code and Customer Code.

Question 6

If the Customer Code is L015 what is Sales Rep Name?

Answer

It could be either Singh or Hempel. You have to know the Product Code as well as the Customer Code to identify a particular row. Try some other combinations like this for yourself until you are sure you understand.

We can **remove** the fields that are **not fully dependent** on both Product Code and Customer Code to their own CUSTOMER table, with **Customer Code** the clear candidate for key field.

Customer Code	Customer Name	Customer Since
A071	Agassi	02/02/95
L015	Laver	05/04/96
W006	Wade	31/10/96
B104	Becker	25/11/94
W015	Wade	13/07/93
L015	Laver	05/04/96
F094	Frentzen	06/08/95
D149	Dumali	02/03/97
F094	Frentzen	06/08/95
W015	Wade	13/07/93
S022	Scholes	17/09/96
H053	Henman	19/05/97

This leaves the PRODUCT/CUSTOMER table looking like this.

Product Code	Customer Code	Sales Rep Code	Sales Rep Name	Credit Status	Discount %
A005	A071	145	Singh	A	10
A005	L015	145	Singh	C	5
A005	W006	172	Michaels	D	5
A005	B104	145	Singh	F	0
A005	W015	172	Michaels	B	7
A006	L015	175	Hempel	E	0
A006	F094	175	Hempel	B	7
A006	D149	175	Hempel	C	5
A007	F094	175	Hempel	A	10
A007	W015	144	Calder	B	7
A007	S022	144	Calder	E	0
A007	H053	175	Hempel	C	5

Here is another an alternative presentation of the story so far. The <u>key fields</u> are <u>underlined</u>.

(The **examiner** uses *this* style in his book, as well as the other alternative presentation shown on the previous page.)

Product Code	Product Code	Customer Code
Product name	Customer Code	Customer Name
	Sales Rep Code	Customer Since
	Sales Rep Name	
	Credit Status	
	Discount %	

Step 5. Convert to **Third Normal Form** by ensuring that **BOTH**:

- all **non-key fields** are **independent** of all other non-key fields; **AND**

- all **key fields** are **independent** of all other key fields.

The PRODUCT table and the CUSTOMER table are already in third normal form.

In the PRODUCT/CUSTOMER table, however, Sales Rep Name is determined by Sales Rep Code and Discount % is determined by Credit Status (but not vice versa: a discount of 5% is given to both grade C and D credit risks, for instance). There are clearly some non-key dependencies.

As for the key fields in the PRODUCT/CUSTOMER table, there is more than one possible value for Customer Code given a single Product Code, and there is more than one possible value for Product Code given a single value of Customer Code. Neither field determines what the other will be so they are independent.

We can now remove the dependencies in the PRODUCT/CUSTOMER table to give the following final result.

PRODUCT	**Product Code,** Product Name
PRODUCT/CUSTOMER	**Product Code, Customer Code,** Sales Rep Code, Credit Status
CUSTOMER	**Customer Code,** Customer Name, Customer Since
SALES REP	**Sales Rep Code,** Sales Rep Name
CREDIT STATUS	**Credit Status,** Discount %

Notice that the PRODUCT/CUSTOMER table retains the fields Sales Rep Code and Credit Status to preserve the links between the tables.

Question 7

Given a particular Customer Code, how would you find out that customer's Discount %?

Answer

You could look up the customer's Credit Status in the PRODUCT/CUSTOMER table, and then look up the Discount % that applied to that status in the CREDIT STATUS table. Again, try any other combinations you can think of.

Section Summary

4.6 Normalisation is a way of **analysing and simplifying the relationships** between items of data (it is also called relational data analysis). This is done in three stages, as follows.

First Normal Form (1NF)	Remove repeating groups
Second Normal Form (2NF)	Remove part-key dependencies
Third Normal Form (3NF)	Remove non-key dependencies and inter-key dependencies

Exam focus point

In the exam it is most likely that you would be given data in the format:

TABLE 1   **Key field,** Non-key field 1, Non key field 2
TABLE 2   **Key field,** Non-key field

You would then be asked to spot problems that prevented the data from being in 3NF and asked how to put them right.

5   LOOKING FORWARD ...

5.1   We are ending this chapter at this point because we think you deserve a rest and a chance to absorb what you have learned so far. Everything in this chapter is highly examinable.

5.2   More systems development techniques are described in the next chapter.

Chapter roundup

- **Dataflow diagrams** are used to record the ways in which data is processed without taking account of physical factors. There are only four symbols used in dataflow diagrams.

- An **entity relationship model** provides an understanding of a system's logical data requirements independently of the system's processes. The ERM uses 1:1, 1:n and m:n relationships.

- An **entity life history** is a diagram of the processes that happen to an entity. It gives a dynamic view of the data, rather than a static view of it. It describes how an entity comes into existence, the processes to which it is subjected and the way in which it is terminated.

- **Normalisation** is a technique used in the creation of a relational database. It allows the complex relationships between entities to be simplified so that all the data for an entity can be held in two-dimensional tables.

Quick quiz

1   Draw and label the four symbols used in a data flow diagram. (see para 1.1)

2   What is a context diagram? (1.12)

3   What connections are not allowed in a DFD? (1.28)

4   What three relationships may be found in an entity relationship model? (2.11)

5   How are sequence, iteration and selection depicted in an ELH diagram? (3.4)

6   What is normalisation? (4.2)

7   What is a 'key' or 'key field'? (4.5)

8   What are the three stages of normalisation? (4.6)

Question to try	Level	Marks	Time
14	Exam standard	10	18 mins

Chapter 13

MORE SYSTEMS DEVELOPMENT TECHNIQUES

Chapter topic list	Syllabus reference
1 Structured English	3(f)
2 Decision trees	3(f)
3 Decision tables	3(f)

Introduction

This chapter is a continuation of the last. Here we look at what are sometimes called **process specification tools.** These set out in detail the logic behind a data process that might simply be described as 'Process order' in a DFD.

Many students are **scared** of Structured English and decision tables. If you try hard to master them, therefore, you stand a good chance of outshining your fellow students on exam day!

1   STRUCTURED ENGLISH

1.1   A 'structured narrative' is a systems design tool which describes the logic of a process in a highly detailed narrative form.

1.2   This method uses **English** as the language but **severely limits the available vocabulary** and tries to follow the layout and logical operation of a computer program.

1.3   This tool is **not particularly easy to use** or to understand. It is best suited for describing **specific activities** or functions, while the broader and more general concerns of system design are typically analysed by using data flow diagrams and decision tables or trees, which are better at simplifying procedures and choices into a presentable format.

Exam focus point
Structured English featured in a question set by the **new** examiner in **December 1997**. The old examiner included it in questions in **June 1994, December 1994** and **June 1995**.

1.4   There are several different kinds of Structured English. What is important is that Structured English has the following features.

(a)   It is more **like spoken English** than normal programming languages and so is easier for programmers and non-programmers to understand.

(b)   It is much **more limited than normal speech,** as it has to follow a **strict logical order**.

(c)   There is a **variety of conventions** for writing it.

1.5   Structured English uses **keywords** (eg IF, ADD) which, by some conventions, are written in capitals and have a **precise logical meaning** in the context of the narrative.

1.6   The logical order in which instructions are performed is sometimes expressed in indentation. As we have seen in the previous chapter, there are **three basic logical structures**.

- Sequencing
- Selection
- Iteration

1.7   The **data elements** which are the subject of processing are, by some conventions, written in lower case and underlined.

1.8   Some conventions begin a description of a system with the word **DO** and finish with **ENDDO** (for example 'DO Process stock delivery ... ENDDO').

Sequence instruction

1.9   For example, the calculation of gross pay from hours worked and rate of pay could be written in structured English. This type of instruction is known as a **sequence** instruction.

> MULTIPLY hours worked by pay rate to get
> gross pay

1.10   It is possible to **aggregate sequence instructions**. For example the computation of gross pay in a program not only involves simple calculation but includes other processes.

(a)   Retrieving master records from a file for the employee reference.

> GET master record

(b)   Counting records so that the next record in sequence is retrieved.

> ADD 1 to counter

Selection instruction

1.11   Most computer programs offer a number of **'choices'** and the consequent action taken depends on the choices being made. In structured English, a choice follows this structure.

```
IF
            THEN
ELSE
            THEN
ENDIF
```

1.12   For example, a company offers **discounts to trade customers only**. How would this be expressed in structured English?

```
IF the customer is a trade customer
            THEN give 10% discount
ELSE (customer is not trade customer)
            THEN no discount given
ENDIF
```

1.13   Sometimes, decisions are more complicated. Assume that the company only offers a 10% discount to trade customers who have been customers for over one year, but other trade customers receive a 5% discount.

> IF the customer is a <u>trade customer</u>
>   IF customer is customer over 1 year
>   THEN 10% discount given
>   ELSE 5% discount given
>   ELSE (customer not a <u>trade customer</u>)
>   THEN no discount given
> ENDIF

1.14   One particular type of decision is a **CASE statement**. Cases are a special type of decision structure to indicate **mutually exclusive possibilities**.

1.15   A case structure is an alternative to the IF-THEN-ELSE-SO structure outlined above, which is satisfactory for making relatively simple decisions, but can become unwieldy when the decision becomes complex.

1.16   For example, we could have expressed the trade credit policy as follows. (END IF ends the case statement.)

> IF customer a <u>trade customer</u>
>   CASE   customer for more than one year
>   give 10% discount
>   CASE   customer for less than one year
>   give 5% discount
> END IF

Iteration

1.17   Sometimes a block or set of instructions may need to be **repeated** until a final condition is reached.

For example, assume we have called a given block out instructions the name Block 1. We wish these instructions to be executed until the number of records processed reaches 100. This requirement is a **condition**, which we can call condition 1. In structured English, this can be written as follows.

> REPEAT
>   Block 1
> UNTIL
>   Condition 1

Exam focus point
If you follow these general principles - sequence, selection and iteration - it does not matter much what specific instruction words you use or how you describe data elements.

2   DECISION TREES

2.1   You may have met decision trees as part of your studies for **Paper 3** in the context of expected values, probabilities and so on. In Paper 5 they are slightly different.

KEY TERM

A **decision tree** is a design tool which provides a **graphic** representation of the various **choices or decisions which are available,** the events which might occur and their consequences.

2.2   EXAMPLE: DECISION TREES

Consider an order processing system. Whenever an order is received the system should first check to determine if payment has been received with the order. There are two possibilities - yes and no - which lead on to differing responses.

(a)   If payment **is included** with the order, the system would then have to check on the availability of the items ordered. Here there are two further possibilities - the items can be in stock or not.

   (i)   If the items are in stock they would then be shipped or delivered to the customer.

   (ii)   If the item is not in stock a record of the customer's order needs to be made so that the item will be despatched when stock becomes available.

(b)   If the customer has **not included** payment with order a similar set of activities would be undertaken but they would be preceded by credit evaluations.

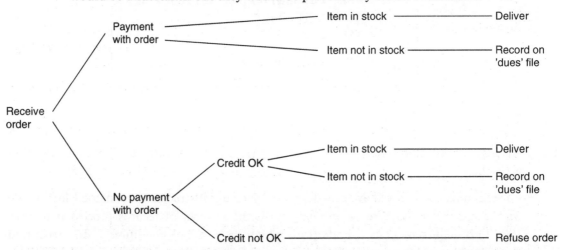

2.3   In the discussion above the focus was upon **imposing an order or structure** upon the decision-making process so that a computerised system could replicate the sequence of **decision-event-decision** as necessary.

2.4   In many cases in business the **likelihood** of various responses or conditions can be predicted or is known. In the example used above, we may know from past experience that most orders are prepaid or are for items held in stock. This information will be useful since it can be **used to predict** which systems functions may be most heavily used.

2.5   Decision trees are methods used to **select the most appropriate or optimum option** at each stage in the process. This approach may also be built into an information system. If the likelihood of various subsequent events may be estimated it is then possible to design the system so that it will attempt to select the option which leads to the best outcome.

Drawing decision trees

2.6   It is conventional to draw decision trees from **left to right**.

2.7   You may also have encountered conventions which use, for example, a box for a decision point and a circle for an **outcome point**. These are more usually associated with decision trees used for statistical or decision-making purposes, where probabilities and expected values are assigned to each outcome.

2.8   Here, we are concerned with representing the **logic** of a process and so it is quite acceptable to draw decision trees **without such conventions**. For example, in the diagram above, the first point does not really represent a decision or an outcome. We are simply showing the two possible states of a customer order: either payment is included with the order or the customer expects to be given credit.

Question 1

Draw a decision tree to represent the following procedure for development of new employees in an organisation.

Employees with a relevant degree may either joint the graduate entry programme or, provided they are in the top 15% in special aptitude tests, undergo accelerated management training. Those with other degrees are eligible for the graduate entry programme only. Employees without a degree but with other qualifications join the main intake stream. Employees without any qualifications are taken on at clerical grades.

Answer

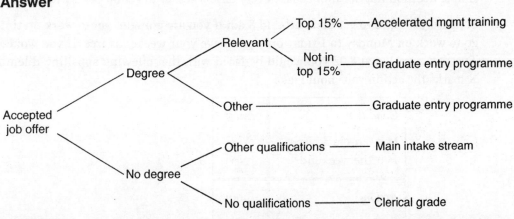

Disadvantages of decision trees

2.9   Decision trees are usually structured so that each decision has a **maximum of two outcomes**. This leads to potential inefficiencies in the use of decision trees.

(a)   An action may result from more than one condition, leading to **repetition**.

(b)   Very **long or complex** processes will be **difficult to adapt** to this method because choices could easily be missed or the tree size could become unmanageable.

(c)   It might take **several runs** through the tree to complete all possibilities. In the exercise above, how would you treat a new employee who has a non-relevant degree, a relevant degree *and* other qualifications?

3   **DECISION TABLES**

3.1   Decision tables are used as a method of defining the logic of a process (ie the processing operations required) in a compact manner. They are **more convenient than decision trees** in situations where a **large number of logical alternatives exist**.

3.2   The basic format consists of four quadrants divided by intersecting double lines.

Condition stub	Condition entry
Action stub	Action entry

3.3   **SIMPLE EXAMPLE: A DECISION TABLE**

The technique is **quite hard to grasp at first** so we shall start by considering a very simple decision that most of us face every day: whether to get up or stay in bed.

Suppose you have to get up at around 8 am if you are going to get to work on time. You go to work on Monday to Friday only and have your weekends free. If you woke up one Tuesday morning at 8.02 you would be faced with the following appalling dilemma. An X marks the action you should take.

Conditions	*Entry*
Is it 8 o' clock yet?	Yes
Is it the weekend?	No
Actions	*Entry*
Get up	X
Stay in bed	

3.4   We can expand this table so that it takes account of **all the possible combinations** of conditions and shows the action that would be taken in each case.

(a)   Because a condition can only apply or not apply (Yes or No), **the number of combinations (or 'rules') is 2^n, where n is the number of conditions.**

Here there are 2 conditions (n = 2) so the number of combinations is $2^2 = 4$. There are four columns.

	1	2	3	4
Is it 8 o' clock yet?				
Is it the weekend?				
Get up				
Stay in bed				

(b) Because the conditions can either have a Yes or No answer (Y or N) **half** of the each row must be filled with Ys and the other half with Ns.

(i) Write in Y for the first half of the columns in row 1 (columns 1 and 2) and N for the other half.

(ii) For row 2, write in Ys and Ns alternately, the number in each group of Ys and Ns being **half** that of each group in the previous row. In this example row 1 has Ys in groups of twos, so row 2 will have Ys in groups of 1.

(iii) If there are more conditions continue **halving** for each row until you reach the final condition, which will always be consecutive Ys and Ns.

	1	2	3	4
Is it 8 o' clock yet?	Y	Y	N	N
Is it the weekend?	Y	N	Y	N
Get up				
Stay in bed				

(c) Now **consider what action** you would take if the condition(s) specified in each column applied. For column 1 it is 8 o'clock but it is the weekend so you can stay in bed. For column 2 it is 8 o' clock but it is not the weekend so you must get up. Explain the logic of columns 3 and 4 yourself.

	1	2	3	4
Is it 8 o' clock yet?	Y	Y	N	N
Is it the weekend?	Y	N	Y	N
Get up		X		
Stay in bed	X		X	X

(d) In more complicated problems you may find that there are some columns that do not have any Xs in the Action entry quadrant because **this combination of conditions is impossible**. You can delete these columns. Question 5 will demonstrate this in a moment.

(e) Other columns have different combinations of conditions, but **lead to the same action**. Columns 1, 3 and 4 in the above example are of this type: they all say you can stay in bed. However, in columns 3 and 4 you can stay in bed because it is not yet 8 o clock.

It is **immaterial** whether it is the weekend or not: the answer can be Y or N. When a condition is immaterial to the decision we replace the Y or N with a **dash** – and **consolidate columns** if possible.

	1	2	3/4
Is it 8 o' clock yet?	Y	Y	N
Is it the weekend?	Y	N	–
Get up		X	
Stay in bed	X		X

(f) This is the final form of the table: it has been simplified as far as possible.

Question 2

L Bones woke up one morning and looked at the clock. It was 8.30. 'Oh no!', he thought, 'What day is it?' He lay in a daze for a moment and then realised it was Sunday.

Some hours later when he got up Mr Bones decided to draw up a decision table that he could use to save all this mental activity when he woke up in future. He identified 3 conditions, mirroring his early-morning thought processes, and 2 possible actions.

Conditions Is it 8 o' clock yet? Is it a weekday? Is it the weekend?

Actions   Get up. Stay in bed.

Draw up and complete the decision table.

Answer

There are 3 conditions so there will be $2^3 = 8$ columns.

	1	2	3	4	5	6	7	8
Is it 8 o' clock yet?	Y	Y	Y	Y	N	N	N	N
Is it a weekday?	Y	Y	N	N	Y	Y	N	N
Is it the weekend	Y	N	Y	N	Y	N	Y	N
Get up		X						
Stay in bed			X			X	X	

Columns 1, 4, 5 and 8 do not have any Xs because, thankfully of course, it cannot be both a weekday *and* a weekend. The impossibility of this combination is intuitively obvious in this simple example, but in more complex or less familiar decision situations it may only become clear that certain combinations are impossible once the table has been drawn up.

In this example we could delete columns 1, 4, 5 and 8 and cross out one or other of conditions 2 or 3, since if one applies the other doesn't. Columns 6 and 7 would be consolidated and we would end up with the same decision table as the one we saw earlier (although with the columns in a different order.)

Check that you understand all of this before continuing. Perhaps try out some other homely examples for yourself.

A more formal explanation

3.5   We can now explain this more formally and look at a business example.

- The purpose of the **condition stub** is to specify the values of the data that we wish to test for.

- The **condition entry** specifies what those values might be.

3.6   Between them, the condition stub and condition entry show what values an item of data might have that a computer program should test for. Establishing conditions will be done within a computer program by means of **comparison checks**.

3.7   The **action entry** quadrant shows the action or actions that will be performed for each rule. The columns are marked with an 'X' opposite the actions(s) to be taken. In the computer program, instructions specify the action to take, given the conditions established by comparison checks.

Exam focus point

Questions by the old examiner in **June 1994** and **December 1994** asked students to contrast decision tables with Structured English and decision trees. In a question in **December 1997** the new examiner asked why Structured English was preferable to a decision table in a particular case.

3.8 EXAMPLE: A DECISION TABLE

Consider the **three conditions** which might be encountered by a sales order processing clerk taking a telephone order.

Account overdue?	Y	Y	Y	Y	N	N	N	N
Credit limit exceeded?	Y	Y	N	N	Y	Y	N	N
New customer?	Y	N	Y	N	Y	N	Y	N

3.9 There are **eight separate rules** (2^3). In this example the three conditions are totally **independent**, that is, the answer to one will not affect the answer to the others. As we have seen, in some tables the conditions are not totally independent and there will be fewer columns.

3.10 Continuing the above example, suppose that the **actions** are as follows.

An order should be placed on hold if the customer's account balance is overdue and it exceeds the customer's credit limit. If the order is processed, a reminder should be generated for overdue balances and a reference should be obtained if the customer is a new one. If the customer is not new, then the appropriate level of discount should be given. New customer orders in excess of the credit limit should be referred to the section head.

3.11 From this description we can isolate six actions

- 'Place on hold'
- 'Process order'
- 'Send reminder'
- 'Obtain reference'
- 'Give discount'
- 'Refer to head'

3.12 Consider the fifth rule in the table below. There is no overdue balance on the account, but a new customer wishes to exceed his credit limit. The action entry will therefore show an X against 'Process order'; 'Obtain reference' and 'Refer to head'.

Rule	1	2	3	4	5	6	7	8
Account overdue?	Y	Y	Y	Y	N	N	N	N
Credit limit exceeded?	Y	Y	N	N	Y	Y	N	N
New customer?	Y	N	Y	N	Y	N	Y	N
Place on hold								
Process order					X			
Send reminder								
Obtain reference					X			
Give discount								
Refer to head					X			

3.13   By considering each rule in turn the table can be completed.

Rule	1	2	3	4	5	6	7	8
Account overdue?	Y	Y	Y	Y	N	N	N	N
Credit limit exceeded?	Y	Y	N	N	Y	Y	N	N
New customer?	Y	N	Y	N	Y	N	Y	N
Place on hold	X	X						
Process order			X	X	X	X	X	X
Send reminder			X	X				
Obtain reference			X		X		X	
Give discount				X		X		X
Refer to head	X				X			

Question 3

Sales orders are processed and approved by a computer. Management has laid down the following conditions. Construct a decision table to reflect these procedures.

(a)   If an order is between £10 and £100 a 3% discount is given, if the credit rating is good. If the customer has been buying from the company for over 5 years, the discount is increased to 4%.

(b)   If an order is more than £100 a 5% discount is given, if the credit rating is good. If the customer has been buying from the company for over 5 years, the discount is increased to 6%.

(c)   If the credit rating is not good in either case the order is referred to the supervisor.

(d)   For orders under £10 no discount is given.

Answer

There are five *conditions*.

(1)   Is the order < £10?
(2)   Is the order £10 - £100?
(3)   Is the order > £100?
(4)   Is the credit rating good?
(5)   Has the customer been buying > 5 years?

Note that the 'cut-off' values must be precisely stated.

There are seven *actions:* approve, refer on, give one of 5 levels of discount.

32 rules are required (2^5). This results in the following table.

	1	2	3	4	5	6	7	8	9	10	11	12	13	14	15	16	17	18	19	20	21	22	23	24	25	26	27	28	29	30	31	32
Order < £10	Y	Y	Y	Y	Y	Y	Y	Y	Y	Y	Y	Y	Y	Y	Y	Y	N	N	N	N	N	N	N	N	N	N	N	N	N	N	N	N
Order £10 - £100	Y	Y	Y	Y	Y	Y	Y	Y	N	N	N	N	N	N	N	N	Y	Y	Y	Y	Y	Y	Y	Y	N	N	N	N	N	N	N	N
Order > £100	Y	Y	Y	Y	N	N	N	N	Y	Y	Y	Y	N	N	N	N	Y	Y	Y	Y	N	N	N	N	Y	Y	Y	Y	N	N	N	N
Rating good	Y	Y	N	N	Y	Y	N	N	Y	Y	N	N	Y	Y	N	N	Y	Y	N	N	Y	Y	N	N	Y	Y	N	N	Y	Y	N	N
5 years	Y	N	Y	N	Y	N	Y	N	Y	N	Y	N	Y	N	Y	N	Y	N	Y	N	Y	N	Y	N	Y	N	Y	N	Y	N	Y	N
Impossible	X	X	X	X	X	X	X	X	X	X	X	X					X	X	X	X									X	X	X	X
Approve													X	X	X	X																
0%													X	X	X	X																
3%																						X										
4%																					X											
5%																										X						
6%																									X							
Refer																							X	X			X	X				

This means unwieldy construction (particularly in an examination). Condition 3 can be removed from the decision table. For example, if the answers to conditions 1 and 2 are NO then the answer to condition 3 must be YES, (unless there is an error) and so it need not be tested. In this way the decision table will be reduced to 16 rules.

Order < £10?	Y	Y	Y	Y	Y	Y	Y	Y	N	N	N	N	N	N	N	N
Order £10 - £100	Y	Y	Y	Y	N	N	N	N	Y	Y	Y	Y	N	N	N	N
Rating good	Y	Y	N	N	Y	Y	N	N	Y	Y	N	N	Y	Y	N	N
5 years	Y	N	Y	N	Y	N	Y	N	Y	N	Y	N	Y	N	Y	N
Impossible	X	X	X	X												
Approve					X	X	X	X								
0%					X	X	X	X								
3%										X						
4%									X							
5%														X		
6%													X			
Refer											X	X			X	X

In addition, the over 5 year condition is only relevant to orders for £10 or more, and so we need not test this condition when the order is below £10. This cuts the number of rules to 10.

Original rule no	13	15	21	22	23	24	25	26	27	28
Order < £10	Y	Y	N	N	N	N	N	N	N	N
Order £10-£100	N	N	Y	Y	Y	Y	N	N	N	N
Rating good	Y	N	Y	Y	N	N	Y	Y	N	N
5 years	-	-	Y	N	Y	N	Y	N	Y	N
Approve	X	X								
0%	X	X								
3%				X						
4%			X							
5%								X		
6%							X			
Refer					X	X			X	X

Three points arise from the above exercise.

(a)   Orders under £10 are processed whether the credit rating is good or not. Although this results in lack of control over small orders, management may feel that the risk is justified by the savings made in processing time.

(b)   After the first construction (the draft) the decision table should be redrawn to take into account:

(i)   the impossible combinations - these rules can be removed;

(ii) take rules which result in identical actions. These indicate which conditions need not be tested by the computer program, and highlight the order in which the conditions should be examined (to save processing time). In the example, rules 13/15 and 23/24 can be combined and it then becomes apparent that credit rating is immaterial if the order is less than £10; but if the credit rating is bad, it is immaterial whether the order is between £10 and £100, or over £100.

(c) For the customer > 5 years check, customers are given an extra 1% discount if they have been with the company over 5 years. Instead of 2 action entries, discount 4% and discount 6%, we can have a single action entry - add 1% to discount. The decision table could be refined still further.

Exam focus point

You are most unlikely to get such a large decision table as the one in Question 3 in the exam. The new examiner has shown a preference for solutions which take a two-table approach to the preparation of decision tables. The most recent question (**December 1997**) was a very simple one with only four rules.

The two-table approach

3.14 Read through the following narrative. (CASE and 4GLs are explained in a later chapter.)

'An organisation which has advertised for a systems analyst has received so many applications that it has devised a set of procedures for drawing up an interview shortlist.

All accredited systems analysts will be interviewed: those with CASE experience during the week commencing 27 June and those without during the following week. A reserve list will be drawn up of applicants with CASE experience but without systems analysis accreditation.

Applicants who are not accredited systems analysts but who have 4GL experience will have their application forms sent to an associated organisation which requires a 4GL expert. Those programmers with 4GL experience in a mainframe environment will be interviewed by this second organisation while others will be placed on a reserve list.

Any other applicants will receive a rejection letter.'

3.15 The standard single table approach to this problem would probably involve the identification of **four conditions**, as follows.

(a) Accredited systems analyst?
(b) CASE experience?
(c) 4GL experience?
(d) Mainframe experience?

3.16 This would give $2^4 = 16$ columns, and a total of **six actions**, as follows.

(a) Interview during w/c 27 June
(b) Interview during w/c 4 July
(c) Reserve list
(d) Interview at associated organisation
(e) Associated organisation's reserve list
(f) Reject

3.17 However, because condition (d) is relevant only to condition (c) and is not independent, and because condition (c) is not relevant if condition (a) applies, this approach is **inefficient**. For all the situations where the applicant is an accredited systems analyst, it simply does not matter whether he or she has 4GL experience, whether on mainframes or not.

3.18   The **recommended approach** is therefore to move **condition (d)** into a **separate table,** together with any **actions** which relate solely to that condition. A **cross-reference** from one table to the other must of course be added.

3.19   This amended approach produces the following tables.

Table A

Accredited systems analyst?	Y	Y	Y	Y	N	N	N	N
CASE Experience?	Y	Y	N	N	Y	Y	N	N
4GL experience?	Y	N	Y	N	Y	N	Y	N
Interview during w/c 27 June	X	X						
Interview during w/c 4 July			X	X				
Reserve list					X	X		
Do *Table B*					X		X	
Reject								X

Reduced Table A

Accredited systems analyst?	Y	Y	N	N	N	N
CASE Experience?	Y	N	Y	Y	N	N
4GL experience?	-	-	Y	N	Y	N
Interview during w/c 27 June	X					
Interview during w/c 4 July		X				
Reserve list			X	X		
Do *Table B*			X		X	
Reject						X

Table B

Mainframe experience?	Y	N
Interview at associated organisation	X	
Associated organisation's reserve list		X

Extended entry and mixed entry decision tables

3.20   Decision tables of the type we have just examined are called '**limited entry**' decision tables. In these, each condition is posed as a question requiring either a YES, NO or 'immaterial' answer and each action is either taken or not taken.

3.21   In an **extended entry decision table** the condition and the action stubs are more general, the exact condition or action being specified in the entry quadrants. A **mixed entry table** consists of both limited and extended entry lines within one table. An example will make this clear.

3.22   EXAMPLE: MIXED ENTRY DECISION TABLES

Reservation requests for the flights of the Caviar and Champagne Airline are dealt with according to the following rules. You are required to construct a mixed entry decision table of the procedure.

(a)   All flights contain both first and second class cabins.

(b)   If a seat is available on the flight of the requested class allocate seat and output a ticket for that class.

(c)   If not, where a first class passenger will accept a seat in the second class cabin and one is available, the seat is allocated and a second class ticket is output. Second class passengers are not offered a seat in the first class cabin.

(d) In cases where no seat is available to meet the request, output 'sorry, no seat' message.

3.23 SOLUTION

A mixed entry decision table is shown below.

Request is for:	1st	1st	1st	1st	2nd	2nd
1st class seat available?	Y	N	N	N		
2nd class acceptable?		Y	Y	N		
2nd class seat available?		Y	N		Y	N
Allocate seat	1st	2nd			2nd	
Issue ticket	1st	2nd			2nd	
Output 'sorry no seat'			X	X		X

3.24 Extended entry and mixed entry decision tables are **more compact** when constructed, and are useful as a **communication** method (eg to show the analysed problem to management).

3.25 However they are **more difficult** than limited entry decision tables to **prepare** and **check** for completeness.

The advantages and disadvantages of decision tables

3.26 The main **advantages** of using decision tables are as follows.

(a) It is possible to check that **all combinations** have been considered.
(b) They show a **cause and effect** relationship.
(c) It is easy to **trace from actions to conditions** (unlike in flowcharts).
(d) They are **easy to understand** and copy as they use a standardised format.
(e) **Alternatives can be grouped** to facilitate analysis.

3.27 However, there are some **disadvantages**.

(a) They are not suited to problems with **unclear** conditions or actions.

(b) They do not present the **step-by-step logic** of a process.

(c) In a case where certain procedures (ie actions) are performed in **every circumstance** (eg calculating a customer's new balance when an order is received) decision tables may get unnecessarily complex. **Structured English** is preferable for simple procedural actions.

Chapter roundup

- **Structured English** is a highly stylised and carefully disciplined version of the English language which seeks to eliminate the ambiguities and complexity of the natural language in order to make it suitable for **describing program operations and processes**. There are three basic logical structures: sequence, selection and iteration.

- A **decision tree** is a design tool which provides a graphic representation of the choices or decisions made in a particular process so long as these are not too numerous.

- **Decision tables** are another method of defining the logic of a process. The basic format consists of four quadrants, with **conditions** in the top half and the **actions** taken, when different combinations of conditions apply, in the bottom half.

Quick quiz

1   When might Structured English be used? (see para 1.3)

2   Explain the terms sequence, selection and iteration. (1.9 - 1.17)

3   What are the disadvantages of decision trees? (2.9)

4   How do you determine the number of columns in a decision table? (3.4(a))

5   What is meant by 'halving' in decision tables? (3.4(b))

6   When can columns in a decision table be consolidated? (3.4(e))

7   How are the tables in the two table approach to decision tables linked up? (3.18 - 3.19)

8   What are the advantages and disadvantages of decision tables? (3.26, 3.27)

Question to try	Level	Marks	Time
15	Exam standard	15	27 mins

Chapter 14

SYSTEMS DESIGN

Chapter topic list		Syllabus reference
1	Input and output design	1(b)
2	Dialogue design	1(b)
3	User-friendliness	1(b)
4	File and database design	3(e), 3(f)
5	Database structures	3(e), 3(f)
6	Data dictionaries	3(e), 3(f)
7	Using a database	3(e), 3(f)
8	CASE tools	3(f)
9	Prototyping	3(a), 3(f)
10	Developments in programming	3(f)

Introduction

As you can see from the topic list this chapter covers a lot of ground. A lot of it is highly examinable, too, so don't attempt this chapter if you are not reasonably fresh.

It might be helpful to take this chapter in three chunks.

- Sections 1 to 3 look at the design aspects of how **users** interact with the system and the relevant **input/output** issues.

- Sections 4 to 7, the **most important** part of this chapter, look at how files and data can be **stored** most efficiently.

- Sections 8 to 10 look at various **software tools** that can help maintain the integrity of the systems design process or help to speed it up.

One or two other areas that might be relevant in this context, such as different technologies available for input, and the choice between bespoke design and off-the-shelf packages have already been covered in Chapters 4 and 8.

1 INPUT AND OUTPUT DESIGN

Input design

1.1 The design of input is important because in most computer systems data is first of all collected in **human-sensible** form and must be 'converted' into computer input.

1.2 People are thus very much involved in providing the data that the computer system will use, and in input design the **requirements of the system** must be balanced with the personal **capabilities of its users**. Input design is closely bound up with data collection and data capture.

1.3 There are a number of different considerations for input design. These are as follows.

(a) Which input data will become **standing** data and which input will be regular **transaction** data? There should be no **unnecessary re-input** of data - for example, if standing file data includes a customer's name, address and code (account) number, it should only be necessary to input the unique **customer code** number with any transaction data for the customer. Transaction records should not contain name and address.

(b) What **volumes** of input are expected? **Large volumes** of input are more likely to lend themselves to a **batch processing** system rather than a random access interactive processing system.

(c) What will be the **frequency** of input? Infrequent transaction data might suggest a random access system from keyboard terminals. With batched input, however, the frequency of input must be considered.

(d) In what **sequence** should batched data be input? For example, data for file maintenance ought to be input in batches before transaction data, to ensure that the standing data is up-to-date before the transaction data is processed.

(e) **Where** will data be collected or captured for input? Where will it be converted into machine-sensible form? In general, it is preferable to capture data as soon as possible and to keep to a minimum the transcription of data from one 'source' document to other document before input.

(f) For computer systems, what should be the **input medium**?

(g) Is the **need for accuracy** very important (are inaccuracies costly or unacceptable?) and so should there be verification of input? How extensive should built-in data validation checks be?

Output design

1.4 The design of output will cover the following factors. These overlap to some extent.

Factor	Comment/Example
Why produced?	Where appropriate, the conditions giving rise to the production of output should be specified - ie what needs to happen first for a particular report or item to be produced as output?
Frequency of production	Is it produced weekly, or daily, or by the hour? Is there any urgency in its production? Response times for keyboard interrogations should be specified.
Volume	If output volumes are very large, high-speed printer output is appropriate.
Sequence	For instance it might be desirable to print out exception reports such as lists of slow payers before a full debtors listing is produced.
Output medium	Output which will be used as input to another program or module will need an electronic medium, such as disk. The choice of output medium will have regard to whether a hard copy is required and what quality the output should be, whether hard copy or VDU display.
Content and format	Printouts and VDU displays must be well designed, because they are the primary point of communication between information systems and users. The layout and contents of any piece of output must be clear and designed to a high standard of presentation.

Factor	Comment/Example
Screen displays	Whenever displays are being designed it is vital to consider their purpose and present the information so that users can quickly see and understand it. The VDU is used as both an input and an output device in many systems. There is more on this later in this Chapter
Identification	All output report documents and VDU screen displays etc must be clearly specified and uniquely identified.

1.5 The **costs and benefits** of output information should also be considered. The user might be asking for information that would be too costly to produce in view of the benefits obtainable from it. The systems designer should discuss these matters with the users.

(a) Is the user asking for **too much information**?

(b) Can two or more required outputs be **combined** into a single multi-use output?

(c) Is the output required as frequently as specified, or can the frequency be reduced?

(d) Should output be produced **automatically**, or only **on demand**?

(e) Does the **response time** have to be so short, or is some delay acceptable?

(f) Does the user need some **control over the format and sequence** of output, or should format and sequence be rigidly designed?

2 DIALOGUE DESIGN

The human computer interface

2.1 Most people operate computers using a keyboard and a screen. The important thing about screen and keyboard is the capacity for **'feedback'** between user and computer that they provide, allowing the system to be highly flexible, interactive and conversational.

2.2 The way the keyboard is used, and what you would expect to see on the screen, will therefore depend on the particular strategy for **'screen dialogue'** that the software adopts.

2.3 This **dialogue** between the system and its users might be a central feature of the running of a program, and the term **conversational mode** describes a method of operation in which the operator appears to be carrying on a continual interactive dialogue with the computer, receiving immediate replies to input messages.

2.4 Broadly speaking, there are three ways of using a keyboard with VDU to input data. Any system is likely to use a combination of the three.

(a) By selecting options from a **menu**.

(b) By filling in a **form**.

(c) Using a **graphical user interface**.

Menu selection

2.5 A menu is a **list of items to choose from**. For example, a main menu for a sales ledger system might include the following items.

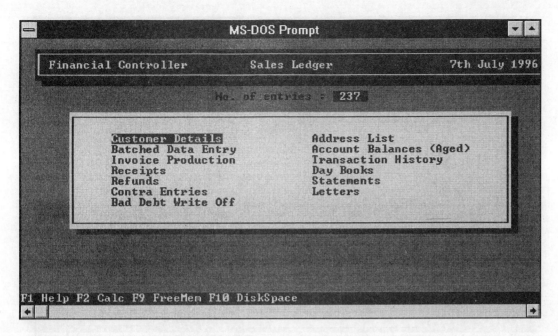

2.6   By selecting **Account Balances (Aged)**, the operator will be specifying that he or she wants to call up a list of account balances. **Another menu** may then be displayed, calling for the operator to narrow down still further the specification of what he or she wants to see, for example by specifying a particular account number or range of codes.

2.7   A menu system is thus a **hierarchical** list of options.

Form filling

2.8   With form filling the screen is landscaped for specific user requirements. Relevant data fields may be set up within an on-screen **skeleton** form.

2.9   **Screen formatting** for this purpose usually includes several features.

- **Different colours** for different screen areas.
- **Reverse video** (where colours in a selected area are the reverse of the rest of it).
- **Flashing** items.
- **Larger characters** for titles.
- Paging or **scrolling** depending on the volume of information.

2.10   Data is entered **automatically** in some fields when codes are entered. Other entries are made by **moving the cursor** from one field to the next and typing in the data.

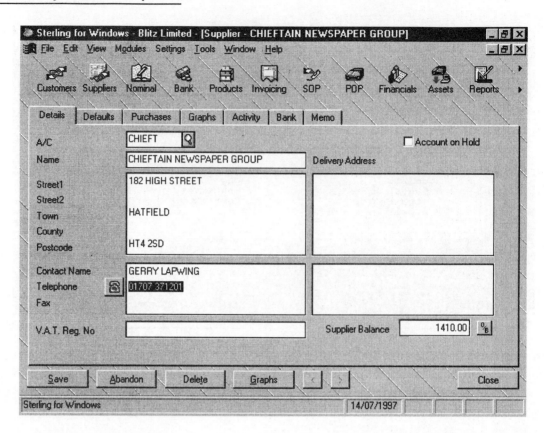

2.11   Recent developments in accounting packages take this further. A purchase ledger clerk wishing to raise a cheque may actually be confronted with a **proforma cheque** on screen. The cursor moves from line to line and the process is almost identical to the completion of a manual cheque.

Graphical user interfaces

2.12   Graphical user interfaces (GUIs) were designed to make computers more '**user-friendly**' to people without experience of using them, and who might have difficulty in using a keyboard, or who might be resistant to the idea of becoming a computer user.

2.13   A GUI involves the use of two design ideas and two operating methods which can be remembered by the abbreviation **WIMP**. This stands for 'Windows, Icons, Mouse, Pull-down menu' and is an environment which offers a **method of accessing the computer without using the keyboard**. Dialogue is conducted through images rather than typed text.

2.14   Graphical user interfaces have become the **principal means** by which humans communicate with machines.

Windows

2.15   This basically means that the screen can be divided into sections, 'windows' of flexible size, which can be opened and closed. This enables **two or more documents to be viewed and edited** together, and sections of one to be inserted into another. For instance figures from an Excel spreadsheet can be pasted directly into a Word word-processing document.

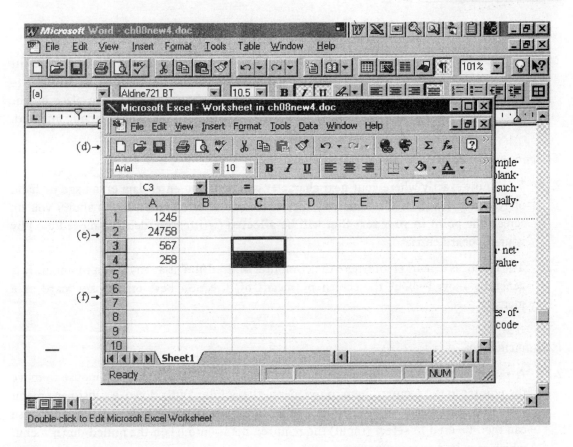

Icons

2.16   An icon is an image of an object used to represent a function or a file in an obvious way. For instance Windows based packages use a **picture of a printer** which is simply clicked to start the printing process. Another common icon is a **waste paper bin** to indicate the deletion of a document.

2.17   Both icons and windows are shown in the illustration below.

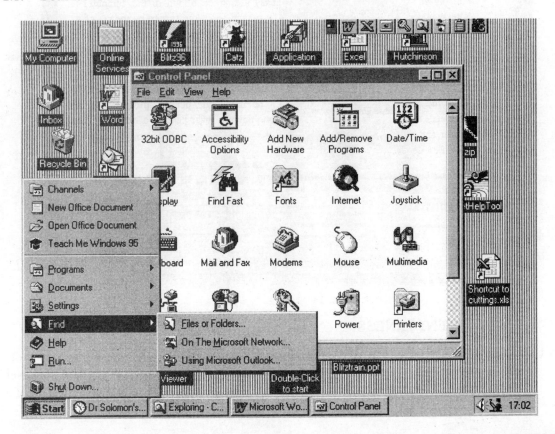

Mouse

2.18 As the mouse moves around on the desktop a *pointer* (cursor) on the screen mimics its movements. A mouse can be used to **pick out and activate an icon or button**, to **highlight** a block of text for deletion/insertion, or to **drag** data from one place on the screen to another. It also has buttons which are **clicked** to execute the current command.

The cursor

2.19 You know exactly where your next character will be if you enter data on a page by hand or typewriter, and in the same way the cursor (an arrow, line or 'blob') shows you on screen the **point in your text that will be affected** (written on, deleted, moved etc.) by your keyboard entries.

2.20 The cursor is a 'marker' of where the **computer's 'attention'** is at any given moment. It is generally moved about the screen by means of direction keys on the keyboard or a mouse.

Pull-down menu

2.21 A **'menu-bar'** will be shown across the top of the VDU screen. Using the mouse to move the pointer to the required item in the menu, the pointer **'pulls down'** a subsidiary menu - somewhat similar to pulling down a roller blind at a window. The pointer and mouse can then be used to **select** (input) the required item (output) on the pulled-down menu, which may lead to more menus.

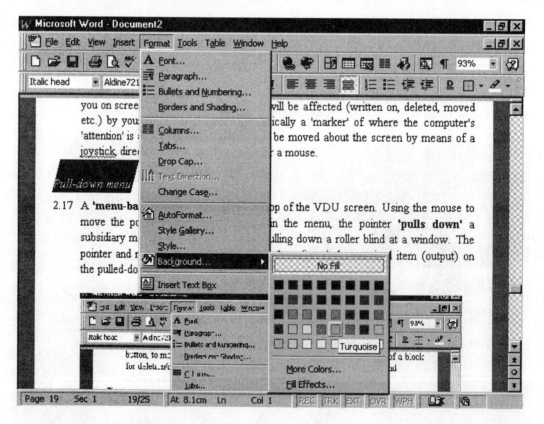

3   USER-FRIENDLINESS

3.1 These days most people in an organisation are likely to use a computer and most of these are not computer professionals. The modern trend, therefore, is towards user friendliness, or **ease of use**. The following features all improve the user-friendliness of a system.

Ease of data entry

3.2   It must be easy for the user to input data into the system. This has several aspects.

(a)   The **data entry screen** should be designed in the **same logical order** as the **input form** (source document).

The user should be able to work down the form in a logical order with the screen cursor moving down the screen to the next input field in the same order. Data entry will be inefficient if the user has to search around for the item to go into the next field.

(b)   The data entry screen should be **clearly designed,** so that, for example, input fields are highlighted, perhaps by **colour, flashing** or **reverse colouring**. The position of the cursor should be clear.

Titles of fields should be **easy to read** and should **match** the titles used on **source** documents.

(c)   **Default entries** should be provided for items such as the date (usually today's date) or the standard VAT rate.

The defaults will then be entered automatically unless the user wishes to change them. This can speed up data entry considerably.

Intuitiveness

3.3   It should be possible for users to make **reasonable guesses about what they need to do**.

3.4   For example in Windows a program is started simply by double-clicking on an **icon** that represents that program in an **obvious** way ('W' for Microsoft Word; a letter tray for e-mail). The user does not need to know where the program is stored on disk or have to type in command words to start up the application.

Design principles consistent with other modules/packages

3.5   Many computer users use **more than one part of a system**. Even in a non-accounting environment, an increasing number of users must be able to operate a spreadsheet and WP, and, in an accounting environment, it is useful for staff to have 'transferable' skills.

3.6   This means that the more systems can **'look and feel' the same** and operate in a similar way (eg F1 is always 'Help', F2 is always 'Save' etc), the easier it will be for users to switch between packages/modules without going through a huge learning curve.

3.7   One of the advantages of the **Windows** environment is that packages specifically written for Windows are generally **similar in design**. This **reduces training time** and costs and makes **skills transferable**.

On-screen help

3.8   It is increasingly common to find software pre-loaded onto computers without manuals being provided or to find that, when manuals *are* provided, they are rarely referred to. This is because packages invariably include **on-screen help**.

3.9   If a user requires help, he or she requests it at the touch of a **single key** (eg **F1**) or by clicking on '**Help**' on a **pull-down menu**. The help screen is usually **context specific**, so that, for example, if a particular dialogue box in a package is open, the system will offer help related to relevant functions and options. Problems can be resolved more quickly and productivity improved.

3.10   Help files are often written in **hypertext**, which provides **links** between topics. The user can click on words that are underlined and move directly to another topic.

Use of dialogue boxes and on-screen prompts

3.11   The more critical the potential effect of a command issued by the user, the more important it is that the user is not allowed simply to **start a process by mistake**.

3.12   Thus where commands such as **delete** a file, **format** a disk or **update** a ledger are being made, user-friendly software should issue a **warning** that such an operation is about to be carried out, *after* the initial command is entered.

3.13   This gives the user a **second chance** to confirm that the command was intended and that the computer is indeed required to carry out the specified process.

3.14   In turn this means that users will spend less time attempting to reverse the effects of **unintentionally-used commands**.

Escapability

3.15   An inexperienced user, or someone 'exploring' in a hit-or-miss way to try to find the right command, might find himself or herself faced with a command which he or she *knows* to be the wrong one.

3.16   It is important that an option is available which offers a **harmless alternative** to following the **unwanted route**. Thus in Windows there is usually a '**Cancel**' button next to the 'OK' button in each dialogue box. Selection of 'Cancel' enables the user to return to where he or she was before the wrong path was taken. An alternative is often the '**Esc**' key on the keyboard. These options are to be preferred to simply switching off the machine, which can have catastrophic consequences.

Customisation

3.17   Many users find that they perform the **same series of actions** so frequently that it becomes tedious to click their way through menus and dialogue boxes. User-friendly software will recognise this and offer **fast alternatives**.

(a)   '**Shortcut keys**' (typically pressing the Ctrl key together with one or more other keys) can be assigned to standard actions so that they are performed literally at the touch of a button.

(b)   A series of actions can be 'recorded' as they are done in the form of '**macros**', which can then be activated using a shortcut key or user-defined button.

Question 1

Look at the various illustrations of screens in this chapter and elsewhere in this book. How many 'user friendly features' can you identify?

Answer

Look at the buttons, menus, keyboard shortcut hints (eg File means press Alt + F on the keyboard to bring up the file menu), scalability of windows, system messages, Help facilities, and so on. You may have found lots of other examples.

4 FILE AND DATABASE DESIGN

4.1 The way in which data is **stored and manipulated** is an important aspect of information systems design. There are three principal approaches to information handling in computer systems.

(a) **Non-integrated** systems.
(b) **Integrated** systems.
(c) **Database** systems.

Non-integrated systems

4.2 A computer application might process **only one sort of data**. A payroll file would process only payroll data and a stock file only stock data. An organisation might end up with separate files and processing subsystems for each area of the business.

4.3 However, in many cases the underlying data used by each application might be the same. A major consequence is that **data items are duplicated** in a number of files. They are input more than once (leading to **errors and inconsistencies**) and held in several files (**wasting space**).

Integrated systems

4.4 An **integrated system,** as you know from Chapter 1, is a system where one set of data is used for more than one application. In an accounting context, it might be possible to integrate parts of the sales ledger, purchase ledger, stock control systems and nominal ledger systems, so that the data input to the sales ledger updates the nominal ledger automatically.

Question 2

What data items might link up a purchase ledger system and a stock control system?

Answer

Refer to Chapter 1 if you have forgotten.

Database systems

4.5 A database provides a comprehensive file of data for a number of different users.

> ### KEY TERMS
>
> The term **database** has a strict and a loose meaning.
>
> - Strictly speaking, a database is a collection of **structured data**. The structure of the data is independent of any particular application. Any item of data can be used as a subject of enquiry. The concept is that programs are written around the database rather than files being structured to meet the need of specific programs.
>
> - Loosely speaking, a database is a **collection of data files** which is integrated and organised so as to provide a single comprehensive file system. The data is governed by rules which define its structure and determine how it can be accessed. The purpose of a database is to provide convenient access to the common data for a wide variety of users and user needs.
>
> A **database management system (DBMS)** is the software that builds, manages and provides access to a database. It is a system which allows a systematic approach to the storage and retrieval of data in a computer.
>
> The independence of logical data from physical storage, and the independence of data items from the programs which access them, is referred to as **data independence**.
>
> Duplication of data items is referred to as **data redundancy**.

The objectives of a database system

4.6   A database should have four major objectives.

(a) **It should be shared**. Different users should be able to access the same data in the database for their own processing applications, and at the same time if required. This removes the need for duplicating data on different files.

(b) **The integrity of the database must be preserved**. This means that one user should not be allowed to alter the data on file so as to **spoil** the database records for other users. However, users must be able to make **valid** alterations to the data.

(c) **The database system should provide for the needs of different users**, who each have their own processing requirements and data access methods.

(d) **The database should be capable of evolving**, both in the short term (it must be kept updated) and in the longer term (it must be able to meet the **future** data processing needs of users, not just their current needs).

The advantages and disadvantages of database systems

4.7   The **advantages** of a database system are as follows.

(a) **Avoidance of unnecessary duplication of data**

It recognises that data can be used for many purposes but only needs to be input and stored once. The drawback to single entry input is that one department only must accept responsibility for the accuracy of the input.

(b) **Multi-purpose data**

From (a), it follows that although data is input once, it can be used for several purposes.

(c) **Data for the organisation as a whole, not just for individual departments**

The database concept encourages management to regard data as a resource that must be **properly managed** just as any other resource. The installation of a database system encourages management to analyse data, relationships between data items, and how data is used in different applications.

(d) **Consistency**

Because data is only held once, it is easier to ensure that it is up to date, so that no department in an organisation uses out-of-date data, or data that differs from the data used by other departments. They should not come to different decisions simply because they were based on different data.

(e) **New uses for old data**

Data on file is independent of the user programs that access the data. This allows greater flexibility in the ways that data can be used. New programs can be easily introduced to make use of existing data in a different way.

(f) **New applications**

Developing new application programs with a database system is easier than developing other applications, because the programmer is not responsible for the file organisation, which is already taken care of by the database management software.

Exam focus point
A question in **December 1995** asked for an explanation of a DBMS and for three advantages of the database approach

4.8   The **disadvantages** of a database systems relate mainly to security and control.

(a) There are problems of **data security** and **data privacy**. The potential for unauthorised access to data creates a serious problem. Administrative procedures for data security must supplement software controls.

(b) Since there is only one set of data, it is essential that the data should be **accurate** and free from corruption.

(c) Since data is held once, but its use is widespread, there are potential problems of recovery of data in the event of a **system failure**.

(d) If an organisation develops its own database system from scratch, initial **development costs** will be high, although the costs of maintaining a database system (keeping the data up to date etc) should be lower than for more traditional systems. 'Off-the-shelf' database management system (DBMS) software packages can be obtained, and so the cost of installing a database can be reduced.

Database administrator

4.9   Control over data and systems development can be facilitated by the appointment of a **database administrator**, who controls and sets standard for:

- the input of data
- its definition, for instance the development of logical data models
- physical storage structures
- system performance
- security and integrity of data, eg maintenance of the data dictionary (see later)
- back-up and recovery strategies

4.10   The principal role of a DBA can be described as ensuring that the database **functions correctly and efficiently** at all times. To achieve these aims the DBA will carry out a variety of tasks, including some or all of those discussed below. The DBA must be a person that is **technically competent** and possesses a **good understanding** of the **business and operational needs** of the organisation.

4.11   The DBA must implement procedures that ensure that **all data** entered onto the system is **complete, current and accurate**. Techniques that can be used to achieve this are data validation and verification procedures such as batch sampling of entered data, software 'traps' to detect the attempted input of wrong data types and completeness checks.

4.12   Database **security** is another important area for the DBA, though some aspects, such as network security, may not be his or her direct responsibility. The database must be protected from possible **physical and logical threats**. The DBA should implement logical access controls such as **passwords** to log-on to the system and, in addition, partition the database so that only **authorised users** can access relevant data. If the database can be accessed from **external sites** it will be necessary for the DBA to implement appropriate procedures, such as **firewalls**, to protect the system from hackers and other unauthorised users.

4.13   Regular **virus checks** should be made and the database users should be prohibited from installing their own programs onto the system.

4.14   Measures to provide **physical security** have been discussed in an earlier chapter. It is also vital that the DBA introduces, and enforces, a strict **back-up routine** with a copy of the data stored in a secure location off-site. (Again, both of these aspects may be handled by a **network administrator** rather than a DBA.)

4.15   The DBA should seek to keep up with **new technical developments**, identify **new user requirements** and their development, review the **performance** of the database and take appropriate action to ensure that the database functions correctly. The DBA will implement effective **maintenance schedules** for the hardware and software. An **audit trail** may be devised and used as an aid to maintaining the database.

4.16   The DBA must make sure that the database is operated legally and complies with the relevant legislation such as the **Data Protection Act**.

4.17   Finally the DBA will have responsibility for producing **system documentation** (technical information, manuals, the data dictionary, user guides, etc) and developing **training programmes** for users of the database, and perhaps for **managing** assistants.

5   DATABASE STRUCTURES

5.1   A number of different models are used in databases.

(a)   The hierarchical model
(b)   The network model
(c)   The relational model

The hierarchical model

5.2 Many relationships are **one-to-many** or **many-to-one** relationships. Such relationships can be expressed conveniently in a **hierarchy**. Each data item is related to only one item above it in the hierarchy, but to any number of data items below it.

5.3 In a customer database, for example, the hierarchical model might be used to show customers and customer orders. An extract from a **parts department database** might be structured as follows.

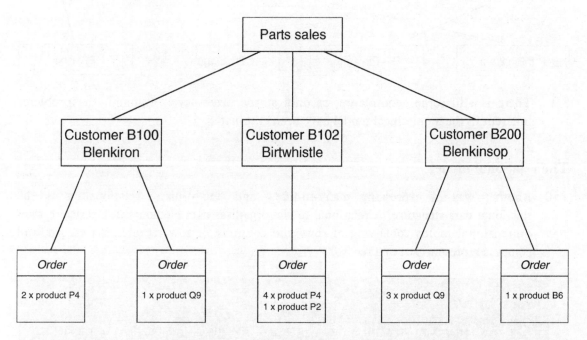

5.4 The biggest **drawback** to a file organised in hierarchical data structure is that the user is limited in the number of ways he or she can look for records: the file organisation makes it much easier to search for certain items in the file records than for others.

5.5 In the example above, to access an order record it is necessary to specify the customer to which it belongs, which is straightforward. However, let us imagine that you wish to obtain a **listing of all customers who have ordered a particular part number**. This would require a search of each customer record - a long process.

5.6 If the hierarchical model had been structured so that **products** were superior to **orders** and each order contained customer data instead of product data, this would be simpler, but the **first** process would be harder!

5.7 This **asymmetrical** character of the hierarchical model makes it **unsuitable for many applications,** especially where there is not a true hierarchical relationship between the data.

The network model

5.8 Whereas a hierarchical data structure only allows a **one-to-many** relationship between data items, a **network** database is a database in which the logical data structure allows **many-to-many** relationships.

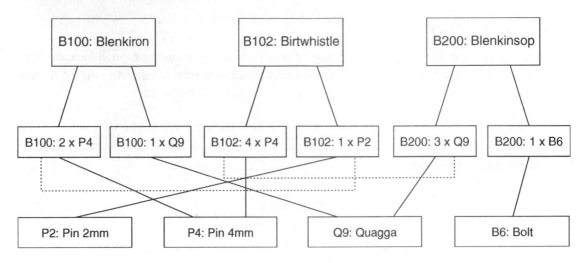

5.9 There is still some **redundancy of data** at the order level, although the problems inherent in the hierarchical model have been eliminated.

The relational model

5.10 Another way of expressing many-to-many and one-to-many relationships is the relational data structure. A relational model organises data elements in a series of **two-dimensional tables** consisting of rows and columns. A row represents a record, and columns represent part of a record.

> ### KEY TERM
>
> In a **relational data structure,** the structure of the file is independent of the actual data. The relationships between different entity types have been determined at the outset, and are not embodied in the records themselves. A relational database thus does not have to navigate through other data before reading the required record.

5.11 You will recognise this technique as **normalisation**, or relational data analysis.

Customer table

B100	Blenkiron
B102	Birtwhistle
B200	Blenkinsop

Product table

B6	Bolt
P2	Pin 2mm
P4	Pin 4mm
Q9	Quagga

Order table

B100	P4	2
B100	Q9	1
B102	P4	4
B102	P2	1
B200	Q9	3
B200	B6	1

5.12 The redundant data in the network model, ie the customer number and part number in the order relation, has been eliminated. Any data element can be recognised by its record number or field name. The **primary key** is used to identify a record.

6   DATA DICTIONARIES

> **KEY TERM**
>
> A **data dictionary** is an index of data held in a database, used to assist in maintenance and any other access to the data.

6.1   A data dictionary is a feature of many database systems and CASE tools (see later). As the term might suggest, it provides a method for **looking up the items of data** held in the database, to establish the following.

(a)   **Field names, types, lengths and default values**. For instance a 'year' field would be numeric with four digits and may have a default value of the current year. (**Note.** If these aspects are defined in the data dictionary they **only need to be defined once**, no matter how often they are applied by other programs using the database.)

(b)   A list of the **entity, attribute and relationship types**.

(c)   A list of the **aliases** (see below).

(d)   A list of all the **processes** which use data about each entity type.

(e)   **How to access** the data in whatever manner is required (a data dictionary is sometimes called a data directory).

(f)   What the **data codes and symbols mean**.

(g)   The **origin** of the data.

(h)   Possible **range of values**.

(i)   **Ownership** of the data.

(j)   Other comments.

6.2   A data dictionary is simply a list or record of each **data store** in the system and each **data flow** in the system showing what items of data they contain. It is easy for different users to give data **ambiguous names**. Thus 'stock number', 'part number' and 'stock code' might be used interchangeably.

6.3   EXAMPLE

In a payroll system, the data store for the **employee name** might be included in a data dictionary as follows.

```
Reference
File: Employee name for payroll system
Ref No of file D2
Data elements
Name:              Employee name
Aliases:           Name
                   Staff name
                   Employee
Description:       The name of an employee, in the form: Last name, first name, other details
Format:            Character
Related data:      Employee address
                   Employee number
Ownership:         Human resources
Users:             Human resources
                   Accounting
                   Payroll
                   Job costing
                   Administration
```

The usefulness of a data dictionary

6.4   The data dictionary is a form of technical documentation; it is a form on **control** and ensures that everyone in the organisation defines and uses the data **consistently**. This consistency is extremely important for large projects which involve several programmers. The opportunity for misunderstandings is so high that the data dictionary becomes essential.

6.5   A data dictionary helps with systems analysis, systems design and systems maintenance.

(a)   During systems analysis a data dictionary helps the analyst to **organise his information about the data elements in the system**, where they come from, where they go to what fields are used (name, type, length).

(b)   During systems design a data dictionary helps the analyst and programmers to ensure that **no data elements are missed** out if they are really needed. In some cases defining data items (ie building the dictionary) is a major part of the process of **producing the physical system**, and some data dictionaries can even generate program code automatically.

(c)   Once the system is operational, and an **amendment** is required to a program, a data dictionary will help the programmer to understand what each data element is used for, so that any amendment he makes does not 'spoil' other parts of the program. This is sometimes called **impact analysis.**

(d)   Future **maintenance** work on the system is unlikely to be carried out by the people who originally wrote it. A data dictionary records the original work and helps to ensure continuity.

6.6   Software packages which **automate the creation of dictionaries** have been developed. The creation of this reference material is tedious and the availability of a computer tool which can determine basic information about the data has increased their use. It is most unlikely that paper records or index cards would be used in a modern environment.

Exam focus point

A question in **June 1995** referred to data dictionaries in the context of CASE tools, described later in this chapter. A question in **December 1997** asked 'What is a Data Dictionary?' and what two of its roles might be.

7   USING A DATABASE

7.1   There are four main operations in using a database.

   (a)   Creating the database **structure**, ie the structure of files and records.
   (b)   **Entering data** on to the database files, and **amending/updating** it.
   (c)   **Retrieving and manipulating** the data.
   (d)   Producing **reports**.

Creating a database structure

7.2   Of the four broad operations involved in setting up and using a database, the most crucial is the creation and structure of the database file or files. As we have seen, the person creating the database file must first carry out an **analysis of all the data** for processing and filing, because a full and accurate analysis of data in the system is crucial to the construction of complete and workable database files.

7.3   It is also necessary to specify what **files** will be held in the database, what **records** (entities) and **fields** (attributes) they will contain, and how many **characters** will be in each field. The files and fields must be named, and the characteristics of particular fields (for example **all-numeric** or **all-alphabetic** fields) should be specified.

Entering and amending data

7.4   When the database structure has been established, the data user can **input data** and create a file (or files) or **derive data** from existing records.

Amalgamating existing data

7.5   Problems in amalgamating data originally stored separately are likely to be numerous.

   (a)   The **compatibility** between systems is not just a matter of whether one system's files are computer-sensible to another system. It may extend to matters such as different systems of coding, different formats for personal data (with/without a contact name? with/without phone or fax number, and so on), different field sizes.

   New standards that apply across the board can be developed, but implementing them is likely to require a great deal of collection of data and inputting. It will be necessary to acquire and test conversion software and ensure that there are sufficient staff to perform and check the conversion.

   (b)   There is great potential for **loss or corruption of data** during the conversion process. Depending on the extent of the loss this could mean a small amount of re-keying or it could be a disastrous, permanent loss of valuable information needed for sales management.

   Full **back-ups** should be taken at the start of the process, and back-ups of information on the old system should continue during any period of parallel running.

   (c)   Existing application-specific systems are unlikely to have sufficient **storage** space to accommodate the combined data. This can easily be resolved, but it must be resolved with an eye to the **future growth** of the business and future use of the database to store both **existing information** and **new information** that has not been available in the past.

   (d)   **Access to data must not suffer**. Operational users will be attempting to extract information from a much larger pool, and the system must be designed in such a way that they do not have to wade through large amounts of data that is irrelevant to them to find what they need. If this aspect is neglected the new system could seriously undermine users' ability to respond to queries.

Those developing the system therefore need to **consult widely with users** at the sharp end of processing to ensure that their current information needs are understood and can be met by the new data architecture.

(e) As well as offering the potential for new kinds of report the system must continue to **support present requirements for management reports** that are essential to the smooth running of the business. Amalgamation could inadvertently break down links between data items and make it impossible to pull off a much needed daily report.

Once more, **extensive consultation** with users is essential.

(f) Once the data has been amalgamated the business faces the task of ensuring that it is **secure**. A systems failure will now mean that no part of the business can operate, rather than at most just one part.

Dealing with this is likely to mean changes in the role and structure of the IT department. New, **centrally administered back-up procedures** will be needed, and contingency arrangements must be worked out and put in place to ensure that the risks to the business of systems disasters are minimised.

7.6 The data must be **kept up-to-date**, and so there will be subsequent insertions of new records, deletions of unwanted records and amendments to existing records. Database packages usually allow the **same field in every record** on file, or **all records** with certain characteristics, to be amended in the same way by means of **a single command**. For example, a single command can arrange for all customers on a sales ledger database file whose account type is type 2, say, to have their credit limit raised by 5%.

Retrieval and manipulation of data

7.7 Data can be retrieved and manipulated in a variety of ways.

(a) Data can be retrieved by **specifying the required parameters** - for example from a database of employee records, records of all employees in the sales department who have been employed for over 10 years and are paid less than £12,000 pa could be extracted. If there are certain search and retrieve parameters that are used regularly, they can be stored on a search parameters file for future use.

(b) Retrieved data can be **sorted** on any specified field (for example for employees, sorting might be according to grade, department, age, experience, salary level etc).

(c) Some **calculations** on retrieved data can be carried out - such as calculating **totals** and **average** values.

Query languages

7.8 A database can be interrogated by a **query language**. A query language is a formalised method of constructing queries in a database system. Basically a query language provides the ways in which you ask a database for data. Some query languages can be used to change the contents of a database.

SQL

7.9 SEQUEL (Structured English Query Language) is the name of the original version of SQL (which is pronounced either as 'sequel' or as separate letters). **SQL** was adopted by the *Oracle* corporation and helped Oracle to become the second largest software company in the world after Microsoft. It is now regarded as the **industry standard** query language.

> **Exam focus point**
> A question in the **June 1997** exam asked for an explanation of SQL.

7.10 SQL (short for **Structured Query Language**) uses an English-like syntax to perform all database operations, including:

(a) **Reading records from the database**. This operation is called a query. You can read records from a table, view, or synonym.

(b) **Inserting, deleting, and updating records**. Through SQL code, you can edit the contents of tables.

(c) **Creating, modifying, and deleting database objects**. You can also write SQL code to change the **tables** that store records as well as other database objects (views, sequences, and so on) that appear in the database.

(d) **Defining transactions**. Using SQL, you can group database operations in a single transaction. This feature helps ensure the integrity of information in cases where several operations need to be performed together, such as subtracting an amount from one bank account and adding it to another. Transactions also give you the chance to reverse (or roll back) changes to the database.

7.11 Although **all relational databases** use some version of SQL, the implementation of SQL often varies by database. Some database vendors have **extended** standard SQL by adding additional programming elements.

7.12 EXAMPLE: SELECT STATEMENTS

To query records from a relational database, you write a SQL statement that begins with the keyword **SELECT**.

7.13 A SELECT statement has the following mandatory components:

SELECT columns FROM record_source

The 'columns' component identifies the columns from which the relational database will return values. For example, if you want to return values from the EMP_ID and EMP_NAME columns in the EMPLOYEES table, you would write the following query:

SELECT EMP_ID, EMP_NAME FROM EMPLOYEES

7.14 In this case, each record would consist of the values queried from the EMP_ID and EMP_NAME columns in the EMPLOYEES table. If other columns exist in the table, the query ignores them and does not return values for them.

7.15 If you want to return values from **all the columns** in a record source, you use the **asterisk** character ⋆ , referred to as a **wildcard**. Therefore, if you wanted to return values from all columns in the EMPLOYEES table, you would write the following SELECT statement:

SELECT ⋆ FROM EMPLOYEES

7.16 EXAMPLE: OTHER OPTIONS

Beyond the required elements of a SELECT statement, you can add syntax that performs the following tasks:

(a) **Filter records**. Using a WHERE clause, you can specify criteria

SELECT * FROM EMPLOYEES WHERE SALARY > 50000)

SELECT * FROM CUSTOMERS WHERE NAME LIKE 'Kath%'

The second example would return all records for customers named Katherine, Kathleen, and so forth.

(b) **Join records** from multiple record sources. You can write the SELECT statement to query records from multiple record sources, using matching values in different columns to determine how to relate similar records in separate tables or views.

(c) **Sort records**. Using an ORDER BY clause, you can specify the columns used to sort records. For example, in a table of customers, you can sort by name, post code, or other information stored for each customer.

(d) **Perform calculations**. Within the SELECT statement, you can perform calculations, so that you can take values from a single or multiple columns, write an expression using these values, and display the result in a separate column. Additionally, you can perform aggregate calculations, such as sums and averages, on all of the values stored in a column.

7.17 Different databases provide **further options**. For example, a common SQL feature is the ability to select unique values using the DISTINCT operator or select all the records in multiple tables using the UNION ALL command.

Microsoft Access

7.18 The illustration below shows the tools available in Microsoft Access for building queries using Visual Basic-like comments. Access also offers the option of using SQL-type queries.

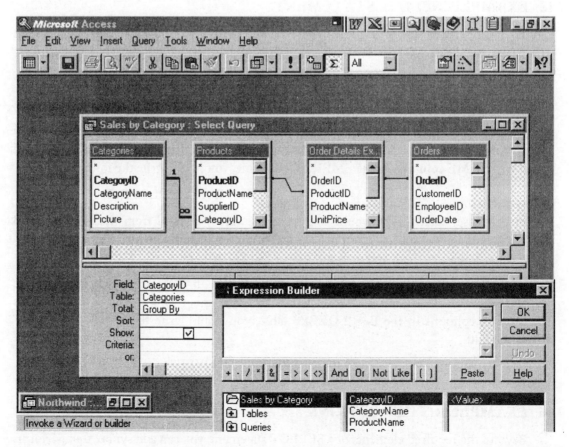

Report production

7.19 Most database packages include a **report generator facility** which allows the user to design report structures so that information can be presented on screen and printed out in a format which suits the user's requirements and preferences. Report formats can be stored on disk, if similar reports are produced periodically, and called up when required.

Question 3

Try to get someone to demonstrate a database package to you - perhaps your marketing department at work uses Access - and if possible learn how to build a query. It is very easy.

---

8   CASE TOOLS

8.1 Systems development methodologies are part of a more general trend towards software engineering, which takes the construction of a program to be similar to constructing a large building, requiring **detailed plans, blueprints and co-ordination** by effective project management. You will have noted that all the methodologies discussed place a heavy reliance on **documentation**. SSADM makes frequent use of DFDs throughout the development process.

Computer aided software engineering

8.2 CASE techniques aim to automate this document production process, and to ensure automation of some of the design operation.

> **KEY TERM**
>
> A **CASE tool** is a software package that supports the construction and maintenance of logical system specification models. They are often designed to support the rules and interaction of models defined in a specific methodology, and more sophisticated packages permit software prototyping and code generation.

8.3 There are two types of CASE tool: analysts' workbenches and programmers' workbenches.

Analysts' workbenches

8.4 These are software which perform several analysis tasks.

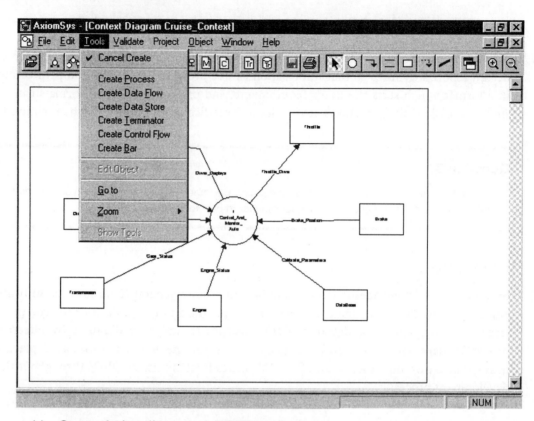

(a)   **Create design diagrams (eg DFDs) on screen**

High quality documentation can be produced, and **very easily updated**. Maintenance of complex models such as DFDs and entity-relationship models is made easy. The diagramming facilities are used with a mouse, in a manner similar to most graphics packages.

Tool kits come with a bank of **pre-designed symbols** including those used in flowcharts and data flow diagrams and, like graphics packages, allow on-screen editing.

Tool kits usually also offer a simple **word processing** package to assist in the preparation of written material including narrative supporting diagrams, the system specification, program specifications and any other reports produced.

(b) **Check adherence to design and development standards**

Standards define how development will be carried out. A CASE tool will **not allow designers to break rules** (such as not linking a data store directly to an external entity) that they could easily break accidentally if working manually.

(c) **Consistencies and relationships**

CASE tools can verify that diagrams are **consistent** with each other and that the **relationships** are correct.

(d) **Documentation**

CASE tools can help generate **specimen input and output documentation** (ie from the data flows identified in the diagrams).

(e) **Data dictionaries**

CASE tools can create a logical data dictionary from the items identified. Entries will be made for entities, data flows, data stores, processes, external entities and individual data items and the dictionary can be **easily maintained**, checked for **consistency, cross-referenced** and analysed. For example it will be possible to produce a listing of all the data flows where a particular data item is used, or cross reference the entities of the entity relationship diagram to the data stores of the DFD.

Programmers' workbenches

8.5 These provide similar features to ensure **consistency of coding** during the later stages of the design cycle.

(a) There is usually a **code-generator facility** to automate the production of code in a high level language from, say, Structured English.

(b) **Diagnostic aids** enable subroutines to be tested independently of other programs.

(c) A library of **subroutines** is also provided. These are **often-repeated procedures** which can be incorporated into programs.

Advantages of CASE

8.6 Advantages of CASE include the following.

(a) The drudgery is taken out of **document preparation** and **re-drawing of diagrams** is made easier.

(b) **Accuracy of diagrams** is improved. Diagram drawers can ensure consistency of terminology and maintain certain standards of documentation.

(c) **Prototyping** (see below) is made easier, as re-design can be effected very quickly and the models are always consistent with the actual system.

(d) **Blocks of code can be re-used**. Many applications incorporate similar functions and processes; if pieces of software are retained in a library they can be used (or modified) as appropriate.

Exam focus point

A question in the **June 1995** exam asked for an explanation of CASE tools and their advantages in various aspects of systems development, compared with manual methods.

9 PROTOTYPING

9.1 One way of ensuring full **user involvement** in, and commitment to, design is the technique of **prototyping**.

> **KEY TERM**
>
> A **prototype** is a model of all or part of a system, built to show users early in the design process how it will appear. As a simple example, a prototype of a formatted screen output from a system could be prepared using a graphics package, or even a spreadsheet model. This would describe how the screen output would appear to the user. The user could make suggested amendments, which would be incorporated into the next model.

9.2 Using prototyping software, the programmer can **write an application program quickly**. (Much software production is repetitive, and this makes the development of prototyping software feasible.) He or she can then **check with the data user** whether the prototype program that has been designed appears to **meet the user's needs**, and if it doesn't it can be amended. Any number of 'prototype' programs can be made for the user to sample, and it is only when the program does what the user wants that the final version of the program is ready.

CASE tools and prototyping

9.3 A CASE tool can support prototyping as follows.

(a) It may allow the logical contents of the data dictionary to be displayed on **demonstration screens** and link these screens together using menus and other dialogue structures. Thus the user sees a demonstration of the system through the CASE software.

(b) Through **converting** the process descriptions of the logical data dictionary into **programs** and the data stores/entities into **files and databases**. The user can then experiment with the software

Advantages and disadvantages

9.4 The **advantages** of prototyping are as follows.

(a) It makes it possible for programmers to present a 'mock-up' version of a program to a data user, to see how it works, **before anyone has to commit substantial time and money** to the project. The data user can judge the prototype before things have gone too far to be changed.

(b) It makes it more economical for data users to get **'custom built' application software,** instead of having to buy off-the-shelf application packages which may or may not suit their particular needs properly.

(c) It makes **efficient use of programmer time** by helping programmers to develop programs more quickly. Prototyping may speed up the 'design' stage of the systems development life-cycle.

(d) A prototype does not necessarily have to be written in the language of what it is prototyping (as an analogy, you can make a prototype car out of wood), and so prototyping is not only a tool, but a **design technique**.

9.5   There are some **disadvantages** with prototyping too.

(a)   Many prototyping software tools assume that the data user is about to **computerise an application for the first time**. This may not be so: some data users might want to transfer an application from an 'old' program to an updated new one, and so transfer data from existing files on to files for the new program.

(b)   Many prototyping software tools produce programs that are **tied** to a particular make of **hardware**, or a particular **database system**, and cannot 'travel' from one system to another without further use of prototyping.

(c)   It is sometimes argued that prototyping tools are **inefficient** in the program codes they produce, so that programs are bigger and use up more computer memory than they would if they had been written by programmers without the aid of prototyping.

(d)   Computer **users may be unimaginative**, and the resulting system may be too similar to what has been the case before.

(e)   Some **specialised program demands cannot be 'automated'** and have to be hand-written. Not all prototyping tools allow programmers to insert hand-written codes into a program.

(f)   A serious criticism is that prototyping tools allow programmers to produce a bigger quantity of **shoddy programs** at a high speed.

(g)   Many prototyping tools do not produce suitable program **documentation** for the user.

Exam focus point
Prototyping came up in the **December 1994** exam and again in the **June 1996** exam.

10   DEVELOPMENTS IN PROGRAMMING

Programming languages

10.1   A **programming language** is neither the 'normal' written language of humans, nor is it usually the machine code language of computers.

(a)   A computer can only deal with data and program instructions which are in **binary form** (the 1 and 0 corresponding to the on and off states of a transistor). So every program must be in a computer's **machine code** before the computer will do anything with it. Writing in machine code is **difficult**, because it takes a long time to learn, and is therefore usually restricted to programs developed by the computer manufacturers themselves.

(b)   A program in a programming language, however, can be translated into machine code. Programming languages are **easier for humans to use**, being more condensed and displaying a logic that humans can understand.

10.2   The program written in a **programming language** is called the **source program**. The translation into machine code is done by a specialised translation program. The translated program in its **machine code** (or machine language) version is called the **object program**.

10.3   **Assembly languages** were a subsequent development from machine code. They are also machine specific, but the task of learning and writing the language is made easier than with machine language because they are **written in symbolic form**. Instead of using machine code operation numbers, the programmer is able to use easily learned and understood operation mnemonics (for example, ADD, SUB and MULT).

10.4 Machine code and assembly languages are sometimes known collectively as **low-level languages**.

10.5 To overcome the low-level language difficulty of machine dependency, high-level (or machine independent) languages were developed. Such programming languages, with an extensive vocabulary of words and symbols are used to instruct a computer to carry out the necessary procedures, regardless of the type of machine being used. The following are examples of **high-level languages**. They are also know as **third-generation languages**.

(a) **COBOL** is used for business data processing.

(b) **PL/1** is also used for business computing.

(c) **BASIC** is designed for beginners, particularly on PCs, although in its latest form, **Visual Basic,** it has become an easy, yet sophisticated, language that is very widely used to write **Windows-based programs**.

(d) **FORTRAN** is a scientific language.

(e). **CORAL** is a language well-suited to on-line real time systems.

(f) **Pascal** is well-suited to programming with structured programming techniques.

(g) **C** is an advanced language, originally used for development in the Unix operating system environment, but also behind much Windows programming.

(h) **C++** is a language derived from C, that is becoming ever more popular. Many **Windows-based programs** are written in C.

(i) **Java** is a programming system similar to C++ which produces software that can run on any computer that has Java enabling software (eg Internet software), in spite of differences in hardware or operating system. A Java programming tool is illustrated below.

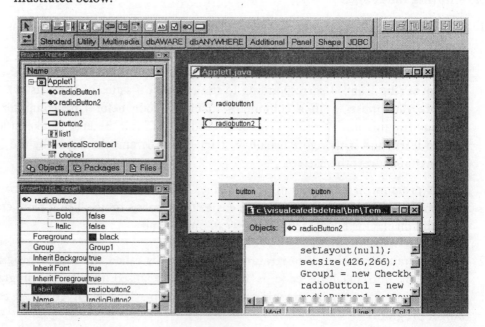

Fourth generation languages (4GL)

10.6 A fourth generation language is a programming language that is easier to use than languages like COBOL, PASCAL and C++. Well known examples include **Informik** and **Powerhouse**

> ### KEY TERM
>
> The term **fourth generation language (4GL)** loosely denotes software which enables systems designers, and even users, to develop their own systems. A 4GL offers the user an English-like set of commands and simple control structures in which to specify general data processing or numerical operations. These programs are then translated into a conventional high-level language such as COBOL or C.

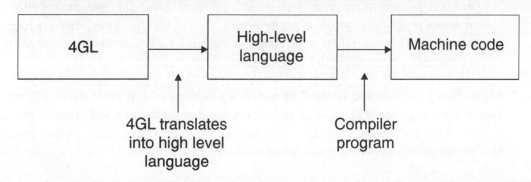

10.7 4GLs arose partly in response to the **applications backlog**. A great deal of programming time is spent maintaining and improving old programs rather than building new ones. Many organisations therefore have a backlog of applications waiting to be developed. 4GLs, by stepping up the process of application design and by making it easier for end-users to build their own programs, helps to reduce it.

10.8 Most fourth generation systems use a mixture of text and graphics, often a **graphical user interface**. A fourth generation system should have the following features.

(a) It should be **easy to learn** and use.

(b) It should contain **on-line 'help'** facility for users.

(c) It should be usable **interactively**.

(d) It should be **'fault' tolerant** (ie any mistakes in data entry should be dealt with easily).

(e) It should be suitable for **document design** work.

Application generators

10.9 An application generator is a type of 4GL used to create complete **applications programs**. The user describes what needs to be done and the data and files which are to be used. The applications generator then translates this description into a program.

10.10 The basis for this process is the recognition that **many of the functions** such as data input, sorting, searching, file management, report writing and the like are **quite similar** in operation even when these program segments are found in quite different applications programs.

10.11 The objective is to use a number of standardised program segments to provide these common functions. This is analogous to the use of **interchangeable parts** in manufacturing which helped stimulate the industrial revolution. Programs no longer need to be entirely custom made since the appropriate use of common modules may significantly reduce the cost and time involved in creating programs.

10.12 The **usefulness** of application generators lies in their ability to provide much of the program **quickly and relatively easily**. The major **drawback** to using these systems results from their inability to cover all possible program requirements. As a consequence application generators are used in two modes.

(a) They may be used to provide **relatively simple programs** in a finished form, this would be appropriate for non-programmers with undemanding requirements.

(b) As programs become more complex or use less common analytical methods the program generators become less useful. In these cases the **generators** provide **common segments** while a **programmer** then adds the **specialised program segments**. This combination of man and machine takes advantage of the relative abilities of each to provide a finished system.

10.13 Application generators can be **used by non-programmers** to develop their own program though some experience or training in programming generally aids the creation process and also allows the user to add in any specialised program segments when needed. Application generators are useful but limited tools.

Report generators

10.14 An example of a tool which is particularly useful for PC users is a report generator. This is a program which gives the non-specialist user a capability of producing reports from one or more files, through easily constructed statements.

10.15 Many software packages (for example for database systems or accounting systems) include a report generator which can be used by non-technical users. The value of a report generator is that it enables PC users to **extract information** from their files - for example in a database or spreadsheet package - **in the form of tabulated reports** which can be presented to management.

Advantages and disadvantages

10.16 The use of 4GLs has the following advantages.

(a) It enhances **end-user computing**, so limiting the work of IS staff.

(b) It taps user **creativity**.

(c) It **diffuses IT** throughout the organisation.

(d) It vastly increases programmer **productivity**, even though it uses more hardware resources.

10.17 There are also potential problems with 4GLs.

(a) **Over-enthusiastic** use by users might overload the main hardware resources.

(b) The information systems department might get overloaded by **training** requirements.

(c) Programs written in a 4GL do make **less efficient use of computer processing power** and memory. This can have the effect of slowing down the execution of a program to unacceptable levels.

Exam focus point

4GLs were mentioned in the scenario question in the **December 1996** exam. Answers could usefully have referred to some of the disadvantages of 4GLs.

Case example: Informix

The following is an extract from current marketing material on the Informix website.

The INFORMIX-4GL Product Family, comprised of INFORMIX-4GL Rapid Development System, INFORMIX-4GL Interactive Debugger, and INFORMIX-4GL Compiler, is a comprehensive fourth-generation application development and production environment that provides power and flexibility without the need for third-generation languages like C or COBOL. INFORMIX-4GL version 4.1 provides more enhancements to the product line than any other release since 4GL was introduced in 1986 giving you more functionality than ever before!

Wouldn't you like to find a self-contained application development environment that:

- provides rapid development and interactive debugging capabilities;

- offers high performance in the production environment;

- integrates all the functionality you could possibly need for building even the most complex applications;

- doesn't require the use of a third-generation language;

- allows you to easily maintain your applications for years to come;

- is based on industry-standard SQL; and

- is easily portable?

Look no further. You've just described INFORMIX-4GL.

The INFORMIX-4GL Product Family gives you all the tools you need to create sophisticated database applications in three easy packages with one consistent interface. Used together, INFORMIX-4GL Rapid Development System and INFORMIX-4GL Interactive Debugger provide the optimal environment for developing applications, while INFORMIX-4GL Compiler provides high-performance application execution in the production environment.

Whether you're building menus, forms, screens, or reports, INFORMIX-4GL performs all development functions, and allows for easy integration between them, eliminating the need for external development packages. Because our INFORMIX-4GL products are source-code compatible, portability is ensured.

Modern trends in programming

10.18 Programming has advanced considerably since computers first started to be used in business in the 1950s. Four key trends can be identified.

(a) **Greater modularity and reusability**. Programmers are encouraged to re-use the work of others and construct programs from pre-existing modules rather than writing everything from scratch. Typical re-usable modules include programs that control windows on a screen, open and close files, find data in databases or perform repetitive calculations.

(b) **Greater non-procedurality**. More modern languages allow people to express *what* should be accomplished instead of *how* it should be done by the computer. It is less necessary to make choices about computer-related details that are unrelated to the business problem being solved.

(c) **Greater machine independence.** Programs are increasingly written using industry standard programming languages and operating systems so that they can be run on a variety of machines from different vendors

(d) **More data independence.** Programs are increasingly written in ways that make it possible to change the physical storage of data without changing the program.

Event-driven programming

10.19 In a **traditional procedural** program, the program itself controls the portions of program code that run (or 'execute', hence the suffix '.exe' that is attached to program files). Execution starts with the first line of code and follows a defined pathway through the application.

10.20 In **event-driven programs**, however, the order in which the code executes depends on which 'events' occur. An event is an action or occurrence that is recognised by a program. Typical events are user actions such as **clicking a mouse button** or **pressing a key**. In other words the order in which the code executes depends on what the user does. This is the essence of **graphical user interfaces** and most modern applications are said to be 'event-driven'.

Object-oriented programming

10.21 Object-Oriented Programming (OOP) is now **the dominant philosophy** for developing new computer programs. Visual Basic is sometimes described as an 'object-oriented language', but this is not strictly correct. The main examples are **C++**, **Smalltalk** and **Java**.

10.22 Traditional procedural program design is based on a model that separates the programming operations from the data on which the operations are performed. This type of programming makes it difficult to manage changes in the data that affect the operations and changes in the operations that affect the data. Thus, instead of focusing on algorithms, the basis of traditional procedural programming, OOP focuses on the **data**.

Exam focus point

In our view the concepts of OOP are beyond the scope of the *Information Analysis* paper, but you may be able to impress the examiner by showing that you know it exists.

Chapter roundup

- **Input design** takes account of matters such as volume of data, frequency of input, need for accuracy. **Output** design has similar concerns.

- **Dialogue design** refers to the messages that the computer system displays on screen and the ways that users can respond. Modern systems use menus, form-filling and graphical user interfaces.

- **User friendliness** is enhanced by good input screen design, intuitiveness, consistency between packages, on-screen help, dialogue boxes, escapability and customisation.

- A **database** has four major **objectives**. It should be shared, its integrity must be preserved, it should provide for the needs of different users and it should be capable of evolving.

- A **database management system** organises the storage of data in the most appropriate way to facilitate its use in different applications. It provides the interface between the logical data and the physical data. A database administrator will often be appointed to look after the structure, physical storage and security of the data.

- **Three different models** are used in databases: the hierarchical model, the network model and the relational model. Each is suitable in different situations.

- Data analysis is vital to the design and construction of database files. It involves identifying the **entities** in a system, the **attributes** of those entities and the **relationships** between them.

- A **data dictionary** is a feature of many database systems. It provides a method of looking up the items of data held in the database and indicates their meaning. It assists with access to the data and is useful in database maintenance, ensuring that all users define and use the data consistently.

- **CASE techniques** attempt to automate the process of producing documentation which is important in many systems development methodologies. Available tools are analysts' workbenches and programmers' workbenches.

- One way of ensuring full user involvement in and commitment to design is the technique of **prototyping**. Prototyping assists programmers by helping them to write application programs much more quickly and easily, and they involve little coding effort on the part of the programmer.

- A program is written in a programming language. **COBOL** was the most popular business language before Windows came along, and is widely found in older systems that are still in use. Modern Windows-type software is usually written in a language such as **Visual C++** or **Visual Basic** (now a very powerful language).

- Modern developments such as **Visual Basic** mean that programming is much easier than it used to be. A **fourth-generation language** is software which enables a systems developer or an end-user to develop his or her own system.

Quick quiz

1   Explain four considerations in input design and four in output design. (See paras 1.3, 1.4)

2   What features might you see in an on-screen skeleton form? (2.9)

3   What are the components of a GUI? (2.13)

4   In what sense should an application be 'intuitive'? (3.3)

5   Why is it useful to be able to customise an application? (3.17)

6   What are the advantages of databases? (4.7)

7   How does a relational database organise data? (5.10)

8   What is a data dictionary? (6.1)

9   What is SQL? (7.9, 7.10)

10   What functions might an analyst's workbench CASE tool perform? (8.4)

11   What are the disadvantages of prototyping? (9.5)

12   What are the advantages of 4GLs? (10.16)

13   What are the key trends in the development of programming? (10.18)

Question to try	Level	Marks	Time
16	Introductory	n/a	20 mins
17	Exam standard	20	36 mins

Chapter 15

SECURITY DESIGN AND OPERATION

Chapter topic list	Syllabus reference
1 Back-up procedures	4(c), 5(c)
2 Controls	4(c)
3 Computer fraud	4(c)
4 Passwords and logical access systems	4(c), 5(c)
5 Hackers and viruses	4(c)

Introduction

In this final chapter on Systems Design we look at the various security and control measures that operate **within** the system (as opposed to security measures relating to the systems environment, covered in Chapters 9 and 10).

1   BACK-UP PROCEDURES

1.1   In spite of everything said in the previous chapter about avoiding duplication, an overriding concern of the system designer will be to provide the required services continuously without a break or deterioration in performance.

1.2   For many applications this will require that some amount of duplication in the system be tolerated or even encouraged. For example, data may be made more secure by using **back-up files** to archive data.

> **KEY TERM**
>
> **Back-up** means to make a copy in anticipation of future failure or corruption. A back-up copy of a file is a duplicate copy kept separately from the main system and only used if the original fails.

Re-creating file data when a file is lost or corrupted

1.3   One of the worst things that could happen in data processing by computer is the loss of all the data on a file or the loss of a program. Files can be **physically lost** (for example, the librarian might misplace a file) or a file may be **stolen,** but it is also possible for a file to become **corrupted** when it is written and so include false data. A file might also be **physically damaged** and become unreadable.

1.4   An important set of procedural controls is therefore to enable a data or program file to be **recreated** if the original is lost or corrupted. To recreate a file, it may be possible to go back to earlier versions, do the data processing all over again and create a new version of the up-to-date file.

Grandfather-father-son security

1.5   The reconstruction of magnetic tape files can be achieved by use of the grandfather-father-son technique of keeping as many **generations** of historical 'master' files, 'transaction' files and 'reference' files as is considered necessary for the security of both the files and the data contained on them.

1.6   It is common to keep three generations (grandfather, father and son) of master files, and sufficient transaction files to re-create the father from the grandfather master file. If the **'son'** tape is found to contain corrupted data, a corrected son file can be recreated by going back to the **'father'** and redoing whatever processing has been done since the father was created.

Disk files

1.7   Disk files are usually overwritten during updating, and so the grandfather, father, son technique cannot be applied. Instead, a copy of the disk file is periodically **'dumped'** on to a back-up tape or disk and all input transaction data after the dump is kept, thereby allowing for file reconstruction if necessary.

Procedures

1.8   Creating back-up files is now a regular routine with PC systems in many offices. The computer's **operating system** will have a back-up command for creating back-up files, and the computer operator will use this. It might not be necessary to back up every disk which holds transaction data, or even some standing data. For example, word processing data is not necessarily of such importance as to warrant back-up copies.

1.9   With networks and larger systems the system can be set up to back up everything, or certain selected files, **automatically** at a regular time each day (say, midnight).

1.10   All **program disks** should have a back-up copy. Some program disks which are bought from software manufacturers are **copy-protected** and cannot be backed up, but in these cases, the manufacturer is normally willing to provide a back-up copy as part of the sales package to the customer.

1.11   Backing up a **hard disk** on to floppy disks can be tedious, because a hard disk holds much more data than a floppy disk. Backing up a hard disk on to a tape is quicker and more convenient, although the user has to go to the expense of buying a **tape streamer** unit. Backing up from hard disk on to tapes is now quite common. It is possible to back up onto **CD-R** or onto a separate hard disk.

1.12   Many back-up routines use some kind of **compression** program so that the backed-up data takes up less space than the original. If the back-up has to be used a **restore** program has to be run to **expand** the data into useable format.

Storage of back-ups

1.13   Back-up copies should be stored **off-site** perhaps at a bank. This means that if there is a fire or a burglary at the business premises the back up copies will not be damaged. In practice many organisations keep one set of back-ups on-site (for speed of access) and a second set at a separate location.

The effectiveness of backups

1.14   The backing-up of data is a critical requirement for systems security. However, data on a back-up file will not itself be entirely secure unless some **additional measures** are used.

1.15   If there is a **hardware fault** which causes data loss of corruption the fault must be diagnosed and corrected before the correct data is put at risk in the system. The usefulness of archived data would be entirely negated if it were fed mindlessly into a faulty system. Systems will need to be repaired and fully tested to ensure that the real data will not be corrupted.

1.16   The back-up data should also be **isolated from the operations staff** so that it is not too readily available. Back-up data which is easily available could be used before system errors have been fully corrected and then the back-up will become corrupted too.

2   CONTROLS

Data integrity and controls

2.1   Data will maintain its **integrity** if it is **complete** and **not corrupted**. This means that:

(a)   the original **capture** of the data must be controlled in such a way as to ensure that the results are complete and correct;

(b)   any **processing and storage** of data must maintain the completeness and correctness of the data captured;

(c)   that reports or other **output** should be set up so that they, too, are complete and correct.

2.2   **Controls** must therefore be put in place to ensure that:

- problems are identified and put right when they occur;

- errors are recognised and eliminated;

- there is a record of all processing that occurs;

- all the data that *should* be processed *is* processed, at the correct time and in the correct order;

- the system is capable of recovery following a breakdown.

Some of these controls may be simple manual **clerical** checks. Others can be performed by the **software**.

Question 1

How might storage of data affect its integrity?

Answer

It might be backed up incorrectly. For example, this chapter is a revision of the chapter that appeared in the previous edition of this book. If this version of this chapter is not included in the material that is backed up once the current edition of the book is completed, or if *last* year's chapter is accidentally included on the *current* year's back up instead, all of the changes will have to be traced and done again next year.

See if you can devise a control system that would ensure that this could not happen.

Controls over input

2.3 **Human error** is the greatest data security weakness in computer systems, and controls ought to be applied to reduce the likelihood of errors, or to identify errors and the loss of data when these occur.

2.4 The extent of the input controls will depend on the **method of processing** input data (eg keyboard input, OCR document input etc) and the **cost** of making an input error. If the consequences of input errors would be costly, the system should include more extensive input controls than it would need if the cost of making input errors were insignificant.

Controls over data capture

2.5 Errors in data capture are difficult to spot once they have been made, because they are often errors on the 'source' document.

(a) They can be reduced by **double-checking**. One person's work might provide a cross-check on the accuracy of another's. For example, errors in recording suppliers' invoices in the purchase day book could be double-checked by getting another person to add up the total amount of invoices received that day, from the invoices themselves.

(b) The system can be designed to reduce the likelihood of errors arising in the first place, by including as much **pre-printed information** on the data recording document as possible, and by giving clear instructions about how data documents should be filled in.

(c) The use of **turnround documents** and **OCR, MICR, bar coding**, or in some applications, **plastic cards** with magnetic strips containing some of the input data, could be used to reduce the need for manually-prepared input data, and so limit the frequency of data capture errors.

Controls over transcribing data

2.6 If input data must be prepared manually, controls can be applied to minimise the number of errors.

(a) Staff who prepare data for input should be **well-trained** and **properly supervised**.

(b) Data **input documents** should be **designed** in a format to help the person preparing the data to fill them in properly.

(c) As we have see, when data is input by keyboard, the **screen** should be designed to help the keyboard operator to input the correct data.

Controls over processing

File identification checks

2.7 A program can check that the **correct file** has been loaded for processing before it will begin its processing operations. It can do this by checking the 'label or 'header' properties of the file, and comparing this data with the equivalent data for the file that it has been instructed to process. In other words, if the computer has been instructed to process file A, it will first of all check that file A has indeed been loaded for processing, and that it is the correct version of the file.

Checkpoints and recovery procedures

2.8   A checkpoint or *restart program* is a utility that **intervenes** at intervals (checkpoints) during the running of a program, and dumps the work done so far on to a **back-up** file.

2.9   Should anything turn out to be 'wrong' with the running of the program or if the system suddenly **crashes**, the checkpoint/restart program can be used to get the program **back to a checkpoint/restart position** before the error occurred, and restart the program with conditions exactly as they were before - for example copying back the contents of the dump file into the memory.

Question 2

Give a modern example of a checkpoint program.

Answer

In Microsoft Office applications there is an **Autosave** utility, which the user can set to save work automatically every, say, 15 minutes.

Control totals

2.10   A control total is the sum of specified fields. It might be any of the following.

(a)   The number of **records** on a file.

(b)   The total of the **values** of a particular field in all the records on a file - eg the total of debts outstanding in all the customer records on a sales ledger file.

(c)   The number of records in a **batch** (batch control total).

(d)   A **hash** total, which is a control total that has no meaning, except as a control check; for example, the **total of supplier code numbers** on a purchase ledger file.

2.11   **Control total reconciliation checks** are often written into programs to ensure that no records have been lost or duplicated, input files have been read fully and all output records have been written to the output files.

Verification and validation

> **KEY TERMS**
>
> **Verification** is the process of ensuring that the data that has been input is the same as the data on the source document.
>
> **Validation** is the process of ensuring that the data that has been input has a value that is possible for that kind of data, for example that a number is not more than a certain amount.
>
> Data should be subjected to both types of control if possible because it may be in a valid form (for example, four digits) but be totally inaccurate.

Data verification

2.12   One method of data verification if data must be converted from one form to another for input (for example from a paper document on to disk) is to **input the data twice** and then get the **software** to perform a **like-for-like comparison.**

2.13   The most common method of verification, however is encouraging staff to **look for errors.** If input is done by keyboard, the input data will be shown on screen, and a **visual check** on the data can be made. For instance if a customer code is keyed in, the screen might display the name and address of the customer automatically and this will alert the user if he has entered the wrong code.

Validation checks

2.14   Many checks on the validity of input data can be **written into the system's programs.**

2.15   When a validation check identifies an error, the record concerned will probably be rejected and **processed no further without correction**. Rejection reports will be printed out or messages displayed on a VDU screen.

2.16   Some data validation checks are outlined below. You ought to be aware what they are and when each type of check would be suitable. Obviously each application will have validation checks which are **relevant** to its particular processing requirements: not all of these checks are necessary in all circumstances.

Exam focus point

Verification and validation featured in a question in **June 1996.** Candidates were expected to give **examples,** so make sure you can do so.

Range checks

2.17   These are designed to ensure that the data in a certain record field lies within **predetermined limits**. For example in a wages application, the program may contain instructions to reject any clock card with 'hours worked' outside the range 10-80 hours, and to print out a special report (for checking) for any clock card with hours worked outside the range 35-60.

Limit checks

2.18   Sometimes called credibility or reasonableness checks, these are very similar to range checks, but **check that data is not below a certain value,** or **above a certain value**. In the previous example, the check on 'hours worked' might be that the value in the record field should not exceed 80 (or, in other words, is in the range 0-80).

- With a **range** check, there is an upper **and** lower bound
- With a **limit** check, there is either an upper **or** lower bound, but not both.

Existence checks

2.19   These are checks to ensure that the data is valid within a particular system. For example if the user inputs a stock code a program would check that the stock code **exists** by looking up the stock code number of the record against a reference file.

Format checks

2.20   Format checks help to ensure that the **format (and size)** of the data in a field is correct, for example:

(a)	check that the format is all numeric	1234	(here, four figures)
(b)	check that the format is all alphabetic	ABCDE	(here, five letters)
(c)	check that the format is alphanumeric	A123	(here, one letter followed by three figures)

Consistency checks

2.21   These involve checking that data in one field is **consistent** with data in another field. For example, in a payroll system, there might be a check that if the employee is a Grade C worker, he or she must belong to Department 5,6 or 9.

2.22   A consistency check is also called a **cross field validation check**.

Completeness checks

2.23   A check can be made to ensure that **all records** have been processed. For example, if a weekly processing run must include one record for each of the 5 working days of the week, a completeness check can ensure that there are 5 input records, one for each day.

2.24   Completeness checks on individual **fields** would be checks that an item of data has not been **omitted** from an input record.

Check digits

2.25   Computer records make extensive use of **codes** but it is very difficult for the human eye to detect an error in a code on a casual inspection.

2.26   By **splitting codes** into several groups of three or four digits, divided by a space or stroke (eg credit card numbers), it makes it easier for the data preparation staff to write codes without making errors. However, coding errors, especially **transposition errors**, may well escape detection before input to a computer system.

2.27   To avoid the situation where the computer treats an incorrect code number as the correct one, systems of **self-checking numbers** are used. The most common have **check digits**. These are digits that are added to the end of the code and give the whole new number some special mathematical property.

2.28   Check digits are commonly used in computer systems for **key field identification** codes (eg customer number, employee number, student number) but may not be considered necessary where the volume is low and/or the code number is less than five digits, because the likelihood of data collection errors or data preparation errors will be much smaller.

2.29   EXAMPLE: CHECK DIGITS

Suppose a product has a code 14875. One way of producing a check digit is the **modulus 11 method**. (This is just one of hundreds of different systems.)

Determine the number of digits, n (here 5) and write this below the first number in the code. Below the second number write (n – 1), and so on.

(a)	Code	1	4	8	7	5
(b)	Multiplier	5	4	3	2	1
(c)	(a) × (b)	5	16	24	14	5

	Sum of (c)	64
	Divide by 11	5
	Remainder	<u>9</u>

The **remainder** is used as the **check digit**, so the final code is 14875-9.

Exam focus point

The question in **June 1996** referred to earlier asked what sort of errors could be prevented by means of check digits (and for an illustration).

Question 3

(a)   What would be the six digit code for a product with the code 24875?
(b)   What would be the six digit code for a product with the code 14876?
(c)   What would happen if a user input a code 148757?

Answer

(a)   24875-3

(b)   14876-0 (The remainder is 10. In this case the digit '0' is added.)

(c)   The system would calculate the check digit as 9 and so not accept the entry. It would display a message telling the user to try again with a valid code.

Question 4

The effectiveness of controls over input is not always as great as a computer user might like. Evaluate the effectiveness of the following five typical checks on input to a purchase ledger system.

(a)   Input transaction displayed on VDU screen with keyboard input, for a visual check by the input clerk.

(b)   Check digit in the supplier account code number.

(c)   Batching records with a batch header control slip.

(d)   Display of supplier account details on screen when the account code is keyed in.

(e)   Double keying-in of all input transactions by different staff.

Answer

(a)   This depends on how good the input clerk is at his or her job. The risk of keying-in errors will be high. Also there is a possibility of a deliberate keying-in error by a dishonest clerk.

(b)   This reduces the risk of error in the input of the account code number. But it is a check on just one field of data, and so is limited in the number of errors it can find.

(c)   Batching is a time-consuming operation, but it should identify the loss of data, or the failure to input data records.

(d) This should prevent errors where the wrong supplier account is updated. However, the error depends on the input clerk checking the screen and looking at the account details displayed. Experience shows that clerks will often not bother to do this when they have a lot of input records to key in.

(e) This should identify most keying-in errors, and also prevent dishonesty or fraud by an input clerk. It is particularly useful where only range and format checks are possible, since these do not necessarily prevent transcription errors. However, double keying-in takes twice the effort and cost of once-only keying-in.

Output controls

2.30 A system should be designed to include certain controls over **output** from computer processing.

(a) In a batch processing system, where data is sent off to a computer centre, there should be a check to make sure that **all batches have been processed and returned.**

(b) All **input** records that have been **rejected** by data validation checks and master file update checks must be looked at to **find out the cause of the error.**

Corrected data should then be prepared for **re-input.** Some errors might need immediate correction, such as rejected input records in a payroll program for preparing the monthly salary payments to staff.

(c) Output should be **correctly distributed**, and a record kept of the distributions that have been made. Careful controls are needed over **confidential** outputs, to make sure that they do not get into the wrong hands.

(d) Output on to tapes, files and CDs should be **properly labelled and stored.**

3 COMPUTER FRAUD

Major categories of computer fraud

3.1 Computer fraud usually involves the **theft of funds** by dishonest use of a computer system.

3.2 The type of computer fraud **depends on the point in the system** at which the fraud is perpetrated.

(a) **Input fraud.**

Data input is falsified; good examples are putting a **non-existent employee** on the salary file or a non-existent supplier to the purchases file.

(b) **Processing fraud.**

A programmer or someone who has broken into part of the system may alter a program. For example, in a large organisation, a 'patch' might be used to change a program so that 10 pence was deducted from every employee's pay cheque and sent to a fictitious account to which the perpetrator had access. A 'patch' is a change to a program which is characterised by its speed and ease of implementation.

(c) **Output fraud.**

Output documents may be stolen or tampered with and control totals may be altered. Cheques are the most likely document to be stolen, but other documents may be stolen to hide a fraud.

(d) **Fraudulent use of the computer system.**

Employees may feel that they can use the computer system for their own purposes and this may take up valuable processing time. This is probably quite rare, but there was a case of a newspaper publisher's computer system being used by an employee to produce another publication!

Recent developments increasing the risk of fraud

3.3 Over the last few years there have been rapid developments in all aspects of computer technology and these have increased the opportunities that are available to commit a fraud. The most important of the recent developments are as follows.

(a) **Computer literacy.**

The proportion of the population which is computer literate is growing all the time. Once people know how to use a computer, the dishonest ones among them may attempt computer fraud. It is much easier to 'hide' an electronic transaction: it is not 'visible', or not in the same sense as a paper-based one, in any case.

(b) **Communications.**

The use of telephone links and other public communication systems has increased the ability of people outside the company breaking into the computer system. These 'hackers' could not have operated when access was only possible on site.

(c) **Reduction in internal checks.**

The more computers are used, the fewer the tasks left to personnel to carry out. A consequence of this is often a reduction in the number of internal checks carried out for any transaction.

(d) **Software controls.**

Improvements in the *quality of software* and the controls available has not kept pace with the improvements in hardware. Distributed systems and networked PCs have become very common but this has caused the control over central databases and programs to be relaxed.

Discovery and counteracting computer fraud

3.4 The management of every company must be conscious of the possibility and costs of computer fraud and everything must be done to avoid it. Employees (including directors) are the most likely perpetrators of fraud. A dishonest employee will be rare, but temptation should be avoided by giving no opportunity or motive to staff.

(a) All staff should be properly **trained** and should fully appreciate their role in the computer function. They should also be **aware of the consequences** of any fraud they might perpetrate.

(b) **Management policy** on fraud should be **clear and firm**. Management should have a positive approach to both the possibility and prevention of computer fraud.

(c) **Risk analysis** should be carried out to examine where the company is **exposed to possible fraud.**

(d) In the computer area itself **controls in the system** and **training** will both be important.

(e) Other areas should also be examined, such as **recruitment and personnel policies.**

(f)   Particular care should be taken when there are **changes in programs** or when **new software and hardware** are acquired.

Controls to prevent computer fraud

3.5   As with all controls in a system, the three areas to examine are **prevention, detection** and **correction**. Here are some possible controls.

(a)   **Access** to computer terminals and to other parts of the computer should be **restricted**.

(b)   **Access** to sensitive areas of the system should be **logged and monitored**.

(c)   **Error logs** and reports should be **monitored and investigated** on a regular basis.

(d)   **Staff recruitment** should include careful vetting, including taking up all references.

(e)   **Expert system** software may be used to **monitor unusual transactions**.

4   PASSWORDS AND LOGICAL ACCESS SYSTEMS

> ### KEY TERM
>
> **Passwords** are a set of characters which may be allocated to a person, a terminal or a facility which are required to be keyed into the system before further access is permitted.

4.1   Passwords can be applied to data files, program files and to parts of a program.

(a)   One password may be required to **read a file**, but another to **write new data** to it.

(b)   The terminal user can be **restricted** to the use of certain files and programs (eg in a banking system, junior grades of staff are only allowed to access certain routine programs).

4.2   In order to access a system the user needs first to enter a string of characters. If what is entered **matches** a password issued to an authorised user or valid for that particular terminal the system permits access. Otherwise the system **shuts down** and may record the attempted unauthorised access.

4.3   Keeping track of these attempts can alert managers to **repeated efforts** to break into the system; in these cases the culprits might be caught, particularly if there is an apparent pattern to their efforts.

4.4   The restriction of access to a system with passwords is effective and widely used but the widespread and growing use of PCs and networks is making physical isolation virtually impossible. The wider **use** of information systems requires that **access** to the system becomes equally **widespread and easy**. Requirements for system security must be balanced by the operational requirements for access: a rigidly enforced isolation of the system may significantly reduce the value of the system.

Problems with passwords

4.5   Passwords ought to be effective in keeping out unauthorised users, but they are **by no means foolproof**.

(a) By **experimenting** with possible passwords, an unauthorised person can gain access to a program or file by **guessing** the correct password. This is not as difficult as it may seem when too many computer users specify 'obvious' passwords for their files or programs. In addition **computer programs** are available that run through millions of possible combinations at lightning speed until the correct one is found.

(b) Someone who is authorised to access a data or program file may **tell an unauthorised person** what the password is, perhaps through carelessness, or because it seems convenient on a particular occasion.

(c) An unauthorised person may simply **observe** someone else keying in their password. Most systems display **asterisks** instead of the actual characters typed, to try to prevent this, although this may not help if the password is a short simple one and the user types very slowly.

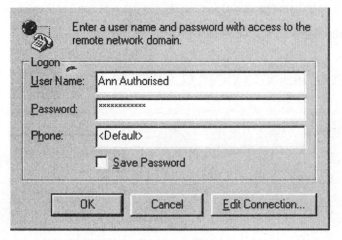

(d) Many password systems come with **standard passwords** as part of the system, such as LETMEIN. It is essential for these to be removed if the system is to be at all secure. Such common passwords become widely known to people in the industry using similar packages.

(e) Password systems they rely upon users to use them **conscientiously**. Users can be extremely sloppy with their security control. Passwords are often left in plain view or 'hidden' beneath keyboards or inside desk drawers where virtually anyone could readily find them. A password system requires both a software system and strong organisational policies if it is to be effective.

(f) A good password, in a form such as **f146PQzH7364** (numbers and letters, upper and lower case), would be very difficult to guess, but it is also very **difficult to remember**! Valuable information may become totally inaccessible if the user assigns a password (to a spreadsheet or database, say) and then forgets it.

Ways of avoiding this include using **mnemonics** for the letters and using numbers that are **significant** to the user for another reason (a cash card PIN number in reverse, say), but not easily guess-able by others.

Exam focus point

Passwords featured in a question in the **December 1997** exam, where candidates were asked to explain what passwords are and what they are for, to identify potential problems, and to suggest how these may be overcome.

> **BPP - Best Password Practice**
>
> Here is a checklist of points to be observed by computer users to whom passwords have been allocated.
>
> - **Keep your password secret**. Do not reveal it to anyone else.
>
> - **Do not write it down**. The second easiest way of revealing a password is to write it on an adhesive label and stick this to the VDU, the desk beneath the keyboard, the inside of a desk drawer or the underside of an overhead filing cabinet.
>
> - **Change your password regularly**. Passwords can become common knowledge, especially if they are associated with a particular PC that has been used by several different people. Passwords should be associated with **users**, not with machines. The ideal option is for passwords to be generated and assigned to users by **computer software**, and to be changed at regular intervals by the password generation program.
>
> - **Be discreet** when you **change and use** your password. Even though a password does not show up on screen, it is easy for onlookers to see which keys are being used. (FRED is a popular password for this reason; the relevant keys are close together on a QWERTY keyboard.)
>
> - **Do not use an obvious password**. FRED is an obvious password. Your name or nickname is another. The best option is a combination of letters and numbers and upper-case and lower-case.
>
> - **Change** your password **immediately** if you suspect that anyone else knows it.

Logical access systems

4.6   Whereas physical access control (doors, locks etc) is concerned with the prevention of unauthorised persons gaining access to the hardware, logical access control is concerned with **preventing** those who already have access to a terminal or a computer from **gaining access to data or software**.

4.7   In a logical access system, data and software, or individual computer systems, will be classified according to the sensitivity and confidentiality of data.

   (a)   Thus **payroll** data or details of the draft corporate budget for the coming year may be perceived as highly sensitive and made available to identified individuals only.

   (b)   Other financial information may be made **available to certain groups** of staff only, for example members of the finance function or a certain grade of management.

   (c)   Other data may be **unrestricted.**

4.8   A logical access system performs three operations when access is requested.

   - **Identification** of the user.
   - **Authentication** of user identity.
   - Check on user **authority.**

Database controls

4.9   **Databases** present a particular problem for computer security. In theory, the database can be **accessed by large numbers of people**, and so the possibility of alteration, unauthorised disclosure or fraud is so much greater than with application-specific files.

4.10   It is possible to construct complicated password systems, and the DBMS can be programmed to **give a limited view** of its contents to particular users or **restrict the disclosure** of certain types of information to particular times of day. It is possible to build a set of **privileges** into the system, so allowing authorised users with a particular password to **access more information**.

4.11   However, there are problems ensuring that individuals do not circumvent the database by means of **inference**. If you ask enough questions, you should be able to infer from the replies the information you are really seeking.

4.12   For example, the database forbids you to ask if John is employee Category A. However, if you know there are only three employee categories, A, B, and C, and there is no prohibition on asking about categories B and C, you can work out the members of category A by process of elimination (ie neither B, or C, therefore A).

4.13   So-called '**inference controls**' exist to make this difficult by limiting the number of queries, or by controlling the overlap between questions.

5   HACKERS AND VIRUSES

Telecommunications dangers

5.1   When data is transmitted over a network or **telecommunications link** (especially the **Internet**) there are numerous security dangers.

(a)   Corruptions such as **viruses** on a single computer can spread through the network to all of the organisation's computers. (Viruses are described at greater length later in this chapter.)

(b)   Staff can do damage through their own computer to data stored on other computers. For example, they may try to transfer a file from their own hard disk to a colleague's hard disk without realising that their colleague has a file with the same name. Unless care is exercised it is easy to **overwrite somebody else's data**.

(c)   Disaffected employees have much greater potential to do **deliberate damage** to valuable corporate data or systems because the network could give them access to parts of the system that they are not really authorised to use.

(d)   If the organisation is linked to an external network, persons outside the company (**hackers**) may be able to get into the company's internal network, either to steal data or to damage the system.

Systems can have **firewalls** (which disable part of the telecoms technology) to prevent unwelcome intrusions into company systems, but a determined hacker may well be able to bypass even these. (There is more on hackers below.)

(e)   Employees may **download inaccurate information** or imperfect or **virus-ridden software** from an external network. For example 'beta' (free trial) versions of forthcoming new editions of many major packages are often available on the Internet, but the whole point about a beta version is that it is not fully tested and may contain bugs that could disrupt an entire system.

(f)   Information transmitted from one part of an organisation to another may be **intercepted**. Data can be 'encrypted' (scrambled) in an attempt to make it unintelligible to eavesdroppers, but there is not yet any entirely satisfactory method of doing this. (See below. The problem is being worked upon by those with a vested interest, such as credit card companies, and will no doubt be resolved in time.)

(g)   The **communications link itself may break down or distort data**. The worldwide telecommunications infrastructure is improving thanks to the use of new technologies, and there are communications 'protocols' governing the format of data and signals transferred (see below). At present, however, transmitted data is only as secure as the medium through which it is transmitted, no matter what controls are operated at either end.

Protocols

5.2 One of the big problems in transmitting data down a public or private telephone wire is the possibility of **distortion or loss of the message**. There needs to be some way for a computer to:

(a) detect whether there are **errors in data transmission** (eg loss of data, or data arriving out of sequence, ie in an order different from the sequence in which it was transmitted);

(b) take steps to **recover the lost data,** even if this is simply to notify the computer or terminal operator to telephone the sender of the message that the whole data package will have to be re-transmitted. However, a more 'sophisticated' system can identify the corrupted or lost data more specifically, and request **re-transmissio**n of only the lost or distorted parts.

5.3 The mechanism used to detect and usually then to correct errors is known as a **communications protocol**. Factors covered by a protocol include the following amongst many others.

- Speed of transmission.
- Format of the data.
- Error detection and correction procedures.

5.4 One set of protocols has been developed by the **International Standards Organisation (ISO)**. It is known as open systems interconnection (OSI).

5.5 As in other areas, however, there is a tendency for the computer industry to prefer *de facto* standards for telecoms. Thus the official OSI standard has not been widely adopted and many suppliers are instead adopting **TCP/IP (Transmissions Control Protocol/Internet Protocol)**.

5.6 TCP/IP is regarded as cheaper and easier to implement than the OSI model. The exponential growth of the **Internet** has probably secured its supremacy.

Encryption and other safety measures

5.7 **Encryption** is the only secure way to prevent eavesdropping (since eavesdroppers can get round password controls, by tapping the line or by experimenting with various likely passwords).

KEY TERM

Encryption involves scrambling the data at one end of the line, transmitting the scrambled data, and unscrambling it at the receiver's end of the line.

5.8 **Authentication** is a technique of making sure that a message has come from an authorised sender. Authentication involves adding an extra field to a record, with the contents of this field derived from the remainder of the record by applying an algorithm that has previously been agreed between the senders and recipients of data.

5.9   **Dial-back security** operates by requiring the person wanting access to the network to dial into it and identify themselves first. The system then dials the person back on their authorised number before allowing them access.

5.10   All attempted **violations of security** should be automatically **logged** and the log checked regularly. In a multi-user system, the terminal attempting the violation may be automatically disconnected.

Hacking

5.11   A hacker is a **person who attempts to invade the privacy of a system**.

5.12   Hackers are normally **skilled programmers**, and have been known to crack system passwords with consummate ease. The fact that billions of bits of information can be transmitted in bulk over the public telephone network has made it **hard to trace** individual hackers, who can therefore make repeated attempts to invade systems. Hackers, in the past, have mainly been concerned to **copy** information, but a recent trend has been their desire to **corrupt it**.

5.13   Phone numbers and passwords can be guessed by hackers using **electronic phone directories** or number generators and by software which enables **rapid guessing** using hundreds of permutations per minute.

5.14   **Default passwords** are also available on some electronic bulletin boards and sophisticated hackers could even try to 'tap' messages being transmitted along phone wires (the number actually dialled will not be scrambled).

5.15   The **Computer Misuse Act 1990** addresses the problems of hacking, but clearly cannot **prevent** it. See Chapter 9.

Viruses

KEY TERM

A **virus** is a piece of software which replicates itself, and which may do damage to data or programs.

5.16   Viruses need an **opportunity to spread**. The programmers of viruses therefore place viruses in the kind of software which is most likely to be copied. This includes:

(a) **free software** (for example software downloaded from the Internet);
(b) **pirated software** (cheaper than original versions); and
(c) **games software** (wide appeal).

5.17   The problem has been exacerbated by the **portability of computers and disks**. Many employees **take disks home** and may work on them on their own personal PCs. Office PCs may be taken home and the opportunity taken to try out games or other software.

5.18   It is consequently very difficult to keep control over **what disks** are inserted into an organisation's computers and similarly **what computers** may be used to retrieve data from or store data to office disks. Some organisations go as far as to disable the floppy disk drive on PCs.

The effect of viruses

5.19 Most viruses are **comparatively harmless**, and may be present for years with no noticeable effect: some, however, may cause **random damage to data files** (sometimes insidiously, over a long period) or attempt to **destroy files and disks**.

5.20 Others cause **unintended damage**. Even benign viruses (apparently non-destructive viruses) cause significant damage by occupying disk space and/or main memory, by using up CPU processing time, and by the time and expense wasted in detecting and removing them.

5.21 An activated virus can **show itself** in a number of ways.

- The **Jerusalem** virus **slows down** the operation of the infected machine so much that it becomes virtually unusable, then deletes files.

- The **Stoned** virus displays a **message** saying 'This computer is stoned - legalise marijuana.

- **Cascade** causes letters on the **screen** to 'fall' to the bottom of the screen and may reformat the hard disk.

- The **Italian** displays a ball which bounces around the **screen**.

- **Casino** displays a one-armed bandit game on screen; if you fail to win the jackpot, your **hard disk is wiped**.

5.22 The most serious type of virus is one which **infects an operating system** as this governs the whole execution of a program. However, many current viruses were designed to run under DOS, and use DOS-specific functions to operate and take advantage of undocumented DOS features. These features have been removed in Windows 95.

5.23 Viruses can spread via data disk, but have been known to copy themselves over whole **networks**. When transmitted over a network into a clean system, the virus continues to reproduce, thus infecting that system.

Type of virus	Explanation/Example
File viruses	File viruses infect program files. When you run an infected program the virus runs first, then passes control to the original program. While it has control, the virus code copies itself to another file or to another disk, replicating itself.
Macro viruses	A macro virus is a piece of self-replicating code written in an application's 'macro' language, which is intended to allow users to automate commonly performed tasks. Many applications have macro capabilities including all the programs in **Microsoft Office**.
	The distinguishing factor which makes it possible to create a virus with a macro is the existence of **auto-execute events**. Auto-execute events are opening a file, closing a file, and starting an application. Once a macro is running, it can copy itself to other documents, delete files, and create general havoc in a person's system. These things occur without the user explicitly running the macro.
	Microsoft Office offers reasonably good protection against this, and you may well have seen a warning such as the following.

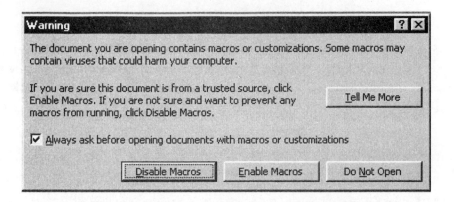

Boot sector viruses

The boot sector is the part of every hard disk and diskette which is read by the computer when it starts up. Most PCs are set up to attempt to boot from the A: drive first. If the boot sector of a diskette is infected, the virus runs when you attempt to boot from the diskette, and infects the hard disk.

For example, if you leave a diskette in the drive overnight and then switch on your PC the next day, a message like the following is displayed: 'Non-system disk or disk error ... Replace and press any key when ready'. However, if the diskette is infected with a boot sector virus, that **virus has already run**, and your PC may **already be infected**.

Overwriting viruses

An overwriting virus simply overwrites each file it infects with itself, so the program no longer functions. Since this is very easy to spot these viruses do not spread very well, and are not a real threat.

Worms

A worm is a program which spreads (usually) over network connections. Unlike a virus, it does not attach itself to a host program. Worms are not normally associated with PC systems.

Dropper

A dropper is a program, not a virus itself, that installs a virus on the PC while performing another function. A typical example is a utility that formats a floppy disk, complete with Stoned virus, on the boot sector.

Trojans

5.24 A Trojan or Trojan Horse is a program intended to perform some covert and usually malicious act which the victim did not expect or want. It differs from a destructive virus in that it **doesn't reproduce** (though this distinction is by no means universally accepted).

(a) **A logic bomb** is a **type of trojan** that is **triggered by certain events**. A program will behave normally until a certain event occurs, for example when disk utilisation reaches a certain percentage. A logic bomb, by responding to set conditions, maximises damage. For example, it will be triggered when a disk is nearly full, or when a large number of users are using the system.

(b) **A time bomb** is similar to a logic bomb, except that it is **triggered at a certain date**. Companies have experienced virus attacks on April Fool's Day and on Friday 13th. These were released by time bombs.

Bugs

5.25 A **bug** is an **unintentional fault** in a program, and can be misinterpreted as a virus. Virtually all complex software contains bugs. Minor bugs merely cause inconvenience, while major bugs can cause catastrophic data loss. There is no way of detecting bugs in advance, and the only defence is to ensure you back up your important data regularly.

Jokes and hoaxes

5.26 Some programs claim to be doing something destructive to your computer, but are actually harmless jokes. For example, a message may appear suggesting that your hard disk is about to be reformatted. Unfortunately, it is **easy to over-react** to the joke and cause more damage by trying to eradicate something that is not, in fact, a virus.

5.27 There are a number of common hoaxes, which are widely believed. The most common of these is **Good Times**. This hoax has been around for a couple of years, and usually takes the form of a virus warning about viruses contained in e-mail. People pass along the warning because they are trying to be helpful, not realising the damage that this does.

Case example: the Good Times hoax

Here is the text of one version (of many) of the well-known 'Good Times' hoax. Read this, see if you can spot the flaws in the argument, and be sure to do Question 5. (*Note.* 'an nth-complexity infinite binary loop' is sheer gobbledegook!)

V I R U S - W A R N I N G

There is a computer virus that is being sent across the Internet. If you receive an email message with the subject line "Good Times," DO NOT read the message, DELETE it immediately.

Please read the messages below. Some miscreant is sending email under the title "Good Times" nationwide, if you get anything like this,

DON'T DOWN LOAD THE FILE!

It has a virus that rewrites your hard drive, obliterating anything on it.

Please be careful and forward this mail to anyone you care about.

WARNING!!!!!!! INTERNET VIRUS

The FCC released a warning last Wednesday concerning a matter of major importance to any regular user of the Internet.

Apparently a new computer virus has been engineered by a user of AMERICA ON LINE that is unparalleled in its destructive capability.

What makes this virus so terrifying, said the FCC, is the fact that no program needs to be exchanged for a new computer to be infected. It can be spread through the existing email systems of the Internet. Once a Computer is infected, one of several things can happen. If the computer contains a hard drive, that will most likely be destroyed. If the program is not stopped, the computer's processor will be placed in an nth-complexity infinite binary loop--which can severely damage the processor if left running that way too long.

Luckily, there is one sure means of detecting what is now known as the "Good Times" virus. It always travels to new computers the same way in a text email message with the subject line reading "Good Times." Avoiding infection is easy once the file has been received simply by NOT READING IT!

The act of loading the file into the mail server's ASCII buffer causes the "Good Times" mainline program to initialize and execute. The program is highly intelligent--it will send copies of itself to everyone whose email address is contained in a receive-mail file or a sent-mail file, if it can find one. It will then proceed to trash the computer it is running on.

The bottom line is:

If you receive a file with the subject line "Good Times", delete it immediately! Do not read it" Rest assured that whoever's name was on the "From" line was surely struck by the virus.

> Warn your friends and local system users of this newest threat to the Internet! It could save them a lot of time and money. Could you pass this along to your global mailing list as well?

Identification of a virus

5.28 There are two ways of identifying a virus. The first is to identify it before it does any damage. The second is to identify it when it is activated.

5.29 It is difficult for the typical user to identify the presence of a virus. There are sometimes **tell-tale signs,** such as slight changes in file lengths as displayed in the directory, or additional disk activity before a program is run, but **more sophisticated controls** than this are needed.

(a) **Anti-virus software** such as Dr Solomon's is capable of detecting and eradicating a vast number of viruses before they do any damage. Upgrades are released regularly to deal with new viruses. The software will run whenever a computer is turned on and will continue to monitor in the background until it is turned off again.

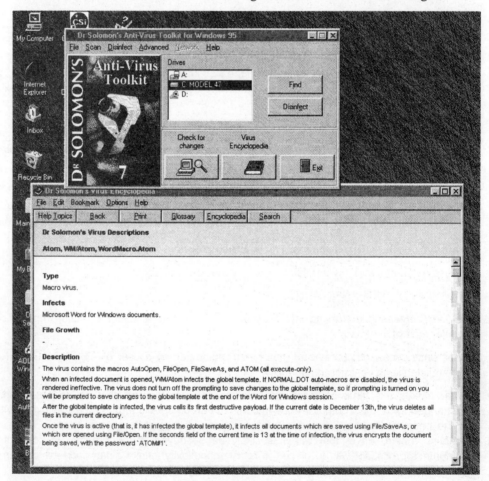

(b) Organisations must have **procedures** to guard against the introduction of unauthorised software to their systems. Many viruses and trojans have been spread on pirated versions of popular computer games.

(c) Organisations, as a matter of routine, should **ensure that any disk received from outside is virus-free** before the data on the disk is downloaded.

(d) Any **flaws in a widely used program** should be rectified as soon as they come to light.

Question 5

A **hoax** is not a virus at all, but simply a spoof warning that such and such a document or program contains a virus. Hoaxes are sent by e-mail to unsuspecting persons and they encourage people to forward the message to anybody else they can think of that might be affected by the spoof virus.

What is the point of this?

Answer

Hoaxes do not do any harm in themselves and there is no point - unless you believe that it is amusing or desirable to create panic and waste the time of organisations. This is precisely what some of the perpetrators do believe. Recent reports suggest that hoaxes are more of a problem now than real viruses.

Chapter roundup

- **Back-up procedures** are essential to guard against deliberate or accidental damage to data. Methods include the grandfather-father-son approach and dumping.

- Back-ups should be **stored off-site.**

- **Controls** should be built in to a system and cover inputs, processes and outputs.

- **Verification** ensures that the data input is the same as the data in the source document.

- A wide variety of **validation** checks can be built into programs and data, including range checks, limit checks, consistency checks and check digits.

- **Computer fraud** usually involves the theft of funds. The opportunities for people to commit fraud are growing as computers become more widespread and computer literacy increases. Clear policies, good training and careful recruitment can help to counteract fraud.

- **Passwords** can be applied to data files. A password is a set of characters which are required to be keyed into a system before further access is permitted. Although password systems can be extremely sophisticated, they all depend on user discipline.

- A **logical access system** is concerned with preventing those persons who have gained physical access from gaining unauthorised access to data or software.

- A **hacker** is a person who attempts to invade the privacy of a system by circumventing logical access controls.

- When data is transmitted over telecommunications links, there are a number of security risks. One method of preventing eavesdropping is **encryption**. Authentication ensures that a message has come from an authorised user.

- A **virus** is a piece of software which corrupts the operation of programs and, given the opportunity, replicates itself throughout a system. **Virus protection** should be a standard part of the internal control system of any organisation.

Quick quiz

1   What is the purpose of a back-up? (see para 1.4)

2   How effective is backing up? (1.14 - 1.16)

3   What controls can be exercised over processing? (2.7 - 2.9)

4   What is a range check? (2.17)

5   What is a format check? (2.20)

6   What types of computer fraud are there? (3.2)

7   What controls can be used to prevent fraud? (3.5)

8   Write out a checklist of best password practice? (4.5)

9   What security dangers arise due to telecommunications links? (5.1)

10   What is encryption? (5.7)

11   What controls are needed to avoid viruses? (5.29)

Question to try	Level	Marks	Time
18	Exam standard	10	18 mins
19	Exam standard	15	27 mins

Part D
Systems implementation, management and evaluation

Chapter 16

PROJECT MANAGEMENT

Chapter topic list		Syllabus reference
1	Project management	3(c), 5(a), 5(b)
2	Reducing the threats through project management	3(c), 5(a), 5(b)
3	Network analysis	3(c), 5(a), 5(b)
4	Gantt charts	3(c), 5(a), 5(b)
5	Project management software	3(c), 5(a), 5(b)
6	The project team	3(c), 5(a), 5(b)

Introduction

We saw in **Chapter 7** how important it is to **choose** projects carefully. In this chapter the topic of **managing** projects is analysed.

The importance of good management of projects cannot be exaggerated as certain recurrent problems may frequently be observed. Any one or combination of these failings leads to wasted time, money and effort.

(a)   New systems do not arrive on **time**.

(b)   New systems often cost a lot more than was **budgeted**.

(c)   New systems do not meet **user requirements**.

This chapter looks at these threats in more detail and at the techniques and tools used to overcome them.

1   PROJECT MANAGEMENT

1.1   The following definition will help you to appreciate why it is necessary to **manage** information systems projects.

> ### KEY TERM
>
> A **project** is a type of work whose end-product is a single item on a very large scale. Examples include the Channel Tunnel and the Millenium project.

1.2   Like these examples, information systems projects involve large numbers of people, long periods of time and large amounts of money.

1.3   However, it is not uncommon for a systems development project to be years late, wildly over budget, and a waste of effort, as the system produced in the end does not deliver the goods. Perhaps the best way of understanding why active management of systems development projects is necessary is by seeing what **problems** arise when they go wrong.

What can go wrong?

1.4 A number of factors can combine to produce these expensive disasters.

Project managers

1.5 Project managers are usually **technicians,** not managers. Technical ability for IS staff is no guarantee of management skill. However, often, the only promotion path available is to a management role. An individual might be a highly proficient analyst or programmer, but **not a good manager.**

1.6 The project manager has a number of **conflicting requirements.**

  (a) The **systems manager,** usually the project manager's boss, wants the project **delivered on time,** to specification and within budget.

  (b) **Users,** and the **management** of the function to which they belong, want a system which does everything they require - but they are **not always certain what they want.** User input is vital to a project, but user management and staff may not be able to take time off from their normal duties to help out. If the project is late, over budget, and does not do all which is required of it, then users will be vocal critics.

  (c) The project manager has to plan and supervise the work of **analysts** and **programmers** and these are rather different roles (see later in this chapter).

1.7 The project manager needs to develop an **appropriate management style.** What he or she should realise is the extent to which the project will fail if users are not consulted, or if the project team is unhappy. As the project manager needs to encourage participation from users, an excessively authoritarian style is not suitable.

Exam focus point

A question might typically present you with a scenario in which a project is clearly failing to deliver and ask for your comments on how the situation might be improved. Such questions came up in **June 1994** and **June 1995.**

Other factors

1.8 Other factors can be identified.

  (a) The project manager **accepts an unrealistic deadline** for having the system up and running. The timescale is fixed too early on in the planning process: the user's idea of when the system would be needed is taken as the deadline, before sufficient consideration is given to the realism of this timescale.

  (b) **Poor or non-existent planning** is a recipe for disaster. Ludicrous deadlines would appear much earlier if a proper planning process was undertaken.

  (c) **Control** is non-existent (ie no performance reviews).

  (d) Users **change their requirements,** resulting in costly changes to the system as it is being developed.

  (e) **Poor time-tabling and resourcing** is a cause of problems. It is no use being presented on day 1 with a team of programmers, when there is still systems analysis and design work to do. As the development and implementation of a computer project may take a considerable length of time (perhaps 18 months from initial decision to operational running for a medium-sized installation) a proper plan and time schedule for the various activities must be drawn up.

Terms of reference

1.9   At the start of a project, once selected, a **Project Initiation Document (PID)** may be drawn up, setting out the **terms of reference** for the project. Typical contents might include the following.

(a)   The **business objectives**. Projects should not be undertaken simply for their own sake: the business advantages should be clearly identified and be the first point of reference when progress is being reviewed, to make sure that the original aim is not lost sight of

(b)   **Project objectives**

(c)   The **scope** of the project: what it is intended to cover and what it is not

(d)   **Constraints,** such as maximum amount to be spent and interim and final deadlines

(e)   The **ultimate customer** of the project, who will resolve conflicts as they occur (for example between two different divisions who will both be using the new system) and finally accept it

(f)   The **resources** that will be used – staff, technical resources, finance

(g)   An **analysis of risks** inherent in the project and how they are to be avoided or reduced (for example, the consequences of replacing the old sales ledger system and only discovering after the event that the new one does not work).

(h)   A **project plan** (targets, activities and so on) and details of how the project is to be organised and managed (see the next section)

(i)   **Purchasing and procurement policy,** perhaps specifying acceptable suppliers and delivery details.

Exam focus point
A question in **June 1996** asked about the likely contents of a project initiation document.

Phases of project management

1.10   Every project is different, by definition, and it is impossible to be prescriptive about what a project involves. According to the very recent *Guideline for the Project Management of the Development of Critical Computer Systems* issued by a leading group of European experts, there are twelve **phases** of project management (following the selection of the project) categorised as follows.

Phase	Comment
1 Preparation 2 Initiation	These phases are likely to involve tasks such as identifying and assembling the **project team** and any **resources** (software tools etc) needed; **making arrangements with the user** of the new system for access to existing systems and staff; agreeing **terms of reference** and **briefing the team** on what is to be done.
3 Specification 4 Design 5 Build	This is the development work described in **Chapters 11 to 15**, probably following a methodology such as SSADM.
6 Integration	**Integration** means pulling the work of all the different people involved in the project together

Phase	Comment
7 Installation	These phases are described in depth in **Chapter 17**.
8 System validation	
9 Handover	
10 Project review	See **Chapter 18** for more on these phases.
11 Operations and maintenance	
12 Decommissioning and replacement	This point comes when a new system to replace this one has been developed and is about to take over. This phase would roughly coincide with Phases 7 to 9 of the **new** project. Obviously it is useful to have members of the original team on hand to run down the old system, but this may not be possible in practice.

2   REDUCING THE THREATS THROUGH PROJECT MANAGEMENT

2.1   A project is affected by a number of factors, often in **conflict** with each other.

(a) **Quality** of the system required, in terms of basic system requirements.

(b) The **resources**, both in terms of staff recruitment and work scheduling, and technology.

(c) **Time,** both to complete the project, and in terms of the opportunity cost of time spent on this project which could be spent on others.

(d) **Costs,** which are monitored and controlled, in accordance with the budget set for the project.

2.2   The requirement to keep to a specified **time** might for example **increase costs**, if there are delays and new staff have to be employed, or **reduce quality** if corners are cut.

2.3   It is with these threats in mind that **management of the project** must be conducted.

The responsibilities of the project manager

2.4   By definition every project is different and so we can only set out the type of tasks project manager is likely to have to perform in general terms.

(a) Devising the Project Quality Plan
(b) Planning the project
(c) Communication
(d) Co-ordination
(e) Monitoring and control
(f) Post project review
(g) People management

Exam focus point

In an exam you might be required to discuss particular problems that a project manager might face in the light of a particular scenario, so be prepared to *apply* these points, not just reproduce them *verbatim*, in exam answers.

There was a question on the responsibilities of a project manager in the **December 1997** scenario question.

Project Quality Plan

2.5 The project manager may flesh out the terms of reference (see above) into a more detailed document which (in Project Management jargon) is sometimes called a **Project Quality Plan**.

2.6 The **project quality plan,** perhaps in conjunction with other documents, describes the following.

   (a) **What** the product **requirement** is (ie what is to be built and delivered by when)

   (b) How **changes** to the requirement are to be **controlled**

   (c) How the requirements are to be met (common management and technical **procedures** which are to be used on the project; **standards** which are to be used by the project)

   (d) How the requirements are to be **seen** to be met

   (e) How **conformance** to the requirements is to be **independently checked**

   (f) What are seen as the **risks** that might prevent the requirements from being fully met

Project planning

2.7 This involves the setting of measurable **targets** from the stated broad objectives.

   (a) Developing project targets such as **overall costs or timescale** needed (ie project should take 20 weeks)

   (b) Dividing the project into **activities** (eg analysis, programming, testing), and placing these activities into the right **sequence**, often a complicated task if overlapping. Section 3 of this chapter deals with this in much more depth.

   (c) Developing a framework for the **organisational procedures and structures** necessary to manage the project (eg decide, in principle, to have weekly team meetings, performance reviews etc)

Detailed planning

2.8 The 'nitty-gritty' of time scheduling and so forth is worked out here, and the exact sequence of individual tasks within activities. Network analysis techniques may be used in this context. There are outputs from the planning process.

   (a) **Time budgets** for tasks, and for team members.

   (b) Identification of **critical activities**.

   (c) Allocation of **resources** to activities (for example computer hardware).

   (d) Arrangement of any **training** which might be needed for certain members of the project team.

   (e) Establishment of **reporting structures and procedures** identified in the outline planning phase (ie decide when to have the weekly team briefings).

Communication

2.9 The project manager must let **superiors** know what is going on, and ensure that members of the project **team** are properly **briefed**. Overall staffing structures must support effective communication.

Co-ordination

2.10 Co-ordinating project activities between the **project team** and **users**, and other **external parties** (for example suppliers of hardware and software) is a vital task.

Monitoring and control

2.11 Project management invariably involves a number of control activities.

   (a) **Planning** and **work scheduling**.

   (b) Establishment of **feedback procedures** to aid the **control and monitoring** of the project (timeliness, keeping to budget, quality control etc).

   (c) Ensuring that the **different members** of staff working on different segments of the project **communicate** with each other, and with the project manager.

   (d) **Quality control** over work done, perhaps enforced through the use of systems development standards.

   (e) **Reporting** to the **steering committee** and/or **senior management** on a regular basis as part of the control procedure, as to how the project is **progressing**. A typical report would show what tasks had now been completed, what tasks were in progress and what tasks were due to start. It would also discuss problems that had arisen or were likely to arise, such as changes in requirements, and what the impact of these problems was likely to be in terms of cost and timescale.

Post project review

2.12 This will entail meetings and document production, organised by the project manager, involving staff who took part in the project and client staff in the user department. It considers matters such as whether the project **delivered what was required** (especially in terms of **cost** and **timescale**), and the **lessons learned** for future projects, both in terms of the new **system** that has been built and in terms of the **organisation** of projects.

People management

2.13 This would include matters such as keeping the staff involved **motivated**, dealing with **conflicts** within the team, and general **personnel** responsibilities such as staff **development** and **appraisal**, awarding **bonuses** or other types of **recognition**, and **hiring and firing**.

3 NETWORK ANALYSIS

3.1 Network analysis, also known as **critical path analysis (CPA)**, is a useful technique to help with planning and controlling large projects, such as construction projects, research and development projects and the computerisation of systems.

3.2 Its aim is to programme and monitor the progress of a project so that the project is completed in the **minimum time** and on **schedule**.

3.3 It pinpoints the parts of the project which are **'critical'**, ie those parts which, if delayed beyond the allotted time, would delay the completion of the project as a whole.

3.4 The technique can also be used to assist in **allocating resources** such as labour and equipment.

> **KEY TERM**
>
> **Network analysis** is used for scheduling and controlling projects where many separate tasks (which collectively make up the whole project) can either happen simultaneously or must follow one after another such that it is difficult to establish the relationships between all the separate tasks. The technique can be applied to any purposeful chain of events involving the use of time, labour and physical resources.

The technique: drawing a diagram

3.5 Network analysis is quite a simple technique. The events and activities making up the whole project are represented in the form of a **diagram**.

3.6 Drawing the diagram or chart involves the following steps.

Step 1. Estimating the time needed to complete each individual activity or task that makes up a part of the project.
Step 2. Sorting out what activities must be done one after another, and which can be done at the same time, if required.
Step 3. Representing these in a network diagram.
Step 4. Estimating the critical path, which is the longest sequence of consecutive activities through the network.

3.7 In an **exam** you would generally only have to do Steps 3 and 4. The other information would have to be given to you.

Activity-on-node presentation

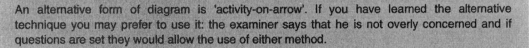

> **Exam focus point**
>
> The current examiner has stated that he suggests the **activity-on-node** type of diagram is used. This is the type produced by popular **project management software** packages such as Microsoft Project.
>
> An alternative form of diagram is 'activity-on-arrow'. If you have learned the alternative technique you may prefer to use it: the examiner says that he is not overly concerned and if questions are set they would allow the use of either method.
>
> In practice it is more likely that you would have to **explain** the technique than draw a diagram. A question requiring explanations was set in the **June 1997** exam.

3.8 The method of drawing network diagrams explained here closely follows the presentation that you would see if you used the **Microsoft Project** software package. It is easier and clearer than old-fashioned methods using circles divided into quadrants, dummy activities and so on.

3.9 EXAMPLE: ACTIVITY ON NODE

Suppose that a project includes three activities, C, D and E. Neither activity D nor E can start until activity C is completed, but D and E could be done simultaneously if required.

This would be represented as follows.

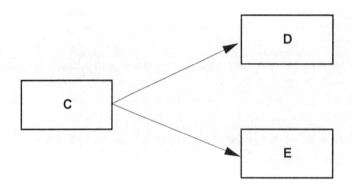

3.10 Note the following.

(a) An **activity** within a network is represented by a rectangular box. (Each box is a **node**.)

(b) The '**flow**' of activities in the diagram should be from **left to right**.

(c) The diagram clearly shows that **D and E must follow C**.

3.11 A second possibility is that an activity cannot start until two or more activities have been completed. If activity H cannot start until activities G and F are both complete, then we would represent the situation like this.

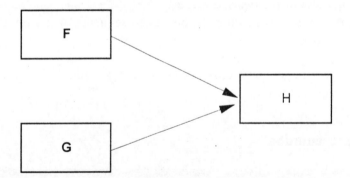

Starts and ends

3.12 In some conventions an extra node is introduced at the start and end of a network. This serves absolutely no purpose (other than to ensure that all the nodes are joined up), and is **potentially highly confusing**, so we recommend that you do not do it. Just in case you ever see a network presented in this way, however, both styles are shown in the next example.

3.13 EXAMPLE: STARTS AND ENDS

Draw a diagram for the following project. The project is finished when both D and E are complete.

Activity	Preceding activity
A	-
B	-
C	A
D	B & C
E	B

3.14 SOLUTION

Microsoft Project style (Right)

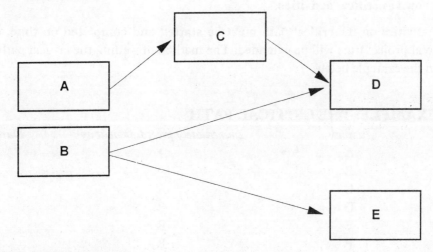

With start and end nodes (Wrong)

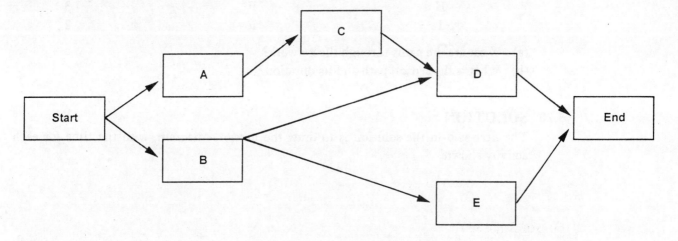

Paths

3.15 Any network can be analysed into a number of different paths or routes. A path is simply **a sequence of activities** which can take you from the **start to the end** of the network. In the example above, there are just three routes or paths.

(a) A C D.

(b) B D.

(c) B E.

The critical path

3.16 The time needed to complete each individual activity in a project must be estimated. This **duration** is shown within the node as follows. The reason for and meaning of the other boxes will be explained in a moment.

Task A	
ID	6 days

3.17 The duration of the whole project will be fixed by the time taken to complete the largest path through the network. This path is called the **critical path** and activities on it are known as **critical activities**.

3.18 Activities on the critical path **must be started and completed on time**, otherwise the total project time will be extended. The method of finding the critical path is illustrated in the example below.

3.19 EXAMPLE: THE CRITICAL PATH

Activity	*Immediately preceding activity*	*Duration (weeks)*
A	-	5
B	-	4
C	A	2
D	B	1
E	B	5
F	B	5
G	C, D	4
H	F	3
I	F	2

(a) What are the paths through the network?

(b) What is the critical path and its duration?

3.20 SOLUTION

The first step in the solution is to draw the network diagram, with the time for each activity shown.

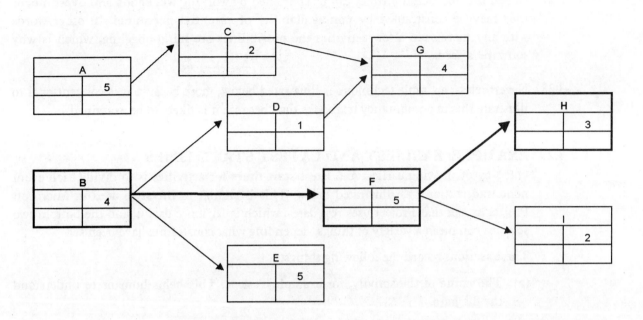

3.21 We could list the paths through the network and their overall completion times as follows.

Path	Duration (weeks)	
A C G	(5 + 2 + 4)	11
B D G	(4 + 1 + 4)	9
B E	(4 + 5)	9
B F H	(4 + 5+ 3)	12
B F I	(4 + 5 + 2 + 0)	11

3.22 The critical path is the longest, **BFH**, with a duration of 12 weeks. This is the **minimum time needed** to complete the project.

3.23 The **critical path** is indicated on the diagram by drawing **thick** (or **double-line**) arrows, as shown above. In Microsoft Project the arrows and the nodes are highlighted in **red**.

3.24 **Listing paths** through the network in this way should be easy enough for small networks, but it becomes a **long and tedious task** for bigger and more complex networks. This is why **software packages** are used in real life.

Earliest and latest times

3.25 Conventionally (at least in accounting exams) it is also felt to be useful to calculate the earliest and latest times for activities to start or finish, and show them on the network diagram. This can be done for networks of any size and complexity.

3.26 Project management software packages offer a much larger variety of techniques than can easily be done by hand. Microsoft Project, for instance allows **each activity** to be assigned to any one of a variety of types: 'start as late as possible', 'start as soon as possible', 'finish no earlier than a particular date', "finish no later than a particular date', and so on. Each different activity may be of a different type and subject to different constraints, just as in **real life**.

3.27   In real life, too, activity times can be shortened by working **weekends and overtime,** or they may be constrained by **non-availability of essential personnel**. In other words with any more than a few activities the possibilities are mind-boggling, which is why software is used.

3.28   Nevertheless, a simple technique is illustrated below, more because it is conventional to illustrate this in accountancy textbooks than because it is likely to be examined.

3.29   EXAMPLE: EARLIEST AND LATEST START TIMES

One way of showing earliest and latest **start** times for activities is to divide each event node into sections, as illustrated below. This is similar to the style used in Microsoft Project except that Project uses real dates, which is far more useful, and the bottom two sections can mean a variety of things, depending what constraints have been set.

These sections record the following things.

(a)   The **name** of the activity, for example Task A. This helps humans to understand the diagram.

(b)   An **ID number** which is unique to that activity. This helps computer packages to understand the diagram, because it is possible that two or more activities could have the same name. For instance two bits of research are done at different project stages might both be called 'Research'.

(c)   The **duration** of the activity

(d)   The **earliest start time**. Conventionally for the first node in the network, this is time 0.

(e)   The **latest start time**.

(**Note**. Don't confuse start times with the **'event'** times that are calculated when using the **activity-on-arrow** method, even though the approach is the same.)

Task D	
ID number: 4	Duration: 6 days
Earliest start: Day 4	Latest start: Day 11

Earliest start times

3.30   To find the earliest start times, always start with activities that have no predecessors and give them an earliest starting time of 0. In the example we have been looking at, this is week 0.

Then work along each path from **left to right** through the diagram calculating the earliest time that the next activity can start.

For example, the earliest time for activity C is week $0 + 5 = 5$. The earliest time activities D, E and F can start is week $0 + 4 = 4$.

To calculate an activity's earliest time, simply look at the box for the **preceding** activity and add the bottom left figure to the top right figure.

If **two or more** activities precede an activity take the **highest** figure as the later activity's earliest start time: it cannot start before all the others are finished!

Latest start times

3.31   The latest start times are the latest times at which each activity can start **if the project as a whole is to be completed in the earliest possible time**, in other words in 12 weeks in our example.

Work backwards from **right to left** through the diagram calculating the latest time at which the activity can start, if it is to be completed at the latest finishing time. For example the latest start time for activity H is 12 - 3 = week 9 and for activity E is 12 - 5 = week 7.

3.32   Activity F might cause difficulties as two activities, H and I, lead back to it.

   (a)   Activity H must be completed by week 12, and so must start at week 9.
   (b)   Activity I must also be completed by week 12, and so must start at week 10.

Activity F takes 5 weeks so its latest start time F is the either 9 – 5 = week 4 or 10 – 5 = week 5. However, if it starts in week 5 it not be possible to start activity H on time and the whole project will be delayed. We therefore take the **lower** figure.

3.33   The final network diagram is now as follows. We have left the ID boxes blank to avoid confusion.

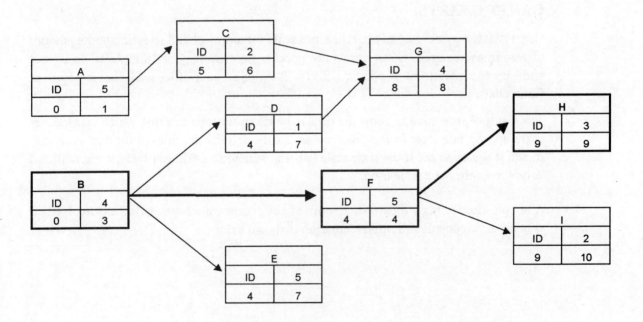

The critical path

3.34   Critical activities are those activities which must be started on time, otherwise the total project time will be increased. It follows that each event on the critical path must have the same earliest and latest start times. The critical path for the above network is therefore **B F H**.

PERT

3.35 Network problems may be complicated by **uncertainty** in the expected duration of individual activities. This may be expressed in terms of a most likely, optimistic and pessimistic time for each activity or in terms of a probability distribution of the expected time for each activity.

3.36 **Project evaluation and review technique (PERT)** introduces a form of time-uncertainty analysis into network analysis. For each activity in the project, optimistic, most likely and pessimistic estimates of times are made, on the basis of past experience, or even guess-work. These estimates are converted into a mean time and also a standard deviation.

3.37 Once the mean time and standard deviation of the time have been calculated for each activity, it should be possible to do the following.

(a) Estimate the **critical path** using expected (mean) activity times.
(b) Estimate the **standard deviation of the total project time**.

Exam focus point
It is **most unlikely** that you will be asked to use PERT in an examination question, but it might be helpful to mention that it exists.

4 GANTT CHARTS

4.1 Gantt charts may be used to plan the **time scale** for a project and to estimate the amount of **resources** required. Gantt charts are popular because they are **simple to construct** and **easy to understand**. If you have a Year Planner on your office wall, that is a form of Gantt chart.

4.2 The Gantt chart is used to show the time to be taken for each activity, which commences at the appropriate stage in the project plan. As the activity is achieved the 'bar' is shaded in and it is easy to see if the time scale is being adhered to. Alternatively, an 'actual' and 'estimated' split bar can be used.

4.3 A simple Gantt chart, illustrating some of the hardware-related activities involved in systems development and implementation is shown below.

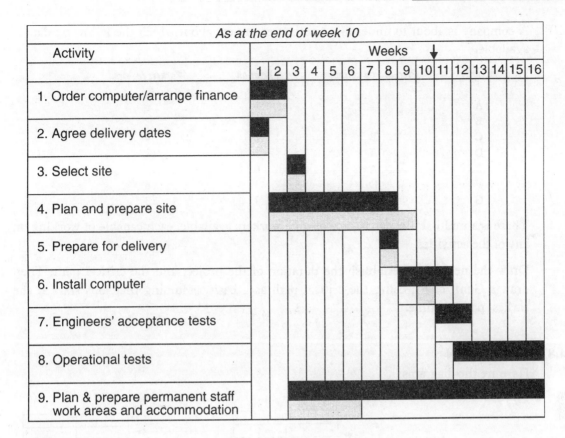

Key

   Estimated

   Actual

4.4 **At the end of the tenth week** Activity 9 is running behind schedule and more resources may have to be allocated to this activity if the staff accommodation is to be ready in time for the changeover to the new system.

4.5 Activity 4 had not been completed on time, and this has resulted in some disruption to the computer installation (Activity 6), which may mean further delays in the commencement of Activities 7 and 8.

4.6 One of the main problems with this type of Gantt chart is that it **does not clearly reflect the interrelationship** between the various activities in the project as does a network diagram. However, a combination of Gantt charts and network analysis might be used for project planning and resource allocation.

4.7 EXAMPLE: GANTT CHARTS AND RESOURCES

This example is provided as an illustration of the use of Gantt charts to manage **resources** (particularly human resources) efficiently, so that you feel happy about **describing** Gantt charts in exams. It is unlikely that you would actually have to deal with a numerical problem.

Exam focus point
A question set in **June 1995** asked for an explanation not a diagram.

A company is about to undertake a computer project about which the following data is available.

Activity	Preceded by activity	Duration Days	Workers required
A	–	3	6
B	–	5	3
C	B	2	4
D	A	1	4
E	A	6	5
F	D	3	6
G	C, E	3	3

There is a multi-skilled workforce of nine workers available, each capable of working on any of the activities.

Draw the network to establish the duration of the project and the critical path. Then draw a Gantt chart, using the critical path as a basis, assuming that jobs start at the earliest possible time.

4.8   SOLUTION

Here are the diagrams.

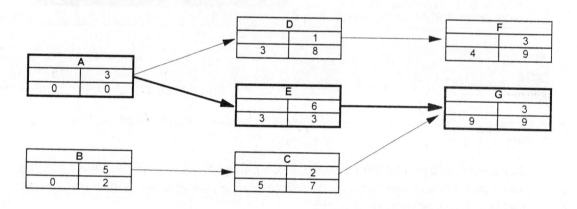

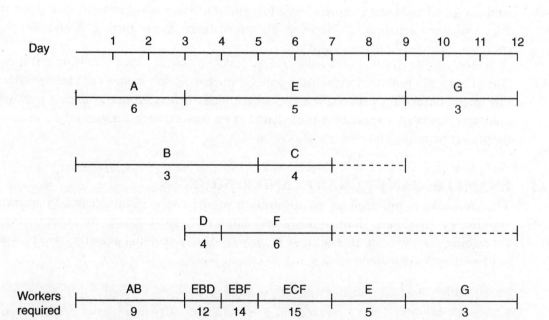

4.9   It can be seen that if all activities start at their earliest times, as many as 15 workers will be required on any one day (days 6-7) whereas on other days there would be idle capacity (days 8-12).

4.10   The problem can be reduced, or removed, by using up spare time on non-critical activities. Suppose we **deferred the start** of activities D and F until the latest possible days. These would be days 8 and 9, leaving four days to complete the activities by the end of day 12.

4.11   The Gantt chart would be redrawn as follows.

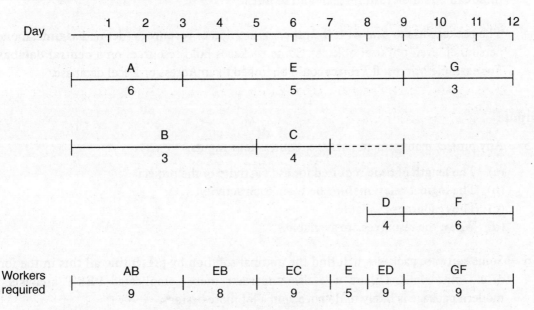

5   PROJECT MANAGEMENT SOFTWARE

5.1   As we have said repeatedly the project management techniques described above are **ideal candidates for computerisation**. Project management software packages have been available for a number of years.

5.2   Software might be used for a number of purposes.

(a)   **Planning**

Network diagrams (showing the critical path) and Gantt charts (showing resource use) can be produced automatically once the relevant data is entered. Packages also allow a sort of 'what if?' analysis for initial planning, trying out different levels of resources, changing deadlines and so on to find the best combination.

(b)   **Estimating**

As a project progresses, actual data will become known and can be entered into the package and collected for future reference. Since many projects involve basically similar tasks (interviewing users and so on), actual data from one project can be used to provide more accurate estimates for the next project. The software also facilitates and encourages the use of more sophisticated estimation techniques than managers might be prepared to use if working manually.

(c)   **Monitoring**

Actual data can also be entered and used to facilitate monitoring of progress and automatically updating the plan for the critical path and the use of resources as circumstances dictate.

(d) **Reporting**

Software packages allow standard and tailored progress reports to be produced, printed out and circulated to participants and senior managers at any time, usually at the touch of a button. This helps with co-ordination of activities and project review.

5.3 Most project management packages feature a process of identifying the main steps in a project, and breaking these down further into specific tasks. For example, one part of a project is a feasibility study. This can be subdivided into a number of tasks. Each of these can be subdivided further, and so forth.

5.4 The package has to deal with the proper allocation of **resources** (defined as time, money, personnel, even physical objects). Some packages hold resources on a **central database**. For example Microsoft Project could be linked to an Access or Excel database.

Inputs

5.5 Any project management package requires four inputs.

(a) The length of **time** required for each activity of the project.
(b) The **logical relationships** between each activity.
(c) The **resources** available.
(d) **When** the resources are available.

5.6 Some software packages will find the optimal solution by presenting all this in the form of a **Gantt chart**. Others will also undertake more complicated **PERT analysis**. A modern package is likely to do both, and a lot more besides.

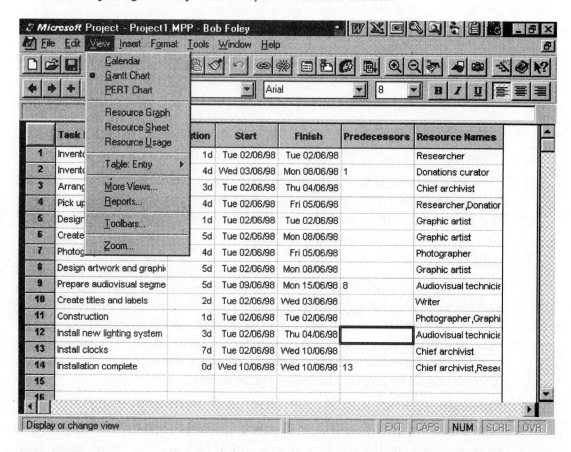

Features

5.7 There are a number of ways of distinguishing between and **choosing packages**.

(a) Does the package show data related to **different aspects** of the project on the **same screen**?

(b) Do projects take their resources from a **central pool of resources**? Effectively this asks whether the package will support more than one project at a time, so that staff-scheduling decisions on one project can be taken into account in another one.

(c) Is there a facility to **record what each individual does**? So, if an individual works on several different projects, is it possible to keep a record of what that individual has done, as well as the progress of the projects?

(d) When updating a project, is a record kept as of the **original plan**, or is it completely overwritten and forgotten?

(e) Does the package deal with **non-human resources**, such as materials?

(f) Does the package **move activities** to get the **most efficient use of resources**, in terms of cost and time?

(g) Is it possible to **consolidate different projects** into one? Or to create sub-projects from the main project? Microsoft Project, for instance, is able to **consolidate** up to 80 projects and 249 sub-projects. A project can have up to 9999 tasks and 9999 resources.

(h) Can you build in **quality control targets** into the project planning.

(i) Is there a feature for **exception planning** (ie if you overrun cost or time targets)?

6   THE PROJECT TEAM

6.1 A project team will have an overall **project manager**, whose role was described in section 2 of this Chapter. It will also have a number of **administrative staff** such as secretaries.

6.2 Essentially, however, developing a computer system can be divided into two parts.

(a) **Designing** a program or programs that will do the data processing work that the user department wants, and to the user's specification (for example about response times, accuracy etc).

This involves deciding what hardware there should be, what the input and files should be, how output should be produced, and what programs there should be to do this work.

This is the task of the **systems analyst**.

(b) **Writing the software**

Systems analysts

6.3 In general terms, the tasks of the systems analyst are as follows.

Systems analysis

6.4 This involves carrying out a methodical study of a **current system** (ie some data processing applications) to establish:

(a) what the current system **does**;

(b) whether it does what it is **supposed to do**;

(c) what the user department would **like it to do**, and so what the required objectives of the system are.

6.5 The analysis of the current system might involve a manual data processing system or a system that is already computerised but could possibly be improved or modernised.

Systems design

6.6 Having established what the proposed system objectives are, the next stage is to design a system that will **achieve these objectives**.

Systems specification

6.7 In designing a new system, it is the task of the systems analyst to **specify** the system in detail.

6.8 This involves identification of inputs, files, processing, output, hardware, costs, accuracy, response times and controls.

6.9 The system design is spelled out formally in a document or manual called the **systems specification** (which includes a program specification for each program in the system).

Systems testing

6.10 The analyst will be responsible for **systems testing**.

Review and maintenance

6.11 Keeping the system under **review**, and controlling and monitoring system **maintenance** with the co-operation of **user** departments.

6.12 The analyst might be responsible for writing and maintaining a user **procedures manual** - ie a manual for employees in the user department - which would:

(a) **explain** the computer system in very general terms;
(b) detail the **procedures** required in the user department to operate the system.

Programmers

6.13 Programmers take over from the systems analysts and have the task of writing the programs. This task involves the following.

(a) Reading the **system specification** and understanding it.

(b) Recognising what the processing requirements of the program are, in other words, **defining the processing problem in detail**.

(c) Having defined and analysed the processing problem, **writing the program** in a programming language.

(d) Arranging for the program to be **tested**.

(e) Identifying **errors** in the program and getting rid of these 'bugs' - ie **debugging** the program.

(f) Preparing full documentation for each program within the system.

The structure of the team

6.14 In a modern organisation it may be that the IS department has a very limited number of staff. An **hierarchical structure** of manager, analysts, programmers, etc may prove to be **very inflexible** in terms of getting individual projects done. For instance, someone who officially has the 'status' of 'Project Manager' may find that he or she has no projects to manage at a particular time but may have four or five projects to manage at another time. Likewise so-called 'Analysts' and 'Programmers'.

6.15 This situation is likely to arise frequently because much of the work of a dedicated IS department is **project-based**. One project may require a considerable amount of programming from scratch, while the next is largely 'tweaking' an existing system, requiring analyst skills, and someone who can motivate staff and control progress but very little programming.

6.16 A solution adopted increasingly in organisations is to organise the IS department according to a **flat** structure that recognises that multi-talented individuals will adopt **different roles at different times** rather than occupying a particular 'status' whether or not there is any work for someone of that status to do. Staff are selected from a pool of available staff and perform different roles depending upon demand.

6.17 To operate such a system the organisation needs to devise a **remuneration system** that recognises **skills** and work done rather than status.

Exam focus point

This point was examined in the **December 1997** exam, where students were asked to justify an IS Director's proposals to adopt a flat structure for his department rather than **outsourcing** IS work to external consultants (see Chapter 6).

The **December 1997** question also offered **two very easy marks** for explaining what was **meant by** a 'flat' structure. Easy, that is, if you have the basics of management theory at your fingertips, in this exam and in all others. If not, go back to your Paper 4 Study Material and do some revision!

Chapter roundup

- **Good management** of projects is vital. Many systems **arrive late, cost more** than was budgeted and **do not meet user requirements**. Project management is concerned with the detailed management of the development of a new system.

- The **project manager** is responsible for outline and detailed planning, communication, co-ordination and control, problem resolution and quality control.

- There are a number of **conflicting pressures** in any project. The most significant are usually the requirement for quality, the available resources, time constraints and finance.

- There are tools available to help with project management. The most widely used approaches are **critical path analysis** and **Gantt charts**.

- **Project management software** is available to automate these procedures.

- The project **team** (besides the overall manager and administrative staff) comprises **analysts** and **programmers.** A modern team may be organised on a very **flat** basis; with different people adopting different roles at different times.

Quick quiz

1   What problems might project managers face? (see paras 1.5 - 1.7)

2   What other factors can make projects go wrong? (1.8)

3   What are the likely contents of a project initiation document? (1.11)

4   What factors are in conflict during a project? (2.1 - 2.3)

5   What is a Project Quality Plan? (2.6)

6   What control activities may be used in project management? (2.8)

7   What is the aim of critical path analysis? (3.2)

8   What is the critical path? (3.17)

9   What are Gantt charts used for? (4.1)

10   What features might be found in a project management software package? (5.7)

11   What does a systems analyst do? (6.3 - 6.12)

12   Why is an hierarchical structure likely to prove problematic? (6.14)

Question to try	Level	Marks	Time
20	Exam standard	15	27 mins

Chapter 17

SYSTEMS IMPLEMENTATION

Chapter topic list	Syllabus reference
1 Installation and implementation	4(a)
2 Testing	5(a)
3 IT Training	5(e)
4 Documentation	5(b)
5 File conversion	5(a)
6 Changeover	5(a)

Introduction

Even if you have designed the best system in the world things can still go horribly wrong when you actually try to put it in place. Implementation covers a **wide range of issues**, ranging from simple things like remembering that computers need desks to sit on and cables to link them up, to strategic issues like whether to change systems overnight or take a softly, softly approach.

1   INSTALLATION AND IMPLEMENTATION

1.1   The main stages in the implementation of a computer system once it has been designed are as follows.

   (a)   Installation of the **hardware and software**
   (b)   **Testing**
   (c)   **Staff training** and production of documentation
   (d)   **Conversion** of files and database creation
   (e)   **Changeover**

1.2   The items in this list **do not** necessarily happen in a set **chronological order,** and some can be done at the same time - for example staff training and system testing can be part of the same operation.

1.3   The requirements for implementation **vary** from system to system as we shall see throughout this chapter.

Exam focus point
A question in **June 1995** asked what measures besides training are necessary at the implementation stage.

Installation of equipment

1.4 Installing a **mainframe** computer or a large network is a major operation that is carried out by the manufacturer/supplier.

1.5 If jut a few PCs are being installed in a small network, the customer may have to install the hardware himself. This should not be difficult, provided that the manufacturer's instruction manuals are read carefully.

Installation of a PC

1.6 The **office accommodation** for PCs and peripheral equipment will also need a little bit of planning.

   (a) PCs can be used in any office environment, but they generate **some heat** when they operate (just like any other machine) and so it is inadvisable to put them in small, hot rooms.

   (b) **Large desks** may be advisable, to accommodate a screen and keyboard and leave some free desk space for the office worker to use.

   (c) There should be plenty of **power sockets** - enough to meet future needs as the system grows, not just immediate needs.

   (d) If noisy printers are being purchased, it may be advisable to locate these in a **separate printer room,** to cut down the noise for office workers.

   (e) There should be a **telephone** close to the computer, for communicating with the dealer or other organisation which provides **system support and advice** when the user runs into difficulties.

   (f) **Cabling** for network connections needs to take account of possible future changes in office layout or in system requirements.

Question 1

In Europe, Health and Safety legislation governs the siting of PCs. What matters do you think employers have to be careful about?

Answer

Provisions cover the sort of chairs and desks provided, the quality of VDUs and lighting, heat and humidity, the need for regular breaks and the importance of proper training.

1.7 When the hardware has been installed, the **software** may then need installing too. To install the software, the computer user must follow the instructions in the user's manual. Installing software used to be tedious and lengthy, taking perhaps half an hour for a package, but most new software is provided on CD-ROM and can be installed in minutes.

1.8 PCs almost invariably come with **operating software** pre-loaded these days, and many suppliers provide other pre-loaded software such as **Microsoft Office.**

1.9 If possible, **back-up copies** should be made of all software.

1.10 Whether or not this is done the software should be **registered** with the manufacturer, either by filling in a registration form and posting it or often, these days, by completing a form on screen and sending it in via telecommunications links.

1.11 **Insurance** should be arranged against losses due to fire or theft. It is also possible to obtain insurance against accidental loss of data. If all the data on a hard disk were lost, for example, it could be a long job to re-enter all the lost data, but with insurance cover, the cost of the clerk to do the re-inputting would be paid for by the insurance.

Installation of a mainframe computer or minicomputer

1.12 If a mainframe or minicomputer installation is to be successful it must be carefully planned. Many of the issues described above, such as furniture needs, cabling and so on, still apply. The **particular problems** of planning a large installation include the following.

Site selection

1.13 The site selected for the main computer might be in an existing or a new building. Factors in the choice of site are the need for the following.

(a) Adequate **space** for computer and peripherals, including servicing room.

(b) **Room for expansion**.

(c) **Easy access** for computer equipment and supplies (it should be unnecessary to knock holes in outside walls, as has happened, in order to gain access for equipment).

(d) **Nearness** to principal **user** departments.

(e) Space available for a **library**, **stationery** store, and **systems maintenance** staff.

Site preparation

1.14 The site preparation may involve consideration of certain potential problems.

(a) **Air conditioning** (temperature, humidity and dust).

(b) Special **electricity supplies**.

(c) **Raised floor** (or **false ceiling**) so that **cables** may pass from one piece of equipment to another.

(d) **Fire protection devices**

(e) **Furnishings**

Standby equipment

1.15 Standby equipment should be arranged, to ensure **continuity of processing** in the event of power or computer failure. Such equipment may include standby **generators** and standby **computers**.

2 TESTING

2.1 A system must be thoroughly tested before implementation, otherwise there is a danger that the new system will **go live with faults** that might prove costly. The scope of tests and trials will again **vary with the size** of the system.

2.2 Three types of testing can be identified: program testing, systems testing and acceptance testing.

Exam focus point

A question in **December 1995** asked for a description of the stages of testing and how each stage should be carried out.

Program testing

2.3   A **diagnostic routine**, or debugging routine, provides for outline program testing and error correction during program development. When a programmer is testing a program, and the program does not operate correctly, he must locate the cause of the error. Diagnostic routines enable him to find out what the program was doing at the time it failed.

2.4   Test data will be prepared of the type that the program will be required to process. This test data will deliberately include **invalid/exceptional items** to test whether the program reacts in the right way and generates the required management reports.

2.5   The anticipated results of processing will be worked out in advance and then after processing the test program, there will be **item for item checking** against the actual computer output to test whether the program has operated as required.

Systems testing

2.6   There will then be testing of the **'interface' between individual programs** in the system, in an overall systems test.

2.7   Various personnel will be involved in system tests.

- The **IS project manager** will have overall responsibility for the project, and must ensure that the tests are planned and executed properly, and the system is fully documented.

- **Systems analysts** must check with their tests that the system achieves the objectives set for it, and do not contain any errors.

- **Programmers** must be on hand to de-bug any faults which the earlier program tests had not spotted.

- The **computer operations manager** will be in charge of data preparation work and operations in the computer room.

2.8   Test data should be constructed to test **all conditions**. For example, dummy data records and transactions should be input which are designed to test all the data validation routines and the **links** between different parts of the system in the system.

2.9   Unusual, but feasible, transactions could be tested, to see how the system handles them - for example two wage packets in the same week for the same employee.

2.10 Many managers prefer to use **historical data** in trials, because it is then possible to check the output of the new system against the output that the old system produced.

Question 2

Where else in this book have we referred to test data?

Answer

Use the index if you can't remember!

Acceptance testing

2.11 Acceptance testing is testing of a system by the **user department**, after the system has passed its systems test. The purposes of having trials conducted by the user department's managers are to:

(a) find **software errors** which exist but have not yet been detected;

(b) find out exactly what the **demands of the new system** are; and

(c) find out whether any **major changes in operating procedures** will be necessary.

2.12 Another aspect of the user department trials (or a subsequent stage of trials) might be to test the system with **large volumes of data,** and at the same time use the tests as an opportunity to **train staff** in the new system and the new procedures.

2.13 These 'bulk' tests on the system involve a range of checks.

(a) **Error correction** procedures (ie user department routines).

(b) The inter-relationship between **clerical and computer procedures**.

(c) The **timing** of computer runs.

(d) The **capacity** of files, file handling, updating and amendment.

(e) Systems **controls,** including auditing requirements.

(f) Procedures for **data capture, preparation** and **input** and the distribution of **output**.

3   IT TRAINING

3.1 Staff training in the use of information technology is as important as the technology itself as **without effective operation** at all levels computer systems can be an expensive **waste of resources** in any business.

3.2 The issue of training raises the wider matter of how to make personnel at all levels competent and willing to use IT. If organisations wish to encourage end-user computing then a training program can be part of a wider **'propaganda' exercise** by information systems professionals.

3.3 Training is not simply an issue that affects operational staff. As PCs are used more and more as management tools, training in information technology **affects all levels** in an organisation, from senior managers learning how to use an executive information system for example, to accounts clerks learning how to use an accounts management system.

The complete training requirement

3.4 A **systematic approach** to training can be illustrated in a flowchart as follows.

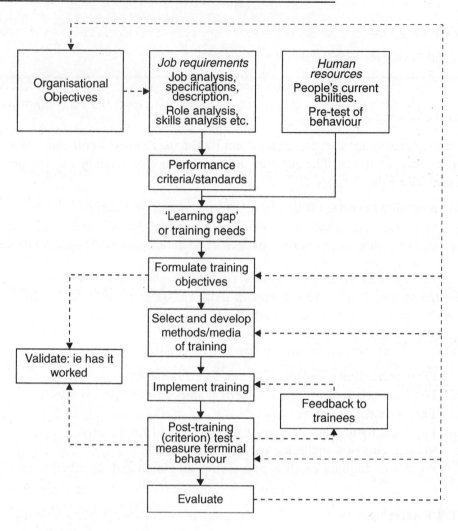

3.5   Note the following points in particular.

(a)   Training is provided primarily to help the **organisation** achieve its **objectives,** not just for the benefit of staff.

(b)   An individual's **training need** is generally defined as follows.

Required level of competence   X
Current level of competence   (Y)
Training need   Z

(c)   Training should be **evaluated** to make sure that it has worked. If not the method may have been wrong. Whatever the cause, the training need still exists.

Senior management training

3.6   Senior management can be 'trained' in a number of ways of varying degrees of formality. The completely **informal** approach might include the provision of information from the following sources.

- **Newspapers** (most of the quality press run regular articles on IT and computing).
- **Subordinates** (getting subordinate members of staff to demonstrate a system).
- **Individual demonstrations** of computer systems for senior executives.

3.7   **Semi-formal** training is of greater value.

(a)   Executive **briefings** (for example presentation before or after board meetings).
(b)   Video **demonstrations** (for example during lunchtime).
(c)   **Short seminars,** designed around an issue that is narrowly defined.

3.8   **Formal sessions** such as day **courses** are necessary if managers are to learn how to use a particular system, for example an EIS or a spreadsheet package.

3.9   Some commentators have argued that senior managers who are knowledgeable about computers and related technologies **make wiser decisions** in the following areas.

(a)   **Allocation of resources** to information systems (especially if the information system gives an organisation competitive advantage).

(b)   **Planning** for information systems.

(c)   Establishing an appropriate **corporate culture** for technological development.

(d)   The establishment of an informed scepticism when dealing with IT professionals means that managers **won't be blinded by science**, and will be able to communicate their needs more effectively.

(e)   Informed managers will have a **better understanding of their subordinates'** work.

Training middle management

3.10   The type of training middle management receives is likely to be **more structured** and **more tailored** to the particular applications within their remit.

3.11   Middle management are responsible for the **correct use of systems** in an age of distributed processing and end-user computing. Middle management are also responsible for implementing in detail the organisation's computer **security policy**.

3.12   The accent is also on the **business issues**. Managers do not necessarily need to know **how** computers work. They need to know **what** computing can do for them.

Training users

3.13   Users need a number of different types of computer and systems training.

(a)   **Basic literacy** in computers such as the concept of a file, updating, maintenance and so forth, might be needed. This might help users relate the workings of a manual system to its computer replacement. Also, some basic ideas as to how to use a computer efficiently can be usefully taught.

(b)   Users also need to get up and running with particular applications **quickly**, even if they do not go into the finer points of it. If the system is complex, such training gives users an **overall view** of the system, commands and procedures.

(c)   Users might sometimes need a **refresher course**, especially if they do not use a particular application regularly.

(d)   Users need training while operating the application (**on-the-job training**).

3.14   Some of these facilities are provided by the computer system itself. For example, many software packages have a **Help facility** which enables a user to learn facts about the system while they are using it.

3.15   **Computer based training** has the advantage of encouraging users to become acquainted with the technology they will be using, and to develop their skills at their own pace. **Multimedia training packages** exist for many widely-used software packages.

3.16   Training can also be provided by:

   (a)   reading the **user manuals**;

   (b)   attending **courses** that the dealer or employer provides;

   (c)   attending **courses** on a leading software package (for example Lotus 1-2-3 for Windows or an operating system such as MS-DOS) provided by third-party training establishment.

3.17   With large computer systems, extensive training of large numbers of staff will probably be necessary, and so further training measures may include other media.

   (a)   **Lectures** on general or specific aspects of the system - possibly with the use of films, video, tape-recordings, slides, overhead projectors etc.

   (b)   **Discussion meetings**, possibly following on from lectures, which allow the staff to ask questions and sort out problems.

   (c)   **Internal company magazines**, to explain the new system in outline.

   (d)   **Handbooks**, detailing in precise terms the new documentation and procedures. Different handbooks for each function will often be prepared by different persons.

   (e)   Using **trials/tests** on the new system to give staff direct experience before the system goes live.

4   DOCUMENTATION

KEY TERM

Documentation includes a wide range of technical and non-technical books, manuals, descriptions and diagrams relating to the use and operation of a computer system. Examples include user manuals, hardware and operating software manuals, system specifications and program documentation.

The systems specification

4.1   The systems specification is a **complete documentation of the whole system** and must always be properly maintained (ie kept up to date) as parts of the system are changed or added to.

4.2   Many of the problems in computer installations arise because of **inadequate** systems and program documentation and controls must be set up to ensure that **updating procedures** are always carried out.

Program specifications

4.3   A program specification, or program documentation, is the complete description of a program, usually including **notes, flowcharts**, a listing of all the **codes,** and perhaps test data and expected results. There should be a program specification for every individual program in the system.

4.4   **Initial specifications** are drawn up by the systems analyst and the programmer then uses the specification as the **basis of writing and testing the required program**.

4.5   When the program has been written and tested, one copy of the **final specification** will form part of the overall systems specification, and a second copy will be retained by the programmer to form part of the programmer's own documentation for the program.

Computer operations manual

4.6   This manual provides full documentation of the **operational procedures** necessary for the 'hands-on' running of the system. Amongst the matters to be covered by this documentation would be the following.

(a)   **Systems set-up procedures**. Full details should be given for each application of the necessary file handling and stationery requirements etc.

(b)   **Security procedures**. Particular stress should be placed on the need for checking that proper authorisation has been given for processing operations and the need to restrict use of machine(s) to authorised operators.

(c)   **Reconstruction control procedures**. Precise instructions should be given in relation to matters such as file dumping and also the recovery procedures to be adopted in the event of a systems failure.

(d)   **System messages**. A listing of all messages likely to appear on the operator's screen should be given together with an indication of the responses which they should evoke.

User manual

4.7   At some stage **before staff training** takes place, the system must be fully documented for the computer **user**. Matters to be dealt with should include the following.

(a)   **Input**. Responsibilities and procedures for preparation of input including requirements for establishment of batch control totals, authorisation etc.

(b)   **Error reports**. Full explanation of nature and form of error reports (eg exception reports for items rejected by data validation checks) and instructions as to the necessary action to be taken.

(c)   **File amendment procedures**. Full explanation of necessary authorisation and documentation required for file amendment.

(d)   **Output**. What this is, what form it takes, what should be done with it etc.

4.8   The user documentation is used to **explain** the system to the user and to help to train staff. Additionally, it provides a **point of reference** should the user have some problems with the system in the future - eg an error condition or a screen message that he or she does not understand.

4.9   When a system is developed in-house, the user documentation might be written by a systems analyst. However, it might be considered preferable for the user documentation to be **written by** a member of the **user's department's staff**, possibly a junior manager who has spent some time with the project development team, learning about the system.

System changes manual

4.10   Amendments to the original systems specification will almost inevitably occur, in addition to the computerisation of additional company activities. The objective of the system changes manual is to ensure that such changes are just as **strictly controlled** as was the case with the original systems development and introduction. Four matters to be covered in this respect would be as follows.

(a)   Recording of the request and **reason** for a change.
(b)   Procedures for the **authorisation** of changes.
(c)   Procedures for the **documentation** of changes.
(d)   Procedures for the **testing** of changes.

5   FILE CONVERSION

> **KEY TERM**
>
> **File conversion,** means converting **existing files** into a format suitable for the new system.

5.1   File conversion may be a **major part** of the systems implementation or it may be largely painless, if upgrading say, from version 1 of a standard package to version 2. If it means the conversion of existing manual file records into a medium used by the **computer** it may be very expensive. It may involve the transcription of records, or parts of them, on to specially designed forms before they are keyed on to the appropriate computer medium.

5.3   Because of the volume of data that must be copied on to the new files, the problem of **input errors** is a serious one, whatever data validation checks may be operating.

5.4   Once the file has been created, **extensive checking** for accuracy is essential, otherwise considerable problems may arise when the system becomes operational.

5.5   Before starting to load live data about customers, suppliers or employees etc, management should check whether the system must be registered under the **Data Protection Act 1984**.

Existing computer files

5.6   If the system is already computerised on a system that the organisation now wishes to abandon, the difficulties of file conversion will usually (though not always) be reduced. When it comes to the actual transcription from the old files to the new computer files the use of a special **conversion program** or **translation program** will speed up the whole process.

5.7   The problem of conversion has reduced significantly as major **software manufacturers** have realised that it may be a barrier to people using their products. Thus an Excel spreadsheet can be saved in Lotus 1-2-3 format, if this is what the user wants.

Question 3

in 1996 Marks and Spencer's stock control system rejected a consignment of corned beef with a sell-by date of 2000 on the basis that it was 96 years old! (00 — 96)

The problem is not limited to ancient programs on old mainframes. MS-DOS and Windows 3.1 are affected, as are versions of popular accounts packages like Sage Sterling bought prior to 1997. Problems are occurring already for people who have just received new credit cards and find that the organisation they are trying to do business with cannot cope with an expiry date of 2000!

Recommend a course of action for an organisation that wants to minimise the **Year 2000 problem.**

Answer

Articles about the problem generally recommend the following action.

(a)   Appoint a Year 2000 compliance manager immediately.

(b)   Set up a project team.

(c)   Catalogue all systems and programmes in use.

(d)   Find out from the manufacturer or writer if the programs and systems are Year 2000 friendly or not.

(e)   Decide what to do about those that are not. The options are to replace the software with something else, upgrade to a newer version, rewrite the existing program or abandon the system entirely.

(f)   Find out whether other organisations with which you have electronic dealings such as EDI and EFT have systems that are Year 2000 compliant, and if not how this might affect your own systems.

Existing manual files

5.8   The stages in file conversion from manual files to computer files, where this is a very complex process, are normally as follows.

(a)   Ensuring that the **original** record files are **accurate and up to date**.

(b)   Recording the old file data on **specially designed input documents**.

This will usually be done by the user department personnel (with additional temporary staff if required) following detailed instructions laid down by the systems designer or software supplier.

The instructions will include the procedures for allocating **new code numbers** (a coding system, including check digits if necessary, may have to be designed by this stage) and for checking **the accuracy and completeness** of the data selected and entered on the input documents (usually verification by another person and the establishment of control totals).

(c)   **Transcribing** the completed input documents on to the **computer media**.

(d)   Data entry programs would include **validation checks** on the input data. The contents of the file must then be printed out and **completely checked** back to the data input forms (or even the original file if possible).

(e)   **Correcting any errors** that this checking reveals.

5.9   Other problems of file conversion which must be considered include the following.

(a)   The possible provision of **additional staff,** or the use of a computer bureau, to cope with the file conversion and prevent bottlenecks.

(b)   The establishment of **cut-off dates** where live files are being converted (should the conversion be during slack times, for example, during holidays, weekends?).

(c)   The decision as to whether files should be converted **all at once,** or whether the conversion should be **file by file** or record group by record group (with subsequent amalgamation).

Question 4

You have been asked to transfer 400 Sales Ledger manual record cards to a microcomputer based system using floppy disks. The program menu has a record create option. Explain how you would set about this process, and the steps you would take to ensure that the task was completed successfully.

Answer

The steps that should be taken are as follows.

(a)   Check the manual records, and remove any dead accounts.

(b)   Assign account codes to each record, ideally with codes that incorporate a check digit.

(c)   If necessary transcribe the data from the card records on to documents which can be used for copying from, for data input.

(d)   Add up the number of accounts and the total value of account balances as control totals.

(e)   Select the record create option from the program menu and key the standing data and current data on to the new computer file. This should ideally be done at a quiet time, perhaps over a weekend.

(f)   Input that is rejected by a data validation check should be re-keyed correctly.

(g)   A listing of the records put on to file should be printed out. This listing should be checked for errors, ideally by someone who did not do the keying in. Errors should be reported, and corrected data keyed in to amend the data on file.

(h)   The program should produce control totals of the number of records put on to the file, and the total value of account balances. These control totals should be checked against the manually pre-listed control totals. Discrepancies should be investigated, and any errors or omissions put right.

(i)   A security back-up copy of the new file should be made.

(j)   The file and the new system should then be ready for use.

---

6   CHANGEOVER

6.1   Once the new system has been fully and satisfactorily tested the changeover can be made. This may be according to one of four approaches.

- Direct changeover
- Parallel running
- Pilot tests
- Phased or 'staged' implementation

Direct changeover

6.2   This is the method of changeover in which the old system is **completely replaced** by the new system **in one move**.

6.3   This may be unavoidable where the two systems are substantially different, or where extra staff to oversee parallel running are unobtainable.

6.4   While this method is comparatively **cheap** it is **risky** (system or program corrections are difficult while the system has to remain operational): management must have complete confidence that the new system will work.

6.5   The new system should be introduced during **slack periods,** for example over a bank holiday weekend or during an office closure such as a factory's summer shutdown or in the period between Christmas and the New Year.

Parallel running

6.6 This is a form of changeover whereby the **old and new** systems are **run in parallel** for a period of time, both processing current data and enabling cross checking to be made.

6.7 This method provides a **degree of safety** should there be problems with the new system. However, if there are differences between the two systems cross-checking may be difficult or impossible.

6.8 Furthermore, there is a **delay** in the actual implementation of the new system, a possible indication of **lack of confidence** in the new system, and a need for **more staff** to cope with both systems running in parallel.

6.9 This cautious approach, if adopted, should be properly planned, and the plan should include the following.

(a) A firm **time limit** on parallel running.

(b) Details of **which data** should be **cross-checked** - all of it? - some of it on a sample basis?

(c) Instructions on how **errors** are to be dealt with - they could be errors in the old system.

(d) Instructions on how to cope with **major problems** in the new system.

Pilot operation

6.10 This is **cheaper** and **easier to control** than parallel running, and provides a **greater degree of safety** than does a direct changeover. There are two types of pilot operation.

(a) **Retrospective parallel running**

This is an approach in which the new system operates on **data already processed** by the old system. The existing results are available for cross-checking and the system can be tested without the problems of staffing and disruption caused by parallel running.

(b) **Restricted data running**

This involves a **complete logical part** of the whole system being chosen and run as a unit on the new system. If that is shown to be working well the remaining parts are then transferred. Gradually the whole system can be transferred in this piecemeal fashion.

For example, one group of customer accounts from the sales ledger might be run on the new system. Again, the planning should involve the setting of strict time limits for each phase and instructions on how problems are to be dealt with. It must be remembered that two systems have to be controlled and additional staff, as well as a longer period for implementation, may be required.

Phased implementation

6.11 Phased implementation takes two possible forms

(a) It can on the one hand resemble **parallel running**, the difference being that only a portion of the data is run in parallel, for example for **one branch** only.

(b) Alternatively, phased implementation may consist of a number of **separate direct changeovers,** for example where a large system is to be replaced and the criteria for direct changeover apply.

6.12 The use of this method of implementation is best suited to very **large projects** and/or those where distinct parts of the system are **geographically dispersed**.

6.13 Where this approach is adopted care must be taken to control any **systems amendments** incorporated in the later phases in order to ensure that the overall system remains totally compatible.

Exam focus point

A question in **December 1994** asked students to recommend an approach to changeover in a specific scenario. As indicated above, key issues are the size of the system, the type of business, the type of system, cost, availability of staff, degree of safety required.

Chapter roundup

- The main stages in the systems **implementation** process are installation of hardware and software, staff training, system testing, file creation and changeover.

- **Installation** of equipment requires careful planning. The **user** may install a small number of PCs, but larger computers will be installed by the **supplier**. Considerations include site selection, site preparation and delivery itself.

- **Training** is a key part of the implementation of a new system. The approach adopted and the medium through which training is given will vary depending on the target audience. **Senior** management are more likely to be interested in the **overall capabilities** and limitations of systems, while **junior** staff need to be taught the **functional** aspects.

- A system must be thoroughly **tested** before implementation, otherwise there is a danger that it may not function properly when it goes live. The nature and scope of testing will vary depending on the size of the system. After **systems testing** is completed, the user department will carry out **acceptance testing**.

- File creation involves the creation or **conversion** of files for use with the new system. This is a major part of systems implementation and must be **fully controlled** to ensure that errors are not allowed to creep into the new files. The process may involve conversion of existing computerised files or may require migration of data from manual records.

- Once the system has been tested and files successfully converted, the system **changeover** can take place. There are four possible approaches: direct changeover, parallel running, pilot tests and phased implementation. These vary in terms of time required, cost and risk.

Quick quiz

1   What matters should be considered when installing a PC network? (see paras 1.6, 1.7)

2   Distinguish between three types of testing. (2.3 - 2.11)

3   How are an individual's training needs defined? (3.5)

4   What kind of training do operational users need? (3.13)

5   What might be found in user documentation? (4.7)

6   Why is a system changes manual maintained? (4.10)

7   What are the stages in converting a large manual system into computer files? (5.8)

8   What is parallel running? (6.6)

9   When might phased implementation be appropriate? (6.12)

Question to try	Level	Marks	Time
21	Exam standard	15	27 mins

Chapter 18

SYSTEMS MAINTENANCE AND EVALUATION

Chapter topic list	Syllabus reference
1 Systems maintenance	4(e), 5(e)
2 User groups	5(d), 5(e)
3 Information centres and help desks	5(d), 5(e)
4 Evaluation	4(b), 4(d)
5 Computer-based monitoring	4(b), 4(d)
6 Systems performance	4(b), 4(d), 5(d)
7 Post-implementation review	4(b), 4(d)

Introduction

This is the final chapter of this Study Text and it looks at what happens once a system is up and running.

Throughout its life, a system should operate effectively and efficiently. To do this, the system needs to be **maintained** and its users need to be **supported**. The first three sections of this chapter look at how this is done.

The last three sections look at **evaluation.** This should be an ongoing process to make sure that the system continues to meet requirements. Once it is implemented, a comparison will be made of the **objectives** and original cost-benefit submissions against actual performance and actual value. The operational characteristics of the system will be reviewed continually.

1 SYSTEMS MAINTENANCE

Types of maintenance

1.1 There are three types of maintenance activity.

- Corrective maintenance
- Perfective maintenance
- Adaptive maintenance

KEY TERMS

Corrective maintenance is carried out when there is a systems failure of some kind, for example in processing or in an implementation procedure. Its objective is to ensure that systems remain operational.

Perfective maintenance is carried out in order to perfect the software, or to improve software so that the processing inefficiencies are eliminated and performance is enhanced. The replacement of a word processing package written for DOS by a package which offers a Windows environment is an example of perfective maintenance.

Adaptive maintenance is carried out to take account of anticipated changes in the processing environment. For example new taxation legislation might require change to be made to payroll software.

1.2 **Corrective** maintenance usually consists of action in response to a **problem**. Much **perfective** maintenance consists of making enhancements requested by **users** to improve or extend the facilities available. The user interface may be amended to make software more user friendly.

1.3 The key features of system maintenance ought to be **flexibility** and **adaptability**.

(a) The system, perhaps with minor modifications, should cope with changes in the computer user's procedures or volume of business.

(b) The computer user should benefit from advances in computer hardware technology without having to switch to another system altogether.

The causes of systems maintenance

1.4 Besides environmental changes, three factors contribute to the need for maintenance.

Factor	Comment
Errors	However carefully and diligently the systems development staff carry out systems testing and program testing, it is likely that **bugs** will exist in a newly implemented system. Most should be identified during the first few runs of a system. The effect of errors can obviously vary enormously.
Changes in requirements	Although users should be consulted at all stages of systems development, problems may arise after a system is implemented because users may have found it difficult to express their requirements, or may have been concerned about the future of their jobs and not participated fully in development.
	Cost constraints may have meant that certain requested features were not incorporated. Time constraints may have meant that requirements suggested during development were ignored in the interest of prompt completion.
Poor documentation	If old systems are accompanied by poor documentation, or even a complete lack of documentation, it may be very difficult to understand their programs. It will be hard to update or maintain such programs. Programmers may opt instead to patch up the system with new applications using newer technology.

Year 2000

1.5 Many organisations' computer systems are having to undergo maintenance because they only allow two digits for the year in date fields (eg 31/12/99), whereas four digits will be needed to maintain the logic of the system once the year 2000 arrives.

Question 1

Is the Year 2000 problem an example of corrective, perfective or adaptive maintenance?

Answer

Strictly it is adaptive, although it is corrective in the sense that it could have been anticipated. However, systems were **designed** with two digit years to save space, so it was not originally an error in programming.

The systems maintenance lifecycle

1.6 Corrective and adaptive maintenance should be carried out **as and when** problems occur, but perfective maintenance may be carried out on a more scheduled system-by-system basis (Sales system in January, Purchases in February, etc).

1.7 Assuming the system is intended to reflect business needs, it ought to be possible to predict with reasonable certainty when business **growth** will make maintenance necessary. It is possible to contend with increasing volumes and communication needs by enhancing the existing computer system on site, on a modular basis.

- Installing **disks** of **greater capacity** and **higher speed**
- Installing a **more powerful processor**
- Changing to **faster printers**
- Installing **additional terminals** or **network facilities**

1.8 As mentioned, systems analysts will always try to design **flexibility** into computer systems, so that the system can **adapt** to change.

1.9 However, there will come a point at which **redevelopment** is necessary, for example where hardware upgrades or the availability of new software make radical change necessary, or following a company restructuring.

In-house maintenance

1.10 With **large computer systems**, developed by the organisation itself, **in-house** systems analysts and programmers might be given the responsibility for **software** maintenance.

1.11 To ensure that maintenance is carried out efficiently, the principles of **good programming practice** should be applied.

(a) Any change must be **properly authorised** by a manager in the user department (or someone even more senior, if necessary).

(b) The new program requirements must be **specified in full and in writing**. These specifications will be prepared by a systems analyst. A programmer should use these specifications to produce an amended version of the program.

(c) In developing a new program version, a programmer should keep **working papers**. He or she can refer back to these papers later to check in the event that there is an error in the new program or the user of the program asks for a further change in the program.

(d) The new program version should be **tested** when it has been written. A programmer should prepare test data and establish whether the program will process the data according to the specifications given by the systems analyst.

(e) **Provisions** should be made for **further program amendments** in the future. One way of doing this is to leave space in the program instruction numbering sequence for new instructions to be inserted later. For example, instructions might be numbered 10,20,30,40 etc instead of 1,2,3,4.

(f) A **record** should be kept of **all program errors** that are found during 'live' processing and of the corrections that are made to the program.

(g) Each **version** of a program (versions that are produced with processing modifications or corrections to errors) should be **separately identified**, to avoid a mix-up about what version of a program should be used for 'live' operating.

Software maintenance

1.12 With **purchased software** (whether off the shelf or bespoke), the **software house** or **supplier** is likely to provide details of any new versions of the software as they are produced, simply for marketing purposes.

Maintenance contracts

1.13 There is also likely to be an **agreement** between the supplier of software and the customer for the provision of a **software support service**. A maintenance contract typically includes the following services.

(a) **Help**

When a customer runs into difficulties operating the system help will initially be given by a **telephone 'hot line'**. If a telephone call does not resolve the problem, the software expert may arrange to visit the customer's premises (within a period of time agreed in the contract), although this would be rare for standard packages.

(b) **Information**

Extra information about using the package may be provided through factsheets or a magazine sent free to subscribers. This may include **case studies** showing how other users have benefited from using the package in a particular way and **technical tips** for common user problems

(c) **Updates**

Free updates are provided to **correct errors** in part of a package, or if there is something **inevitable** that will mean that some aspect of a package **has to be changed**.

For example payroll software has to reflect the latest Finance Act, and users of version 4 of Sage Sterling's payroll package who took out a SageCover contract could expect to receive version 4.0 initially , and then versions 4.1, 4.2 etc as tax legislation changed.

(d) **Upgrades**

When the **whole package** is revised the contract often provides for subscribers to get the new version at a heavily **discounted price**. Upgrades usually include **new features** not found in the previous versions or updates.

(e)   **Legal conditions**

We saw an example of some of these in the licence agreement in **Chapter 8**. There will be provisions about the **duration** of the contract and in what circumstances it terminates, about the **customer's obligations** to use the software in the way it was intended to be used, on the right sort of hardware, and not to make illegal copies. The **liability of the supplier** will also be set out, especially regarding consequential loss.

Exam focus point
A question in the June 1997 exam asked about what support entailed for a payroll package.

Hardware maintenance

1.14   Computer **hardware** should be kept serviced and maintained too. Maintenance services are provided:

(a)   by the computer **manufacturers** themselves; or

(b)   by **third-party** maintenance companies.

1.15   Maintenance of hardware can be obtained in two ways.

(a)   On a **contract** basis. PC maintenance contracts are usually negotiated annually.

(b)   On an *ad hoc* basis - ie calling in a maintenance company whenever a fault occurs.

2   USER GROUPS

End-user computing

2.1   End-user computing has been fuelled by the introduction of **PCs** to user departments, by **user-friendly software**, and by **greater awareness** of computers and what they can do.

KEY TERM
End-user computing is the direct, hands-on use of computers by users - **not indirect** use through systems professionals or the data processing staff. **End-users include** executives, managers, professional staff, secretaries, office workers, salespeople and others.

2.2   Accounts staff designing and using **spreadsheet models** is an example of end-user computing.

User groups

2.3   The concept of user groups has existed in the computer industry for some time.

KEY TERM
A **user group** is a forum for users of particular hardware or, more usually, software, so that they can **share ideas and experience** and, on occasions, acting as an **arbiter** in disputes with the supplier.

2.4   User groups are usually set up either by the software manufacturers themselves (who use them to **maintain contact** with customers and as a source of **new product ideas**) or by groups of users who were not satisfied with the level of support they were getting from suppliers of proprietary software.

2.5   Users of a particular package can meet, or perhaps exchange views over the **Internet** to discuss solutions, ideas or 'short cuts' to improve productivity. An (electronic) newsletter service might be appropriate, based view exchanged by members, but also incorporating ideas culled from the wider environment by IT specialists.

2.6   Sometimes user groups are set up **within** individual organisations. Where an organisation has written its own application software, or is using tailor-made software, there will be a very **small knowledge base** initially, and there will obviously not be a national user group, because the application is unique.

2.7   'Interested parties', including, as a minimum, representatives from the **IT department** and **users** who are familiar with different parts of the system can attend monthly or quarterly **meetings** to discuss the **operation** of the system, make **suggestions for improvements** (such as the production of new reports or time-tabling of processing) and raise any **queries**.

Exam focus point

User groups featured in the **June 1997** question mentioned above.

Question 2

Trends in IT such as distributed processing, increased use of PCs and wide availability of sophisticated general purpose packages have resulted in more responsibility for information processing being transferred to end-users. It is important that end-user computing is supported by management. What do you think are the main problems faced by organisations which experience a significant amount of end-user computing?

Answer

You may have drawn on personal experience here. Here are some suggestions.

(a)   Lack of user education about personal computing.

(b)   User requests for assistance that overwhelm the IT department.

(c)   Lack of user knowledge or concern about PC control measures such as file back-up.

(d)   Lack of integration in micro-mainframe data exchange and control.

(e)   Poor maintainability of user-developed systems.

(f)   Mismatching of user problems and computing alternatives (personal computing, mainframe packages, etc) for systems development.

(g)   Lack of centralised management of corporate data resources that support personal computing.

(h)   Lack of integration in IT management of personal computing and mainframe end-user computing.

(i)   Lack of user concern about equipment security.

(j)   Lack of user-friendly mainframe software to compete with PCs.

3   INFORMATION CENTRES AND HELP DESKS

> ### KEY TERM
>
> An **information centre (IC)** is a small unit of staff with a good technical awareness of computer systems, whose task is to provide a support function to computer users within the organisation.

3.1 Information centres are particularly useful in organisations which use **distributed** processing systems or **PCs** quite heavily, and so have many 'non-technical' people in charge of hardware, files and software scattered throughout the organisation.

Help

3.2 An IC usually offers some kind of **Help Desk** to ensure that staff time is spent on their real work rather than on IT problems. Help may be via the **telephone**, or **visits** may have to be arranged if sites are widely dispersed. Networks mean that help can be made available directly through users' computers, using an **e-mail** system for queries and responses. Common problems and their solutions can be posted on a **bulletin board** for all to read

3.3 Alternatively, or in addition, **remote diagnostic software** is available which will enable staff in the IC to 'take control' of a computer whose user is having problems and sort out the problem for them without leaving their desk, in the same way that they would if they paid the user a visit. Again this will speed up the problem-solving process.

3.4 The help desk needs sufficient **staff and technical expertise** to respond quickly to problems with hardware or software. This means that it must also maintain good contacts and relationships with **suppliers** to ensure that they fulfil their maintenance obligations and their maintenance staff are quickly on site when needed.

Problem solving

3.5 The IC will maintain a **record of problems** and identifies those that occur most often. If the problem is that users do not know how to use the system, **training** is provided. Training software can be developed or purchased and made available over a network from a central server.

3.6 Training applications often contain **analysis software**, drawing attention to trainee progress and **common problems** (the Software Toolworks *Mavis Beacon* typing tutor is a well-known example), and the availability of such information will enable the IC to identify and address specific **training needs** more closely.

3.7 If the problem is with the system itself, a solution is found, either by **modifying the system** or by investment in **new hardware or software**.

Improvements

3.8 The IC can also consider the viability of **suggestions for improvements** to the system and brings these into effect, where possible, for all users who stand to benefit.

Standards

3.9   The IC is also likely to be responsible for setting, and encouraging users to conform to, common **standards**.

(a)   **Hardware standards** ensure that all of the equipment used in the organisation is **compatible** and can be put into use in different departments as needed.

(b)   **Software standards** ensure that information generated by one department can easily be **shared** with and worked upon by other departments.

(c)   **Programming standards** ensure that applications developed by individuals to help them perform their jobs (for example word-processing macros or spreadsheets for data analysis) follow **best practice**, are **easy to modify**, and are **circulated** to others in the organisation where this is of benefit.

(d)   **Data processing standards** ensure that certain conventions such as the format of **file names** are followed throughout the organisation. This facilitates **sharing** and **storage and retrieval** of information by as many users as possible.

Security

3.10   The IC may help to preserve the **security** of data in various ways.

(a)   It may develop **utility programs** and recommended **procedures** for company-wide use, to ensure that **back-ups** are made at regular intervals. If second copies of back-up files are stored off site (as they should be), this system of **archiving** may well be operated and maintained by the Information Centre.

(b)   The IC may help to preserve the company's systems from attack by computer **viruses**, for instance by ensuring that the latest versions of **anti-virus software** are available to all users, by reminding users regularly about the **dangers** of viruses, and by setting up and maintaining **'firewalls'**, which deny access to sensitive parts of the company's systems, except to authorised .

Applications development

3.11   Many users who develop their own applications have **little or no formal training** in programming, consequently their programs might be extremely crude and virtually incomprehensible.

3.12   While these programs may work they will be very **difficult to modify** and they will very often be the personal property of the individual who developed the system, with **no wider use**. This is highly undesirable from the organisation's viewpoint: a great deal of time and energy is going into producing inefficient programs which are unusable by anyone other than their developer.

3.13   An IC can help to remedy this situation by providing **technical guidance** to the developers and to encourage comprehensible and well documented programs. **Understandable** programs can be maintained or modified more easily by people other than the system developer. **Documentation** then provides a means of teaching others how the programs work. These efforts can greatly extend the usefulness and life of the programs that are developed.

4   EVALUATION

4.1   In most systems there is a constant need to maintain and improve applications and to keep up to date with technological advances and changing user requirements. A system should therefore be **reviewed** after implementation, and periodically, so that any unforeseen problems may be solved and to confirm that it is achieving and will continue to achieve the desired results.

4.2   The system should have been designed with clear, specified **objectives**, and justification in terms of **cost-benefit analysis** or other **performance criteria**.

4.3   Just as the feasibility of a project is assessed by reference to **technical, operational, social and economic factors**, so the same criteria can be used for evaluation. We need not repeat material that you have covered earlier, but here are a few pointers.

Cost-benefit review

4.4   A cost-benefit review is similar to a cost-benefit analysis, except that **actual** data can be used.

4.5   For instance when a large project is completed, techniques such as **DCF appraisal** can be performed **again**, with *actual* figures being available for much of the expenditure.

Question 3

A cost-benefit review might categorise items under the five headings of direct benefits, indirect benefits, development costs, implementation costs and running costs.

Give two examples of items which could fall to be evaluated under each heading.

Answer

Direct benefits might include reduced operating costs, for example lower overtime payments, and higher turnover resulting from increased order processing capacity from a new system.

Indirect benefits might include better decision-making and the freeing of human 'brainpower' from routine tasks so that it can be used for more creative work.

Development costs include systems analysts' costs and the cost of time spent by users in assisting with fact-finding.

Implementation costs would include costs of site preparation and costs of training.

Running costs include maintenance costs and software leasing costs.

Efficiency and effectiveness

4.6   In any evaluation of a system, two terms recur. Two key reasons for the introduction of information systems into an organisation are to improve the **efficiency** or the **effectiveness** of the organisation.

KEY TERM

Efficiency can be measured by considering the resource **inputs** into and the **outputs** from a process or an activity.

4.7   An activity uses **resources** such as men, money and materials. If the same activity can be performed using **fewer resources**, for example fewer men or less money, or if it can be completed **more quickly**, the efficiency of the activity is improved. An improvement in efficiency represents an improvement in **productivity**.

4.8 Automation of an organisation's activities is usually expected to lead to greater efficiency in a number of areas.

(a) The **cost** of a computer system is lower than that of the manual system it replaces, principally because jobs previously performed by human operators are now carried out by computer.

(b) The **accuracy** of data information and processing is improved, because a computer does not make mistakes.

(c) The **speed** of processing is improved. Response times, for example in satisfying customer orders, are improved.

> **KEY TERM**
>
> **Effectiveness** is a measurement of how well the organisation is achieving its objectives.

4.9 Effectiveness is a **more subjective** concept than efficiency, as it is concerned with factors which are less easy to measure. It focuses primarily on the relationship of the organisation with its environment. For example, automation might be pursued because it is expected that the company will be more effective at **increasing market share** or at satisfying **customer needs**.

4.10 Computing was originally concerned with the automation of **'back office'** functions, usually aspects of data processing. Development was concerned with improving **efficiency**.

4.11 Recent trends are more towards the development of **'front office'** systems, for example to improve an organisation's decision-making capability or to seek competitive advantage. This approach seeks to improve the **effectiveness** of the organisation.

5   COMPUTER-BASED MONITORING

5.1 Computers themselves can be used in systems evaluation. Three methods used are hardware monitors, software monitors and systems logs.

Hardware monitors

5.2 Hardware monitors are devices which measure the presence or absence of electrical signals in selected circuits in the computer hardware.

5.3 They might measure **idle time** or **levels of activity** in the CPU, or peripheral activity. Data is sent from the sensors to counters, which periodically write it to disk or tape.

5.4 A program will then **analyse** the data and produce an analysis of findings as output. It might identify for example **inefficient co-ordination** of processors and peripherals, or **excessive delays** in writing data to backing storage.

Software monitors

5.5   Software monitors are computer programs which **interrupt the application in use** and record data about it. They might identify, for example, **excessive waiting** time during program execution. Unlike hardware monitors, they may slow down the operation of the program being monitored.

Systems logs

5.6   Many computer systems provide automatic log details, for example **job start and finish** times or which employee has used which program and for how long. The systems log can therefore provide useful data for analysis.

     (a)   Unexplained **variations in job running** times might be recorded.

     (b)   Excessive machine **down-time** is sometimes a problem.

     (c)   **Mixed workloads** of large and small jobs might be scheduled inefficiently.

6   SYSTEMS PERFORMANCE

Performance measurement

6.1   It is not possible to identify and isolate every consequence of a project and the impact of each on organisational effectiveness. To achieve some approximation to a complete evaluation, therefore, certain **indirect measures** must be used.

     (a)   **Significant task relevance** attempts to observe the results of system use.

        For example, document turnround times might have improved following the acquisition of a document image processing system, or minutes of meetings might be made available and distributed faster following the addition of a company secretarial function to a local area network.

     (b)   The **willingness to pay** of users might give an indication of value.

        Users can be asked how much they (their department) would be prepared to pay in order to gain the benefit of a certain upgrade, for example the availability of a particular report. Inter-departmental pricing will be a critical factor in the success of this approach.

     (c)   **Systems logs** may give an indication of the value of the system if it is a 'voluntary use' system, such as an external database.

     (d)   **User information satisfaction** is a concept which attempts to find out, by asking users, how they rate their satisfaction with a system. They may be asked for their views on timeliness, quality of output, response times, processing and their overall confidence in the system.

     (e)   The adequacy of system **documentation** may be measurable in terms of how often manuals are actually used and the number of errors found or amendments made. However, low usage of a user manual, for instance, may mean either that the manual is useless or that the system is so good that it is self-explanatory.

Question 4

Operational evaluation should consider, among other issues, whether input data is properly provided and output is useful. Output documents are often considered by users to be of marginal value, perhaps of use for background information only. In spite of this there is a tendency to continue producing existing reports.

How might you identify whether a report is being used?

Answer

The method chosen depends on how imaginative you are.

You could simply cease production of the report and see if anyone asks for it when it fails to appear. (If they ask for it simply in order to add it to a file, you can draw your own conclusions.)

A study could be carried out to see what each recipient of the report does with it and assess its importance.

A report pricing structure could be implemented - this would be a strong incentive to functional management to cancel requests for unnecessary output.

6.2 Performance reviews will vary in content from organisation to organisation, but the matters which will probably be looked at are as follows.

(a) The **growth** rates in file sizes and the number of transactions processed by the system. Trends should be analysed and projected to assess whether there are likely to be problems with lengthy processing time or an inefficient file structure due to the volume of processing.

(b) The clerical **manpower** needs for the system, and deciding whether they are more or less than estimated.

(c) The identification of any **delays** in processing and an assessment of the consequences of any such delays.

(d) An assessment of the efficiency of **security** procedures, in terms of number of breaches, number of viruses encountered.

(e) A check of the **error rates** for input data. High error rates may indicate inefficient preparation of input documents, an inappropriate method of data capture or poor design of input media.

(f) An examination of whether **output** from the computer is being used to good purpose. (Is it used? Is it timely? Does it go to the right people?)

(g) Operational **running costs**, examined to discover any inefficient programs or processes. This examination may reveal excessive costs for certain items although in total, costs may be acceptable.

Improving performance

6.3 **Computer systems efficiency audits** are concerned with improving **outputs** from the system and their use, or reducing the costs of system **inputs**. With falling costs of computer hardware and software, and continual technological advances there should often be **scope for improvements** in computer systems, which an audit ought to be able to identify.

Outputs from a computer system

6.4 With regard to outputs, the efficiency of a computer system would be enhanced in any of the following ways.

(a) **More outputs** of some value could be produced by the **same input** resources.

For example:

(i) if the system could process **more transactions**;

(ii) if the system could produce **more management information** (eg sensitivity analysis);

(iii) if the system could make information **available to more people** who might need it.

(b) **Outputs of little value** could be **eliminated** from the system, thus making savings in the cost of inputs.

For example:

(i) if reports are produced **too frequently**, should they be produced less often?
(ii) if reports are **distributed too widely**, should the distribution list be shortened?
(iii) if reports are **too bulky**, can they be reduced in size?

(c) The **timing** of outputs could be better.

Information should be available in good time for the information-user to be able to make good use of it. Reports that are issued late might lose their value. Computer systems could give managers **immediate** access to the information they require, by means of file enquiry or special software (such as databases or spreadsheet modelling packages).

(d) It might be found that outputs are not as satisfactory as they should be, perhaps because:

(i) **access** to information from the system is limited, and could be improved by the use of a **database** and a **network** system;

(ii) available outputs are is **restricted** because of the **method of data processing** used (eg batch processing instead of real-time processing) or the **type of equipment** used (eg stand-alone PCs compared with client/server systems).

Question 5

What elements of hardware and software might restrict the capabilities of a system?

Answer

A system's capabilities might be limited by the following restrictions.

(a) The size of the computer's memory.
(b) The power of the processor.
(c) The capacity of the computer's backing storage.
(d) The number of printers linked to the computer.
(e) The number of terminals.
(f) The software's capabilities.

Inputs to a computer system

6.5 The efficiency of a computer system could be improved if the same volume (and frequency) of output could be achieved with **fewer input** resources, and at **less cost**.

6.6 Some of the ways in which this could be done have already been mentioned.

(a) **Multi-user** or **network** systems might be more efficient than stand-alone systems.

Multi-user systems allow several input operators to work on the same files at the same time, so that if one person has a heavy workload and another is currently short of work, the person who has some free time can help his or her busy colleague - thus improving operator efficiency.

(b) **Real-time** systems might be more efficient than batch processing.

(c)   Using computers and external storage media with **bigger storage** capacity.

A frequent complaint is that '**waiting time**' for the operator can be very long and tedious. Computer systems with better backing storage facilities can reduce this operator waiting time, and so be more efficient.

(d)   Using more **up to date software**.

6.7   Management might also wish to consider whether time spent **checking and correcting** input data can be eliminated. An **alternative method of input** might be chosen. For example bar codes and scanners should eliminate the need to check for input errors.

7   POST-IMPLEMENTATION REVIEW

7.1   **Post-implementation review** should establish whether the objectives and targeted performance criteria have been met, and if not, why not, and what should be done about it.

7.2   In appraising the operation of the new system immediately after the changeover, comparison should be made between **actual and predicted performance**. This will include (amongst other items):

(a)   consideration of **throughput speed** (time between input and output);

(b)   use of computer **storage** (both internal and external)

(c)   the number and type of **errors/queries**;

(d)   the **cost** of processing (data capture, preparation, storage and output media, etc).

7.3   A special **steering committee** may be set up to ensure that post-implementation reviews are carried out, although the **internal audit** department may be required to do the work of carrying out the reviews.

7.4   The post-implementation measurements should **not be made too soon** after the system goes live, or else results will be abnormally affected by 'teething' problems, lack of user familiarity and resistance to change.

The post-implementation review report

7.5   The findings of a post-implementation review team should be formalised in a **report**.

(a)   A **summary** of their findings should be provided, emphasising any areas where the system has been found to be **unsatisfactory**.

(b)   A review of **system performance** should be provided. This will address the matters outlined above, such as run times and error rates.

(c)   A **cost-benefit review** should be included, comparing the forecast costs and benefits identified at the time of the feasibility study with actual costs and benefits.

(d)   **Recommendations** should be made as to any **further action** or steps which should be taken to improve performance.

Chapter roundup

- There are three types of systems maintenance. **Corrective** maintenance is carried out following a systems failure, **perfective** maintenance aims to make enhancements to systems and **adaptive** maintenance takes account of anticipated changes in the processing environment.

- **User groups** enable personnel who come into contact with a particular system (not just users) to meet and share their views on the system in question. User groups are a useful forum for generating ideas, suggesting improvements and resolving problems.

- Some organisations have an **information centre** to support and streamline end-user computing. An information centre is a small unit manned by staff with a good technical knowledge. Their task is to provide a link between users and computer operations.

- The criteria for **systems evaluation** mirror those used in the feasibility study. A system can be evaluated by reference to technical, operational, social and economic factors. Similarly, the techniques used are similar to those already employed. A cost-benefit review can be performed and compared with the original cost-benefit analysis, and investment appraisal techniques are still applicable.

- **Efficiency** is a measure of how well **resources** have been utilised irrespective of the purpose for which they are employed. **Effectiveness** is a measure of whether the organisation has achieved its **objectives**.

- Systems evaluation may use **computer-based monitoring**. Methods include the use of hardware monitors, software monitors and systems logs.

- **Performance reviews** can be carried out to look at a wide range of systems functions and characteristics. Technological change often gives scope to **improve** the quality of outputs or reduce the extent or cost of inputs.

- During the **post-implementation review**, an evaluation of the system is carried out to see whether the targeted performance criteria have been met and to carry out a review of costs and benefits. The review should culminate in the production of a report and recommendations.

Quick quiz

1   What factors contribute to the need for maintenance? (see para 1.4)

2   What are the principles of good programming practice? (1.11)

3   What provisions might you find in a software maintenance contract? (1.13)

4   What is a user group? (2.3)

5   How does a help desk operate? (3.2 - 3.4)

6   What standards might be enforced by an information centre? (3.9)

7   What criteria are used for systems evaluation? (4.2, 4.3)

8   What is a hardware monitor? (5.2 - 5.4)

9   What matters might a performance review consider? (6.2)

10   How can outputs be improved? (6.4)

11   What would you expect to see in a post-implementation review report? (7.5)

Question to try	Level	Marks	Time
22	Introductory	n/a	20 mins
23	Exam standard	15	27 mins
24	Exam standard	55	99 mins

Exam question bank

1　FINANCIAL SYSTEMS　　*30 mins*

(a)　Design a computer screen that could be used for entering details of receipts from customers.

(b)　Explain briefly what part of the financial system your receipts-entering screen would be part of and how it would be linked to other parts of the system.

2　INFORMATION　　*20 mins*

The managing director of a manufacturing company is learning about information and systems theory. He has asked you to do the following.

(a)　Define and distinguish between data and information.

(b)　Identify and comment on each of the factors which give information its value when used in management reports.

3　CATEGORIES OF INFORMATION SYSTEM (15 marks)　　*27 mins*

Computers have been used as tools to support managerial decision-making for more than twenty years, and the various tools/decision aids can be grouped into the following categories.

(a)　Transaction processing systems.
(b)　Management information systems.
(c)　Decision support systems.
(d)　Expert systems.

(a)　Define and distinguish between these categories, ensuring that each is considered under the headings of applications served, database facilities, decision capabilities, type of information available and level of organisation served.　　(9 marks)

(b)　In the context of typical computer-based information systems in an organisation's personnel department, identify tasks which might be carried out for each of the categories of information system listed above.　　(6 marks)

4　OPEN AND CLOSED LOOP CONTROL (15 marks)　　*27 mins*

(a)　Explain the difference between open and closed loop control, illustrating each case with the aid of a diagram.　　(9 marks)

(b)　For a manufacturing company discuss whether an open or closed loop model would be appropriate in the case of:

(i)　the total organisation;
(ii)　a mechanised manufacturing unit.　　(6 marks)

5　MEMORIES ARE MADE OF THIS (15 marks)　　*27 mins*

(a)　Explain why it is necessary to divide computer storage into main storage and backing storage.　　(7 marks)

(b)　What are the major considerations which govern the choice of the type of hardware storage for a given file.　　(8 marks)

6　THE ELECTRONIC OFFICE (15 marks)　　*27 mins*

The general manager of a manufacturing company is intending to update its clerical procedures with the introduction of an office automation system.

(a)　Describe the hardware and software systems which make up 'the electronic office'.　　(9 marks)

(b)　Discuss the ways in which developments in communications and information technology (IT), such as telecommuting and teleconferencing, have increased the possibility of an employee working from home.　　(6 marks)

7   **PAPERWORK PLC (15 marks)**   *27 mins*

A small chain of thirty book shops, owned by Paperwork plc, currently have a manual records system to handle day-to-day transactions, invoicing, stock control and ordering. The shops are all situated in a geographical area of radius 150 kilometres. The management of Paperwork plc believes that a computerised system is now necessary to improve the efficiency of the above operations. They also believe that a distributed processing system would be a better option than a centralised system.

They have engaged you as a consultant to advise them.

Required

(a) Distributed processing requires computer networks. Outline your recommendations for the networks required for this application.   (7 marks)

(b) What are the advantages and disadvantage of distributed processing versus centralised processing for the proposed system?   (8 marks)

8   **COST-BENEFIT ANALYSIS TECHNIQUES (10 marks)**   *18 mins*

You are the project manager charged with the task of carrying out a cost-benefit analysis exercise on a proposed new computer-based application.

What techniques would you make use of to demonstrate the costs and benefits of your proposed new system?

9   **ACE MACHINE TOOLS (15 marks)**   *27 mins*

Ace Machine Tools is a medium sized engineering company. The sales director proposes to purchase a stand alone computer to automate the sales department's quotation and customer order processes. You believe that there may be further advantages to be gained by linking the new software to the existing stock control and accounting software.

Required

You have a choice of purchasing standard applications packages and adapting them for use, or commissioning a software company to write a dedicated suite of programs for your company. Compare and contrast the two approaches.

10   **PHYSICAL SECURITY**   *20 mins*

The power and flexibility of computers often makes them indispensable to an organisation. In these circumstances continuity of service is imperative so physical security and disaster planning are of vital importance to the users.

Identify five different physical risks to which a computer system is exposed, describe steps you would take to minimise these risks, and give details of recovery plans that you would prepare in the event of disaster.

11   **REVIEWING DEVELOPMENT (15 marks)**   *27 mins*

There have been extensive press reports and discussions recently of the failure of major computer projects, or their abandonment at a late stage in their development. Examples in the United Kingdom include the London Ambulance Service, Performing Rights Society and the Stock Exchange.

Required

(a) Explain what steps a management board should take to ensure that any proposed major computer development does produce a workable and acceptable system.   (7 marks)

(b) Explain the various responsibilities of internal audit in reviewing the approval of a new computer system and the detailed development of such a system.   (8 marks)

12   FACT FINDING   *20 mins*

An important aspect of systems analysis is the 'fact finding' stage of a systems investigation. Depending on the circumstances and the system being studied, several different methods of fact finding may be used.

You are required to:

(a)   state three methods of fact finding;

(b)   give their advantages and disadvantages and the circumstances in which each might be used.

13   WRAY CASTLE (15 marks)   *27 mins*

Wray Castle is an engineering company which is about to implement a new production planning and control system. There is at the same time a lot of pressure from the marketing department, which wishes to invest in a computerised market planning and research system. The marketing director was told, when the company's sales order processing system was developed, but it does not do so. The system was delivered late and documentation is poor. The company plans to continue to follow the traditional systems development cycle for all its systems development.

Required

(a)   Explain what is meant by the terms logical and physical design.   (7 marks)

(b)   How could the features of a structured systems methodology be applied to overcome the problems previously experienced by the company?   (8 marks)

14   DATA FLOW DIAGRAM (10 marks)   *18 mins*

The registrar's office at a college of further education maintains a set of files which it uses in the administration of student courses each year. Application forms are placed in a *pending tray*. Details of those students called for interview are placed in a *holding file* and others are placed in a *rejections box*. Student details for those who are accepted are held on the *student records database*. There is a *courses file*, which details the structure and objectives of all courses offered, and a *headcount list*, which shows the maximum student numbers for each course. Unfilled places are logged in a weekly *courses available list*.

You have been asked by the registrar to analyse the existing system with a view to computerising it. Draw a data flow diagram which shows the likely student acceptance procedures at the college, incorporating as many of the files (shown in italics) as necessary.

15   PROCEDURE SPECIFICATION (15 marks)   *27 mins*

(a)   A systems analyst may make use of decision tables, decision trees or structured narratives to specify procedures precisely. Describe each of these methods, giving an indication of their merits and drawbacks.   (6 marks)

(b)   The training and development programme of CS plc recognises four categories of new employee and gives them certain options as to their development.

Employees with a relevant degree may either join the graduate entry programme or undergo accelerated management training. Those with other degrees are eligible for the graduate entry programme only. Employees without a degree but with other qualifications join the main intake stream, while those who have a degree and other qualifications may join either the main intake stream or the programme to which their degree entitles them. Employees without any qualifications are taken on at clerical grades.

Using *one* of the methods described in part (a), define the logic of CS plc's training and development programme for new employees.   (9 marks)

16   DATABASE   *20 mins*

Some computer installations, particularly the larger, more sophisticated ones, are using databases in which to store the organisation's data.

(a)   Define a database.

(b) List and explain briefly five of the advantages claimed for a well-designed database.

(c) Explain briefly three of the major problems associated with the implementation and operation of a comprehensive database.

17 BUTTERLEDGE PUBLISHING (20 marks) *36 mins*

Butterledge Publishing specialise in academic books and journals particularly in engineering and design. Recently, the senior executive decided to instigate a full review of their information systems. It needs noting that the existing computer system had reached the end of its useful life. Since they print, publish and market a wide range of books and journals they have selected SSADM to analyse their many requirements and facilitate the design. With many new titles scheduled for production in the next few months there is great urgency to have a properly developed, implemented and tested system as soon as possible.

Required

(a) Explain how CASE tools (computer aided software engineering) may assist to meet the need for rapid development. (7 marks)

(b) A proposed database for a book order processing system will have four tables.

Customers
Customer orders
Order details
Books

Suggest what fields these tables might contain. (5 marks)

(c) Draw an entity relationship model for the books order processing system. (8 marks)

18 SECURITY (20 marks) *36 mins*

A manufacturing company has three divisions, all of which operate from the same site. The company's main finished goods warehouse is located about one mile away. The main manufacturing site is the location for all other functions, including the IT department.

The company runs a corporate database on a mainframe computer with networked terminals. The terminals do not at present have any independent processing capacity.

The warehouse stock records are maintained on a minicomputer in the warehouse. Each morning, details of the previous day's sales orders taken are sent by courier to the warehouse. The data, which is stored on a floppy disk, is downloaded to the warehouse system, which generates despatch documentation, including invoices, and picking lists. The warehouse's 'free' and 'allocated' stock records are updated.

At the end of each day, details of stock movements are sent to the main site and the mainframe's stock records are updated. These are referred to by sales order processing staff to ensure goods are in stock when booking orders. Copy invoices are also sent to the accounts department for posting to customer ledgers.

Required

What controls should be adopted to retain the integrity and the security of the data in the system?

19 CONTROLS (15 marks) *27 mins*

Detail the main areas of consideration by the management of an organisation when examining the security and efficiency of control of data processing operations.

20 PROJECT (15 marks) *27 mins*

The Chief Executive of a large organisation, which is planning a major systems analysis and design project, has read a recent article in a computer journal suggesting that many system development projects are not satisfactory upon completion. Symptoms which are highlighted in the article include:

(a) development costs which exceed the budget;
(b) completion in excess of planned timescales;
(c) systems which do not meet users' requirements;
(d) systems which are unreliable and difficult to maintain.

You are required to draft a report to the Chief Executive of the organisation identifying the problems which may be faced by the systems development section of the organisation when carrying out its major analysis and design project.

21   SYSTEMS IMPLEMENTATION (15 marks)   *27 mins*

A company which services all its customers (dealers) from one central warehouse has decided to computerise the stock control, order processing and sales accounting procedures. It has also been decided to close the central warehouse and establish five regional warehouses, each of which will be based on a central mainframe computer with on-line links to regional warehouses where data entry of customer orders and stock replenishment will take place.

You have the responsibility of planning the implementation of the above system. Describe the issues which would need consideration, paying particular attention to the method of changeover which you would recommend.

22   SUPPORT PROVISION   *20 mins*

Your organisation is proposing a rapid increase in the number of personal computers deployed in administrative departments. Illustrate the nature and type of support provision administrative staff would need to enable them to cope with the likely changes.

23   DETERIORATION IN PERFORMANCE (15 marks)   *27 mins*

The company for which you work operates a real-time order entry system. Orders and enquiries can be made in person, by telephone or by post. When the system was installed, response time was in the range two to five seconds and the system was performing well. The system has now been running for two years. During the last six months the response time has deteriorated, at peak times it now takes up to 40 seconds to get a response. Staff and customers are unhappy.

What factors would you examine to determine the cause(s) of the problem?

24   ACCOUNTING ACADEMY (55 marks)   *99 mins*

This case study, which was written by the new examiner for Paper 5, was first published in the March 1995 edition of the Student's Newsletter. It reflects the new format for Section A questions, comprising compulsory questions based on a case study.

The Accounting Academy (AA) is a specialist ACCA training company offering Study Schools in Foundation, Certificate and Professional Stage examination papers. It was formed eight years ago by the charismatic lecturer and author Jon Lowe to offer courses that helped students prepare for the examinations. The courses are essentially pre-revision courses intended to concentrate students' minds for the final revision phase. The company currently organises 15 courses in 7 different countries for each examination sitting. These courses are residential and are held in universities or conference centres. The Foundation Stage is covered in a five day course and the Certificate and Professional Stages combined in a nine day course. The average attendance is 30 on a Foundation course, 25 on a Certificate and 50 at the Professional level.

Jon Lowe is currently Course Director of the Accounting Academy and the only full-time lecturer. All other lecturers are employed on a freelance basis. Courses are advertised in accounting publications throughout the world. The Study Schools achieve pass rates well above the national average.

The company's headquarters are in London where three administrative assistants handle enquiries, take course bookings, send out joining instructions, photocopy lecture notes and book conference facilities and lecturers. A further administrative assistant maintains the accounting records on a single user personal computer (PC). The office suite occupied by AA is divided into the Admin. Office, a small Accounts Office, a meeting room and Jon Lowe's office. The total space occupied is about 1200 sq. feet.

A year ago Jon Lowe decided to seek new investment in the company. Initial meetings with an investment group were successful and the investors commissioned a business review to identify the company's strengths and weaknesses. The review summarised these as follows:

Strengths
Consistent achievement of high pass rates
International reputation of Jon Lowe
High quality residential conference centre provision
Focus on ACCA examinations
Pre-payment for courses leads to strong cashflow position

Weaknesses
Inconsistency in the quality of course material produced by individual freelance lecturers
Strong seasonal variation in cash flow
Over-reliance on the lecturing of Jon Lowe
Time-consuming administrative procedures
Inadequate and untimely financial information

As a result of their review the new investors in the company have suggested that the company should begin to employ full-time lecturers and offer an all year round course programme covering full-time courses, Study Schools and Revision Courses. Their plan also suggests that ways should be found to exploit related markets. The plan has been accepted by Jon Lowe and the company's bankers.

However, it is envisaged that there well be a six-fold increase in student numbers in the next three years and hence a thorough review of the company's administrative procedures has been recommended because it is recognised that these are unlikely to be adequate to meet the requirements of the newly expanded company. A preliminary interview has been held with administrative staff and the results of this meeting is summarised below:

Administrative arrangements

The three staff in the Admin. Office all undertake the following tasks:

They take telephone and written enquiries from students about the Study Schools. Each enquiry is logged on a standard form giving the enquirer's name, address, details of the enquiry itself, action taken and the source of the enquiry. The last piece of information is particularly important as it allows the Academy to target its advertising more carefully. Consequently, the assistant must look at a standard Source List while processing the enquiry and code it accordingly. Typical codes are:

0001 The Accounting Professional
0002 Accountants Training Update
0003 Accountancy Today... etc
0020 Personal recommendation

The enquiry forms are stored in order of receipt until the end of the week. On the following Monday one of the administrative assistants goes through each enquiry form to create an Enquiry Summary List which is sent to Jon Lowe. This is a list of each source code, the source description and the number of enquiries logged the previous week for each source. This information is taken into consideration by Jon Lowe when he is reviewing his advertising strategy.

Completed application forms from students are also handled in this office. The application form is checked against the Course list to make sure that valid dates and courses have been booked. It is a rule of the company that the application form must be accompanied with a cheque or bankers draft for the full Study School fee. If a payment is not enclosed or invalid dates or courses have been booked then the application form is returned to the student with an explanatory note about the error or omission. However, if the course details are correct and a payment has been enclosed then the application form is copied and the copy sent with the payment to Edith Donaldson who handles accounting and financial matters. She will also deal with any over or under-payment of the course fee. The original copy of the application form is filed in the appropriate section of a ring binder and a booking confirmation letter is sent to the student. This is produced on an electronic typewriter.

Four weeks before the course, joining instructions are sent to each student due to attend the Study School. These are currently prepared on an electronic typewriter. The assistant checks the venue (from the Course List) and calls in a set of standard paragraphs concerning administrative and travel arrangements for that venue. The student's name and address is found on the application form in the binder and is individually typed in. A Delegate List is also typed up and sent to the

Lecturer showing delegate name, company and any special dietary requirements. A copy of this is also sent to the conference centre where the course is being held.

Once the course is completed the lecturer collects post-course questionnaires from the students and sends them to the Admin. Office. Theses are stored until time allows one of the assistants to type up a one-page summary report to send to Jon Lowe. This report is essentially a statistical summary of the questionnaires together with positive and negative comments entered by the delegate. Particularly adverse statements will be followed up by Jon Lowe.

Questions

The company intends to undertake a feasibility study to identify the costs and benefits of computerisation.

(a) Identify and briefly describe four areas of the current or proposed business that you recommend should be included within the scope of such a study. (8 Marks)

(b) Justify your selection of the business areas by discussing the business benefits that should result from their computerisation. (8 Marks)

(c) The head of the investment group is keen for the rapid computerisation of the company. He has indicated that he wishes to fulfil system requirements using 'off-the-shelf' application software packages rather than commissioning a bespoke software solution. Discuss four potential disadvantages or problems of adopting this approach at the Accounting Academy.

(12 Marks)

(d) It is likely that the system will be implemented with a PC network linked to a central file server. What are the security and audit issues raised by this type of implementation and what steps and precautions might be taken to address these? (12 Marks)

(e) Draw a Data Flow Diagram of the administrative arrangements described in the notes summarising the preliminary meeting with staff of the Accounting Academy. (15 Marks)

Exam answer bank

1   **FINANCIAL SYSTEMS**

(a)   Your screen should have looked something like this:

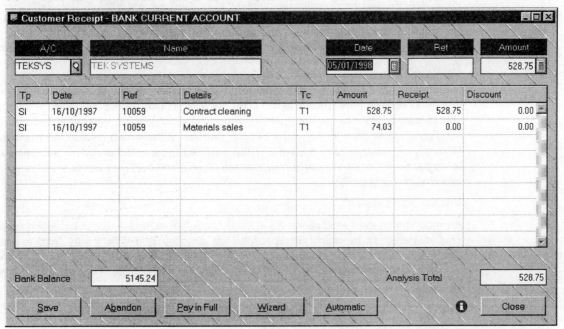

(b)   This would be part of the cash book, with links to the nominal ledger and the sales ledger systems.

2   **INFORMATION**

(a)   *Data* refers to raw, unprocessed facts. *Information* is the meaningful interpretation which is obtained after applying a specific process (such as sorting, adding or collating) to raw facts (data) or to facts which have been subjected to some other processing. The resulting interpretation (or information) is used as the basis for making decisions.

For information to be generated the processing which is applied must generate results which are meaningful and useful to the recipient. Incorrect results, excessively voluminous results and unnecessary results are all just more facts. They may be different from the original data, but because they do not convey meaning they are not information.

Examples of data are the registration numbers of cars passing under a bridge, the account balances of a company's debtors and a list of house addresses and their values in a certain area. By classifying, or sorting, the house data by value, one set of information that might be derived from data is that a certain road contains a majority of high value homes.

(b)   For information to have value it must lead to a decision to take action which results in for example increased profitability, better utilisation of resources, prevention of fraud or an improved understanding of the business. The benefits of such action must exceed the costs of acquiring the information and taking the action. If information is to have value when used in management reports, it must have a number of features. The factors which give information its value and which promote those features are as follows.

Timing

Information must be available in time for a decision to be made. If it is not, it will only be useful for comparisons or longer-term control purposes. Thus a 'flash' report of monthly sales might be available on the first working day after the month end, management accounts after five to ten working days and financial accounts for Head Office within two to three weeks of the month end. If the company's sales director has a quarterly target, he must know how monthly sales have performed very quickly if he is to be given time to react. On the other hand, management of the company are less likely to make across-the-board strategic changes on the basis of the previous month's figures and so a greater delay is acceptable in order to ensure a reasonable degree of accuracy in the figures provided to them.

Accuracy and completeness

Information should be accurate; use of inaccurate information could have serious consequences. Management will also require a complete picture in any report.

Information needs to be accurate enough for its purpose. A report for middle management might be prepared to the nearest £100 or £1,000, so that they can review revenues and costs on a line by line basis. Senior management might be satisfied with reports including information to the nearest ten thousand pounds or to the nearest £0.1 million. Reports must be complete, for example a credit control department cannot operate effectively using out of date sales ledger prints, as those will not include latest cash postings or credit note issues.

Relevance

If information is to have value in a report, the report must be relevant to the purpose for which it is to be used. It should keep to the point and not contain excess information. Information should also be sent to the right person. A common problem in many organisations is the sending of information to the wrong people, who are at the wrong level in the management hierarchy. A manager may receive a report intended to be acted on by his subordinate and fail to pass it on, or an employee may likewise receive and hold, or attempt to act on, a report intended for his superior.

Volume of information

An important concept which adds value to information in reports is that of exception reporting. This is a process by which actual results are only reported if they vary from forecast or expected results by more than a certain factor. Thus for example a quality control report will identify the batches which are not within set tolerance levels; it does not need to enumerate all the satisfactory batches produced.

3   **CATEGORIES OF INFORMATION SYSTEM**

(a)   A management information system may be divided into four separate levels of information system. At the lowest level is the *transaction processing* system. A transaction processing system performs routine tasks which are usually carried out a large number of times. A computerised transaction processing system eliminates the need for performance of repetitive and (from the human viewpoint) uninteresting tasks, and also provides a superior performance capability to that achievable under a manual system. The main purpose of such a system is operational, but an important feature is its ability to provide management information in the form of summaries or analyses of data processed. Typical applications include a sales system, purchasing system, stock control system and payroll system. Database facilities are unique to the individual system.

The transaction processing system is used at the clerical level and at the lower management level. The information it provides is likely to be unsorted and unanalysed, typically a listing by date or account number of transactions processed. It is not a useful tool for decision-making. It is in its interaction with the second category of system that it provides information which can be used to advantage.

At the second level is the *management information* system itself; this is developed from the fundamental operational system by the introduction of features which are not in themselves essential to the basic processing function. Thus middle management may rely on exception reporting generated from the transaction processing system. Similarly they may utilise analyses of actual results against budget or forecast. In this case the 'actual' data is generated from the transaction processing system and is analysed against budget data held by the management information system, which also provides suitable sorting and editing facilities. This kind of management information system is typically used at the operational level and at the tactical level. Information available encompasses all that held by the individual transaction processing systems, but includes additionally summaries showing for example a position at different points in time or analysed by age. A management information system commonly uses a database facility for storage and retrieval of information.

It is at this second level that the system begins to provide information for decision-making. It is not a formalised process; at this stage human intervention dictates what decisions are made, for example, a decision can be made to act on an exception report if the variance shown is above a certain percentage.

The third level of the MIS is the *decision support* system. This does not actually make decisions; it is designed to allow the manager at the tactical or strategic level to consider alternative options and evaluate them under a variety of conditions. For example a manager may prepare a cash flow forecast using a spreadsheet and may then apply a number of assumptions (eg variations in cash payments and receipts cycles, new assumptions on bad debt exposure, different interest rates) to understand the ramifications of different actions.

A typical decision support system consists of three elements, a language subsystem, a problem processing subsystem and a knowledge subsystem. The knowledge subsystem holds internal data and is thus dependent on a database.

The *expert* system is a form of decision support system which is sophisticated enough to indicate what decision is most appropriate in a given set of circumstances. This is possible because the expert system holds a large amount of specialist data on file, eg credit reference and payment pattern data, or tax rules and regulations, and this database can be drawn on for a decision. Expert systems have evolved as an 'add-on' to management information systems, rather than as an integral element of them.

Although the expert system may appear sophisticated, it is not necessarily targeted at higher levels of management. Indeed, because it uses expert knowledge and information to give advice, it can be used at the operational level to reach preliminary decisions which can then be reviewed.

(b)　(i)　*Transaction processing system*

The most likely application would be in the maintenance of personnel records, which would include such data as name, address, department, basic salary, tax code, department and date commenced.

If the personnel department was also responsible for holding data for the payroll department, then in addition to basic salary data, this system would hold details of overtime rates, deductions authorised (eg union dues, save-as-you-earn, give-as-you-earn, loans etc), pension arrangements and other data necessary for calculating net pay.

(ii)　*Management information system*

This system would provide headcount information (total, departmental, movements etc) and total salary information. Information on union membership, average age of workforce (to plan future recruitment patterns) and courses attended/qualifications would also be available. Again, if the system is linked to the payroll system, then full analysis of and reports on actual staff costs could be obtained.

(iii)　*Decision support system*

The most useful applications of a DSS in this department would be in the areas of forecasting, particularly to enable reviews to be carried out examining the effects of (i) changes in headcount and (ii) changes in rates of pay.

Thus costs and benefits of courses of action could be clearly reviewed using a 'what if' approach.

(iv)　*Expert system*

An expert system would be of immense value in showing costs of personnel related actions, eg redundancies. A database of legal and taxation rules would enable calculation of the costs and benefits of any course of action.

An expert system could also have training applications

4　OPEN AND CLOSED LOOP CONTROL

(a)　Control is the process by which outputs from a system are kept in line with a plan or program, subject to system inputs. Control *systems* can be built into any system to ensure that control is exercised. This is true for social as well as physical systems.

A control system typically contains the following.

(i)　A *sensor* receives inputs to the control system.

(ii)　A *plan* contains the predetermined system objectives.

(iii)　A *comparator* compares information or data received from the sensor against the plan.

(iv)　An *effector* exercises control action.

In physical systems, control is built into their design and is exercised by physical means. In social systems, information is vital for the control process. As a business organisation, for example, is a social system, the generation of information about its activities is vital to control it.

Control systems can be classified as either open loop control systems or closed loop control systems. The concept of open and closed loops refers to the extent of the control information available to the system. Feedback is system output which is reinput to the system. It is used as information to control the system. Single loop feedback merely highlights deviations from system plans or objectives. Double loop feedback on the other hand is used to consider the appropriateness of the system itself, or the plans controlling it, to changing environmental circumstances.

A closed loop control system only uses feedback, as defined above, as control information. It has no *direct* contact with the environment. Many mechanical systems (eg thermostats in water heaters) are totally closed loop systems.

Closed loop control system

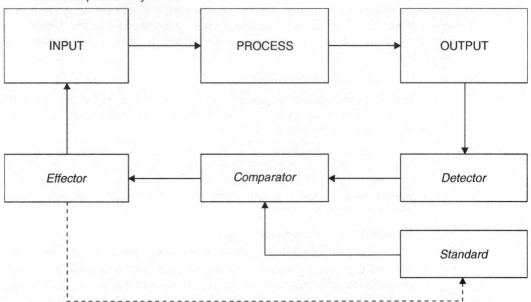

In an open loop system, control exercised does not *depend* on the output of the system. Control information can be provided by the environment. Control action is not automatic. Open loop systems are essential where the system has to interact with an environment that is not predictable, though there is no reason why an open loop system should not contain some feedback element.

An organisation, viewed without people, is an open loop system. Feedback, in the form of a human operator comparing input and output and making connections based on the differences between actual and plan, would cause the system to become a closed loop system.

Open loop control system

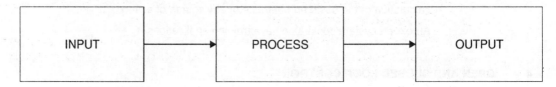

(b)   (i)   *Total organisation*

The total organisation exists in an environment. Its whole *raison d'être* in this case is to make outputs to the environment in the form of its manufactured products, and to do so it must receive inputs from it (eg raw materials, sales revenue). Consequently, the organisation cannot in principle rely on information generated internally describing its own processes to indicate the performance of the organisation as a whole. The type of information required will be that relating to environmental factors that affect the organisation over the long term, but which are largely outside its control (eg state of the economy, government policy, social trends). Over the short term, the total organisation needs to be responsive to immediate market reactions, raw materials price changes, interest rates and so forth, all of which are determined by outside forces. All of these will be used to control the system. An open loop control system is therefore appropriate. The total organisation will not be able to function without environmental control information.

(ii)   *Manufacturing unit*

The manufacturing unit in the organisation is likely to be fairly self-contained. The inputs it receives from elsewhere in the organisation, or from outside, will be controllable. Outputs from such a system will also be predictable. For example, from the controlled input of raw materials, a predictable output of 'product' is produced. It is therefore a closed system. Any control function in such a unit, whether it be over costs or quality, will be one which is responsive to the unit's actual performance according to planning targets set for it. A closed loop control system is therefore appropriate. This is because in a closed system the best source of information about the system is the system itself.

5 MEMORIES ARE MADE OF THIS

(a) Computer storage is divided into main storage and backing storage. A computer has a limited amount of internal (main) storage, more often referred to as *memory*. Most computer applications require more data and processing capacity than can be provided by the memory. External (backing) storage holds the data, in machine form, which is not required by the CPU. This division also helps to maximise the efficiency of the system and to ensure adequate security of data.

The main storage of a computer (also called memory or immediate access storage) holds programs, some input/output data and has a work area to process data. Data is held in main storage in two principal forms; read only memory (ROM) is normally used for start-up programs and other fixed data, and random access memory (RAM) (more important from the point of view of the user) has a read/write capability and is essential for effective main memory. The primary feature of main storage is fast processing speed. The larger the main storage, the more expensive the configuration, so the limited size of main storage results in the need for external storage, held on hard disk or perhaps peripheral devices.

Backing storage devices hold large quantities of data in machine form until required by the CPU for some form of processing. The data is accessed and transferred to the main storage for processing and then transferred back to the backing store when the operation is complete. Hard disks, although sometimes located in the same 'box' as the CPU, are a form of backing storage.

Another application for backing storage is in the maintenance of duplicate records in case of data loss or corruption on the main system; this is an important feature of most computer systems. The ability to recreate data following system failure or other disaster should always be given a high priority in any computer system.

Main storage is physically made up of electronic integrated circuits or silicon chips, which are cheap to produce, small in size and can hold large amounts of data. Backing storage devices are either in disk or tape form and use magnetic or optical technology.

(b) The choice of hardware storage medium for a given file might be considered initially as a matter of choosing between disk media (hard or floppy disk, and fixed or exchangeable disk, magnetic or optical) with tape backup.

Tape files must be processed serially (one after another in turn, from the start through to the end of the file), and so are nowadays used more often as backup to disk files, although they are still used in batch processing systems.

Access to records on a *disk file* can be either serial or direct. Direct access means that records can be read or written individually by means of an index or address generation system.

The core of any solution to a decision like this should concentrate primarily on the requirements of the application. The major considerations are as follows.

(i) *Response time.* If the user wants a quick response time in obtaining information from file, direct access will be required.

(ii) *'Conversation' with the computer.* If the user wishes to obtain information and input new data at the same time, in an interactive process with the computer, direct access will be required.

(iii) If the user wishes to process information immediately and to be able to use files that are always fully *up-to-date* (ie to operate in real time) direct access is again essential.

(iv) If the file contains information that must be, or could be, processed in serial order, then either tape or disk files could be used. The choice between the two should possibly depend on which would provide the fastest processing:

(1)   disks have a faster transfer rate, in moving data from backing store to main memory and back;

(2)   when the 'hit rate' (ie the ratio of records on file to be processed during a computer run as a proportion of the total number of records on file) is high using a tape master file would provide faster processing speeds.

The choice between different types of storage medium will also depend on:

(i)   the eventual *size* of the file (cassettes and floppy disks are for smaller files, and so generally for smaller computers);

(ii)   the *hardware* that the manufacturer or selling company tends to sell with the basic processor. Some computer systems are sold 'ready packaged' with either tape or disk backing storage.

Two final influential considerations might be:

(i)   the *existing hardware* owned by an organisation. If an organisation is planning to design a new system, it might opt to use its existing hardware for the new system - ie to make the best use of what is available;

(ii)   *incremental cost*. If new equipment must be purchased, the user might opt for what is currently the cheapest on the market.

6   THE ELECTRONIC OFFICE

(a)   The electronic office has been brought into existence by advances in computer and communications technology. The term 'electronic office' is used to describe an office environment which makes use of these twin technologies in the course of data processing and information handling. The typical electronic office will have a number of visible features and underlying processes not inherent in the non-automated office environment.

The first obvious feature of the electronic office is likely to be the PC. There may be as many as one per desk. A workstation will consist of a PC (basic module, keyboard and VDU), connected to a printer. Printers may be shared between a number of PCs. Each microcomputer is unlikely to be a stand-alone machine. In a typical electronic office it will be connected to an internal communications system and to an external communications system. The internal communications system is provided by means of a local area network (LAN). This links the user to other similar computers so that users can make use of common data and communicate with one another. The external communications system is provided by means of telecommunications links, and terminals include fax and telex machines and telephones.

The hardware in the electronic office is used to run applications software programs. There will be a number of pieces of pre-packaged software in any electronic office. Pre-packaged software is cheap by comparison with tailor-made packages and is generally very user-friendly.

The most important package in the electronic office is likely to be a word processing package. This allows the user to input text and store it for subsequent retrieval or editing. The user can produce high quality documents. If the user has a desktop publishing package, which is based on a WP package, he will be offered a range of additional features including a graphics application and a page layout function. This will provide suitable output for reports and tender documents.

A manufacturing company will also be able to make use of spreadsheet packages, for example Lotus 1-2-3. A spreadsheet package will enable staff to perform a range of tasks from basic calculations and preparation of tables through to complex financial modelling. A spreadsheet is effectively an electronic piece of analysis paper, divided into rows and columns. Each row and column configuration represents a cell, into which the user can insert data, formulae or labels. A typical package also offers sophisticated menus, help screens, edit functions and statistical and mathematical functions.

The company may also be looking to computerise its accounting function, in which case it will require an accounts package. In their most basic form accounts packages are simply a series of electronic ledgers. Complete accounts packages are usually fairly cheap single-user systems; more sophisticated packages may be modular in nature, allowing a gradual build-up to a complete system.

The company may also use a database package. This will enable users to share common data for different purposes.

For internal communications the company may consider the use of electronic mail. This enables memos and letters to be sent from department to department by registered users without the necessity for hard copy to be generated. E-mail is a feature frequently available on integrated packages, which also offer spreadsheeting, wordprocessing and a database in a single package.

For external communications the company will use facsimile for transmitting and receiving text, diagrams and charts and telex for text. The company may also link up to external information services such as Viewdata, Textline and the Internet.

(b)   It is now quite possible technically for employees of many descriptions to work from home. A PC sited at home enables a user to handle data just as if he were in the office, using spreadsheet and word processing packages. Links to the office provide a means of transmitting information and receiving new data. Links are provided by means of a modem at each end of the telephone line. The modem, or modulator-demodulator, converts the digital signals used by the computer to analogue signals for transmission along the telephone line; at the other end of the line they are reconverted by the second modem. A network enables communication with the office by e-mail. Sophisticated e-mail systems allow whole documents (eg reports) to be sent as attachments to memos.

Advantages of telecommuting are the savings of office space and the elimination of travelling time. A disadvantage is the loss of face-to-face contact, which can be very important in meetings and negotiations and is not fully compensated for by mail or by phone calls. A means of overcoming this is teleconferencing. Teleconferencing involves the use of video technology. Each party sits in front of a video camera and looks at a video monitor sited next to the camera. This configuration is mirrored by the other party to the conference, so that each can see and be seen. This overcomes a lot of the psychological difficulties of parties not meeting face-to-face. It is particularly useful for international meetings.

7   PAPERWORK PLC

(a)   The recommended wide area network configuration for this organisation would be as shown below.

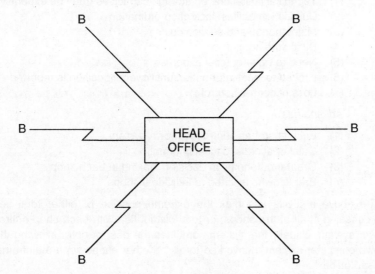

Branches (B) would each be responsible for their own processing of transactions. They would be able to ascertain their own stock levels and sales figures at any time. A PC or PCs would be located at each branch and would be connected to a central computer (probably a minicomputer) at head office via telecommunication lines. Larger branches might have an installed local area network with a server computer running LAN services for a number of PCs and linking into the WAN. Details of all transactions, sales order, enquiries would be sent to the central computer at head office at the end of each day. Head office would use the data from each branch to update the database and send back to the branches details of the overall position with regard to stock availability.

It would be possible to operate the network on-line and in real-time thus allowing each shop to enquire of the up-to-date position at any time. Each transaction would go immediately to the central database for up dating. The solution may be too expensive relative to Paperwork's needs, and a batch system (on-line) might be more appropriate. Updating could then be done overnight, while communications costs are lower.

Strictly, distributed processing means that each branch acts autonomously but their inter-dependence is such that a network and central database would greatly benefit the business. As to whether to invest in an on-line system, much will depend on the speed required, particularly in relation to stock turnover.

If the company wished to make full use of available technology, it could use EFTPOS technology, allowing data capture at point of sale using bar codes (book details and price) and magnetic stripe cards (customer payments). Terminals could link into local computers via the LAN, and a separate communications link to the appropriate banking network would be required for transactions authorisation/money transfer purposes.

    (b)   *Centralised*

        (i)   *Advantages*

                (1)   Uniformity of files
                (2)   Easier security and control
                (3)   Head office kept up-to-date
                (4)   May be cheaper approach than network
                (5)   Ease of administration
                (6)   Draw on head office experience
                (7)   Better control over daily cash/working capital position
                (8)   Power of central mainframe or minicomputer

        (ii)   *Disadvantages*

                (1)   Delay in receiving results of processing
                (2)   Shops dependent on head office
                (3)   Vulnerable to breakdown of common system

      Distributed

        (i)   *Disadvantages*

                (1)   Technical limitations on storage capacities (may be expensive to overcome)
                (2)   Duplication of flies, lack of co-ordination
                (3)   Maintenance and service costs
                (4)   Difficult to administer
                (5)   Need to train for local expertise
                (6)   Limited to local information until overall position is reported
                (7)   Loss of central control

            Advantages

                (1)   Each shop has control over own system
                (2)   Quicker access to local information
                (3)   Greater autonomy in decision making at each shop
                (4)   Breakdowns isolated to individual shops

The above analysis assumes the extreme position of either total centralisation, with no processing at all at the shops, or total distribution with each shop entirely responsible for its own system. Usually the system combines the best of both: allowing the shops to use their own computer system, networked to all the other shops via a mainframe or minicomputer at head office.

8   COST-BENEFIT ANALYSIS TECHNIQUES

Techniques which might be used to evaluate the costs and benefits of a new system include the following.

(a)   *Cash flow analysis.* At the end of the project the result should be that the project produces a positive balance. The problem with this is that although many costs will be tangible, many benefits will be intangible, and might need to be estimated in order to establish any kind of sensible figure.

(b)   *Payback period.* Assuming that the result of implementing the system is positive then after some period of time the benefits outweigh the costs. This is the payback period. The shorter the payback period the more attractive the project. If target payback periods are set and capital project approval only given to projects meeting the target, it will be necessary to apply different periods to different scales of investment. Differences in payback patterns must also be taken into account.

(c)   *Return on investment.* This is the method of quantifying the benefit in terms of the rate per year expressed as a percentage of the costs. Normally all costs and benefits are totalled and the result spread over the anticipated life of the project, giving the ROI figure. No attempt is made to account for the value of holding the investment in the project.

(d)   *Discounted cash flow.* The discounted cash flow takes into account the timing of both payments and benefits, and returns a figure which more meaningfully estimates the value of the project taking into account both the sums involved and their timings. Flows are discounted so that their present values are obtained.

The results from the analysis methods above might be compared to results which could be obtained from using the same funds elsewhere, to establish whether there were compelling financial reasons to proceed with the project.

Each of the sets of figures from the accounting mechanisms listed above could be perhaps better presented graphically rather than in tabular form. This would visually emphasise that the project was going to make a 'profit', and over what period (which is what in essence the figures illustrate).

9   ACE MACHINE TOOLS

The comparison and contrast may be seen by reference to the table below.

Applications package	*Custom built software*
• Less costly to produce	Potentially very expensive to produce
• Rapid installation with little or no debugging	Longer development time
• Some compromises likely in terms of business requirements	May be written to encompass all present and anticipated future business needs
• Likely to be compatible with other software	Knowledgeable programmers needed to write compatible systems.
• Probably supported by supplier as technology advances	Difficult to support as technology advances
• Supplied with documentation and possibly on-screen tutorials for training	Documentation and training needs to be developed: most costly
• Developed as user-friendly	User-friendly features to be addressed
• Modifications may be difficult, time consuming and expensive to introduce	Written to meet optimum needs, modifications less likely
• May be easy to integrate with other standard applications in the future	May be harder to integrate with future applications
• Relatively easy to maintain and upgrade	Expensive to maintain and upgrade
• Basic security features	More sophisticated procedures for security may be written

In summary Ace would certainly save money by buying and possibly modifying packages but may need to sacrifice some quality elements in meeting their needs. However since their business needs would appear to be for quite straightforward commercial functions, they should consider purchasing well supported and tested application packages.

10 **PHYSICAL SECURITY**

Physical security comprises two sorts of controls, protection against natural and man made disasters, such as fire, flood and sabotage, and protection against intruders gaining physical access to the system. These threats can be grouped alternatively as accidental and deliberate.

The physical environment has a major effect on information system security, and so planning it properly is an important precondition of an adequate security plan.

(a) Fire is the most serious hazard to computer systems. Destruction of data can be even more costly than the destruction of hardware. A proper fire safety plan is an essential feature of security procedures, in order to prevent fire, detect fire and put out the fire. Fire safety includes:

    (i) site preparation (eg appropriate building materials, fire doors);

    (ii) detection (eg smoke detectors);

    (iii) extinguishing (eg sprinklers);

    (iv) training for staff in observing fire safety procedures (eg no smoking in computer room).

(b) A proper environment must be provided for mainframes. Mainframe computers in particular are susceptible to damage from poor atmospheric or environmental conditions. A typical installation would provide air-conditioning, a dust-free environment (provided by use of special clothing and double sets of sealed doors), antistatic protection and 'clean' power supplies. Power supplies must be protected from both loss of power and irregularities in supply, both of which can corrupt data and processing activities.

(c) Other natural disasters include flooding and abnormal weather conditions. It is difficult to envisage the form and effect of these, but certain steps can be taken. It may be unwise to site a computer in a basement, even if this is considered to be a more suitable location for machines than people, as this is likely to be the first area affected by flooding. Lightning may adversely affect power supplies.

(d) The other main area of physical security is access control, to prevent intruders getting anywhere near the computer equipment or storage media. Methods of controlling human access include:

    (i) personnel (security guards);

    (ii) mechanical devices (eg keys, whose issue is recorded);

    (iii) electronic identification devices (eg card-swipe systems, where a card is passed through a reader).

(e) Theft is also a problem, particularly where so much computer equipment is easily portable. A PC need not be larger than a briefcase and even a laser printer can be carried by one person. To some extent this can be guarded against by means similar to those described in (d), but with much equipment located in ordinary offices and no longer kept in a single secure location other measures must be taken. Regular 'stock controls' or physical inspections may be necessary, and a strictly imposed form of bookings used when staff take PCs off-site, either to customers or home.

One possible approach to disaster recovery is to use the services of a specialist disaster recovery company. These companies are becoming more widespread as computer users are made more aware of the potential dangers of a major disaster. These companies offer office premises with desks, telephones and storage space which are equipped with hardware, including terminals, of the same type as that used by their customers. In the event of a disaster, the customer can 'invoke' standby procedures and load backups of software to carry on essential business.

Disaster standby companies generally offer services to users of one hardware manufacturer's equipment only, and clearly require a number of subscribers if they are to offer a cost effective service. The upper limit on subscribers is governed by the probability that two customers require facilities at once; this is determined by insurers.

Alternatively, computer bureaux can agree to make their own systems available in the event of an emergency. Such an arrangement has to be specified in advance, as there might be other demands on a bureau's resources.

However, the key is to draw up a formal disaster recovery plan and to ensure maximum staff awareness of the appropriate procedures.

11   REVIEWING DEVELOPMENT

> *Tutorial note.* You may find this question easier if you are also studying for Paper 6.

(a)   The management board must remain in overall control of such new developments, not allowing decisions and costs to be dealt with at too low a management level. The new system must fit in with the overall system development of the entity and the appropriate systems development programme must be identified and properly implemented.

It would normally be customary to appoint one or two board members to be in overall control of any new computer development. They would:

(i)   report back to the board on a regular basis;

(ii)   be responsible for the day to day decisions about the project.

The board should also be responsible for:

(i)   setting up any necessary working parties from the relevant affected departments and ensuring that they have the necessary time and resources;

(ii)   ensuring a wide consultation among all users and any available expertise, both internal and external (for example the external auditors);

(iii)   fixing and adhering to a timetable with fixed reporting periods.

When reviewing the development of a new system, at various points in the process the board should make specific decisions and recommendations. At the very least, these should be at the stages of specification, selection, completion and implementation.

The internal audit department and/or the audit committee could be used for providing regular feedback, but it is up to the board to institute and maintain communication in this way.

Expenditure authorisation is obviously very important. Rather than authorising overall expenditure on the project, the board should authorise each significant component of hardware and software, to make sure that it complies with the overall specification.

Reports from external consultants, or from internal audit, would be of vital help in objectively assessing the system. The external auditors may be involved if the impact of the system significantly affects the company.

(b)   The internal auditor should be involved in all stages of the design of the new accounting system. There are three main stages of development:

(i)   feasibility studies;

(ii)   system development;

(iii)   system specification and construction.

At each of these stages the internal auditor is in an ideal position to ensure that:

(i)   all the proper controls which are required have been built into the system design; and

(ii)   the system meets company standards along with the design process itself.

The controls to be identified will fall into two distinct categories:

(i)   internal controls, such as segregation of duties, etc (all the SOAPSPAM controls); and

(ii)   computer controls, including data input controls, processing controls and so on.

In effect, the internal auditor is doing the same job as usual: evaluating the system's effectiveness according to the company's criteria and ensuring all necessary controls are present. In this case, the system has not yet been constructed so the internal auditor cannot test it. However, the auditor can look for key attributes in the system design.

(i)   Is the benefit worth the cost of the system?

(ii)   Is the system complete?

(iii)   Are all outputs (reports, invoices, and so on) relevant and are they produced in a timely manner?

(iv)   Is the system secure from internal and external tampering?

(v)   If staff training is necessary, has it been planned? (Courses, manuals and so on.)

During the feasibility stage, the auditor should ensure that all user departments have been consulted. The auditor should assess the reasonableness of any assumptions made, for example future trading growth.

As the development stage commences, the auditor needs to check that all of the development phase is properly documented. This is also the phase where audit matters become important, in terms of audit trails, control requirements and so on.

The audit requirements of the system are also important in the final phase when the auditor will be involved in testing the new system. The testing should be properly recorded. At this stage the auditor should be aware of all the documentation relating to the system. Clear and complete documentation will make it easier to train staff in user departments on the new system.

Note that, although the internal auditor must monitor the whole process of systems development, he must not take part in its implementation, as this would partly invalidate his audit of the system at a later date. The auditor must not become involved in operational matters.

12   FACT FINDING

(a)   Three methods of fact finding are:

    (i)   interviews;
    (ii)   questionnaires;
    (iii)   observation.

Interviews involve face-to-face discussions between the analyst and individuals with knowledge of the system. The analyst asks questions and obtains answers, comments and suggestions.

Questionnaires are written lists of questions. These can be used by a systems analyst in an interview, or given to respondents, who will be asked to write answers in their own time and return the completed questionnaire.

Observation involves the analyst in watching the system in operation as an observer.

(*Note*. A fourth method of fact finding that could also be discussed is the study of historic records and documents. This is a form of observation.)

(b)   The advantages and disadvantages of these three methods are as follows.

    (i)   *Interviews*. As a fact finding technique, interviewing will to some degree be appropriate in almost all situations. It may be particularly useful where the proposed system will involve a number of related areas in the existing system. This is because it is usually the case that only by talking to all parties involved will the analyst gain a total view and proper understanding of the interaction of the various parts of the system.

         Interviewers need background information on those interviewed and many find this valuable later on during implementation. It gives an opportunity to discuss in-depth opinion as well as fact and he may learn of suggestions that are worth looking into further. However, interviewing is an acquired skill and depends upon the cooperation of those being interviewed. It can be costly in time and effort and the rewards are unpredictable.

    (ii)   *Questionnaires*. In many ways, the ideal solution to the problem of fact finding will involve a certain amount of direct contact between the analyst and those members of staff concerned with the day to day running of the system. However, it may sometimes be physically impossible, or at least highly impractical, for the analyst to personally talk with all staff members. This may either be because of the sheer numbers of staff involved and/or the decentralised nature of the business organisation. It is in such situations that the use of questionnaires may have to be considered.

         Questionnaires can sample a wide range of opinion and collect useful statistics in a short space of time, particularly if those questioned cover a large geographical area. There are potentially many problems with a questionnaire. The response rate may be poor, analysis of a lengthy questionnaire can be costly and design of a good questionnaire is not easy, particularly if consistency of answer is needed to be checked by cross referencing answers.

         Where questionnaires are to be distributed for completion by staff members, it is essential that the questions themselves have been designed in such a way that ambiguities are avoided. There is also a danger with questionnaires that staff may give the reply which they feel is expected of them, rather than perhaps what they see as the answer in 'real life'. For these reasons, questionnaires should only be used where the system details which the analyst is enquiring about are comparatively simple.

A questionnaire might be used to survey a new product when the potential customer base numbers many thousands.

(iii) *Observation.* Studying by observation requires a base level of knowledge about a system and should provide experience of the details of the system which is needed if changes are to be introduced. It can be a cheap means of gaining knowledge of a system and has the advantage of showing what actually happens, not what you expect or believe to be happening. On the other hand, direct observation is time consuming and may provoke a reaction in those observed which makes it difficult to allow normal working practice to go ahead as normal. It is for this reason that it would perhaps be necessary to make a number of separate observations, at random intervals, rather than forming an opinion based upon a single visit.

Observation is a useful 'follow-up' procedure, used to gain confirmation that a system is outlined 'in theory', perhaps in an interview does actually work 'in practice'.

It might be used for example whenever the flow of documents through a system needs to be assessed for efficiency.

13   WRAY CASTLE

(a)   It is possible to describe a system in a number of ways. A system can be analysed in terms of its components (ie a collection of hardware and software items). Alternatively, a system can be examined in terms of what it does (eg the detail of the processing operations it performs). Finally a system can be viewed abstractly, in terms of its logical design.

The *logical design* of a system is the design of the system in concept, what the system is meant to achieve, rather than detailed implementation. The *physical design* of the system not only specifies hardware, but also the exact design as to how a particular procedure will be implemented in software. Theoretically, it is not impossible for one logical design to be implemented in more than one physical way (use different hardware, different programming languages).

The distinction between logical and physical design is at the heart of a commonly used design methodology, structured analysis.

Structured analysis is a formal methodology which begins with the *logical* design of the system and progresses, step by step towards physical implementation, with each stage completed before the next is commenced. The final output from each stage is used as the starting point for the next stage.

In the design of a computer system, seven stages can be outlined.

(i)   *Problem definition.* In this stage, the problem is outlined, and ends with a statement of the scope and objectives of the proposed system, although it might only go as far as to recommend a feasibility study.

(ii)   A *feasibility study* is carried out, to see if there is a feasible solution to the problem outlined in stage (i).

(iii)   After this stage, a rough *outline of a proposed system* will prepared. This will contain no details of physical implementation, and may for example simply consist of a number of dataflow diagrams. Were implementation issues to be discussed at this stage, the valuable contribution that users can make to systems design would be made less effective, as they would be unable to suggest amendments to a design which is too technical.

(iv)   A stable logical model of the system is prepared. Once the logical model has been agreed, a number of *outline designs* will be made, with perhaps a cost/benefit analysis for each.

(v)   The system is now *designed in detail.* Typical documents produced at this stage are the systems specification, program specifications etc.

(vi)   The system is now *designed, tested and implemented.* Programs may be designed using structured narratives (for example, structured English, which follows certain prescribed logical rules).

(vii)   Maintenance involves the regular *review* and updating of the computer system.

(b)   A structured systems methodology could be applied to avoid the problems previously experienced by Wray Castle. An example of such a methodology is Structured Systems Analysis and Design Methodology, or SSADM. The key features of SSADM are set out below. Most of these could equally well be attributed to any structured systems methodology.

Project management

The structured framework of a methodology helps with planning. It defines the tasks to be performed and sets out when they should be done. Each step has an identifiable end product. This allows control by reference to actual achievements rather than to estimates of progress.

Techniques

Three techniques are used in SSADM: dataflow diagrams, logical data structures and entity life histories. These allow information to be cross-checked between diagrams and ensure that the delivered system is close to the final system, in other words that the necessity for later enhancements is minimised. For example, an event in an entity life history will match data flows which trigger processes on the dataflow diagrams. These techniques and others are available in different methodologies.

The specification

A logical design is produced that is independent of hardware and software. This logical design can then be given a physical design using whatever computer equipment and implementation language is required.

Users

Users are involved with development work from an early stage. Their involvement is a critical factor in the success of any development. SSADM encourages better communication between users and developers.

Documentation

Documentation is produced throughout the project. This gives a comprehensive and detailed picture of the system and helps understanding of the system. This makes the consequences of proposed changes clear.

Contractors

SSADM and other commercial methodologies are used widely enough to be known to many systems professionals. This is obviously an advantage, as it reduced dependence on individual suppliers or contractors.

Methodology

A methodology provides a set of development standards to which all parties can adhere.

Emphasis on graphical techniques

The emphasis on diagramming makes it easier for relevant parties to understand the system than if narrative descriptions were used. Some narrative can be used; however if this is excessive, the advantage of the diagramming techniques is lost.

14   DATA FLOW DIAGRAM

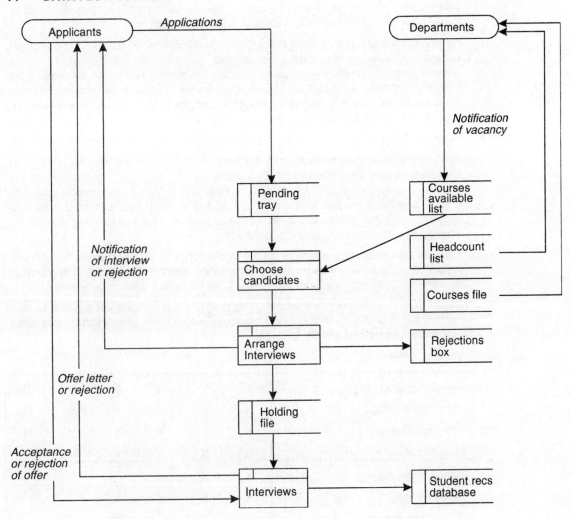

15   PROCEDURE SPECIFICATION

(a)   (i)   *Decision tables*

Decision tables define the logic of a process by presenting conditions and actions laid out in quadrants. Tables can be used for presenting complex processes and program operations. They are suited to problems which have a large number of alternative options. Tables can be easily checked to see that all alternatives have been considered.

Decision tables can be standardised, which may allow different scenarios to be considered and presented. For instance, they could be used to compare the processing logic of different computer systems. The cause and effect of individual results can be easily identified using decision tables; this may be useful for assessing program logic.

Decision tables are not suited to problems with unclear conditions or actions; the table would be incomplete or inaccurate. Priorities are difficult to allocate in tables and they do not present the step by step logic of a process; they are therefore unsuited to tasks such as procedure writing which may require each step in a process (like sales ordering) to be clearly stated. Chronology may, in certain circumstances, be incorporated by the use of a series of tables.

(ii)   *Decision trees*

Laid out as a graphical representation of a decision making process, decision trees highlight all available choices and the steps which must be taken to arrive at any given result.

The sequence of events is highlighted, and the consequences of decisions can be clearly seen. This method is suitable for procedure writing; using the previous example, several checks may be made before a sales order is processed. Procedures set out using this method make decisions easier to assess if the available choices are clearly understood. The clarity of decision trees means that they can be used to present overall system design or individual program operations.

However, very complex or long processes may be difficult to adapt to this method because choices could easily be missed or the tree size could become unmanageable. A process with many alternatives is more suited to the decision tables described above. Because each tree diagram is unique it is not possible to standardise them and therefore comparisons of operations or processes are not appropriate for this method.

(iii)   *Structured English*

This method describes operations in the form of instructions and results. Structured English eliminates the ambiguity inherent in the English language. The statements are made in limited English and are written in similar logical form to a computer program. This is a detailed method of presentation and is suitable for describing individual program functions. End-users could use this method when developing macros or simple programs in spreadsheets or databases.

Program instructions and their results can be checked by simply reading through the logic of the narrative which is easily understood although there are a number of conventions and keywords (such as IF, THEN, ELSE) which need to be learned.

Larger or more complex processes such as system overviews are not suitable for this method because the level of detailed employed would fail to simplify the procedures and choices into a presentable format.

(b)   (i)   *Decision table*

Relevant degree	Y	Y	N	N	N	N
Other degree	N	N	Y	Y	N	N
Other qualification	N	Y	N	Y	Y	N
No qualification	N	N	N	N	N	Y
Management training	X	X				
Graduate entry	X	X	X	X		
Main intake stream		X		X	X	
Clerical grades						X

(ii)   *Decision tree*

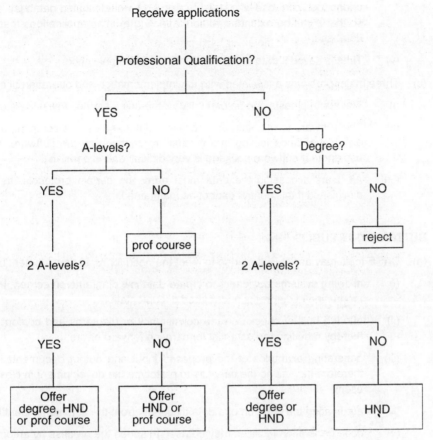

(iii)   *Structured English*

IF <u>Applicant</u> has non-degree qualification

    IF <u>Applicant</u> has degree

        IF <u>Applicant</u> has relevant degree
        THEN Offer management training, graduate entry or m.i.s.
        ELSE Offer graduate entry or m.i.s.

    ELSE Offer m.i.s.

ELSE <u>Applicant</u> has no non-degree qualification

    IF <u>Applicant</u> has degree

        IF <u>Applicant</u> has relevant degree
        THEN Offer management training or graduate entry
        ELSE Offer graduate entry

    ELSE place in clerical grade.

16   DATABASE

(a)   A database could be defined as a collection of any type of data with a structure that removes the need for the duplication of files and meets the information needs of a large section of an organisation. It is defined in the CIMA's Computing Terminology as: 'in its strict sense...a file of data structured in such a way that it may serve a number of applications without its structure being dictated by any one of those applications, the concept being that programs are written around the database rather than files being structured to meet the needs of specific programs'.

(b)   Five advantages of a well designed database are:

    (i)   If duplication of information is removed, then updating information is made easier with fewer errors.

    (ii)   The amount of file storage space for data is reduced.

    (iii)   The time taken to access different parts of the same database should be less than accessing separate files.

(iv) The database can be extended to bring in new data in a structure that is well understood by those who need to use it. (A well-designed database should be flexible so that it can be extended without affecting existing applications that already use this database.)

(v) Time is saved if data are entered into a system only once.

(c) Three major problems associated with the implementation and operation of a database are:

(i) The start-up costs can be prohibitive if the gains are not well understood or defined.

(ii) The software to maintain and access a database can be complex, and also rigid and expensive. Once locked into a structure imposed by the software, then changing to use another software package is very difficult and expensive.

(iii) All users accessing the data must agree on certain protocols. Its effectiveness is diminished if this control cannot be maintained.

17 BUTTERLEDGE PUBLISHING

(a) CASE tools may assist Butterledge to meet the need for rapid development by:

(i) allowing systems designers to create dataflow diagrams on screen, thus speeding the production of diagrams and related documentation;

(ii) offering built in checks on the consistency of diagrams and conformity to standards, thereby reducing the potential for carrying forward errors;

(iii) generating examples of the proposed input and output documentation and screens, therefore increasing the capacity to prototype the development in close liaison with the users;

(iv) automating the creation of a data dictionary from the data items identified;

(v) code generation facilities may be used to speed the process by automating production and importing ready prepared sub-routines;

(vi) toolkits for diagramming and editing will improve efficiency and enhance user friendliness.

Butterledge may benefit from a whole range of existing and developing tools to speed and ease the work of the analyst and programmer across all components of the systems life cycle. In their quest to run a cost-effective publishing business, they may wish to give particular attention to the order processing system.

(b) CUSTOMERS   <u>Account code</u>, name, address, credit limit, delivery address

CUSTOMER ORDERS   <u>Order no</u>, account no, date

ORDER DETAILS   <u>Order no, book codes</u>, number required

BOOKS   <u>Book code</u>, book title, author, edition, year, price

(c) *Entity attribute relationship model*

See diagram on following page.

ENTITY   RELATIONSHIP

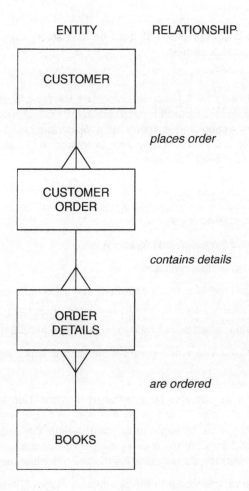

18   **SECURITY**

Information is a vital resource of any organisation, and steps have to be taken to ensure its security and integrity as if it were any other valuable asset. Just as there are systems to ensure against theft or destruction of tangible assets, so too are measures taken to protect data and information.

Physical access

It is possible to enumerate any number of threats to the integrity and privacy of data held in any system. There are basic physical dangers such as fire which need guarding against. Controls to minimise risk include fireproof cabinets where important files are kept. Also, there are basic measures relating to physical access by unauthorised people to an organisation's premises. These physical controls relate both to the equipment and the storage media. In a database system like the one described, this is likely to be a random access storage medium. Both backup copies and backup systems can be maintained in case of disasters.

Particular risks at SWM Ltd relate to the use of couriers and floppy disks to transfer data between sites. Assuming back-ups are available, it is still possible that loss or corruption of disks could retard processing by 24 hours.

In a new multi-user database system, the database file will be held centrally, and the problem of physical access to the medium on which the data is stored will not be multiplied over several sites. Also, it will be easier to keep backup copies of one set of files than of several.

Logical access

The database contains data relating to a number of different applications, some of which might be for restricted viewing only. Access to the entire database should be restricted also, for the same reasons. The type of control that will serve both functions is a password system, in which each user is given a unique code. The password can determine entry to the database, and also restrict users to specific views of it. A further measure would be to restrict an individual user to one terminal, so that the password keyed in from that terminal could be checked to see that it corresponds in some way to the terminal itself.

For this system to work, passwords must be kept strictly confidential between users, and also as far as outsiders are concerned.

Communications

If data is transferred over a telecommunications link (as proposed earlier in this solution), controls should be made as far as possible to minimise the risks of hacking. Data sent over the link can be subjected to encryption and authentication procedures. Dial-back modems can be used: they request callers to hang up and they then telephone the caller ensuring that the number is taken from the modem's pre-set database.

Communications software is written with security and integrity in mind. As an example, Novell's Netware includes the following.

(a) Duplication of directories.

(b) Duplication of file allocation tables (FATs).

(c) Read-after-write disk verification.

(d) Hot fix, which redirects faulty data from the disk's main storage area to a separate part of the disk.

(e) Disk mirroring, which allows data to be written to two different disks.

(f) Transaction tracking, which reverses out transactions interrupted by hardware errors.

Errors

The integrity of data can also be threatened by error. Human error can occur both in systems design and programming. Controls in the design stage, to avoid bugs, include adherence to programming standards, testing and so forth, before the database system is implemented. The same can be said for controls over system maintenance and updating. Proper documentation, testing and authorisation should minimise the risk of further design error.

Other forms of error can occur in the operational stage. There can be programmed controls over data input. These include check digits, range checks, format checks and so forth. The user interface can be so designed to make input of data strictly guided. As noted, re-input of invoice details is a source of possible data input errors; use of automatic updating will reduce this risk.

Personnel

Controls over personnel relate to a separation of functions as far as possible between programming staff and operational staff, so that operational staff do not have the opportunity to amend programs fraudulently, and so that programming staff do not get the opportunity to interfere with live data for fraudulent ends. For sensitive positions strict recruitment procedures should be followed.

With end-user computing, some of these controls are hard to maintain. In the situation outlined in this case, however, control over the database is maintained centrally so this is not so much of a problem.

19 CONTROLS

(a) Management must consider the various possible risks to data in a system, and the potential consequences if an error happens. The risks to data can be listed, in general terms, as errors arising from:

(i) human error;
(ii) technical error;
(iii) natural disasters;
(iv) deliberate actions (fraud or malicious damage) by individual members of staff;
(v) commercial espionage;
(vi) industrial action.

(b) With these risks in mind, management should assess the adequacy of:

(i) controls over hardware;

(ii) processing controls over the workings of the software;

(iii) controls over the data:

(1) input controls;
(2) file controls;
(3) output controls;
(4) data transmission controls;

(iv) controls over the administrative aspects of the system;

(v) controls over system design and development and over program amendments.

(c) *Controls over hardware*

Controls over hardware should be sufficient to prevent (or reduce the likelihood of) a situation where costly errors occur due to a hardware fault. Hardware controls include parity checks, overflow checks, file masks and terminal readiness checks.

Management should be satisfied that routine maintenance is carried out regularly on equipment, and that for urgent data processing, there are 'back-up' items of equipment available for use in the event of a breakdown of the CPU or a peripheral unit.

There should be in-house engineers to repair breakdowns or a satisfactory arrangement for using the services of an external firm of engineers.

(d) *Controls over software*

Controls over software should be sufficient to prevent or identify errors whereby records are 'lost' by the computer, or whereby a program processes the wrong file of data. Management should be satisfied that there are sufficient:

(i) file identification checks, whereby a program will not run until a check has been made that the correct file has been loaded for processing;

(ii) control totals, to check against the loss or duplication of records.

The operating system should minimise the operator intervention, to reduce the likelihood of human error by the operator in giving the computer instructions.

(e) *Input controls*

Management should be satisfied that there are sufficient controls over input to ensure that the level of accuracy of input data is sufficient of the system's needs. The requirement for accuracy will vary from system to system, but controls over input data can include:

(i) data validation checks, including batch control totals;
(ii) verification of input data;
(iii) use of turn-round documents;
(iv) a high level of staff training to improve the quality of the work of user department staff;
(v) visual checking of input data, perhaps by reading through a printed listing.

(f) *File controls*

Management should be satisfied that there are adequate controls to minimise the risk of loss or corruption to files and of unauthorised access to files. If files are lost or corrupted, there should be adequate facilities for re-creating the lost or corrupted data. The range of controls to consider includes:

(i) keeping back-up files;
(ii) keeping 'old' generations of files;
(iii) physical safeguarding of files in a fireproof safe or cabinet;
(iv) control over the environment in which equipment is used;
(v) passwords to prevent unauthorised access.

(g) *Output controls*

There is a need to make sure that input is guarded against distribution to the wrong person, or unauthorised access. Controls will include making a person responsible for the safeguarding and despatch of output (a data control clerk). Procedures for correcting errors should also be enforced.

(h) *Data transmission controls*

In systems where data is transmitted over a telecommunications link or network, there should be controls against unauthorised access. Encryption and authentication procedures can be used.

20   **PROJECT**

REPORT TO CHIEF EXECUTIVE

Scope

This report identifies the problems which may be faced by the company's systems development section when carrying out the forthcoming major analysis and design project.

Introduction

The project will have two distinct stages. The systems analysis element will involve a study of current operations and problems followed by the preparation of a specification of requirements. The systems design stage will involve design of data, processes and physical elements.

As the project is a major one it will be led by the systems development section, but users have an important part to play at all stages.

Study of current operations and problems

During the first phase of systems analysis the project team will acquire detailed information about the existing system. This may lead to difficulties as the existing system environment is continually changing, as are the requirements of the users. The analysts and users will have to understand each others' requirements: the analysts to comprehend the users' operational view of the system, and the users to appreciate the way in which analysts operate and handle information. This process will require a high degree of co-operation between the two groups.

Because the project is complex, the analysts will need to adopt a structured approach to the acquisition of information, and they must consider how they will control the process of fact-finding and recording of data. This is an area which can lead to cost overruns if it is not adequately controlled.

The analysts will need to ensure throughout this process that they corroborate information and explanations received from users. They will be likely to use a selection of techniques including interviews and questionnaires. In either of those, users may interpret questions in unexpected ways or may be unintentionally misleading, particularly if they are subject to particular sensitivities about the future of their job or their job definition.

Specification of requirements

This phase of the analysis also requires close co-operation between analysts and users. The users will specify what they want the new system to do and give details of required data input and information output. The analyst has to prepare the specification with due regard to those requirements. The users have to be persuaded to 'buy in' to the specification, and so the analysts have to prevent problems by striking a balance between producing a specification which is too vague and therefore not a satisfactory foundation for design work and preparing a specification which is too formal for the users to understand, in which case they may be unwilling to commit to what is being developed. If they do not commit to the development they may restate the requirements and this will lead to time and cost overruns.

Systems design

One of the key issues at the design stage is the necessity for a clear demarcation between design elements. What is critical, following the specification of requirements, is the design of data and of processes. It is important that this process, that of defining the functional specifications, is kept distinct from the process of defining non-functional specifications. Non-functional specifications set out not what the system is to do but how it is to do it, for example extent of use of existing hardware and any constraints such as response times, data volumes and cost. If the new system is to meet user requirements it is important that data design and process design are considered before physical design. If this is not done, then systems will not meet users' requirements and may also be unreliable, as a result of sacrifices made at the design stage.

Recommendations

The planned system analysis and design project is a complex one and it is recommended that the company adopts a framework within which this project should be controlled. It is recommended that a formal system analysis and design methodology is used throughout the project; this will help break it down into stages so that effort is directed at each task as appropriate.

21   SYSTEMS IMPLEMENTATION

The following changeover strategies are possible.

(a)   *Direct changeover* involves the total replacement of the old system by the new at one point in time. The main advantage are that it is probably cheaper to implement than those implementation strategies which run both systems in parallel, on either all or part of the system. Confusion caused by the concurrent operation of two systems is therefore minimised. However, a crucial disadvantage is that it places too much reliance on system testing, as there may be unforeseen problems which only emerge after implementation. Additionally, all staff must be trained at the same time, which may cause a certain amount of disruption.

(b)   A *parallel running* strategy would mean that both systems are run at the same time for a period. This has the advantage that the results of the new system can be checked against the results of the old, and that should the new system break down, then the old can be run until the problem is sorted out, without any impairment of the organisation's data processing. A disadvantage is that the extra time involved is considerable. This method may not be suitable for situations where not only has the system changed, but also the organisational structure in which it operates.

(c)   Another alternative is a *pilot operation* in which the entire system is run in one location, or part of the system is run in all locations, so that any bugs can come to light before wholesale implementation. Once these difficulties have been ironed out, then each of the other locations can be changed over to the new system immediately.

(d)   *Phased* or *staged* implementation is a strategy which sets out a detailed timetable, so that each location is changed over separately. This has the advantage that the short term disruption is minimised, in comparison to a direct changeover. Also, the change over is easier to manage, by those systems professionals, if any, and management, required to supervise it. Within phased implementation, individual locations may be switched over by parallel running or direct changeover as appropriate.

The appropriateness of any particular strategy depends on the context. In this case a crucial factor is that both the computer systems and the company's entire method of distribution are changing. Parallel running is not really possible, given that the two situations are so different. The same could be said both for a pilot operation and a strategy based on a phased implementation. Direct changeover is the only viable option.

Whatever implementation strategy is adopted, the following issues will be crucial to its success:

(a)   system testing before changeover;
(b)   file conversion, with old files reconciled to new;
(c)   full staff training;
(d)   organisation of backup and standby facilities;
(e)   liaison with third parties for proper communications and data links;
(f)   proper project management, to ensure smooth implementation

22   SUPPORT PROVISION

If there is a rapid increase in the number of PCs in use, there will be a serious problem with large numbers of relatively inexperienced computer users, who will need training, advice and other assistance to help them to get used to their new ways of working. The staff would need substantial support, which could be provided by an Information Centre or similar unit.

The type of support that would be needed is as follows.

(a)   Training. Administrative staff should be given thorough training in the use of PCs, and in the use of the software systems that they will have to operate. The training requirements will include basic operations such as:

(i)   switching on the PC and loading in the required programs and files;
(ii)   making file copies;
(iii) loading and using a printer;
(iv)   the use of passwords;
(v)   the use of a keyboard (the function keys and other special keys etc).

(b)   Training in the use of applications software will be needed simply to enable staff to do their job properly. Since it takes time to become fully familiar with a system, initial training programmes should be backed up by a subsequent support and advice service. An Information Centre's staff should provide this through:

(i)   a telephone hot line;

(ii) a drop-in advice centre.

(c) Expert staff (eg Information Centre staff) should be given the responsibility of monitoring the system in use, to check that end-users are making full and efficient use of the system. Advice should be given on how to get more out of the system, as users become more proficient, such as:

(i)   using report writers;

(ii)   using query languages;

(iii) using application generators (fourth generation languages).

(d) The opportunity should be provided for end-users to discuss their experiences and difficulties with each other. This could be done by arranging semi-informal meetings and discussions between staff of different user groups.

(e) Since information technology is continually developing, staff should be kept aware of improvements in hardware, or network systems, and new versions of software packages. Continuing education in computer technology could be provided by circularising an in-house IT journal, or regular IT magazines, to give staff a chance to read about current changes.

23   DETERIORATION IN PERFORMANCE

The point must first be made that a 40-second response time is inappropriate. It is frustrating for customers whose telephone bills are increased as a result. It is also frustrating in the office environment, as staff have to wait for their requests to be processed. This means that they cannot deal with any other customers. With a wait of this length, and assuming say, another minute for further order processing, this means that a maximum of thirty to forty telephone requests can be dealt with per hour. With only a five second delay, the company would experience an immediate 50% increase in order-processing capability. There are clear costs associated with this inefficiency: extra staff to cope with the volume of work, and dissatisfied customers.

An assessment of the causes of the increase in response time and the consequent deterioration in the overall performance of the system can concentrate on a number of areas.

(a) *Technical*

(i)   Are there particular problems with items of hardware not functioning properly? Mechanical breakdown, or a failure inside the CPU, may inhibit processing speeds. If there is no other reason to explain the poor performance then the hardware should be examined.

(ii)   Any new equipment should be assessed for malfunction.

(iii) As far as software goes, the computer might have to process several applications, with consequent demands on CPU resources (eg multiprogramming)

(iv)   New system enhancements to the operating system and/or application programs and/or DBMS may have been implemented improperly

(b) *Communications and network configuration*

If the company uses the telecommunications network to send data between offices, perhaps there are problems on the data link. If a networking system is used, perhaps the server is not powerful enough for the number of desktop PCs. Alternatively, there may be too many terminals for the communications network to deal with properly, if these are all connected to a central mainframe or minicomputer.

(c) *Work loads*

Point (b) above leads on to the volume of transactions being processed. It is possible that the capacity level of the system has been breached in the last six months, and it is having to cope with transaction volumes for which it was not designed. In this case, a logical step would be to examine current transaction volumes and compare these with what was originally specified.

However, the long response times may only occur at certain times of the day in conditions of peak usage. In this case, the total demands made on the computer should be assessed.

(d)   *Other operational*

Poor operating procedures might result in increased response times. The CPU might be used more efficiently if the some of the processing were performed on intelligent workstations (if a system based around a network, rather than a mainframe-terminal configuration). Changes in other operating procedures might have resulted in performance deterioration.

Staff may be on a learning curve, so part of the decline might have been caused by poor training. However, this is unlikely to be the case if the activity is quite simple, or if most of the staff are experienced.

Summary

A detailed analysis of the system needs to be made in terms of:

(a)   operating procedures;
(b)   transaction volumes;
(c)   system configuration (too many terminals);
(d)   hardware failure

24   ACCOUNTING ACADEMY

(a)   The areas of the business recommended for inclusion within the scope of the feasibility study are as follows.

(i)   *Production of course material.* Inconsistencies in quality have been identified. Greater control is required over individual freelance lecturers. A 'house style' could be imposed and a central databank of material maintained to enable use of material in appropriate modules.

(ii)   *Finance.* Since there are strong seasonal variations in cashflow, a cashflow forecasting model should be a key part of this. The opportunity should also be taken to review accountancy procedures; including invoicing and cash handling. 'Inadequate and untimely financial information' is a key area to address.

(iii)   *Marketing.* There is potentially useful data available in the organisation in the form of the source data about the origin of student enquiries. This data is not really being used to its full potential. The Academy should also consider mailshots, an obvious target for computerisation.

(iv)   *Administration.* As the DFD in part (e) below shows, administrative arrangements are fairly complex. A review of this area of the business would be extremely useful. WP in particular is needed, as various pieces of mail are sent to each student.

(b)   Areas where business benefits could be identified are as follows.

(i)   *Increased income (and profitability).* If marketing activities are improved to make them more focused, attendances could rise further than anticipated. The six-fold increase referred to is presumably 'across-the-board'. Good marketing could help attract students who might otherwise select rival courses.

(ii)   *Cost savings.* An area often identified as being justification for computerisation of business activities is cost-cutting. There is certainly scope for this here. The small size of personnel in administrative operation makes redundancies unlikely, but it is likely that the same staff, once trained, will be able to take on *more* work, so that when student numbers increase, fewer new staff will be required than would be the case under the current system.

(iii)   *Improved control of financial position.* Computerisation will overcome the problem of inadequate and untimely financial information, allowing better planning in the light of available and forecast cash resources. Reliance on such factors as short-term overdrafts may be eliminated if these are a feature.

(iv)   *Improved quality.* Improvements in the quality of material (as identified in (a) above) may help to enhance the image of the Academy, as will word processed (as opposed to typewritten) documents/letters.

(c)   Disadvantages of off-the-shelf packages are as follows.

(i)   The *requirements* of the Accounting Academy are extremely *varied*. It may be difficult to identify suitable packages for all these requirements. WP is probably the least problematic as modern packages will provide facilities such as mailmerge and address labelling. A spreadsheet *could* be used for cashflow forecasting, but a dedicated package would probably be preferable. As for finance, given the status of the Academy and the nature of its operation it might be difficult to identify a suitable package. Some tailoring of packages might be necessary; alternatively some amendments to the company's operations could be necessitated if the package solution is inadequate.

(ii)   Given that one package will not satisfy all the Academy's requirements, the issue of *compatibility* arises. The company will have to consider whether different packages might produce incompatible data. A further problem, whether or not date is compatible is the issue of interface. If data needs to be transferred between packages, they will need to be able to recognise each other's file formats. The requirement for different packages might result in *duplication* of data, for example student and lecturer names and addresses might be held in more than one package. This would make file maintenance difficult.

(iii) Use of a package (or packages) involves reliance on the supplier of the package. Not all suppliers have the reputation and stability of, say, Microsoft, Lotus or Borland. Suppliers can go out of business or change their strategic direction (eg from products into services) and this can leave a package without support. This results in it not being upgraded while rival packages improve and possibly in the loss of technical support. If an organisation buys a bespoke package, the organisation becomes the 'owner' and, provided that the package is of a certain standard, the owner can commission upgrades and enhancements. In addition, some packages are supplied with poor *documentation* and without tutorial facilities. These, while not affecting the package's functionality, can impede users wishing to use the package effectively.

(iv)   The decision to purchase a package can be made without adequate *recognition* of the organisation's *requirements*. The Academy is going through a period of change and it might be difficult to identify the organisation's requirements clearly (let alone meet them, as described in (i)). If the requirements analysis is poor or non-existent, the package might be purchased for the wrong reasons, for example, it is a good offer or it has a 'nice' interface! This could lead to a package which is inappropriate for actual business requirements being acquired.

(d) Physical security comprises two sorts of controls, protection against natural and man made disasters, such as fire, flood and sabotage, and protection against intruders gaining physical access to the system. These threats can be grouped alternatively as accidental and deliberate. The physical environment has a major effect on information system security, and so planning it properly is an important precondition of an adequate security plan.

Fire is the most serious hazard to computer systems. Destruction of data can be even more costly than the destruction of hardware. A proper fire safety plan is an essential feature of security procedures, in order to prevent fire, detect fire and put out the fire.

The other main area of physical security is *access control*, to prevent intruders getting anywhere near the computer equipment or storage media. Methods of controlling human access include:

(i)   personnel (security guards);

(ii)   mechanical devices (eg keys, whose issue is recorded);

(iii) electronic identification devices (eg card-swipe systems, where a card is passed through a reader).

Theft is also a problem, particularly where so much computer equipment is easily portable. A PC need not be larger than a briefcase and even a laser printer can be carried by one person. To some extent this can be guarded against by means similar to those described above, but with much equipment located in ordinary offices and no longer kept in a single secure location other measures must be taken. Regular 'stock controls' or physical inspections may be necessary, and a strictly imposed form of bookings used when staff take PCs off-site, either to customers or home.

Hacking has received newspaper coverage in recent years. The use of telecommunications links across, and between, large organisations, whether multinational companies or national defence departments, makes them vulnerable to determined hackers. Again the risk varies from 'nuisance value' to potential loss of material either through destruction or to competitors. Certain companies in London now advertise a service by which for a fee, they can obtain bank account details and financial information about any named individual for customers: this kind of illegal activity is made easier by the use of IT.

Another risk is from *viruses*. These may be carried on games software or pirated software; they can be also spread on computer networks. At best, they are a nuisance; at worst tremendously harmful to data to the extent of to wiping hard disks clean. All disks coming into an organisation and, periodically, all computers, should be checked using proprietary anti-virus software.

In smaller companies the security officer is normally responsible for the whole computer function and is often the finance manager or equivalent. System security may be less formal especially where the officer knows all the users personally. Nevertheless it is advisable that at least a basic password structure is applied to the system.

Data integrity can be corrupted by system faults and user error as well as unauthorised access. The regular back up of data should be a disciplined procedure for all computer systems. This may happen daily and the copies are often kept off premises. Security copies of the system programs may be kept at a bank or with solicitors (possibly at the request of insurers). Proper shut down procedures should also be carried out only by authorised personnel and the network should not be left on and unattended.

Data integrity will also be maintained by keeping information on the system to a realistic minimum. This will involve deleting or archiving redundant data. This has the additional benefits of improving response times and reducing the time taken for back-up procedures. Random checks and reconciliations of data from audit trails or system enquiry will also highlight, by exception, problems which have occurred.

(e)

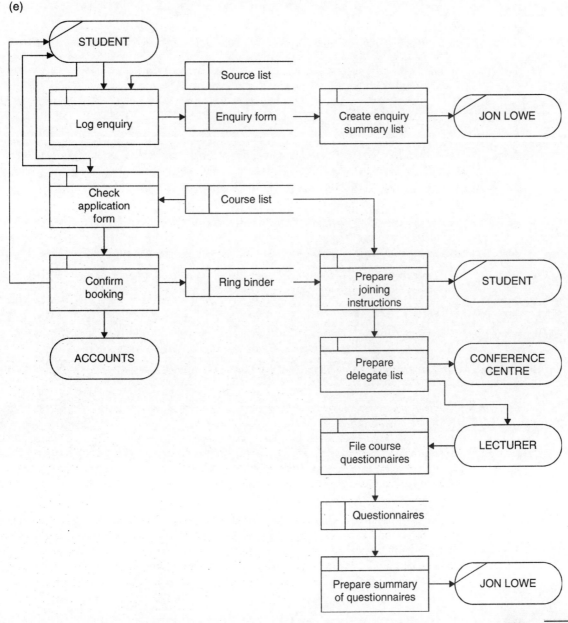

Lecturers' question bank

1 FLEXIBILITY

'A properly designed information system needs to be flexible, and be responsive to change.'

How important is this statement when identifying the information flows needed for development of strategic, tactical and operational systems?

2 FEEDBACK (15 marks)   *27 mins*

A feature of general systems theory and of all managerial control systems is the existence of feedback control loops. The normal feedback loop, sometimes termed single loop feedback, is the most formalised, yet, from a systems viewpoint. Higher level feedback, sometimes termed double loop feedback, can be said to be of equal importance.

You are required to:

(a) describe a single loop feedback control cycle, identifying each element in the loop; (6 marks)
(b) discuss the importance of feedback in the control of systems;   (5 marks)
(c) describe the role of double loop feedback.   (4 marks)

3 COMPUTER SYSTEMS

(a) The general manager of an organisation with many PCs which are used for a wide variety of administrative tasks has decided to perform a review of software usage to evaluate the effectiveness of current purchasing arrangements. He has called you in to do the following.

   (i)   Describe briefly the major categories of software which the organisation is likely to have on its stand-alone PCs, giving an example from each category.

   (ii) Explain the criteria which the organisation should use in selecting its software.

(b) What are the primary considerations when choosing the most appropriate method for data capture?

4 FEASIBILITY REPORT (15 marks)   *27 mins*

(a) Outline the main sections of a feasibility report and briefly explain the purpose of the typical contents of each section.   (6 marks)

(b) An important part of any feasibility report is a section giving a financial justification for the proposed system. Describe in detail the matters dealt with in this section and the role of the accountant in its preparation.   (9 marks)

5 DATA ANALYSIS (15 marks)   *27 mins*

A large multinational company is considering implementing a large-scale corporate database. The Chief Executive has been told that the company must carry out a data analysis exercise and choose a logical database model.

You are required:

(a) to identify the advantages for the company of using a systems analysis technique based on data analysis rather than on the detailed analysis of processes;   (4 marks)

(b) to identify the main features of the following logical database models;

   (i)   the relational model
   (ii) the hierarchical model
   (iii) the network model.   (11 marks)

6 DATA FLOW DIAGRAM (15 marks)   *27 mins*

The South Bank is planning a systems analysis and design project with a view to improving its customer service.

Customers are divided into two groups - savers and borrowers - with a department of the bank for each group.

Savers have an account into which deposits may be made and from which withdrawals may be taken. Interest on savings is paid to the savers twice a year. Tax on interest is paid directly to the Government. A saver who becomes overdrawn on his or her account technically becomes a borrower and is charged interest until the overdraft is cleared.

Borrowers may take out a loan by sending an application to the loan department which will, depending on the borrower's status, send a cheque for the loan amount to the borrower and create new records in the central accounts and borrower file. The borrower may pay interest payments by cash or cheque. Accounts are monitored closely to pick up arrears as soon as possible. Where an account goes into arrears a warning is sent to the borrower.

You are required to produce a data flow diagram for the current system described above.

7   DECISION TABLE (10 marks)   *18 mins*

A company wishes to grade its employees in accordance with a new grading structure given below:

Grade 'A' employees must satisfy at least two of the following requirements:

(a)   they must possess acceptable academic qualifications;
(b)   they must have completed a training programme;
(c)   they must have the commendation of their departmental head.

Failure to achieve a Grade 'A' rating automatically means a grading of 'B'.

However, if employees qualify for Grade 'A' ratings but have not received their heads' commendations they are classed as 'Grade 'A' under review' and referred to the Personnel Officer for further investigation.

Employees who are classed as Grade 'B' but who have obtained their heads' commendations are classed as 'Grade 'B' provisional' and are required to undertaken further training.

You are required to prepare a limited entry decision table describing the grading system.

8   THE DATABASE APPROACH   *45 mins*

A company manufactures motor components and sells them to car manufacturers and also has a growing market in direct supply of parts to dealers. The computer users' group within the company is currently considering the design and development of an integrated information system based on a corporate database. The use of a corporate database would enable the company to meet its management information needs in all areas of the business at all levels of management, if it were correctly designed and administered.

Senior management would like eventually to allow dealers who purchase from the company to have terminals allowing direct access to relevant parts of the database for ordering purposes. There is, however, some concern about security if staff who are not employees of the company are allowed to use the system.

(a)   Discuss the advantages of the database approach when compared to the design of systems using files which are dedicated to a specific application.

(b)   Write a memorandum to the computer users' group, setting out the implications of higher levels of management becoming end-users and using computer-based information systems, in terms of systems design, software flexibility and the user interface.

9   FILE CONVERSION (15 marks)   *27 mins*

File conversion (or file creation) is always a major practical problem when a new computer-based system is being implemented.

Assume that a new computer-based accounting system is to be implemented and source data are at present held in various types of clerical files in several locations.

You are required to describe:

(a)   the objectives of file conversion;   (3 marks)
(b)   the typical problems that would be encountered in the situation outlined;   (5 marks)
(c)   the way the file conversion process should be planned and controlled.   (7 marks)

10 END-USER COMPUTING

The promotion of so called end-user computing requires not only support from the information centre but the provision of suitable software aids.

What is meant by the respective terms 'end-user computing', 'information centre' and 'software aids'.

11 PRIVACY AND SECURITY (15 marks)   *27 mins*

For some people the difference between the privacy and the security of information stored on a computer system becomes a confused issue. Explain, in detail, the separate issues that privacy and security give rise to, and, where appropriate, methods by which computer systems may be protected.

12 FILE SECURITY (15 marks)   *27 mins*

File security is essential in any organisation to prevent important business information being overwritten or accidentally erased.

(a) Explain how the generation method may be used to provide file security for magnetic tape.
(5 marks)

(b) Explain the meaning of dumping as a method of file security for magnetic disk.   (4 marks)

(c) Describe the methods of protecting important information on floppy disk from being overwritten.   (6 marks)

List of Key
Terms and index

These are the terms which we have identified throughout the text as being KEY TERMS. You should make sure that you can define what these terms mean; go back to the page highlighted here if you need to check.

Accounting rate of return, 154

Adaptive maintenance, 353

Analogue, 95

Analytic decision, 29

Application controls, 189

ASCII, 63

Audit trail, 198

Back-up, 291

Batch processing, 81

Benchmark tests, 162

Bespoke package, 167

Bit, 63

Business system, 39

Bytes, 63

CASE tool, 279

Character, 63

Client, 137

Closed system, 44

Communication, 4

Comparator, 47

Computer, 56

Computer bureau, 181

Contingency, 196

Corrective maintenance, 352

Data, 23

Data dictionary, 273

Data flow, 225

Data independence, 268

Data processes, 226

Data redundancy, 268

Data store, 225

Data structure, 233

Data subject, 181

Data users, 181

Database, 268

Database management system (DBMS), 268

Decision tree, 246

Desktop publishing (DTP), 93

Digital, 95

Discounted cash flow, 155

Distributed system, 133

Documentation, 344

Effectiveness, 29, 361

Effector, 48

Efficiency, 29, 360

Encryption, 305

End-user computing, 356

Entity, 225

Entity life history (ELH), 234

Entity relationship model (ERM), 233

Entropy, 52

Exception reporting, 26

External auditor, 187

Facsimile transmission, 97

Fax, 97

Feasibility study, 146

Feedback, 48

File conversion, 346

Filtering, 50

Fourth generation language (4GL), 285

General controls, 189

Hardware, 56, 76

Heuristic decision, 29

Information, 23

Information centre (IC), 358

Integrated systems, 17

Internal auditor, 188

Inventory, 12

Invitation to tender (ITT), 159

Job sensitivity analysis, 195

Key field, 237

Management control, 29

Management information system (MIS), 7

Methodology, 207

Negative feedback, 48

Network, 135

Network analysis, 321

Test data, 201, 340
Testing, 334
Theft, 178
Thin client, 139
Third Normal Form, 240
Timing, 26
Touch sensitive pads, 66
Touch-sensitive screens, 66
Trackball, 66
Training, 164, 341
  of middle management, 343
  plan, 343
  software, 358
Transaction files, 80
Transactions processing, 7
Trojans, 308
TUPE, 126
Turnround documents, 67

Unauthorised modification of data, 185
Uniform Resource Locator (URL), 106
Unix, 77, 138, 141
  flavours of, 77
Unstructured data, 107
Unstructured decision, 28
URL, 105
Usenet, 108
User groups, 356
User manuals, 345
User requirements, 123
User validation., 192
User-driven development, 216
User-driven methodologies, 216
Utility software, 164

Validation, 295
VDU, 65, 69, 72
Vendor proposals
  obtaining, 159

Verification, 295
Video cards, 65
Videoconferencing, 100
Viruses, 304, 306
  checks, 270
  identification of, 310
Visa, 68
Visual Basic, 278
Visual display unit (VDU), 65
Voice mail, 99
Voice messaging, 99
Voice recognition, 69
Volume, 26

Warranty, 164
Water, 175
Websites, 102
What if? analysis, 90
Wide area networks, 136
Wildcard, 277
WIMP, 262
Windows, 66, 77, 262
Windows 95, 77
Windows 98, 78, 140
Windows NT, 77, 138, 141
Word processing, 91
Word processing, 91
Words, 63
Workstations, 59
World Wide Web (www), 102
Worms, 308
www, 106
WYSIWYG, 91

Yahoo!, 105
Year 2000 problem, 347

Zip drive, 72

ORDER FORM

To order your ACCA books, you can phone us on 0181 740 2211, email us at publishing@bpp.co.uk, fax this form to 0181 740 1184 or cut this form out and post it to the address below.

To: BPP Publishing Ltd, Aldine House, Aldine Place,
London W12 8AW

Tel: 0181-740 2211
Fax: 0181-740 1184

Forenames (Mr / Ms): _____   Surname: _____

Daytime delivery address: _____

_____

Post code: _____   Date of exam (month/year): _____

Please send me the following books:

	Price			Quantity			Total
	6/98 Text £	1/98 Kit £	1/98 Passcards £	Text	Kit	Passcards	£
Foundation							
The Accounting Framework	18.95	8.95	4.95	....	....	....	....
The Accounting Framework (Int'l)	18.95	8.95★		....	....		....
The Legal Framework	18.95	8.95	4.95	....	....	....	....
Management Information	18.95	8.95	4.95	....	....	....	....
The Organisational Framework	18.95	8.95	4.95	....	....	....	....
Certificate							
Information Analysis	18.95	8.95	4.95	....	....	....	....
The Audit Framework	18.95	8.95	4.95	....	....	....	....
The Audit Framework (Int'l)	18.95	8.95★		....	....		....
The Tax Framework FA 98 (7/98 Text, 8/98 P/c, 8/98 Kit)	18.95	8.95	3.95	....	....	....	....
Managerial Finance	18.95	8.95	4.95	....	....	....	....
Professional							
Information for Control and Decision Making	19.95	9.95	5.95	....	....	....	....
Accounting and Audit Practice A: Accounting	15.95	9.95	5.95	....	....	....	....
Accounting and Audit Practice A: Accounting (Int'l)	15.95	9.95★		....	....		....
Accounting and Audit Practice B: Auditing	13.95			....			....
Accounting and Audit Practice B: Auditing (Int'l (Kit and Passcards cover both accounting and auditing)	13.95			....			....
Tax Planning FA 98 (7/98 Text, 8/98 P/c, 8/98 Kit)	19.95	9.95	5.95	....	....	....	....
Management and Strategy	19.95	9.95	5.95	....	....	....	....
Financial Reporting Environment	19.95	9.95	5.95	....	....	....	....
Financial Reporting Environment (Int'l)	19.95	9.95★		....	....		....
Financial Strategy	19.95	9.95	5.95	....	....	....	....

Postage and packaging:

UK: Texts £3.00 for first plus £2.00 for each extra   ....

Kits and Passcards £2.00 for first plus £1.00 for each extra   ....

Europe (inc ROI & CI): Texts £5.00 for first plus £4.00 for each extra   ....

Kits and Passcards £2.50 for first plus £1.00 for each extra   ....

Rest of the World: Texts £20.00 for first plus £10.00 for each extra   ....

Kits and Passcards £15.00 for first plus £8.00 for each extra   ....

(Single Kits/Passcards are airmailed. All other parcels are sent by courier and should arrive in not more than six days.)

★ International Stream Kits will be published in Autumn 1998   Total _____

I enclose a cheque for £ _____ or charge to Access/Visa/Switch

Card number | - | | | | | | | | | | | | | | | | | | |

Start date (Switch only) _____   Expiry date _____   Issue no. (Switch only)___

Signature _____